Studies in European Economic Law and Regulation

Volume 4

Series Editor
Kai Purnhagen
Law and Governance Group, Faculty of Law
Wageningen University, Erasmus University
Wageningen and Rotterdam, The Netherlands

AF769481

The series shall focus on studies devoted to the analysis of European Economic Law. It shall firstly embrace all features of EU economic law in general (e.g. EU law such as fundamental freedoms and their relationship to fundamental rights, as well as other economic law such as arbitration and WTO law) and more specifically (antitrust law, unfair competition law, financial market law, consumer law). This series shall cover both classical internal analysis (doctrine) as well as external analysis, where European Economic Law and Regulation is the subject of analysis (Law and Economics, Sociological Analysis, Comparative Law and the like).

The series accepts monographs focusing on a specific topic, as well as edited collections of articles covering a specific theme or collections of articles by a single author. All contributions are accepted exclusively after a rigorous double-blind peer-review process.

More information about this series at http://www.springer.com/series/11710

Javier Plaza Penadés • Luz M. Martínez Velencoso
Editors

European Perspectives on the Common European Sales Law

Springer

Editors
Javier Plaza Penadés
Department of Civil Law
University of Valencia Faculty of Law
Valencia
Spain

Luz M. Martínez Velencoso
LL.M. Humboldt Universität Berlin
University of Valencia
Valencia
Spain

ISSN 2214-2037 ISSN 2214-2045 (electronic)
ISBN 978-3-319-34832-2 ISBN 978-3-319-10497-3 (eBook)
DOI 10.1007/978-3-319-10497-3
Springer Cham Heidelberg New York Dordrecht London

© Springer International Publishing Switzerland 2015
Softcover reprint of the hardcover 1st edition 2015
This work is subject to copyright. All rights are reserved by the Publisher, whether the whole or part of the material is concerned, specifically the rights of translation, reprinting, reuse of illustrations, recitation, broadcasting, reproduction on microfilms or in any other physical way, and transmission or information storage and retrieval, electronic adaptation, computer software, or by similar or dissimilar methodology now known or hereafter developed. Exempted from this legal reservation are brief excerpts in connection with reviews or scholarly analysis or material supplied specifically for the purpose of being entered and executed on a computer system, for exclusive use by the purchaser of the work. Duplication of this publication or parts thereof is permitted only under the provisions of the Copyright Law of the Publisher's location, in its current version, and permission for use must always be obtained from Springer. Permissions for use may be obtained through RightsLink at the Copyright Clearance Center. Violations are liable to prosecution under the respective Copyright Law.
The use of general descriptive names, registered names, trademarks, service marks, etc. in this publication does not imply, even in the absence of a specific statement, that such names are exempt from the relevant protective laws and regulations and therefore free for general use.
While the advice and information in this book are believed to be true and accurate at the date of publication, neither the authors nor the editors nor the publisher can accept any legal responsibility for any errors or omissions that may be made. The publisher makes no warranty, express or implied, with respect to the material contained herein.

Printed on acid-free paper

Springer is part of Springer Science+Business Media (www.springer.com)

Preface

The Proposal for a Common European Sales Law (CESL), published by the European Commission in 2011, has the aim of introducing an optional regime for cross-border sale of goods for the European Union.

The publication of this Proposal has given rise to a lot of interest not only in the academic community, but also in the world of the practitioner. The aim of this Commentary is to present a coherent view of the subject from the perspective of a number of scholars from different European countries, of whom will compare the text of the CESL with their own national law and other European legal texts. This Commentary offers a serious comparative study of the CESL alongside other instruments, such as the CISG, and also pre-existing instruments including the Draft Common Frame of Reference (DCFR) and the Principles of European Contract Law (PECL).

In the future application of the CESL it is anticipated that problems will arise in relation to the uniformity that is intended by such a European legal text requiring homogeneous application by the different national courts. The drafters of the CESL have sought uniformity in order to avoid the complexity of a European sales law resulting from the application of the different sales laws of each Member State. This Commentary, coordinated by legal scholars, whom of which are members of the Valencian Study Group for the Study of European Private Law (GEVDPE)[1], will contribute towards the achievement of this desired uniformity.

Firstly, the process of the enactment of the CESL will be analysed, in conjunction with its scope of application, covering areas such as sale of goods, supplying (licensing) of digital content, supply of trade-related services, and consumer protection. International aspects concerned with the application of the CESL will also be analysed in this Commentary, particularly as one of the main features of the CESL—unlike other international instruments—is its optional nature, i.e. the parties must agree upon its application in order for this instrument to govern the particular contract.

[1] This Book has been prepared within the framework of the Research Project DER2013-42526-R ("New legal challenges of the digital society: property, contracts, data and electronic registers"), funded by the Spanish Ministry of Science and Innovation and Prometeo Program 2011, PROMETEO 2011/23, ("Technological model of the Valencian Community").

The structure of the CESL determines the structure of this Commentary. The subjects that are regulated by the CESL may be divided into three groups: (i) aspects related to the conclusion of the contract and its content; (ii) aspects related to the performance of obligations by both parties; and (iii) aspects related to remedies in case of non-performance, including the issue of prescription of claims and other rights. The CESL adopts a simpler structure (compared to the Draft Common Frame of Reference) that is more accessible to traders and consumers. This Commentary focuses on the main aspects of the Common Sales Law proposal in more detail. In particular, the regulation of the CESL with regards to issues such as: pre-contractual information duties, unfair contract terms, the notion of conformity with the contract and the remedies in case of non-performance of obligations.

[1] Issues concerning the conclusion of contract.

Firstly, the CESL regulates matters relating to the conclusion of a contract. The provisions cover the pre-contractual information requirements. This includes the pre-contractual information required in the contract between the involved traders, the contract concluded by electronic means, the provisions that regulate conclusion of contract by the offer and its acceptance, and the provisions concerning the right to withdraw in distance provisions on the content of the contract and on unfair contract terms.

One of the questions related to the pre-contractual phase is the integration of advertising into contracts in Article 69 of the CESL where the necessary requirements of the professional supplier's pre-contractual statements are fixed, or the statements of a third party about the characteristics of the product to be incorporated into the content of the contract.

Another significant issue to take into consideration is that conclusion of contract regulated in the CESL is based on a combination of concepts derived from various legal systems. The textual part of the CESL combines some elements of common law and some elements taken from the European system. For that reason, future application of the rules will provide interesting insights into the mechanism of the reception of law into different legal cultures.

In relation to unfair contractual terms, there is a long-standing European tradition of law demanding good faith and fair dealing in contractual relationships. Therefore, this Commentary will analyse how to deal with contract terms that are considered unfair.

In addition to this, a chapter is also dedicated to the right of withdrawal that appears in the context of contractual obligations as a more modern development of the principle "pacta sunt servanda". Nowadays the right of withdrawal is considered as an exceptional facility of only one of the parties of the contract, the consumer, enabling him or her to terminate "ad nutum", meaning with no reason, and with retroactive contractual effect.

[2] Issues concerning performance.

Parts IV and V of the CESL are based on the approach of the CISG, containing the obligations and remedies of the parties to a sales contract, and related services contracts. In both cases, the respective provisions are preceded by a set of provisions that apply to both parties alike (Chaps. 9 and 15).

The subject of performance of the obligations is regulated in Chap. 10, which addresses the seller's obligations. Chapter 12 (Articles 123–130 of the CESL) relates to a buyer's obligations, and Chap. 14 addresses the passing of risk. Chapter 15 regulates the obligations of the parties in a service contract.

In Article 87 of the CESL the general definitions about the notions of "non-performance" and "fundamental non-performance" are recorded. This regime constitutes a unitary concept of breach of contract and, therefore, closely follows the European standard based on CISG, PECL and DCFR. In the corresponding chapter of this Commentary this question has to be analysed as the result of a development of uniform law starting with the CISG and ending so far with the notion of breach of contract in the DCFR. Similarly, the solution proposed by the CESL has to be compared to the diverging approaches of the national legal orders and the history of emergence of what will become a common European notion of breach of contract in a legal sense.

Along these lines the concept of conformity is one of the most important topics in modern Contract Law, especially concerning sales contracts, and other types of contracts for goods and services. This is particularly concerning for the CESL, where the lack of conformity constitutes a case of non-performance and in this situation makes the recourse to the panoply of remedies typical for non-performance possible.

Likewise, another issue to consider is that of the passing of risk, which is one of the most problematic topics regarding contract sales law. National laws usually link the passing of risk to abstract and general concepts, such as the conclusion of the contract, the transfer of ownership, or the transfer of the physical possession of the goods. However, these concepts are rigid and unsuited to international commercial practice. For these reasons, the CESL has opted to follow the "analytical approach" set out in the CISG. In this way Chap. 14 of CESL regulates the passing of risk in sales involving carriage of goods, when the goods are sold in transit or when the goods are placed at buyer's disposal. The CESL also expressly distinguishes between B2B and B2C contracts, ensuring a high level of consumer protection in this field.

The legal doctrine of the change of circumstances is also analysed in this Commentary. In accordance with Article 89 of the CESL, when the exact fulfilment of a contract becomes disproportionate due to an unexpected change of circumstances, the consequence is the duty to renegotiate. If, within a reasonable period of time, the parties do not reach an agreement, they may request the assistance of the court or an arbitrator. The judge may decide to adapt the contract taking into account the hypothetical will of the parties, or declare the termination of the contract and lay down the conditions for doing so. In the corresponding chapter it will be concluded that the application of Article 89 of the CESL should not be problematic in different European countries, as there are a lot of similarities between the various European legal systems in this field.

With regard to service contracts, however, the CESL only regulates those service contracts whose existence is justified by their direct link to sales contracts. This is different to the regulated under the DCFR where it provided a more exhaustive coverage. The aim of this regulation in the CESL is to maximise the added value of the common European sales law, which justifies the inclusion in its material scope of certain services provided by the seller that are directly and closely related to the specific goods or digital content supplied on the basis of the said rules.

There is also a chapter concerned with the topic of the contract for the supply of digital content and its main aspects. This can be seen as the most novel part of the CESL and also a very important part.

[3]. Final part. General contract law issues.

The final three parts of the CESL are concerned again with general contract law issues, certain remedies (damages and restitution) and prescription.

Concretely, Part VI "Damages and interest" contains supplementary common rules on damages for loss and on interest to be paid for late payment. Part VII "Restitution" explains the rules that apply on what must be returned when a contract is avoided or terminated. Part VIII "Prescription" regulates the effects of the lapse of time on the exercise of rights under a contract.

The CESL contains, in Chapter 17 (arts. 172-177) rules relating to the scope and manner of exercising a restitution claim of whatever was supplied under a contract that has been subsequently avoided or terminated. The CESL regulates jointly restitution arising from avoidance and termination. The aim of the corresponding chapter of this Commentary is to analyse the most relevant aspects of this proposal, highlighting certain gaps in the text that could cause problems of interpretation and application.

The next chapter is dedicated to the issue of whether a remedy of compensation of damages as the right to rescind the contract and to withhold or reduce the price does not fully compensate the creditor for his loss in every case.

Finally the Commentary deals with the prescription regulated in a very complete way in the CESL, although this proposal is limited in its application to the sale of goods. This regulation takes into account several new tendencies that have emerged from a number of national legal systems. Prescription is undoubtedly a necessary doctrine; not only for obligations derived from contracts but for all types of obligations, and so its regulation in the Common European Sales Law could go on to form the basis of its regulation in a future European Civil Code.

To conclude, this Book seeks to offer a commentary on the main aspects of the CESL from the perspectives of scholars of different European countries, so that the intended impact of the CESL may be achieved in practice.

Editors
Javier Plaza Penadés
Luz M. Martínez Velencoso

Contents

Contributors

Carmen Azcárraga Monzonís University of Valencia, Valencia, Spain

María Paz García Rubio University Santiago de Compostela, Santiago de Compostela, Spain

Ana Sofia Gomes Universidade Lusíada de Lisboa, Lisbon-Portugal

Raquel Guillén Catalán University of Valencia, Valencia, Spain

Francisco Infante Ruiz University Pablo Olavide Sevilla, Sevilla, Spain

Matthias Lehmann Martin-Luther University Halle-Wittenberg, Halle, Germany

Hans Fredrik Marthinussen University of Bergen, Bergen, Norway

Luz M. Martínez Velencoso LL.M. Humboldt Universität Berlin, University of Valencia, Valencia, Spain

Andrew O'Flynn LL.M. Cambridge University, Valencia, Spain

Francisco Oliva Blázquez University Pablo de Olavide, Sevilla, Spain

Guillermo Palao Moreno University of Valencia, Valencia, Spain

Javier Plaza Penadés University of Valencia, Valencia, Spain

M. José Reyes López University of Valencia, Valencia, Spain

Martin Schmidt-Kessel University of Bayreuth, Bayreuth, Germany

Adela Serra Rodríguez University of Valencia, Valencia, Spain

Eva Silkens University of Bayreuth, Bayreuth, Germany

Jakub J. Szczerbowski University of Social Sciences and Humanities, Warszawa, Poland

Chapter 1
The Proposal for a Regulation on a Common European Sales Law (CESL): An Introduction

Ana Sofia Gomes

Abstract The Common European Sales Law proposal, is the first legislative initiative to come out of the European contract law debate. For more than two decades, there was an intense change of opinions and knowledge about the virtues of uniform legislation for contract law considering the legal traditions of the Member States, but also the good functioning of the internal market.

The proposal for a Regulation on a Common European Sales Law, has resulted from an effort to unify contract law, this having been established as a priority in European Union Law. This instrument would be the first establishing an optional regime of special substantive rules for cross-border contracts.

This is the latest in a series of harmonisation projects. Previous efforts include the Franco-Italian Project; and global efforts such as the CISG, the UNCITRAL and the UNIDROIT. Europe-wide projects include the Principles of European Contract Law—PECL—Lando Group—the European Contracts Code—Gandolfi Project—and the European Civil Code—Von Bar—; whilst similar initiatives relating to legal science are the Common Core of European Private Law and the Acquis Group.

1.1 Introduction

The Common European Sales Law proposal, is the first legislative initiative to come out of the European contract law debate. For more than two decades, there was an intense change of opinions and knowledge about the virtues of uniform legislation for contract law considering the legal traditions of the Member States, but also the good functioning of the internal market (Knöfel and Bray 2012/2013).

The proposal for a Regulation on a Common European Sales Law[1], has resulted from an effort to unify contract law, this having been established as a priority in

[1] COM (2011) 635 final.

A. S. Gomes (✉)
Universidade Lusíada de Lisboa, Rua da Junqueira, 198, 1350-004 Lisbon-Portugal
e-mail: 13000574@edu.ulusiada.pt

© Springer International Publishing Switzerland 2015

J. Plaza Penadés, L. M. Martínez Velencoso (eds.), *European Perspectives on the Common European Sales Law,* Studies in European Economic Law and Regulation 4,
DOI 10.1007/978-3-319-10497-3_1

European Union Law. This instrument would be the first establishing an optional regime of special substantive rules (Mankowski 2012) for cross-border contracts.

This is the latest in a series of harmonisation projects. Previous efforts include the Franco-Italian Project; and global efforts such as the CISG, the UNCITRAL and the UNIDROIT. Europe-wide projects include the Principles of European Contract Law -PECL—Lando Group—the European Contracts Code—Gandolfi Project—and the European Civil Code—Von Bar—; whilst similar initiatives relating to legal science are the Common Core of European Private Law and the Acquis Group.

In the field of EU harmonisation, there are some Directives with impact on European Contract Law, representing a first step to a greater objective.

The strengthening of the internal market and the promotion of the cross-border sales in the EU, were also the concerns tacked into account on the adoption of some regulations in the field of the law of obligations, even if it was in a purely conflict of laws perspective—the Rome I[2] and Rome II regulations[3]—or in a jurisdictional perspective—the Brussels I regulation[4].

1.2 Background

In the Resolutions of 26 May 1989[5] and 6 May 1994,[6] the European Parliament supported the establishment of a Common European Code of Private Law.

This position led to the development of various studies, some which were already being prepared by various working groups. Some of the scholars involved in UNIDROIT, led by Ole Lando, came together to form the Committee on European Contract Law, and began, in 1982, a new project: the development of the Principles of European Contract Law, which was completed in 2003 (Lando and Beale 2000; Lando et al. 2003).

---

[2] Regulation (EC) No. 593/2008, on the law applicable to contractual obligations (Rome I), published in OJ No. L 177, of 17.06.2008, in force from 24th of July 2008. This Regulation applies only in the event of a conflict of laws, between B-SME's 2C or B-SME's 2-SME's-B.

[3] Regulation (EC) No. 864/2007, on the law applicable to non-contractual obligations (Rome II)—OJ No. L 199, 31.07.2007, in force from 11th January 2009.

[4] Regulation (EC) no. 44/2001, on jurisdiction and the recognition and enforcement of judgments in civil and commercial matters, published in OJ No. L 12, 16.01.2001. This Regulation will be substitute by Regulation (EU) No. 1215/2012, on jurisdiction and the recognition and enforcement of judgments in civil and commercial matters (recast), published in OJ No. L 351 of 20.12.2012 that shall apply from 10th January 2015, with the amendments introduced by The **Regulation (EU) No 542/2014 of the European Parliament and of the Council of 15 May 2014 amending Regulation (EU) No 1215/2012 as regards the rules to be applied with respect to the Unified Patent Court and the Benelux Court of Justice, published in** OJ L 163, 29.5.2014, pp. 1–4.

[5] "Resolution on Action to Bring into Line the Private Law of the Member States", published in OJ C n. 158 of June 26, 1989, p. 400 ff.

[6] "Resolution on the approximation of the civil and commercial law of the Member States", published in OJ C 205 of 25 July 1994, p. 518 ff.

In parallel, the European Academy of Private Law, based in Pavia, coordinated by Giuseppe Gandolfi, prepared a draft of a European Contract Code (Gandolfi 2008). In 1998, Von Bar headed another major project developed by the Study Group on a European Civil Code, which drafted a European Civil Code (Von Bar 2001).

The Common Core of European Private Law was formed under the direction of Ugo Mattei and Mauro Bussani, in 1995. Later on, in 2002, the European Research Group on Existing EC Private European Law (Acquis Group) took the responsibility of drawing up the Principles of the Existing EC Contract Law (Acquis Principles) (Research Group on the Existing EC Private Law (Acquis Group) 2009). The members of the "Study Group on a European Civil Code" and those of the "Acquis Group", cooperated in the framework of the "Joint Network on European Private Law" (Palao 2011).

The European Council meeting in Tampere on 15–16 October 1999, found it necessary to "achieve a higher degree of compatibility and convergence between the legal systems of the Member States",[7] and instructed the Council of the European Union to conduct until 2001, "an overall study on the need to approximate Member States' legislation in civil matters in order to eliminate obstacles to the good functioning of civil proceedings".

The concerns about the proper functioning of the internal market led the European Parliament[8] stated that "greater harmonisation of civil law has become essential in the internal market and calls on the Commission to draw up a study in this area… ".[9] The Commission begin to work on it[10], considering fundamental "to find out if the coexistence of national contract laws in the Member States directly or indirectly obstructs functioning of the internal market, and if so to what extent."[11]

The Commission took into account the existence of potential impediments to cross-border transactions, based on the disparity of laws in force in the Member States. Such obstacles include conflicts between mandatory rules of the different Member States that prevent freedom of choice from clauses that lead to the current practices of Member States, especially when formalised in standard contracts. Furthermore, the ignorance of the diversity of legal systems by any Contracting Parties may prevent their willingness to conclude cross-border procurement, and also prove onerous to the party whose law is not applicable to the contract, either because the right choice has not been made, or because it is not their national law that is applicable in the absence of choice of law. All of the above constitute obstacles. This burden arises from the need to obtain legal advice either seeking prior information regarding its implementation and eventual litigation monitoring, which may

[7] Point 39.

[8] In the Resolution of 16 March 2000, point 28.

[9] Point 28.

[10] As it results from it Communication to the Council and the European Parliament on European contract law (2001/C 255/01), on 11 July 2001, published in OJ C 255 of 13/09/2001, pp. 1–44.

[11] Concluding that such obstacles do exist, the European institutions may be called on to take appropriate action".

constitute a competitive disadvantage "in a situation where a foreign supplier is competing with a supplier established in the same country as the potential client."[12]

It was important to note that at that time, that an horizontal measure providing for the complete harmonisation of contractual law provisions may be considered for adoption at Community level where there are contractual obstacles that cannot be resolved through the principle of subsidiarity.[13]

Following the European Parliament point of view[14], and after its communication to the European Parliament and the Council on "A more coherent European contract law",[15] the Commission presented an Action Plan[16], proposed the adoption of specific measures and sectorial regulatory and non-regulatory measures to address the problems posed by the existence of different laws regarding contracts. The objective of these measures is to improve the consistency of the acquis in the context of contract law, by launching two lines of action: improving the quality of existing legislation,[17] and developing a common frame of reference,[18] with the aim of creating a common pattern in contractual matters, composed of common principles on procurement, which could serve as the future basis for reflection on an instrument within European contract law. Moreover, the Commission found that "the creation of a common frame of reference is an intermediate step to improve the quality of the Community acquis in the area of contract law"[19] and that "an improved acquis should enhance the uniform application of Community law and to facilitate the

[12] Point 32 of the Notice.

[13] The Commission recognizes in this document (paragraph 42) the existence of limits to the capacity of Community intervention once "Every measure must be in accordance with the principles of subsidiarity and proportionality, as laid down by Article 5 of the Treaty and the Protocol on the application of the principles of subsidiarity and proportionality."

[14] Stressed on it Resolution on the approximation of the civil and commercial law of the Member States, COM (2001) 398, published in OJ C 140E/538 of 13.6.2002. In that document, it calls on the Commission to draw up an action plan in this area, accompanied by measures to be taken. Furthermore, the European Council adopted its position on the matter, and adopted a report on the need to approximate Member States' legislation in civil matters; dated November 16, 2001 and available on http://register.consilium.eu.int/pdf/en/01/st12/12735en1.pdf. It invited the Commission to submit any observations and considerations deemed appropriate.

[15] Published in OJ C 63, 15.03.2003, pp. 1–44.

[16] In which "…summarizes the problems identified during the consultation process, which concern the need for uniform application of EC contract law as well as the smooth functioning of the internal market."

[17] Applying the Communication from the Commission of 5 June 2002, Action Plan "Simplifying and improving the regulatory environment" [COM (2002) 278 final], submitted on 5.6.2002, that identifies various tools that meet the objectives of the Treaties, with increased simplification of legislation, which are co-regulation, self-regulation, voluntary sectoral agreements, OMC, financial measures and information campaigns.

[18] This should make proposals for common terminology and rules; for example, those relating to fundamental concepts such as contract, but also with regard to other concepts such as damage, and the identification of the set of rules to apply in case of breach of contract.

[19] Point 53.

proper functioning of cross-border transactions and, therefore, the completion of the internal market."[20]

The development of the Principles of European Contract Law and the improvement of the quality of legislation[21], as well as the development[22], and the adoption of a Draft CFR—by 2009—as a tool to improve the coherence and quality of EU legislation—with regard to material standards of EU procurement[23], where considered by the Commission.

Following an invitation for an expression of interest,[24] a network of CFR experts was formed. Some members were part of the Study Group on a European Civil Code and others joined the new European Research Group on Existing EC Private Law (Acquis Group),[25] for the preparation of the draft CFR, and the submission of a proposal by the end of 2007. A draft version was completed during this time and published in 2008 (Von Bar et al. 2008). The definitive version of the Draft Common Frame of Reference (DCFR) prepared by the Study Group on a European Civil Code and the Research Group on Existing EC Private Law (Acquis Group) was published in 2009 (Von Bar et al. 2009).

However, and despite the early adoption of a CFR by 2009,[26] this was never adopted, and the Commission opted to prepare a Green Paper "On policy options for progress towards a European contract law for consumers and businesses."[27] The Commission stressed, in this document, the importance of filling in gaps in contract law, by adopting suitable instruments for removing the disparities between national laws, harnessing the potential of the internal market, and meeting the economic targets set by the EU instruments, whilst also recovering from the economic crisis.[28]

The main goal of the Green Paper was to expose the options on how to strengthen the internal market by making progress in the area of European contract law.

---

[20] Point 57.

[21] Communication on European Contract Law and the revision of the acquis: the way forward COM (2004) 651 final, of 11.10.2004. In this document, the Commission considered that the common frame of reference enables the revision of the acquis communautaire and enhances the coherence of new draft laws.

[22] In the First Annual Report on the progress made in the field of European Contract Law and the Acquis Review (COM (2005) 456 final) of 23.09.2005, the Commission announced the development of a Draft CFR by the end of 2007 and mentioned the initial operation of the CFR network as well as the work undertaken in relation to the Consumer Acquis. The adoption of an optional regime for European Contract Law was noted from the point of view of its opportuneness.

[23] Communication from the Commission to the Council and the European Parliament—The Hague Programme: Ten priorities for the next five years The Partnership for European renewal in the field of freedom, security and justice (COM/2005/0184 final) of 10.05.2005.

[24] As Sect. 2.2.1 of the Communication, p. 3, which was published in the OJ S 148 of 31.07.2004.

[25] With the support of the sixth Framework Program for research and technological development.

[26] For the DCFR, cf. Beale, Hugh—European contract law: The Common Frame of Reference and Beyond, In Twigg-Flesner, ed.—European Union Private Law, Cambridge, Cambridge University Press; 2010.

[27] COM (2010) 348 final, dated 1.7.2010.

[28] Document COM (2010) 348 final, p. 4, ensuring that citizens benefit fully from the advantages of the internal market (p. 1).

Despite basing its legitimacy on the Stockholm Programme (2010–2014),[29] in which the Council invites the Commission to present a proposal for the CFR and to continue its examination of the question of contract law, the Commission recognised that this action may give rise to sensitive issues of subsidiarity and proportionality.[30] In order to identify sensitivities with regard to strategic options, the Paper identified seven potential points of contention regarding the legal nature of the instrument of European contract law. Among those initiatives were options of soft law and hard law, conducing to harmonisation[31], *stricto sensu* unification[32], and standardisation[33].

In the opinion of the Committee on the Green Paper,[34] it can be seen that this institution was advocating the adoption of a "Toolbox", an optional regulatory regime providing more favourable circumstances for contracting parties, and an alternative to national provisions, provided that all of these options are available in all EU languages.

Other initiatives were important in this field such as the Communication "A Common European Sales Law to facilitate cross-border transactions in the single market"[35] and the Communication "Europe 2020"[36] and the "European Digital Agenda".[37]

However, the DCFR 2009, has been very important once it was the last step of the Draft CESL, prepared by the "Expert Group" for a Common Frame of Reference on European Contract Law, appointed by de Commission,[38] which presented a "feasibility study", for an European contract law for consumers and businesses.[39]

[29] Council Act of December 2, 2009, no. 17024/09, available at http://www.europa.eu.

[30] Clearly identifying the issue as to whether to adopt a regulation establishing a European contract law, bearing in minds the existence of increased sensitivity of both this principle and the option of adopting a Regulation establishing a European Civil Code with its more comprehensive framework.

[31] The publication of the results of the expert group, the creation of an official "toolbox" for the legislator, and the adoption of a Commission Recommendation on European contract law, all fall within the set of non-binding measures and, therefore, risk a less vigorous approach to the outlined objectives. As far as a harmonising measure is concerned, this is provided for by the option of adopting a Directive on European Contract Law.

[32] It is expected that these will adopt a regulation that provides for an optional measure—a unifying measure in a strict sense.

[33] The decision to adopt a regulation establishing a European contract law or a regulation establishing a European Civil Code instrument, i.e. measures contributing towards uniformity.

[34] Published in OJ C 84 of 17.03.2011.

[35] COM (2011) 636 final.

[36] COM (2010) 2020 final.

[37] COM (2010) 245 final.

[38] Commission Decision of 26.04.2010 establishing a group of experts for a common frame of reference (2010/233/EU), published in OJ L 105 of 27.04.2010.

[39] Available at: http://ec.europa.eu/justice/contract/files/feasibilty_study_final.pdf, accessed 15.06.2014.

The proposal for a Regulation of the European Parliament and the Council on a Common European Sales Law[40], was presented following the absence of agreement regarding an instrument establishing a compulsory scheme. The legislative process hasn't been linear[41], but the adoption by the European Parliament of a legislative resolution of 26 February 2014 on the proposal for a regulation of the European Parliament and of the Council on a Common European Sales Law[42], seems to indicate that the concretization of this first challenge, is getting closer. The Commission presented the proposal as an internal market legal basis, i.e. the article 114.1 of Treaty for the Functioning of the European Union (TFEU)[43], which enables the European Institutions to: "adopt the measures for approximation of the provisions laid down by law, regulation or administrative action in Member States which have as their object of establishment and functioning of the internal market." That have the effect of triggers the application of the ordinary legislative procedure.[44] Although the legal basis of the proposal met some criticism (Fleischer 2012; Wendehorst 2012; Micklitz and Reich 2012; Sánchez Lorenzo 2011), Council left the assumption of a final position on this matter to the final forecast of the structure and the scope of the proposal[45] and the European Parliament on its Legislative Resolution of 26.02.2014[46], maintains the legal basis of the proposal.

[40] COM (2011) 635 Final.

[41] As it results, specially, from the (draft) opinion of the Internal Market and Consumer Protection Committee, of 24.09.2012, rapporteurs for opinion Evelyne GEBHARDT and Hans-Peter MAYER, PE 505.986v01-00, available at: http://www.europarl.europa.eu/committees/en/imco/draft-opinions.html#menuzone, accessed 15.06.2014, and the amendments suggested by the co-rapporteurs, PE 505.986v01-00, available at: http://www.europarl.europa.eu/committees/en/imco/amendments.html#menuzone, accessed 15.06.2014, the opinion of the Committee on Economic and Monetary Affairs, of 9.10.2012, rapporteur Marianne THYSSEN, PE 491.011v02-00, available at http://www.europarl.europa.eu/committees/en/econ/opinions.html#menuzone; accessed 15.06.2014, and the opinion of the Legal Affairs Committee, of–.02.2013, draft Report, co-rapporteurs Klaus-Heiner LEHNE and Luigi BERLINGUER, PE505.998v02-00, http://www.europarl.europa.eu/committees/en/juri/draft-reports.html#menuzone, accessed 15.06.2014 (Following the working document of 10.2012, PE497.786v01-00, available at: http://www.europarl.europa.eu/committees/en/juri/working-documents.html#menuzone, accessed 15.06.2014), and the Report on the proposal for a regulation of the European Parliament and the Council on a Common European Sales Law, of 24.09.2013, A7-0301/2013, available at: http://www.europarl.europa.eu/document/activities/cont/201309/20130925ATT71873/20130925ATT71873EN.pdf, accessed 15.06.2014.

[42] http://www.europarl.europa.eu/sides/getDoc.do?type=TA&language=EN&reference=P7-TA-2014-0159, accessed 15.06.2014.

[43] Recital 6 of the proposal.

[44] This implies the involvement of the European Parliament and the Council.

[45] The Council also stated that diverging views on the question of the legal basis should not present an obstacle to starting work on examination of the Annex. See the press release of the Justice and Home Affairs Council of 7–8 June 2012, available at http://europa.eu/rapid/press-release_PRES-12-241_en.htm?locale=en, accessed 15.06.2014.

[46] Following the Report on the proposal for a regulation of the European Parliament and the Council on a Common European Sales Law, of 24.09.2013, and the position taken so far by the legal services of all institutions involved.

In which concerns the establishment and functioning of the internal market, the ECJ consider[47] that "(…) a measure adopted on the basis of article 100a of the Treaty [now article 114 TFEU] must genuinely have as its object the improvement of the conditions for the establishment and the functioning of the internal market".

Taken into account the objectives of the proposal, it seems to be the result of the proposal, as identified in art 1, paragraphs 2 and 3. The ECJ also consider that the use of such legal basis confers, in its scope of application, a discretion to choose the most appropriate harmonization technique.[48] The forecast of the CESL as a second contract law regime[49], idea that has been underlined by the Legislative Resolution of the European Parliament,[50] creates a real way to approximate de legislation of the Member States Knöfel and Bray (2012/2013).

1.3 Objective and Subject Matter

The purpose of the regulation is to improve the conditions for the establishment and the functioning of the internal market by making available[51] a uniform set of contract law rules for cross-border transactions for the sale of goods, supply of digital content and for related services, where de parties to a contract agree to do so (art 1).

In which concern the benefits resulting from the implementation of the regulation, paragraph 2 identifies the reduction of unnecessary costs of the cross-border transactions and an implementation of a high level of legal certainty[52].

The future regulation is also supposed to guarantee (…) a high level of consumer protection, to enhance consumer confidence to internal market and encourage consumers to shop across borders" (paragraph 3). The possibility of achievement of those objectives was object of several critical comments (Eindenmuller 2012; Smits 2012).

---

[47] In the judgment by which the tobacco advertising Directive was annulled, Case C-376/98, Germany vs European Parliament and Council, [2000] ECR I-8419.

[48] Case C-217/04, United Kingdom vs Parliament and Council, [2006] ECR I-3771.

[49] Recital 9.

[50] See amendment to article 1, paragraph 1 "(…)making available within the legal order of each Member State, a uniform set of contract law rules(…)".

[51] The Legislative Resolution of the European Parliament of 26.02.2014, following the Report of the European Parliament of September 2013, suggests the amendment above mentioned. If that suggestion will be considered in the final version, that contributes to clarify the role of the Proposal. This reference is in line also with the Amendment proposed by the European Parliament to the recital 9.

[52] The Legislative Resolution of the European Parliament, in the same sense that the above mentioned Report, introduce the expression "in particular small or medium-sized enterprises (SME'S)", in order to clarify the interest of the CESL for traders.

1.4 Scope of Application

a. Personal Scope of Application The Commission didn't identify any reason of concern as regards contracts concluded between natural persons (C2C) and those concluded between B2B, since one of the B is not a SME.

In this context, the parties covered are: the seller, or the supplier, who is a trader, and the other is either a C or an SME. The parties under the scope must be in some commercial relations as B2C or B2SME only (art 7). The definitions of consumer (art 2 (f) of CESL Proposal), trader (Article 2 e) and SME (Article 7 (2)), are essential to determine the personal scope of application.

The trader is any natural or legal person who is acting for purposes relating to that person's trade, business, craft, or profession. The trader could be a big enterprise or a SME under the criteria of art 7 points (a) and (b). In which concerns the contracts B2B with a part SME, it has been point out that the non SME part would have some practical difficulties to determine whether the other part fulfil the criteria or not, to be considered a SME (Knöfel and Bray 2012/2013). Due to the optional nature of the future regulation, the question related to false statements, can arise from the information provided by the parties, especially if the contract is a B2SME, is not solved by the regulation. That's not a question of lack of interest by the European legislator[53], but only a tentative of not having more hesitations by their addresses. It was also noted that once more or less 90 % of the enterprises are SME, the question won't have a huge importance.

The service provider is a seller of goods or supplier of digital contents who undertakes to provide a customer with a service related to those goods or that digital content (art 2 point b)[54]. The consumer is any natural person who is acting for purposes which are outside that person's trade, business, craft or profession[55]. This concept was criticized due to the lack of connexion with other similar provisions (Sánchez Lorenzo 2013), for not considering elements frequently used by the acquis (Behar-Touchais 2012), such as the possibility of considering a B acting as a C if the professional objective doesn't prevail, and also for not including the non-profit making entities (Knöfel and Bray 2012/2013), and it is expected to achieve some improvements. The Legislative Resolution of the European Parliament of 26.02.1014[56], suggest the introduction of the following text to the final part of the provision: "where the contract is concluded for purposes partly within and partly

[53] In that sense, Wenderhorst (2012).

[54] Point fa of the Legislative Resolution of the European Parliament of 26.02.2014, has it has been suggested by the same institution in its earlier Report.

[55] In the Legislative Resolution of the European Parliament of 26.02.14, following the Report of the same institution of 24.09.2013, is suggested the introduction of a final part of the provision: "Where the contract is concluded for purposes partly within and partly outside that person's trade and the trade purpose is so limited as not to be predominant in the overall context of the contract, that person shall also be considered to be a consumer;", introduce an amendment in order to clarify the interest of the CESL for traders, mainly "in particular small or medium-sized enterprises (SME'S)".

[56] Above mentioned.

outside that person's trade and the trade purpose is so limited as not to be predominant in the overall context of the contract, that person to be a consumer." The adoption of this suggestion will be in line with the critics, but it's not granted.

Nevertheless, the possibility of application to B2B depends on the position of the Member State (art 13b).

The application of the future regulation to business to business contracts was one of the questions in discussion, and it's not excluded so far that a change to the prevision of article 7 will be made[57]. The argument in favor of that solution is that the CESL is an offer to the parties and there must be no limitation to the parties included, as it has been pointed out by the rapporteurs of the Committee on Legal Affairs[58].

b. Territorial Scope of Application—Crossborder Contracts The CESL proposal is applicable to Cross-border contracts. The art. 4 provides so[59]. On the same time this provision contains the territorial scope of application of the regulation (Wendehorst 2012). Apparently, this proposal won't be applicable to purely domestic situations, as long as each Member State doesn't decide for the internal application of the regime (art. 13 a), what could be a first step towards a future adoption of a code in Europe. This provision that has never been considered by the expert groups (Schulte-Nölke 2011), and is criticized due to the difficulty to distinguish between cross-border and purely domestic contracts (Knöfel and Bray 2012/2013), was introduced to the proposal by the European Commission. The idea of create a new optional regime to be in force in all Member States, even in purely domestic situations, would have had an effect more inefficient on the legislative procedure (Knöfel and Bray 2012/2013). Although that, the fact that the cross-border nature of the contract might be incidental, and also considering that mobility is growing each day, and that contributes to a possible qualification of a contract as cross-border, without have relevant connecting elements with more than one State. It has been said that especially the large enterprises can created a cross-border situation if they want the CESL to be applied (European Law Institute 2012). Nevertheless, the experience about B2B transactions seems to be that big enterprises usually prefer to decide which regime to apply using the party autonomy, under the scope of application of the Rome I or Rome II Regulations, or choosing the arbitrage, and submitting the contracts to other principles such as Unidroit (Zanobetti 2011) or

[57] The Report and the legislative Resolution of the European Parliament, from 24.09.2013 and 26.2.2014, respectively, don't maintain the prevision of the final part of the first paragraph of the article (7.0) neither the second paragraph. So that could mean, if a final version would be approved with that prevision, that no obstacles would be consider to transaction between business to business parties, and also the difficulties that could arise, in practical terms to a part of a contract, in order to qualify the other part as a SME or not, will disappear.

[58] On the working document PE497.786v01-00, available at: http://www.europarl.europa.eu/committees/en/juri/working-documents.html#menuzone, accessed 15.06.2014.

[59] The Legislative Resolution of the European Parliament introduce a suggestion in this aspect, considering the application of the regulation to distance contracts, especially to on line contracts—see amendment to recital 9.

the *lex mercatoria, e.g.* The question to know what a cross-border contract is[60], is similar to that one that arises from the scope of application of Rome I Regulation (Behar-Touchais 2012).

Considering only the application of this future regulation, a greater similarity can be found with the regime of the Vienna Convention on the International Sales of Goods (Wendehorst 2012). The qualification of the contract depends on the characterisation of the transaction: between traders (B2B) or between a trader and a consumer (B2C), differently the PECL, DCFR and the Acquis Group do not distinguished between concluded contracts with consumers and commercial contracts—in the last case save for some— (Moss 2010).

If the transaction occurs between traders having their habitual residence in different countries of which at least one is a Member State,—and also the European Economic Area (EEA) (Wendehorst 2012), the contract is considered to be cross-border. In which concerns the consumer, it is possible to choose the relevant residence and thus to submit the contract to a certain national regime and then to apply CESL, given to its artificial cross-border nature.

The habitual residence of a legal person is in the same place where the central administration is located. The European legislator followed, in general, the concept previously adopted by Rome II Regulation (art. 23), and the full provision in that matter by the Rome I Regulation (art. 19). The paragraph 4 of art. 4 states that: "Where the contract is concluded in the course of the operations of a branch, an agency or any other establishment of a trader" the habitual residence shall be considered at that place of the secondary establishment. If the trader is a physical person, his habitual residence is the principal place of business.

However, and despite the possibility given to the consumer to create a cross-border contract, due to the choice of the place that should be considered his habitual residence, CESL only applies under the conditions of article 4, and the other assumptions[61].CESL cannot apply by virtue of the CESL Regulation (Hartley 2013). If the traders have their habitual residence outside the EU, or the applicable law is one of a non-Member State of the EU, the choice of the CESL would be a material reference to this regulation, only applied in the terms that the applicable state law consents (Lagarde 2013; Hartley 2013).

While enforcing the contractual law in the EU, the traders of outside will need to conduct additional risk assessments when contracting with EU parties (Kenny et al. 2011).

c. Substantive Scope of Application This regulation proposal refers to its substantive scope of application in articles 5 and 6. Art. 5 bargain for the application of the proposal to the transactions for the sales of goods, for the supply in digital content and for related services[62]. Mixed-purposed contracts and contracts linked to con-

[60] And to the discussion that still exists between the juridical concept of international contract and the economical one.

[61] e.g. art. 2 and 8.

[62] The Legislative Resolution of the European Parliament, as well as the Report of the same institution, suggest an amendment to this provision in order to include the reference that CESL can be

sumer credit are expressly excluded from the substantive scope of application of the proposal (art. 6)[63]. Searching for a solution of legal certainty and predictability, considering the internal previsions of each Member State, the proposal defines those contracts for the effects of the application of the future regulation. The definitions are of outstanding importance[64], taken into account the needs of the uniform application of that future regime. For the same reason, the importance of the recitals must be empathized as an important element of interpretation (Wendehorts 2012)[65]. Considering that the proposal is part of the acquis communautaire (Sánchez Lorenzo 2013; Schmidt-Kessel 2012), some questions related to its interpretation can arise in that field, due to the absence of a strong connexion with the other legal dispositions in force (Sánchez Lorenzo 2013), and due to the necessity of interpreting the concepts with the same sense in all the European Union legislation (Garcimartín Alférez 2013). As it has already been said relatively to other regulations (Lima Pinheiro 2009), and is also bargain for this regulation[66], all the concepts are subjected to an autonomous interpretation, regarding national laws. The ECJ[67], with the cooperation of national judges, has the last responsibility in matters of unification of the interpretation of the European Union law (Moura Ramos 2002), via de use of preliminary questions (Nogueira Serens 2011)[68]. This institution has always mentioned and applied the need of such interpretation. Moura Ramos (2013)[69] The legal culture on this topic already exists, but the regulation proposal demonstrates a real concern about its coherent application, implementing a new mechanism, foreseen in art. 14 (Communication of judgements applying this regulation). Therefore, in order to have a uniform application of this future regime, it is important that the interpretation of the ECJ, as well as the decisions of the national courts are known (Doralt 2001; Wendehorts 2012).[70] The CESL applies only to contract law

used for distance contracts, including online contracts, this new scope is also suggested for the supply of digital content, in paragraph 1, point b, with the addition "…or through any other means…" before "whether supplied on a tangible medium,…."

[63] The Legislative Resolution of the European Parliament of 26.02.14, as it was already considered at the Report of the same institution of 24.9.2013, makes reference to Linked Contracts and mixed-purpose contracts. These documents also contain some amendment suggestions to this provision and in which concerns the mixed purpose contracts the amendment suggested to paragraph 1 c, is intend to clarify that if the situation includes an element which does not fall within the scope of the CESL, such as transport services, this element will be treated as a linked contract.

[64] Even if omnis definitio in jure periculosa est.

[65] Mainly, Recitals 16–20.

[66] Recital 29.

[67] This concern about the uniform and autonomous interpretation of the concepts, was contemplated in the Treaty of Rome, prevision that has always remains in the Treaties (art TFUE).

[68] This means that no judge will interpret this regulation proposal according to the interpretation rules and standards of its internal law, but only according to the regulation, which as to regard the other legal dispositions of the European Union.

[69] See ECJ decision of 17.09.2013, File C-184/12 UNAMAR, recital 31.

[70] However, the Legislative Resolution and the Report of the European Parliament, from 26.2.2014b and 24.09.2013, respectively, don't maintain this prevision, following the regulations in conflict of laws in force (Rome I and Rome II Regulations).

matters[71]. Nevertheless, according to Recital 27 of the proposal, the future regime won't be applicable to "…legal personality, the invalidity of a contract arising from lack of capacity, illegality or immorality, the determination of the language of the contract, matters of non-discrimination, representation, plurality of debtors and creditors, change of parties including assignment, set-off and merger, property law including the transfer of ownership, intellectual property law and the law of torts. Furthermore, the issue of whether concurrent contractual and non-contractual liability claims can be pursued together falls outside the scope of the Common European Sales Law." In that case, the internal law applicable would be the one identified by the Rome I or Rome II Regulations[72]. All other questions related to matters not regulated by CESL, even if not included in the above mentioned recital, are solved by the applicable law, as determined following the criteria of the regulations Rome I or Rome II (Hartley 2013).

Within its scope of application and with a valid agreement of the parties to use it, due to its optional nature[73], matter that will be treated in other chapter, the CESL would apply instead the national contract law regimes, and it will be the only regime that should govern the matters falling within its scope[74].

This is an ambitious project that, while not solving all difficulties and barriers within the internal market, will provide, and will surely achieve, greater balance between the level of consumer protection and the protection of the interests of the other party who may feel that the scheme will not be unfavourable (Alpa et al. 2012). It is also a model that is achievable, bearing in mind the difficulty of agreement on the initiative and its lack of legal force, and with the same interpretation problems as the other Regulations and Directives (Gebauer 2013). The approval and the entry in force of such a regime, will certainly left the door open for future harmonisation initiatives in EU contract law.

References

Alpa, Guido et al., The proposed Common European Sales Law—the Lawyer's View, Sellier: 2012.

Behar-Touchais, "The functioning of the CESL within the framework of the Rome Regulation", pp. 1–90 (http:www.europarl.europa.eu/RegData/etudes/join/2012/462477/IPOL-JURI_ET (2012) 462477_EN.pdf), 2012.

COMMISSION OF THE EUROPEAN COMMUNITIES, COMMUNICATION FROM THE COMMISSION TO THE COUNCIL AND THE EUROPEAN PARLIAMENT ON EUROPEAN CONTRACT LAW, COM(2001) 398 final, of 11.07.2001.

COMMISSION OF THE EUROPEAN COMMUNITIES, COMMUNICATION FROM THE COMMISSION, Action plan "Simplifying and improving the regulatory environment", COM(2002) 278 final, of 11.07.2001.

---

[71] Recitals 26 and 28.

[72] Recital 27.

[73] The optional nature of the instrument is in keeping with the internal choice of the applicable law according to conflict of laws rules (art. 3).

[74] See amendment proposed by the European Parliament to recital 12 of the proposal.

COMMISSION OF THE EUROPEAN COMMUNITIES, COMMUNICATION FROM THE COMMISSION TO THE EUROPEAN PARLIAMENT AND THE COUNCIL, European Contract Law and the revision of the acquis: the way forward, COM(2004) 651 final, of 11.10.2004.

COMMISSION OF THE EUROPEAN COMMUNITIES, REPORT FROM THE COMMISSION, First Annual Progress Report on European Contract Law and the Acquis Review, COM(2005) 456 final, of 23.9.2005, Published OJ C 49, 28.02.2006.

Doralt, Walter, "The Optional European Contract Law and why success or failure may depend on the scope rather than substance". Max Planck Private Law Research Paper n.º 11/9, pp. 1–26 (http://ssrn.com/abstract=1876451), 2011.

Eindenmüller H., What can be wrong with an option? An optional Common European Salles law as a regulatory tool", pp. 1–15, (http://ssrn.com/abstract=2102827), 2012.

EUROPEAN COMMISSION, GREEN PAPER FROM THE COMMISSION on policy options for progress towards a European Contract Law for consumers and businesses, COM(2010)348 final, of, 1.7.2010

EUROPEAN COMISSION, Proposal for a REGULATION OF THE EUROPEAN PARLIAMENT AND OF THE COUNCIL on a Common European Sales Law, COM (2011) 635 final, dated 11.10.2011.

European Law Institute, Statement of the European Law Institute on the Proposal for a Regulation on a Common European Sales Law COM (2011) 635 final, (http://www.europeanlawinstitute.eu/fileadmin/user_upload/p_eli/Publications/S-2-2012_Statement_on_the_Proposal_for_a_Regulation_on__a_Common_European_Sales_Law.pdf), 2012.

Fleischer, H. "Optionales Europaisches Privatrecht "28 Model", Max Planck Research Paper n.º 12/5, pp. 1–21, (www.reei.org), 2012.

Gandolfi, G. ed.—Code Europeén des Contrats: avant-project, Giuffré: 2007.

Garcimartín Alférez, Francisco J., "Hermeneutic Dialog between Rome I and Rome II", In A Commitment to Private International Law—Essays in honour of Hans Van Loon, pp. 169–180, Intersentia, 2013.

Gebauer, Martin, Gemeinsames Europäisches Kaufrecht—Anwendungsbereich und kollisionsrechtliche Einbettung, GPR, Sellier: 2013.

Hartley, Trevor C., "Conflict of laws and the common european sales law", In Entre Bruselas y la Haya, Estudios sobre la unificación internacional y regional del Derecho internacional privado, Liber Amicorum Alegría Borrás, J. Forner Delaygua, C. González Beilfuss, R. Vinãs Farré (coords.), pp. 525–533, Marcial Pons, 2013.

Kenny, Mel; Gillies, Lorna; Devenney, James;"The EU optional instrument, : Absorbing the Private International Law Implications of a Common European Sales Law, Yearbook of Private International Law, Vol. 13, 2011.

Knöfel, Susanne; Bray, Robert, The Proposal for a Common European Salles law: a Snapshot of the Debate, YPIL, 14, pp. 385–407, 2012/2013.

Lagarde, Paul; "Instrument optionel international et droit international privé –subordination ou independence?", In A Commitment to Private International Law – Essays in honour of Hans Van Loon, pp. 287–298, Intersentia, 2013.

Lando, O.; Beale, H., eds.—Principles of European Contract Law Parts I and II. The Hague, Kluwer: 2000.

Lando, O., Clive, E; Prüm, A., Zimmermann, R., eds.—Principles of European Contract Law Part III. The Hague, Kluwer: 2003.

Lima Pinheiro, Luís, Direito Internacional Privado, Voll. II, Almedina , 2009.

Mankowski, P. "Der vorschlag fur ein Gemeinsames Europaisches Kauftrecht (CESL) und das International Privatrecht", Recht der Internationalen Wirtschaft, pp. 97–105, 2012.

Micklitz and Reich, "The Commission Proposal for a regulation on a Common European Salles Law (CESL)—To broad or not to broad enough?", EUI Working Paper Law 2012/04, pp. 1–93 (http://cadmus.eui.eu/bitstream/handle/1814/20485/LAW_2012_04_ERPL_03.pdf), 2012.

Moss, Guiditta Cordero, "Commercial contracts and European private law", In The British Companion to European Union Private Law, Edited by Christian Twigg-Flesner, pp. 147–159, Cambridge University Press: 2010.

Moura Ramos, Rui Manuel, "O Tribunal de Justiça das Comunidades Europeias e a teoria geral do direito internacional privado, desenvolvimentos recentes", In Estudos em Homenagem Ã Professora Doutora Isabel Magalhães Collaço, Vol. I, pp. 431–467, Almedina, 2002.

Moura Ramos, Rui Manuel, "Lugar da prestação habitual do trabalho e direito internacional privado da União Europeia", In Revista de Legislação e de Jurisprudência, Ano 112.º, N.º 3981, pp. 385–400, Coimbra Editora, Julho-Agosto 2013.

Nogueira Serens, M., A obrigação de reenvio prejudicial decorrente do art.º 234, § 3.º (Ex- art. 177, § 3.º) do Tratado CE, In Estudos de homenagem ao Professor Doutor Carlos Ferreira de Almeida, Comissão organizadora José Lebre de Freitas, Rui Pinto Duarte, Assunção Cristas, Vítor Pereira das Neves e Marta Tavares de Almeida, Almedina, 2011.

Palao Moreno, "El Marco Común de Referencia como sistema opcional 28ª: algunas reflexiones desde el Derecho internacional privado", In: Blasco Gascó et al., Estudios en homenage a Vicente L. Montés Penadés, Vol. II, pp. 1905–1922, Tirant lo Blanch, 2011.

Research Group on the Existing EC Private Law (Acquis Group) ed., "Principles of the Existing EC Contract Law (Acquis Principles) – Contract II: General Provisions, Delivery of Goods, Package Travel and Payment Services, Munich, Sellier: 2009.

Sánchez Lorenzo, Sixto A. , "La propuesta de Reglamento relativo a una Normativa Común de Compraventa Europea y el Derecho International Privado", Anuario Espãnol de Derecho Internacional Privado, N.º XI, pp. 35–61, 2011.

Sánchez Lorenzo, Sixto A. , "De Bruselas a la Haya, passando por Roma y Viena: La normativa común de compraventa europea", In Entre Bruselas y la Haia, Estudios sobre la unificación internacional y regional del Derecho internacional privado, Liber Amicorum Alegría Borrás, J. Forner Delaygua, C. González Beilfuss, R. Vinãs Farré (coords.); pp. 821–832, Marcial Pons, 2013.

Schmidt-Kessel, M., "Anwendungsbereich, Ausgestaltung der Option und andere Fragen zur Verordenung", In Schmidt-Kessel et al., Ein einheitliches europäisches Kaufrecht? (Eine Analyse des Vorschlags der Kommission), pp. 35–45, Sellier, 2012.

Schulte-Nölke, "Scope and Function of the Optional Instrument in European Contract Law", In Schulze et al., Towards a European Contract Law, pp. 35–45, Sellier, 2011.

Smits, Jan, "Party choice and the Common European Salles Law or: how to prevent the CESL from becoming a lemon on the law market", Maastricht European Private Law Institute Working Paper n.º 2012/13, pp. 1–21 (http://ssrn.com/abstract=2060017), 2012/2013.

Von Bar, Christian–Le groupe d' Études sur un Civil Code Européen. In Revue International de Droit Comparé, Volume 53, Numero 1, pp. 127–139, Année 2001.

Von Bar, Christian; Clive, Eric and Schulte-Nölke, Hans (eds.)—Principles, Definitions and Model Rules of European private Law, Draft Common Frame of Reference (DCFR), Interin Outline Ed. Munich, Sellier: 2008.

Von Bar, Christian; Clive, Eric and Schulte-Nölke, Hans (eds.)—Principles, Definitions and Model Rules of European private Law, Draft Common Frame of Reference (DCFR), Outline Ed. Munich. Sellier: 2009.

Wendehorst, (2012), "Articles 1–16", In Schulze (ed.), Common European Sales Law (CESL)—Commentary, pp. 9–84, Beck/Hart/Nomos, 2012.

Zanobetti, Alessandra, Unidroit's recent work: an appraisal, Yearbook of Private International Law, Vol. 13, 2011. 345–365

Chapter 2
Some Private International Law Issues

Guillermo Palao Moreno

Abstract The Draft CESL is not only intended to cover intra-European transactions, but will also be applicable to contracts linked to third countries. This twofold effect raises interesting legal questions that are going to be analysed in this chapter from the perspective of Private International Law.

During the final stages of the legislative process, certain decisive decisions must be adopted. In particular, from the perspective of Private International Law, there are some key aspects which should also be clarified. Attention should be paid, for example, to certain significant issues such as its relationship with Rome I and II Regulations, or with the CISG; as well as the applicability of the European instrument when a cross-border transaction would be governed by the law of a third country that is not a Member of the EU.

Keywords European Private International Law · Cross-border transactions · Conflict-of-laws aspects · Consumer protection rules

2.1 Legal Context of the Proposal

The proposal for a Regulation on a Common European Sales Law (CESL)[1] is an important step forward in the direction of creating a harmonized normative legal framework for contracts in the European Union (EU). This initiative is also closely linked to the development of a "European Contract Law". In that respect, some recent and definitive landmarks connected with this European initiative are worth mentioning:

a. As a starting point and from an academic point of view, the Draft Common Frame of Reference (DCFR) of 2009 must be highlighted (Von bar et al. 2009). This work was the result of several decades of study and discussion carried out

[1] COM (2011) 635 final.

G. Palao Moreno (✉)
University of Valencia, Valencia, Spain
e-mail: guillermo.palao@uv.es

© Springer International Publishing Switzerland 2015
J. Plaza Penadés, L. M. Martínez Velencoso (eds.), *European Perspectives on the Common European Sales Law,* Studies in European Economic Law and Regulation 4,
DOI 10.1007/978-3-319-10497-3_2

by hundreds of academics and practitioners from all the EU Member States—in particular, those involved in the "Study Group on a European Civil Code" and the "*Acquis* Group", who cooperated in the framework of the "Joint Network on European Private Law" (Palao Moreno 2011). The DCFR 2009 has been an important precedent of the Draft CESL, which was prepared by the "Expert Group" for a Common Frame of Reference on European Contract Law, appointed by the European Commission,[2] which presented a "feasibility study" for a future instrument in the field of European Contract Law in 2011 (Gómez Pomar and Gili Saldaña 2010).[3]

b. Additionally, and from an institutional perspective, the European institutions have recently produced various definitive documents that have stimulated this process; *inter alia*: the Communication "An area of freedom, security and justice serving the citizen",[4] the Green Paper "On policy options for progress towards a European Contract Law for consumers and businesses"[5] or, even more recently and directly related to the Draft CESL, the Communication "A Common European Sales Law to facilitate cross-border transactions in the single market".[6] Other decisive documents that should also be taken into account in relation to this process are the Communication "Europe 2020"[7] and the "European Digital Agenda".[8]
c. These notable initiatives have, as their main objective, the strengthening of the Internal Market as well as promoting cross-border sales within the EU and, more particularly, e-commerce. Therefore, all of them are closely linked to the development of a "European Private International Law" in the field of the Law of Obligations, a legal sector where some important Regulations have also been adopted from a purely conflict-of-laws perspective—the Rome I and Rome II Regulations,[9] as well as from a jurisdictional perspective—the Brussels I Regulation, which has been recently "recasted"[10].

This intense legislative process has not finished yet. Thus, any reflection on it can only be provisional in nature. However, it is not difficult to observe the strong po-

---

[2] *OJ* No L 105/109, 27.1.2010.

[3] Available at: http://ec.europa.eu/justice/contract/files/feasibility_study_final.pdf, accessed 9.12.2013.

[4] COM (2009) 262 final.

[5] COM (2010) 348 final.

[6] COM (2011) 636 final.

[7] COM (2010) 2020 final.

[8] COM (2010) 245 final.

[9] Respectively, Regulation (EC) No 593/2008, on the law applicable to contractual obligations (Rome I)—*OJ* No L 177, 17.6.2008; and Regulation (EC) No 864/2007, on the law applicable to non-contractual obligations (Rome II)—*OJ* No L 199, 31.7.2007.

[10] Regulation (EC) No 44/2001, on jurisdiction and the recognition and enforcement of judgments in civil and commercial matters—*OJ* No L 12, 16.1.2001, "recasted" by Regulation (EU) No 1215/2012, on jurisdiction and the recognition and enforcement of judgments in civil and commercial matters (recast)—*OJ* No L 351, 20.12.2012.

litical interest underlying the development of a future CESL. In this respect, the fact that the European Parliament has recently published a definitive Report on the Proposal (at the end of September 2013) is highly significant. This new document enables us to consider that the end of this journey is getting closer.[11]

According to art. 1.1 (*Objective and subject matter*), the Draft CESL basically aims "(...) *to improve the conditions for the establishment and the functioning of the internal market by making available a uniform set of contract law rules as set out in Annex I ('the Common European Sales Law')*".[12] These are a set of rules that "(...) *can be used for cross-border transactions for the sale of goods, for the supply of digital content and for related services where the parties to a contract agree to do so*".[13] Amongst the benefits to be derived from the future instrument, paragraph 2 refers to: "*(...) reducing unnecessary costs while providing a high degree of legal certainty*", and paragraph 3 mentions the importance of guaranteeing "*(..) a high level of consumer protection, to enhance consumer confidence in the internal market and encourage consumers to shop across borders*", (Recitals 1–8). However, various authors have made critical comments to the reality of being able to fulfil these objectives (Posner 2012; Eidenmüller 2012; Smits 2012; see however, Mak 2012).

The proposal for a Regulation finds its legal basis in art. 114.1 Treaty for the Functioning of the European Union (TFEU)—instead of the other available alternatives—something that has been met with criticism by the authors: Fleischer (2012); Micklitz and Reich (2012), and Sánchez Lorenzo (2011). This provision enables the European institutions to "(...) *adopt the measures for the approximation of the provisions laid down by law, regulation or administrative action in Member States which have as their object the establishment and functioning of the internal market*".

2.2 Main Elements of the Proposal

The Draft CESL consists of 16 Articles, 37 Recitals and 2 Annexes. In particular, from the perspective of Private International Law, this instrument can be characterised as a "special substantive rule" (Mankowski 2012a; Sánchez Lorenzo 2013), aimed at regulating the contracts covered by the instrument when they enjoy a cross-border nature. Due to the objective of this particular chapter, only the conflict-

---

[11] *Report on the proposal for a regulation of the European Parliament and the Council on a Common European Sales Law*, of 24.9.2013 (A7-0301/2013). Available at: http://www.europarl.europa.eu/document/activities/cont/201309/20130925ATT71873/20130925ATT71873EN.pdf, accessed 9.12.2013.

[12] The Report of the European Parliament of 24.9.2013, refers to the expression "*within the legal order of each Member State*", to underline its consideration of a "second national regime" (*cit.*, p. 42), as it will be analysed later (see infra 2, D).

[13] In the Report of the European Parliament of 24.9.2013, this aspect has been made more specific as it refers to the necessity that those contracts be "*conducted at a distance, in particular online*" (*cit.*, p. 23).

of-laws aspects of the future European instrument will be analysed. Thus, the rules of applicability, confined to the first provisions of the so-called "*chapeau*" of the proposal for a Regulation, will constitute the principal focus of this chapter.[14]

2.2.1 Substantive Scope of Application

To summarise, as this question will be analysed later in other chapters of this Book, the Draft CESL refers to its substantive scope of application mainly in arts. 5 (*Contracts for which the Common European Sales Law can be used*), and 6 (*Exclusion of mixed-purpose contracts and contracts linked to a consumer credit*); (Illescas Ortiz and Perales Viscasillas 2012; Wenderhorts 2012). Nevertheless, art. 2 (*Definitions*) and the related Recitals of the Proposal should also be taken into account (Recitals 16–20) (Wenderhorts 2012), in order to determine which type of transactions are covered by this future European instrument. Needless to say, all those provisions are of outstanding interest from the perspective of Private International Law.

On the one hand, art. 5 provides that transactions for the sale of goods, for the supply of digital content and for related services, are covered by the Proposal.[15] On the other hand, art. 6 establishes that mixed-purpose contracts and contracts linked to consumer credit should be excluded from its scope of application.[16] In relation to this, art. 2 aims to define those contracts in order to meet greater legal certainty and predictability, in the face of the conceptual disparities that can be found among the legal systems of Member States.

In that respect, and specifically from a cross-border standpoint, it must be emphasised that those concepts should be subject to an autonomous and independent interpretation, as mentioned in Recital 29. Thus the European Court of Justice (ECJ) must be the institution responsible for laying down uniform parameters for the concepts used in the Draft CESL, *via* the use of preliminary questions. However, the future instrument will ultimately be applied by the national courts of the Member States; an issue that is of importance for the fulfilment of the goals of the Draft CESL. In this respect, any divergent national application of the future instrument may have the effect of undermining legal certainty, if the different legal traditions within the EU are considered (Dimatteo 2012).

Therefore, it is important that not only the decisions arrived at by national courts be made accessible to the rest of the national jurisdictional authorities—to promote a coherent application of the CESL—but also that the information mechanism fore-

[14] In the Report of the European Parliament of 24.9.2013, this is called Part I under the name "*Application of the instrument*", in order to avoid confusion and to establish a robust connection with the Annexes.

[15] These contracts should be "*distance contracts, including online contracts*" as underlined by the Report of the European Parliament of 24.9.2013 (*cit*., p. 23).

[16] However, in the Report of the European Parliament of 24.9.2013 it is stated that this exclusion, present at art. 6.1, makes reference to "*Linked* contracts and *mixed-purpose contracts*".

seen in art. 14 (*Communication of judgments applying this Regulation*) be made applicable (Doralt 2011; Wenderhorts 2012).[17]

From another perspective, it can be seen that the Draft CESL concentrates exclusively on Contract Law matters (as stressed in Recital 28) and also mentions which issues should (Recital 26) or should not (Recital 27) be regulated by the future European instrument.[18] Again, this delimitation of the issues covered (or excluded) by the Draft CESL, is of a great importance from the perspective of Private International Law. In this respect, it has to be taken into consideration that those issues not covered by the Draft CESL should be governed by the applicable Private International Law system, in accordance with the issue in question (Hesselink 2012). Therefore, the interaction between the future Regulation and other Private International Law rules would gain practical importance.[19]

2.2.2 *Cross-Border Contracts*

Article 4 of the Draft CESL has been entitled "Cross-border contracts".[20] This provision is of outstanding interest, since it would determine whether or not the parties would be able to agree to the application of the future instrument to their contract. Besides, and as mentioned in Recital 13, it is in the context of cross-border situations "that the disparities between national laws lead to complexity and additional costs and dissuade parties from entering into contractual relationships".[21] Therefore, and in principle, the parties to those transactions would only be able to ask for the application of the Draft CESL to their cross-border contracts and not to purely domestic situations. it should be noted that the inclusion of this option is the sole responsibility of the European Commission and that it was not analysed by the Expert Group (Schulte-Nölke 2011).

---

[17] Nevertheless, this obligation has been suppressed in the Report of the European Parliament of 24.9.2013.

[18] The Report of the European Parliament of 24.9.2013 clarifies some of these elements. In this respect, its Recital 27 refers to the possibility that the CESL determine which issues would be included or excluded in order to clarify this issue. In relation to this objective, a new art. 11 (*Matters covered by the Common European sales Law*) would be added to specify those issues that are covered (paragraph 1) and those that are not covered (paragraph 2).

[19] This question was clarified—in the negative—in the Report of the European Parliament of 24.9.2013, with the following wording in art. 11.1: "*Where the parties have validly agreed to use the Common European Sales Law for a contract, only the Common European Sales Law shall govern the matters addressed in its rules, instead of the contract-law regime that would, in the absence of such an agreement, govern the contract within the legal order determined as the applicable law*".

[20] This also should have been qualified as "*distance contracts which are cross-border*", according to the Report of the European Parliament of 24.9.2013.

[21] In addition, the Report of the European Parliament of 24.9.2013 added: "(…), and that distance trade, in particular trade online, has a high potential".

However, despite the literal wording of art. 4, this provision does not only establish the main elements that would enable a contract to be considered as cross-border, but it also allows for the determination of the territorial scope of application of the future instrument (Wenderhorts 2012). This delimitation would depend on the characterisation of the transaction as being a contract between traders (B2B) or between a trader and a consumer (B2), due to their different nature and policy involved, in accordance with the contacts that each transaction maintains with the Member States of the UE—in a similar way that art. 1 of the Vienna Convention on Contracts for the International Sale of Goods of 1980 (CISG)[22] operates to determine its territorial scope of application (Wenderhorts 2012). This delimitation is also compatible with the one contained in art. 1 Rome I Regulation, according to Behar-Touchais (2012).

With regard to B2B transactions, art. 4 refers to those situations where "(…) *the parties have their habitual residence in different countries of which at least one is a Member State*". Hence, when the habitual residence of the traders is to be found in different countries and at least one of those countries is a Member State of the EU—and in the opinion of Wenderhorts (2012), this should mean both the EU and the European Economic Area (EEA)—the parties to the contract would be allowed to opt for the application of the future CESL.

In that respect, a crucial element to consider would be the determination of the place where the habitual residence of the traders is located. This operation would not always be easy to undertake because it is a personal and subjective element which can vary from one country to the other, and its location may depend on the circumstances of each case. So when traders are involved in a B2B transaction, their particular situation must be taken into account.

a. Firstly, where the trader is a legal person, it should be understood, in general terms, that its habitual residence is in the same place where its central administration is located. The equivalence between habitual residence and central administration here is not a novelty in EU Law, as a precedent can be found in art. 23.1 Rome II Regulation. However, a different approach was established in art. 60 Brussels I Regulation—for the determination of the internationally competent national jurisdiction—as this provision provides for an option of either the statutory seat, the central administration, or the principal place of business.
b. Secondly, if the trader, who is a legal person, is acting through a secondary establishment—a branch, an agency or other secondary establishment—it must bear in mind that its habitual residence will be considered to be where the secondary establishment was situated, if the transaction was concluded "*in the course of the (its) operations*" (*cf* Wenderhorts 2012). This solution resembles the one currently provided in art. 23.1 Rome II Regulation; and, from a jurisdictional perspective, it is also similar to art. 5.5 Brussels I Regulation.

[22] Available at: http://www.uncitral.org/pdf/english/texts/sales/cisg/V1056997-CISG-e-book.pdf, accessed 9.12.2013.

c. Third and finally, for those cases where one of the traders is a physical person, his/her habitual residence should be located in the place where that person was carrying his/her principal commercial activity. Article 23.2 Rome II Regulation is similar in this respect; but there are differences between them since the latter refers to the place of the principal establishment of the trader.

When the determination of the cross-border nature of a B2C transaction is at stake, the operation that must be carried out to identify the possible contacts between the transaction and the EU territory is even more complex. First of all, whether one of the following elements of the relationship was situated outside of the country of the trader's habitual residence should be verified: either the address indicated by the consumer, the delivery address of the goods or the billing address. In addition, at least one of those countries must be a Member State of the EU.

Consequently, if the above mentioned requirements are satisfied, the transaction will be considered cross-border in nature, and the future CESL could be applicable. However, this provision does not clarify if the habitual residence of the consumer must be located in a Member State of the EU or not. Again, it has been argued that EU and EEA countries should be made equivalent in this respect (Wenderhorts 2012; Scmidt-Kessel 2012). This solution warrants the following comments:

a. On the one hand, the option chosen by the European legislator can be criticised as having a highly subjective nature, as it exclusively depends on the information the consumer provides to the trader (Fernández Masiá 2012; Micklitz and Reich 2012). Therefore, it would be advisable for the parties to act cautiously in order to avoid undesirable results. This is not only because of possible false statements concerning such information—an aspect to which the EU legislator shows no interest at all, in the opinion of Wenderhorts (2012)—but also with regard to an undesired and unconscious "internationalisation" of the transaction.
b. On the other hand, and less important in practice, this provision does not take into account the habitual residence of the consumer in any way. This personal element, however, enjoys a central consideration in other EU instruments in the field of civil justice, such as the example offered by art. 6 Rome I Regulation; or similarly, albeit considering domicile, in art. 59 Brussels I Regulation.

Various other issues arising from art. 4 also deserve serious analysis. Firstly, and from a terminological perspective, certain authors have criticised some of the expressions found in this provision—e.g. the word "use" instead of other more usual legal expressions such as "apply"—since in so doing the EU legislator clearly highlighted and stressed the idea that the future CESL could be considered as a legal "product" or as a "commodity", to be chosen by the parties in cross-border transactions (Hesselink 2012).

Additionally, it should also be taken into consideration—as the provision itself so states—that these elements should be determined at the moment in which the parties agree to submit the contract to the CESL. Therefore, once the parties have agreed on the application of the European instrument and from then on, any subsequent change of the said elements would be of no importance (Wenderhorts 2012).

Moreover it could be concluded, from the wording of art. 4 and the different situations that may be envisaged, that the future CESL should be applicable to both intra- and extra-EU relationships (Mankowski 2012a; Sánchez Lorenzo 2003). This possibility of this happening could produce some unbalanced effects for those companies established in the territory of the EU, compared to those located in third countries, as highlighted by Wenderhorts (2012).

Hence, on the one hand, this provision could offer a competitive advantage to large companies over small or medium-sized enterprises (SME)—as defined in art. 7—within the internal market, as the former could operate in a third country through a secondary establishment, and connect all their transactions to consumers situated in the EU not to two legal regimes, but to just one: the CESL. On the other hand, all traders established in a third country could also enjoy the same benefit over those established in a Member State of the EU, unless that Member State had decided that the future European instrument should also be made available for the parties to "domestic" transactions, according to that established in art. 13 Draft CESL (Recital 14). This is a possibility that has attracted certain positive endorsements (Doralt 2011; Wenderhorts 2012).

2.2.3 Optional Character

The possibility for parties to apply the Draft CESL to their contract can be found in art. 3 (*Optional nature of the Common European Sales Law*). In this regard, arts. 8 (*Agreement on the use of the Common European Sales Law*) and 9 (*Standard Information Notice in contracts between a trader and a consumer*) determine the requirements of the agreement for the application of the future instrument to be valid.[23]

First of all, and again from a purely terminological perspective, the reference made to expressions such as "use" in these provisions has been criticised, as it would support the aim of the EU legislator to consider a future CESL as a new "commodity" available in the "market" of "legal products" for the regulation of international sales of goods—although not fully confined to those contracts (Hesselink 2012). Additionally, and from a more general point of view, the reference made in art. 8.1 to the fact that the agreement (contemplated in art. 3) should be made "*to that effect*" must be highlighted. With this qualified option, the European legislator would have had intended that *the future CESL* would adopt an *opt-in model*, in line with other international instruments available in that "market"—just as the UNIDROIT Principles of International Commercial Contracts 2010[24] (Wenderhorts 2012).

[23] This aspect would be made much clear in the Report of the European Parliament of 24.9.2013, thanks to the expression added to Art. 3 "*subject to the requirements laid down in Articles 8 and 9*".

[24] As an example, in its Preamble it is established that "*They [The Principles] shall be applied when the parties have agreed that their contract be governed by them*". Accessible at: http://www.unidroit.org/english/principles/contracts/main.htm, accessed 9.12.2013.

Nevertheless, the Draft CESL neither makes any reference to any other specific elements in respect to the scope of those requirements, nor mentions significant aspects of the agreement—such as, for example, the determination of the moment when the parties make such agreement (Hesselink 2012). This silence obliges us to take into account, separately, whether the transaction would be considered as a B2B or B2C, in order to determine those elements of the agreement required to choose the future instrument.

Looking at this from a general perspective, and also what is directly applicable to B2B contracts, art. 8 establishes that the parties should reach an agreement as to the effect of the CESL be applicable to their contract. However, there are several questions related to such an agreement that must also be answered. For a start, it should be clarified whether, not only express, but also tacit, agreements—deriving from the elements of the contract—would be accepted. This problem has been met with different solutions in the legal literature: in favour is Hesselink (2012); and against Sánchez Lorenzo (2011). Bearing in mind that a clear answer cannot be found in the future Regulation, this issue must be approached cautiously when the parties set out the terms of the contract, in order to avoid an unnecessary level of unpredictability.[25] However, and from another perspective, the acceptance of an "incorporation by reference" should not create serious difficulties in the future European instrument.[26]

Moreover, partial agreements would also be accepted, enabling the parties to fragment the legal regime of the contract—with the exception of the mandatory provisions of the Draft CESL (Wenderhorts 2012).[27] In this sense, it should be taken into consideration that the Proposal does not make any mention of the necessity of having an agreement in favour of the instrument as a whole for B2B transactions, apart from the need to observe those mandatory rules that have been incorporated in the Proposal. Additionally, it must be understood that no problem would arise if the parties modified their decision in relation to the applicability of the CESL, either during the conclusion of the contract or subsequently, as long as this change were to respect the mandatory rules and the rights of third parties.

However, it should also be stressed that his generous acceptance of party autonomy in relation to the application of the CESL for B2B transactions could also entail legal uncertainty (Behar-Touchais 2012). Therefore, a cautious use of this possibility is advisable, so that parties minimize that risk and endeavour to incorporate an adequate level of foreseeability in their dealings in relation to the legal regime applicable to their contract.

[25] The new wording given to Recital 9 *in fine* in the Report of the European Parliament of 24.9.2013, clarifies this question, opting for an express choice, when it states that: "The Common European Sales Law should apply on a voluntary basis, upon an express agreement of the parties, to a cross-border contract" (*cit.*, p. 7).

[26] According to Recital 13 Rome I Regulation.

[27] Again, the Report of the European Parliament of 24.9.2013 would clarify this aspect, as it would provide a new wording of art. 8.3, which would sate that: "In relations between traders, the Common European sales Law may be chosen partially, provided that exclusion of the respective provisions in not prohibited therein".

On the other hand, with regard to B2C transactions, the applicable legal framework for the validity of the agreement can be found in art. 8, paragraphs 2 and 3, and art. 9 Draft CESL. These provisions aim at guaranteeing an informed consent by the consumer; however, in these situations, the choice of the CESL would be mainly made by the trader (Doralt 2011; Whittaker 2012) and protecting themselves in relation to cross-border transactions, even when general contract terms are used (Hesselink 2012). This choice would not be directly controlled by the obligations imposed in the Draft CESL, and nor by Directive 93/13 (Basedow 2012). Authors such as Behar-Touchais (2012), estimate that the future instrument would guarantee a high level of protection as compared with current national legislations in many situations. In this respect, the following should be noted.

a. First of all, art. 9 lays down the obligations that could be imposed on the trader, in relation to information that should be made available to the consumer, before entering into the agreement to apply the CESL. Hence, this provision contemplates the necessity to provide the consumer with a "Standard Information Notice" (available in Annex II), which could also be made available in electronic format and free of charge. In this respect, the Internet should be considered an adequate environment for these transactions and the fulfilment of this requirement—through pressing the so-called "Blue Button" (Schulte-Nölke 2011; Fernández Masiá 2012). In case this duty to provide information is not satisfied, the consumer would not be bound by the agreement to apply the future CESL.
b. In addition, and according to art. 8.2, the agreement for the application of the CESL should be only valid if it was expressed through "*an explicit statement which is separate from the statement indicating the agreement to conclude a contract*". Moreover, from the perspective of the trader, this party should "*provide the consumer with a confirmation of that agreement on a durable medium*".
c. Finally, art. 8.3 establishes that parties can only choose the CESL "*in its entirety*". Hence, partial agreements of the future instrument would not be acceptable for B2C transactions. This obligation derives from the objective pursued by the future Regulation to create "a complete set of fully harmonised mandatory consumer protection rules" (Recital 11).[28] The exclusion of a partial choice would benefit both parties, as it would not only guarantee a uniform level of protection for consumers at EU level, but also would favour traders who could benefit from a single legal regime for the whole internal market—a uniform normative framework which would operate as a "Trustmark" within the EU (Mankowski 2012a).

As a consequence, a tacit choice of the future CESL by the parties would not be allowed, as arts. 8.2 y 9 stress the need for an explicit agreement by the consumer (Esteban de la Rosa and Olariu 2013); nor would it be possible for there to be a partial choice of the legal regime of the contract, according to art. 8.3. Moreover, any change in the choice of the CESL, or indeed its exclusion after the conclusion of the contract, would be considered invalid (Esteban de la Rosa and Olariu 2013; Fornasier 2012). Thus, where these conditions are not fulfilled, the agreement will, in principle, be invalid.

[28] The Report of the European Parliament of 24.9.2013 has incorporated a new Recital (11a) with a definition of "consumer" for the CESL (*cit.*, p. 9).

However, it should be born in mind that the non fulfilment of the conditions imposed on the trader, could have a harmful affect on the interests of the consumer. A good example of this is a case in which the consumer visits a website and, as a result, clicks on the "Blue Button" confirming his/her interest in concluding the transaction with the application of the CESL, but the trader fails to provide the confirmation of that agreement to the consumer. In those situations, the agreement would be considered invalid despite the legitimate expectations of the consumer that the CESL is applicable to the transaction, after confirming his/her interest to conclude the contract. For this reason, some authors would prefer to maintain the binding nature of the agreement for the benefit of the consumer, instead of the radical invalidity of applying the CESL in those situations (Esteban de la Rosa and Olariu 2013; Wenderhorts 2012).

The optional nature of the Draft CESL also raises the question of its relationship with other international and competitive instruments, which also have an optional nature, as it happens with the Vienna Convention 1980, on Contracts for the International Sale of Goods (CISG) (Huber 2003), a Convention that has significant practical importance in current International Business Law (Magnus 2012).

In this respect, some authors have questioned the real need to develop a future CESL—particularly in relation to B2B transactions—since there is already an international instrument available; and also in order to avoid unnecessary complexities in this particular field (Illescas Ortiz and Perales Viscasillas 2012; Kornet 2012; Lando 2011; Mankowski 2012b; Schwenzer 2013). Again, it can be seen that the priorities of the EU political agenda justifies this very much criticised decision.

a. On the one hand, it has to be taken into consideration that there may be some amount of overlapping between the two instruments, in relation to several aspects. In this respect, there would be a partial concurrence of both their substantive and territorial scopes of application. However, in relation to the first aspect, the future CESL would go beyond what has been established for the CISG, as far as the former would not only cover more, and different, types of transactions as compared to the second—which is limited to sales of goods—but also because the CISG does not regulate certain specific issues covered by the future European instrument; such as, for example, the pre-contractual period (Fogt 2012; Magnus 2012). With regard to the second aspect—the territorial scope of application—while the Draft CESL would be applicable in all Member States of the EU, the CISG has not been ratified by all of them; notable exceptions being Ireland, Malta, Portugal and the United Kingdom.
b. On the other hand, it is also important to highlight the different ways in which these international instruments are considered to be applicable. With regard to arts. 3, 8 and 9, the future CESL would be a non-compulsory instrument based on an opt-in model. In comparison, even though the CISG is not a binding instrument for the parties, it can be teased out from the wording of arts. 1 and 6 that this instrument is based on an opt-out model: provided that the transaction falls within the scope of application of the Convention, the parties can decide not to apply the international instrument.

With these previous considerations in mind, the relationship between the two instruments—both potential competitors in the international market of legal products—and the possible dialogue between them can be seen more clearly. Moreover, they can also offer some clues for the determination of the following questions: what happens when none of the instruments would be considered as applicable; or under which circumstances they can be jointly applicable? In relation to this, the legal character of each text and the consequences deriving from this should be carefully considered (Fogt 2012). The answer to these issues is to be found in Recital 25 Draft CESL, under which "*the choice of the Common European Sales Law should imply an agreement of the contractual parties to exclude that Convention*".

Even if this approach may be deemed simple at first sight, its consequences are not only more complex to ascertain (Mansel 2012), but also create some practical problems (Fogt 2012). Moreover, it is important to stress that the afore-mentioned Recital has a different meaning and scope in its different linguistic versions (Sánchez Lorenzo 2013). It can be drawn out from most of the linguistic versions—notably the English one—that the option in favour of the future CESL would imply the direct exclusion of the CISG. By contrast, in other languages—and this is actually the case with the Spanish version—this exclusion is not contemplated in such a straight forward way, so that a statement in the agreement in favour of the Draft CESL is also required. Thus, those different approaches to this issue lead to an undesirable level of unpredictability because there is not a clear priority rule between those two instruments.

If the first mentioned approach is supported, it could be considered as an *ultra vires* action of the EU in relation to the CISG (Sánchez Lorenzo 2013). In that respect, it has been stressed that the conditions determining the applicability of the CISG must be found solely in the Convention itself and not in other instruments (Kornet 2012). As a consequence, and in order to avoid the uncertainties which the Recital could create, it would be advisable for the parties to clearly state that they expressly opt for the future CESL, and also clearly exclude the application of the CISG (Hesselink 2012). Moreover, and also with this objective in mind, partial choices should be avoided if possible.

2.2.4 Material Choice

As emphasised in the Recital of the Draft CESL, the agreement in favour of the future instrument has to be understood as a "material choice", because "The agreement to use the Common European Sales Law should therefore not amount to, and not be confused with, a choice of the applicable law within the meaning of the conflict-of-laws rules and should be without prejudice to them".[29] Nevertheless, in

[29] Again, the Report of the European Parliament of 24.9.2013 clarifies this aspect by providing the following wording to Recital 10 "The agreement to use the Common European Sales Law results from a choice between two different regimes within the same national legal order. That choice, therefore, does not amount to, and should not be confused with, a choice between two national

order to grasp the extent of the meaning of this statement, the various choices available to the European legislator in order to provide for the applicability of the future instrument have to be considered (Rühl 2012).

a. Firstly, the EU institutions could have developed an optional and uniform CESL, which could have been conceived as a "28th regime" (currently, "29th"), and would have been made applicable through the choice of the parties following a conflict-of-laws approach (Palao Moreno 2011). This could have been made possible in accordance with art. 3.1 Rome I Regulation, and in particular, its Recital 14. However, if a consumer were to be involved in the transaction, art. 6.2 Rome I Regulation would also need to have been considered; and, as a result, this provision would mean the exclusion of the possibility of a uniform application of the CESL within the EU (Wenderhorts 2012).
b. Secondly, the production of an optional European Convention of uniform law could have followed another of the possibilities available to the EU institutions: a "1st regime" (Rühl 2012). However, again with this approach, a similar result to the above option would have been achieved. This European instrument could have also included those provisions that would determine its scope of application—substantive, personal and territorial—with the possibility of establishing an *Opt-out* model, following the example of art. 1.1(a) CISG (Fogt 2012). Nonetheless, apart from the problems concerning the legal basis of this approach, it would not have been able to avoid the application of art. 6.2 Rome I Regulation, and, as a result, it would have not been possible for the parties to choose the future CESL "*in its entirety*" in relation to B2C transactions.
c. Finally, there is the option selected by the European legislator, which is based on an opt-in model where parties agree upon the application of a "second national legal regime" within each Member State's legal order (Fornasier 2012). Here, the choice of the future CESL would be possible not only when the transaction was under its scope of application (Wenderhorts 2012), but also when the law applicable to the contract was the legislation of a Member State (Esteban de la Rosa and Olariu 2013). In this respect, the future CESL has to be considered as a legal "hybrid", because it has a European origin but it is characterised as national law (Hesselink 2012). However, the sole responsibility for the development of such a "second regime" model lies with the European Commission, as this option was not present in the Study presented by the Expert Group (Schulte-Nölke 2011).

As a consequence of the above, an agreement in favour of the future CESL would result in the development of a "second" national regime within every Member State, which would co-exist with the "first" national legal system, and which would have been considered as a less invasive approach (Recital 9).[30] Therefore, this European

legal orders within the meaning of the conflict-of-law rules and should be without prejudice to them. This Regulation will therefore not affect any of the existing conflict-of-law rules such as those contained in Regulation (EC) No 593/2008" (*cit.*, pp. 7–8).

[30] The Report of the European Parliament of 24.9.2013 stresses that it is to be considered as a "second regime" when determining that: "This *directly applicable* second regime *should be an*

instrument would allow a certain amount of competition within Member States, in relation to the transactions covered by the future Regulation (Müller-Graff 2012). This result could only happen if the following conditions are met: (a) the parties should have *opted-in* to the future European model (in accordance with arts. 3, 8 and 9); (b) the transaction should be characterised as 'cross-border' (as established in art. 4); (c) the contract should be one of those covered by the substantive scope of application of the future Regulation (as determined by arts. 5 y 6); and (d) the legal relationship should be within the personal scope of application of the future instrument (defined in its art. 7) (Wenderhorts 2012).

From the perspective of Private International Law, this characterisation of the future European instrument would allow the Draft CESL to be considered not only as national law (Mankowski 2012a), but also as a "dependent" "special substantive rule" (Mankowski 2012a; Sánchez Lorenzo 2013). This is because its application would rely on the law of a particular Member State being held applicable under the Regulations Rome I and II—the later because the future instrument would also cover the pre-contractual period (arts. 3, 4 and 6 Rome I Regulation and art. 12 Rome II Regulation), (Wenderhorts 2012). In this sense, the agreement in favour of the Draft CESL would not only affect the existing conflict-of-laws rules, but would also be totally compatible with them.[31]

Despite all the problems that this approach attempts to resolve, it has also been severely criticised by some authors. On the one hand, it has been reported that there has not been any successful example of this "second regime" model in the past (Lando 2011). Moreover, on the other hand, it has also been stressed that this model will result in an unnecessarily complicated and expensive system, particularly for consumers who operate internationally within the EU (Sánchez Lorenzo 2013; Wenderhorts 2012).

Apart from that, the wording of this provision does not offer a clear answer in relation to extra-European situations, where the law of a third country applies. In that respect, it should be taken into account that the agreement in favour of the future CESL may be found to be invalid in that type of situations, but could be accepted as an "incorporation by reference", if so accepted by the Private International Law system of that third country (Scmidt-Kessel 2012). Nevertheless, such situations may be equivalent to those cases where standard contract terms had been chosen (Magnus 2012).

In this respect, Recital 10 states that: "This Regulation will therefore not affect any of the existing conflict-of-law rules". As a consequence, and in principle, the choice of the future CESL would not affect Private International Law rules. Thus, the selection of this instrument would have to be done through a "double choice"

---

integral part of the legal order applicable in the territory of the Member States. In so far as its scope allows and where parties have validly agreed to use it, the Common European Sales Law should apply instead of the first national contract-law regime within that legal order. It should be identical throughout the Union and exist alongside the pre-existing rules of national contract law" (*cit.*, p. 7).

[31] Recital 10 *in fine*. In this sense, see: Recitals 12 and 14 Rome I Regulation.

mechanism. In relation to this, the determination of a national legal system *per* Rome I and II Regulations would be the first choice, and the second would refer to the agreement in favour of the CESL, in accordance with arts. 3, 8 y 9 as analysed above (Fernández Masiá 2012). Therefore the determination of the national applicable law would not only operate as a "gateway" for the application of the future CESL, but also would be the residual applicable law for those questions not covered by the CESL (Wenderhorts 2012). However, it should be stressed that this model might imply the application of foreign laws in the Member States (Whittaker 2012), and the national solutions in that respect still differ from one Member State to another (Esplugues et al. 2011).

Additionally, Recital 12 underlines the idea that the application of the future CESL would imply the deactivation of provisions such as art. 6.2 Rome I Regulation, because they would have "no practical importance for the issues covered by the Common European Sales Law".[32] Besides, the application of the Draft CESL would be intended to exclude the application of mandatory rules—art. 9.2 Rome I Regulation—since the future instrument would be made applicable "*in its entirety*" for B2C transactions (Scmidt-Kessel 2012).

Nevertheless, this exclusion would meet with certain significant limitations, because choice-of-law rules would play an important role in some circumstances. This would, therefore, create an intense relationship between the future CESL and the rest of the Private International Law system (Fogt 2012). In that respect, as mentioned earlier, the application of the future European instrument would not only be made dependent on choice-of-law rules, but these would also be used to cover the "external gaps" of the CESL; e.g. those questions excluded from its substantive scope of application (Fornasier 2012; Mansel 2012). This could create new uncertainties and extra costs, as highlighted by Eidenmüller (2012). In contrast, the "internal gaps" of the CESL would be addressed by using the principles underlying that instrument. However, some authors have argued that this option might bring certain difficulties (Magnus 2012; Sánchez Lorenzo 2013).

Apart from that, it should also be taken into account that the normal application of the conflict-of-laws rules could result in the application of the national law of a third country—in relation to B2B transactions *per* arts. 3 or 4 Rome I Regulation—so that it should be clarified what might happen in those situations where the parties had chosen to apply the CESL.

[32] This question has been clarified by the Report of the European Parliament of 24.9.2013 offering a new wording for that Recital: "Once there is a valid agreement to *use the Common European Sales Law, only the Common European Sales Law should govern the matters falling within its scope.* Since the Common European Sales Law contains a *comprehensive* set of *uniform* harmonized mandatory consumer protection rules, there will be no disparities between the laws of the Member States in this area, where the parties have chosen to use the Common European Sales Law. Consequently, Article 6(2) of Regulation (EC) No 593/2008, which is predicated on the existence of differing levels of consumer protection in the Member States, has no practical *relevance to* the issues covered by the Common European Sales Law, *as it would amount to a comparison between the mandatory provisions of two identical second contract-law regimes*" (*cit.*, pp. 9–10).

The relationship between the future CESL and the rest of the Private International Law system must be highlighted with regard to art. 6 Rome I Regulation and its framework of B2C transactions (Esteban de la Rosa and Olariu 2013; Mankowski 2012a).

a. On the one hand, if the consumer had his/her habitual residence in a Member State, there are several situations in which the relationship between the future CESL and art. 6.2 must be addressed. First of all, if the trader directs his/her activity to the Member State where the consumer habitually resides and the parties had chosen the law of that (or a different) Member State—according to the conditions imposed by art. 6 Rome I Regulation—the agreement for the application of the CESL would be considered as valid (Micklitz and Reich 2012). Hence, in those circumstances, art. 6.2 Rome I Regulation would be neutralised, as established in Recital 12.

However, the proposal for a Regulation does not clarify what would happen if the law of a third country is considered to be the applicable law of a particular contract, in accordance with arts. 3 and 6 Rome I Regulation. In other words, the Draft CESL does not clearly determine, whether, under those circumstances, the application of the CESL would be impossible, nor if the CESL would be available *via* an "incorporation by reference". Moreover, the proposal does not makes it clear whether the future CESL could be made applicable for those cases not covered by art. 6 Rome I Regulation; e.g. transactions involving "active" consumers, which are excluded from its substantive scope (Sánchez Lorenzo 2013).

b. On the other hand, difficulties could also arise where the consumer has his/her habitual residence in a third country, and the law of that country was considered to be applicable according to the rules of Rome I Regulation. For those cases—in which the European instrument could be considered as non-operative in practice (Fernández Masiá 2012)—would the European legislator suggest not only that the parties should not have chosen the CESL, but also that they should consider the application of the Private International Law system of that third country as being competent determine the validity of such an agreement (Recital 14)?

However, Recital 14 does not offer a global analysis of this problematic situation. For example, it is questionable as to whether this would result in it being impossible for the parties to agree upon the application of the CESL in those cases where the consumer habitually resided in a third country and where this person purchased a product from a trader who operated out of a Member State, with the law of that third country being considered as the applicable law to the transaction (this being the most favourable for the consumer) (Micklitz and Reich 2012; Wenderhorts 2012).

2.3 Concluding Remarks

The Draft CESL significantly improves the current complex legal situation, benefiting the interests of traders and consumers who operate within the European internal market. However, the future instrument is not only intended to cover intra-European transactions, but will also be applicable to contracts linked to third countries. This twofold effect raises interesting legal questions that have been analysed in this chapter from the perspective of Private International Law. However, it is impossible to predict what will be the definitive answer to these questions since the process for the development of the Regulation has not yet finished.

During the final stages of this process, certain decisive decisions must be adopted. These legislative considerations should address certain issues, such as the correctness of the terminology used; the lack of coherence, within the instrument, between some of the matters already decided; and its relationship with the European *acquis* in the field of Consumer Law. In particular, from the perspective of Private International Law, there are some key aspects which should also be clarified within the future developments of the CESL. Attention should be paid, for example, to certain significant issues such as its relationship with Rome I and II Regulations, or with the CISG; as well as the applicability of the European instrument when a cross-border transaction would be governed by the law of a third country that is not a Member of the EU.

References

Basedow (2012), "The Optional Instrument of European Contract Law: Opting-in through Standard Terms—A Reply to Simon Whittaker-", *European Review of Contract Law* 2012, 1, pp. 82–87.

Behar-Touchais (2012), "The functioning of the CESL within the framework of the Rome Regulation", 2012, pp. 1–90 (http://www.europarl.europa.eu/RegData/etudes/etudes/join/2012/462477/IPOL-JURI_ET(2012)462477_EN.pdf).

Dimatteo (2012), "The Curious Case of Transborder Sales Law: A Comparative Analysis of CESL, CISG, and the UCC", in: Magnus et al., *CISG vs. Regional Sales Law Unification. With a Focus on the New Common European Sales Law*, Munich, Sellier, 2012, p. 25–55.

Doralt (2011), "The Optional European Contract Law and why success or failure may depend on scope rather than substance". *Max Planck Private Law Research Paper no 11/9*, pp. 1–26 (http://ssrn.com/abstarct=1876451).

Eidenmüller (2012), "What can be wrong with an option? An Optional Common European Sales Law as a regulatory tool", pp. 1–15 (http://ssrn.com/abstract=2102827).

Esplugues et al. (2011), *Application of Foreign Law*, Munich, Sellier, 2011.

Esteban de la Rosa and Olariu (2013), "La aplicación de la Normativa Común de Compraventa Europea (CESL) a los contratos de consumo: nuevos desafíos para el sistema de Derecho internacional privado europeo", *InDret* 2013, pp. 1–32 (www.indret.com).

Fernández Masiá (2012), "Optando por la Normativa Común de Compraventa Europea", 2012, no 23, pp. 1–21 (www.reei.org).

Fleischer (2012), "Optionales europäisches Privatrecht "28 Modell", *Max Planck Private Law Research Paper no 12/5*, pp. 1–20 (http://ssrn.com/abstarct=2000110).

Fogt (2012), "Private International Law Issues by Opt-out and Opt-in Instruments of Harmonization: A Comparison between CISG and CESL", in: Bonell et al., *Liber amicorum Ole Lando*, Copenague, DJØF, 2012, pp. 117–149.

Fornasier (2012), ""28" versus "2 Regime"—Kollisionsrechtliche Aspekte eines optionalen europäischen vertragsrecht", *RabelsZ* 2012, pp. 401–442.

Gómez Pomar and Gili Saldaña (2010), El futuro instrumento opcional del Derecho contractual europeo: una breve introducción a las cuestiones de formación, interpretación, contenido y efectos, InDret 1/2012, pp. 1–27 (www.indret.com).

Hesselink (2012), “How to Opt into the Common European Sale Law? Brief Comments on the Commission’s Proposal for a regulation”, *European Review of Private Law* 2012, 1, pp. 195–212.

Huber (2003), “European Private International Law, Uniform Law and the Optional Instrument”, *ERA-Forum* 2/2003, pp. 85–98.

Illescas Ortiz and Perales Viscasillas (2012), “El Reglamento Opcional en material de compraventa en el ámbito de la Unión Europea (CESL): crítica a su ámbito de aplicación”, *Derecho de los Negocios* 2012, No 265/266, pp. 1–17.

Kornet (2012), “The Common European Sales Law and the CISG. Complicating or simplifying the legal environment?”, *Maastricht European Private Law Institute Working Paper no 2012/4*, pp. 1–18 (http://ssrn.com/abstarct=2012310).

Lando (2011), “Comments and Questions Relating to the European Commission’s Proposal for a Regulation on a Common European Sales LAW”, European Review of Private Law 2011, 6, pp. 717–728.

Magnus (2012), “CISG v. CESL”, in: Magnus et al., *CISG vs. Regional Sales Law Unification. With a Focus on the New Common European Sales Law*, Munich, Sellier, 2012, pp. 97–123.

Mak (2012), “In Defense of CESL” (http://www.law.uchicago.edu/files/files/Mak%20paper.pdf).

Mankowski (2012a), “Der Vorschlag für ein Gemeinsames Europäisches Kauuftrecht (CESL) und das Internationale Privatrecht”, *Recht der Internationalen Wirtschaft* 2012, pp. 97–105.

Mankowski (2012b), P., “CESL, who needs it?”, *Internationales Handelsrecht* 2012, 2, pp. 45–53.

Mansel (2012), “Der Verordnungsvorschlag für ein Gemeninsames Europäisches Kauftrecht—Teil I”, *Zeitschrift für Wirtschafts- und Bankrecht* 2012, 27, pp. 1253–1267.

Micklitz and Reich (2012), “The Commission proposal for a Regulation on a Common European Sales Law (CESL)”—Too broad or not broad enough?”, EUI Working Paper Law 2012/04, pp. 1–93, pp. 4–11 (http://cadmus.eui.eu/bitstream/handle/1814/20485/LAW_2012_04_ERPL_03.pdf).

Müller-Graff (2012), “Ein fakultatives europäisches Kauftrechts als Instrument der Markordung?”, in: Schulte-Nölke et al. *Der Entwurf ein optionales europälsches Kauftrecht*, Munich, Sellier, 2012, pp. 21–46.

Palao Moreno (2011), “El Marco Común de Referencia como sistema opcional 28ª: algunas reflexiones desde el Derecho internacional privado”, in: Blasco Gascó et al., *Estudios en homenaje a Vicente L. Montés Penadés*, Valencia, Tirant lo Blanch, 2011, Vol. II, pp. 1905–1922.

Posner (2012), “The Questionable Basis of the Common European Sales Law: The Role of an Optional Instrument in Jurisdictional Competition”, *Chicago Institute for Law and Economic Working Paper no 597 (2d Series)*, Mayo 2012, pp. 1–12 (http://ssrn.com/abstract=2049594).

Rühl (2012), “The Common European Sales Law: 28th regime, 2nd regime or 1st regime?”, *Maastricht European Private Law Institute Working Paper no 2012/5*, pp. 1–14 (http://ssrn.com/abstract=2025879).

Sánchez Lorenzo (2003), “La unificación del Derecho contractual europeo vista desde el Derecho internacional privado”, in: Palao Moreno et al., *Derecho patrimonial europeo*, Aranzadi, Cizur Menor, 2003, pp. 363–381.

Sánchez Lorenzo (2011), “La propuesta de Reglamento relativo a una Normativa Común de Compraventa Europea y el Derecho Internacional Privado”, *Anuario Español de Derecho Internacional Privado* 2011, No XI, pp. 35–61.

Sánchez Lorenzo (2013), “De Bruselas a La Haya, pasando por Roma y Viena: la Normativa Común de Compraventa Europea”, in: Forner Delaygua et al., *Entre Bruselas y La Haya. Estudios sobre la unificación internacional y regional del Derecho internacional privado. Liber Amicorum Alegría Borrás*, Madrid/ Barcelona/ Buenos Aires/ Sao Paulo, Marcial Pons, 2013, pp. 821–832.

Scmidt-Kessel (2012), “Anwendungsbereich, Aussgestaltung der Option und andere Fragen zur Verordnung”, in: Schmidt-Kessel et al., Ein einheitliches europäisches Kauftrecht?”, Munich, Sellier, 2012, pp. 29–50.

Schulte-Nölke (2011), “Scope and Function of the Optional Instrument n European Contract Law”, in: Schulze et al., *Towards a European Contract Law*, Munich, Sellier, 2011, pp. 35–45.

Smits (2012), "Party choice and the Common European Sales Law or: how to prevent the CESL from becoming a lemon on the Law Market", *Maastricht European Private Law Institute Working Paper no 2012/13*, pp. 1–21 (http://ssrn.com/abstract=2060017).

Schwenzer (2013), "Global oder regional –CISG oder CESL?", in: Bruns et al., *Festchrift für Rolf Stürner zum 70 Geburstag*, Tubinga, Mohr Siebeck, 2013, T. 2, pp. 1059–1070.

Von bar et al. (2009), *Principles, Definitions and Model Rules of European Private Law. Draft Common Frame of Reference (DCFR)*, Munich, Sellier, 2009.

Wenderhorts (2012), "Articles 1 to 15", in: Schulze et al., *Common European Sales Law (CESL)—Commentary,* Baden-Baden, Beck/Hart/Nomos, 2012, pp. 9–84.

Whittaker (2012), "The Proposed "Common European Sales Law": Legal Framework and the Agreement of the Parties", *Modern Law Review* 2012, pp. 578–605.

Chapter 3
Formation of Contract

Jakub J. Szczerbowski

Abstract Formation of contract in the Common European Sales Law is based on a mix of concepts derived from various legal systems. The rules governing conclusion of contract are an important piece of the puzzle of contractual freedom. Achieving balance between the description of social customs and the needs for abstraction expected from a normative system requires not only a clear legal text but also a legal culture built around it. The textual part of the CESL combines some of the elements of common law and some of the elements of the European system. Future application of the rules will, therefore, provide interesting insights into the mechanism of the reception of law into different legal cultures. This text compares the rules of the CESL to some of the existing legal systems and underlines the most important differences between them.

Keywords "Causa" · Consideration · Contract formation · Offer · Acceptance · Negotiations · Auction

3.1 Introduction

The Common European Sales Law (CESL) devotes its Chapter 3 to contract formation. The drafters decided to adapt the model of offer and acceptance, which is known on both sides of the Atlantic. The model does not exclude other means leading to the conclusion of a contract, such as negotiations, auctions or tenders, as the main emphasis is put on reaching a consensus that is intended to create a legal bond where its content is sufficient for this purpose. (Article 30 of the CESL states: "A contract is concluded if: (a) the parties reach an agreement; (b) they intend the agreement to have legal effect; and (c) the agreement, supplemented if necessary by rules of the Common European Sales Law, has sufficient content and certainty to be given legal effect."[1])

[1] Cfr. Amendment 108 European Parliament legislative resolution of 26 February 2014 on the Proposal for a regulation of the European Parliament and of the Council on a Common European

J. J. Szczerbowski (✉)
University of Social Sciences and Humanities, Warszawa, Poland
e-mail: jjs@data.pl

© Springer International Publishing Switzerland 2015

J. Plaza Penadés, L. M. Martínez Velencoso (eds.), *European Perspectives on the Common European Sales Law,* Studies in European Economic Law and Regulation 4,
DOI 10.1007/978-3-319-10497-3_3

This is a very minimalist set of rules. The model of offer and acceptance is considered to be sufficient as a description of all social facts leading to the conclusion of a contract. This is similar to the understanding of offer and acceptance in the Common Law. Auctions and negotiations are viewed as various configurations of offer and acceptance. The reducibility of auctions and negotiations to offer and acceptance makes the reduction desirable. Along with consideration, i.e. the giving of something of value, offer and acceptance are the only requirements for the formation of a contract (Silva 2004, p. 106). In the Common Law, contrary to the view of the legal systems of continental Europe, offer and acceptance are not dependent on higher layers of abstraction such as legal acts and declarations of will.

This model lies on the basic principle of freedom of contract (art. 1.1 CESL: "Parties are free to conclude a contract and to determine its contents, subject to any applicable mandatory rules."). The principle of freedom of contract covers both the conclusion of the contract and its contents; and is further developed by the principle of the freedom of form (art. 6 CESL: "Unless otherwise stated in the Common European Sales Law, a contract, statement or any other act which is governed by it need not be made in or evidenced by a particular form."). Freedom of form is sometimes limited in various jurisdictions dependent on the value of the contract or on the nature of the thing conveyed (Philippe 2004, p. 364).

Another underlying principle is the principle of good faith expressed in art. 2.1 CESL: "Each party has a duty to act in accordance with good faith and fair dealing". This principle has to be interpreted as relating not only to the performance phase of the contractual relationship but also as governing the pre-contractual obligations of potential parties. Good faith in pre-contractual relations was already present implicitly in Roman law, but its full development is owed to the nineteenth century German legal science, (for a detailed analysis of the development of the pre-contractual duties doctrine based on the analysis of German Gemeines Recht, see Bauknecht 2014, p. 75 et sqq.).

3.2 "Causa", Consideration and the Intention to be Legally Bound

It is important in every system of contract law to distinguish between agreements that create only social or moral obligations and legally binding contracts. The answer to this important question has been given in a couple of different ways. A legal system may only recognise a closed number of contracts, and all agreements not having the features of one of the contracts would not be considered legally relevant. Roman law developed a similar solution, but even then there existed other legal devices, such as 'form' (on the role of form in the early Roman law of unilaterally

---

Sales Law (COM (2011) 0635-C7-0329/2011-2011/0284 (COD): "Agreement is reached by acceptance of an offer". It has removed the following sentence: "Acceptance may be made explicitly or by other statements or conduct".

binding contracts, see Sacconi 1989, p. 4) and '*causa*', which allowed a legally binding promise to be distinguished from a purely moral obligation. Moreover, the Romans preferred contracts to be concluded by the passing of possession; most of the Roman contracts were "real" contracts. Only contracts, in which the nature of the obligation made it impossible to require the passing of a thing, such as the *societas* or mandate, were binding by mere agreement. In the Common Law, its functional equivalent is the concept of consideration, understood on the European continent as onerosity. This understanding is not exact as consideration does not equal the conveyance of rights to the other party (Gamage and Kedem 2006, p. 1299).

The conceptual framework of the CESL rejects both *causa* and consideration following the path indicated by the DCFR. The DCFR consciously omits the requirements of *causa* or consideration and states they serve no sufficiently important purpose to fit a modern contract law. According to the DCFR, both concepts have only "residual" functions that are fulfilled by other rules. One example given by the DCFR is the one-sided character of a contract (von Bar et al. 2009, p. 290). Also, the DCFR considers *causa* and consideration to be legal devices that work against efficiency (von Bar et al. 2009, p. 75). The efficiency argument is partly convincing (for an extensive review of literature on efficiency in contract law, see Golecki 2003, p. 2 et seq.) as both concepts prove to be complex and difficult to understand for lawyers, but according to Jansen and Zimmermann the model of DCFR is even more obscure (2011, p. 6).

Consideration and *causa* were not intended to prevent exploitation but to establish the legal existence of promises. For this reason, it is hard to share the view of the DCFR. In the CESL the substitution of *causa* and consideration for the intent to be legally bound is sensible. In the contract of sale, by definition, there always exists consideration on both the part of the seller and the purchaser. For this reason, the exclusion of the doctrine of consideration does not raise any doubts. However, the future interpretation of the intention to be legally bound is uncertain. One of the possibilities is that the courts will revert to the old rules they have previously used to assess the validity of a contract. This is not necessarily a bad thing, as gradual change in private law is usually better than a revolution.

3.3 Models of Contract Formation

From a historical perspective, consent is the most important element for the formation of a contract (for example, art. 1341 of the French Civil Code or art. 1261 of the Spanish Civil Code). Legal systems usually deal with the mode of reaching consent as a secondary issue.

The succinct model of the CESL can be contrasted to the baroque model of the Polish Civil Code. The Polish regulation is one of the richest systems of contract formation. Unfortunately, conceptual richness, where there is no need for such complexity can be just a source of difficulties in interpretation. The regulation of art. 66 to 72 of the Polish Civil Code contains three main modes of contract formation:

offer and acceptance, auction and negotiations. Article 66[1] provides a special set of rules for offer and acceptance in electronic form. The form of auction is also divided into (oral) auctions and (written) tenders.

In the Germanic legal tradition, the rules on contract formation belong to the general part of civil law (Kocot 2013, Chap. 1). In the French and Spanish codes, conclusion of contract is regulated in brief. French law provides general requirements for the validity of contract in art. 1108 of the Civil Code. (Four conditions are essential for the validity of an agreement: the consent of the party who binds himself; his capacity to contract; a certain object forming the matter of the obligation; and a lawful *causa* of the obligation). The Spanish Civil Code provides a similar list in its art. 1261. (There is no contract unless the following requisites are jointly met: (1) consent of the parties; (2) certain object of contract; and (3) *causa* of the obligation that is established).

3.3.1 Offer and Acceptance

The unification efforts preceding the CESL emphasise the offer and acceptance model. The Principles of European Contract Law (PECL) define 'offer' in art. 2:201: "Offer (1) A proposal amounts to an offer if: (a) it is intended to result in a contract if the other party accepts it, and (b) it contains sufficiently definite terms to form a contract. (2) An offer may be made to one or more specific persons or to the public". The definition contained in the DCFR is an exact copy of the one from the PECL (art. II.–4:201 DCFR).

The definition has been changed in the CESL to address the difference between the general needs of contract law and the particular needs of the sales contract: (art. 31: "Offer 1. A proposal is an offer if: (a) it is intended to result in a contract if it is accepted; and (b) it has sufficient content and certainty for there to be a contract. 2. An offer may be made to one or more specific persons. 3. A proposal made to the public is not an offer, unless the circumstances indicate otherwise.")[2]. In the CESL proposals made to the public are considered to be an offer only by way of an exception. This flexible solution allows sellers to continue to offer goods in their usual place of sale and still retain separation between sales and unilateral undertakings similar to the public promise of a reward or unilateral contract.

This model of offer and acceptance is the most prototypical mode of concluding a contract. Present in major legal systems and influencing the wording of CESL, it basically states that one potential party expresses the will to conclude a contract and another potential party, consequently, expresses his or her will to conclude

[2] Cfr. Amendment 109 European Parliament legislative resolution of 26 February 2014 on the Proposal for a regulation of the European Parliament and of the Council on a Common European Sales Law (COM (2011) 0635-C7-0329/2011-2011/0284 (COD): "(b) it has sufficient content and certainly for there to be a contract. In relation between a trader and a consumer, an offer shall only be considered to have sufficient content and certainty if it contains an object, a quantity or duration, an a price".

the contract as well, in this case as seller and buyer. The rules of the CESL do not specify if the parties have to play the roles of offeror and offeree, or whether the future parties may be both offerors and offerees with regards to partial conditions of the contract.

3.3.2 Negotiations

Emphasis on consensus, or the so-called 'meeting of the minds', is also rational from the practical point of view. The modern, often electronically aided, commerce relies on multi-stage processes of reaching consensus (Kocot 2013, p. 2). Even in case of the sale, parties may not behave in a way that can be easily reduced to offering and accepting. Consequently, the CESL does not exclude other modes of contract formation, such as negotiations, from its model.

Negotiation is a process where parties to a potential complex contract come to consensus in a way that is not reducible down to an exchange of offers and counter-offers. In common parlance, negotiations signify any act of two parties communicating in order to reach a compromise. The legal meaning of the term consists of the exchanging of opinions about the final content of contract. The proposals of the parties might not always be serious, in the sense that they might exaggerate in order to cause the other party to lower their demands.

Negotiations may be treated by a legal system as a factual matter; i.e. an informal process in which two persons exchange opinions and, only when they agree on the final draft of the contract, one of them proposes an offer and the other one accepts. This configuration allows the negotiators to assess the draft in full. Another approach, represented by Polish law, forces the negotiators to be careful in agreeing to a particular term since the contract becomes valid the very moment they agree on the essential terms (art. 72.1 Polish Civil Code: If parties conduct negotiations aimed at the conclusion of a certain contract, the contract is concluded, when parties agree on all the terms, which were the subject of the negotiations.). Contracts concluded in this way might be difficult to reconstruct both for the parties and for the court. The common practice is, therefore, to make an additional preliminary contract regarding the negotiations, which stipulates that the parties will be bound only by a final contract celebrated in certain form.

Negotiations are a potential source of economic loss to the parties. They belong to a broader category called *culpa in contrahendo*. This harm might be intentional if one of the parties, from the beginning, lacks the will to reach consensus, or without any reason breaks the negotiations. Such issues pose difficulties for legal systems. One of the crucial features of negotiation is the possibility to walk away if consensus is not reached, or if during the negotiations a better offer appears. Lawmakers need to find the right balance between freedom of negotiation and the economic interests of the parties. It is common that law addresses the issue by reference to other normative systems such as usages and practices of fair dealing or to the legal concept of good faith.

Another potential pathology related to negotiations is the illicit use of information acquired during the negotiations. Information such as know-how, or future business strategies, may leak out during negotiations and legal rules should protect the good faith of the negotiator in order to increase the efficiency of contract law. Lack of such protection results in more effort being put by the parties into regulating the negotiations by means of preliminary contracts.

The CESL model is tacit about negotiations, which can be interpreted in such a way that, according to this model, negotiations are a fact and agreements during negotiations do not result in the conclusion of a contract. Various articles of the CESL mention negotiations as a fact of legal relevance. Negotiations form a part of the circumstances taken into account in the interpretation of the contract. Also, individually negotiated terms take precedence over standard terms, usages and practices. The concept of individually negotiated terms is relevant in cases of B2C contracts.

In the opinion of Kocot, the rule of art. 72. § 1 of the Polish Civil Code is based on the assumption that if parties commenced negotiations in order to form a contract, and if they agreed on the terms, then the contract is concluded. In his view, the rule serves as an interpretative provision and does not impose an obligation to agree on all the terms mentioned during the negotiations since they do not carry the same weight (Kocot 2013, Chap. 1). It is submitted that this view is correct; however, the radical wording of art. 72 § 1 Polish Civil Code does not prohibit the negotiators from forming an offer at any moment. The other side of the rule makes it possible for one of the parties to inadvertently conclude a contract if they agree on all the terms in the course of many meetings, which can be significantly spread out in time. During this process, the economic and legal circumstances might change and, assuming that the formerly agreed upon terms stand, this just burdens the parties with an unnecessary obligation. Keeping the negotiations in the realm of fact would be more efficient.

3.3.3 Auction

Auction is defined in art. 2 of the introductory provisions to the CESL: "'Public auction' means a method of sale where goods or digital content are offered by the trader to the consumer who attends or is given the possibility to attend the auction in person, through a transparent, competitive bidding procedure run by an auctioneer and where the successful bidder is bound to purchase the goods or digital content." This method is comprised of bids, which are similar in nature to offers, but do not have the same binding character as only the highest bid is binding.

German law is very succinct in regulating auctions (§ 156 of the German Civil Code states: "At an auction, a contract is not entered into until the fall of the hammer. A bid lapses if a higher bid is made, or if the auction is closed without the fall of the hammer."). Again, Polish law regulates auctions in considerably more detail (art. 70^{1-5} Polish Civil Code). Two types of auctions are defined: auctions and tenders. The Code regulates many of the procedural aspects of auctions: (a) when and how the caution deposit should be paid; (b) rules for the announcement of the auction; (c) special rules for nullity of contracts concluded in this manner; and others on which it is not necessary to comment here.

3.4 Modified Acceptance

The core of the problem with modified acceptance lies in the observation of customs related to the exchange of offer and acceptance. Allowing for modified acceptance increases the potential interpretative problems related to the declarations of the parties. The range of possible solutions is limited. Modified acceptance could be treated as a new offer, being the model most associated with the Common Law,[3] but also present to some extent in many legal systems (for example: art. 68 Polish Civil Code: "Acceptance which implies changed terms is considered to be a new offer"; and also present in art. 38 CESL: "1. A reply by the offeree which states or implies additional or different contract terms which materially alter the terms of the offer is a rejection and a new offer. 2. Additional or different contract terms relating, among other things, to the price, payment, quality and quantity of the goods, place and time of delivery, extent of one party's liability to the other or the settlement of disputes are presumed to alter the terms of the offer materially.").

Any departure from the strict model is usually connected to dealings between merchants. Such a model can be found in Polish law (art 68^1 Polish Civil Code states: "§ 1. In relations between traders a reply to an offer that implies changes or additions that do not change the essential contents of the offer is considered to be an acceptance. In this case the parties are bound by the contract whose terms were specified in the offer including the changes contained in the reply. § 2. The preceding paragraph does not apply if the offer specified can be accepted solely without changes, or if the offeror immediately contested the proposed changes, or if the other party made a condition to accept the offer only if the offeror agrees to the changes and the offeror did not agree."); and also in the Uniform Commercial Code (art. 2-207 (2) UCC (Sec): "The additional terms are to be construed as proposals for addition to the contract. Between merchants such terms become part of the contract unless: (a) the offer expressly limits acceptance to the terms of the offer; (b) they materially alter it; or (c) notification of objection to them has already been given or is given within a reasonable time after notice of them is received."), although the UCC model treats the modified acceptance as a proposal of additional contract terms. The Draft Common Frame of Reference and the CESL (arts. 38.3 and 38.4) contains a similar set of rules: (art. II.–4:208 DCFR: "Modified acceptance (1) A reply by the offeree which states or implies additional or different terms which materially alter the terms of the offer is a rejection and a new offer. (2) A reply which gives a definite assent to an offer operates as an acceptance even if it states or implies additional or different terms, provided these do not materially alter

[3] See Hyde v Wrench [1840] EWHC Ch J90.

the terms of the offer. The additional or different terms then become part of the contract. (3) However, such a reply is treated as a rejection of the offer if: (a) the offer expressly limits acceptance to the terms of the offer; (b) the offeror objects to the additional or different terms without undue delay; or (c) the offeree makes the acceptance conditional upon the offeror's assent to the additional or different terms, and the assent does not reach the offeree within a reasonable time."). The DCFR and the CESL differ from the UCC in how the additional terms are treated. In the DCFR/CESL model, the additional or different contract terms become a part of the contract, whereas in the UCC they form a proposal that has to be accepted by the offeree.

References

Bauknecht AW (2014) Culpa in contrahendo wobec unifikacji prawa prywatnego w Europie, ePubli, Berlin.

Gamage D, and Kedem A (2006) Commodification and Contract Formation: Placing the Consideration Doctrine on Stronger Foundations. *U Chi L Rev* 73:1299.

Golecki MJ (2003) SYNALLAGMA AND FREEDOM OF CONTRACT—The Concept of Reciprocity and Fairness in Contracts from the Historical and Law and Economics Perspective. *German Working Papers in Law and Economics* 2003.

Jansen N, and Zimmermann R (2011) Contract Formation and Mistake in European Contract Law: A Genetic Comparison of Transnational Model Rules. *Oxford Journal of Legal Studies* 31:625–662.

Kocot WJ (2013) *Odpowiedzialność przedkontraktowa*, C.H. Beck.

Philippe JM (2004) French and American Approaches to Contract Formation and Enforceability: A Comparative Perspective. *Tulsa J Comp & Int'l L* 12:357.

Sacconi G (1989) *Ricerche sulla stipulatio*, Jovene.

Silva A (2004) The role of consent in the formation of contract in comparative private law. *International Journal of Baltic Law* 1:117–127.

Von Bar C, Clive E, and Schulte-Nölke H eds. (2009) *Principles, Definitions and Model Rules of European Private Law. Draft Common Frame of Reference (DCFR)*, Munich.

Chapter 4
The Mandatory Nature of the Right of Withdrawal

Carmen Azcárraga Monzonís and Raquel Guillén Catalán

Abstract One of the main features of the CESL—unlike other international instruments—concerns its optional nature, i.e. the parties must agree upon its application in order for this instrument to govern the particular contract. However, once the parties have agreed upon its application, certain aspects of this instrument have a mandatory nature where the relevant contract is concluded between a consumer and a trader, one of these being the right of withdrawal. The aim of this chapter is to consider the regulation of this right of consumers in the Proposal on a CESL and in certain other instruments devoted to the harmonisation of contractual obligations in Europe.

Keywords Right of withdrawal · Information duties · Mandatory nature of the right of withdrawal · Withdrawal period · Effects of withdrawal

4.1 Introduction

The right of withdrawal granted to consumers in certain situations (also known as the "cooling-off period", (Ebers and Arroyo i Amayuelas 2006) appears in the context of contractual obligations as a more modern development of the principle of binding force (or *pacta sunt servanda*), which traditionally only operated when performance of contractual obligations became impossible for reasons that could not have been foreseen without the fault of one of the parties.

Today, the right of withdrawal is not based anymore on the impossibility of performance of the obligations. It is an exceptional facility of only one of the parties in the contract, the consumer, enabling him to terminate the contract *ad nutum*, with no reason, and with retroactive effect (Klein 1997). In other words, it refers to the ability of the consumer and user to revoke the contract by notice to the counterparty within the period established for exercising this right without having to justify the

C. Azcárraga Monzonís (✉) · R. Guillén Catalán
University of Valencia, Valencia, Spain
e-mail: carmen.azcarraga@uv.es

R. Guillén Catalán
e-mail: raquel.guillen@uv.es

© Springer International Publishing Switzerland 2015
J. Plaza Penadés, L. M. Martínez Velencoso (eds.), *European Perspectives on the Common European Sales Law,* Studies in European Economic Law and Regulation 4,
DOI 10.1007/978-3-319-10497-3_4

decision and without penalty (art. 68 Spanish Royal Legislative Decree 1/2007, of 16 November, approving the consolidated text of the General Law for the Defence of Consumers and Users and other complementary laws—TRLGDCU hereinafter—recently amended by Law 3/2014 of 27 March).

The grounds for this exception vary, but they can be seen in the specific situations where such rights of withdrawal exist. The inferior position of the consumer may arise in some situations where traders might have used certain commercial practices that push him into taking decisions without thinking about them (Klein 1997). For instance, the right to withdraw from contracts negotiated away from business premises (i.e. on the doorstep) exists where the consumer may have been taken by surprise or have been less attentive than he or she would have been in a shop. A further example is provided by certain complex contracts (i.e. timeshare contracts) where consumers may need an additional period for reflection (Von Bar et al. 2009).

The Legislations of EU Member States have traditionally regulated consumer rights in general, and the right of withdrawal in particular, differently due to the minimum amount of harmonisation in Directives in this area adopted so far in the EU, which allows each one to adopt, or maintain in force, more exacting provisions than the ones contemplated in the European instruments.

The right of withdrawal is actually the paradigm of inconsistent EU legislation, for instance, in terms of the period within which it can be exercised, the procedure that must be followed in order to exercise it, or the charges that may be imposed on a consumer who decides to withdraw. These inconsistencies appear as a consequence of the divergent rationale for granting this right in different pieces of legislation (Twigg-Flesner 2008).

Recently, nevertheless, Directive 2011/83/UE of the European Parliament and of the Council, of 25 October 2011, on Consumer Rights (OJ L 304 of 22.11.2011; DCR hereinafter) has completely harmonised certain aspects that will be considered in this contribution, including the pre-contractual information which must be provided to consumers, and their right of withdrawal in distance and off-premises contracts.

Following this Directive, the significance of the Proposal for a Regulation of the European Parliament and of the Council on a Common European Sales Law (COM(2011) 635 final; CESL hereinafter) reaffirms the will of the European legislator to attain a high level of protection for consumers because it establishes mandatory provisions in this field that cannot be modified by the parties to the detriment of the consumer; and this is true not only in those transactions where the habitual residence of both contracting parties is located in EU Member States—a situation that would be covered by the previously mentioned Directive—but also in those situations where the contract is concluded between one party who is residing in a Member State and the other party in a third country.

The main objective of this contribution is to consider the right of withdrawal in the CESL and to undertake a comparative analysis of the legal regime of this concept in the Spanish legal system as well as in some other European harmonising proposals, such as the Acquis Principles (ACQP hereinafter; Arroyo i Amayuelas

2008) and the Draft Common Frame of Reference (DCFR hereinafter). The Principles of European Contract Law (PECL) will not be included because they do not deal with the right of withdrawal.

This chapter will examine the basic general elements on which this right is constructed: its definition, mandatory and binding nature for traders, withdrawal period and the restitution of the supplies or services following the exercise of this right. In addition to these general issues we will focus on certain specific types of contract where this right is legally granted; in particular, distance and off-premises contracts. Furthermore, taking into account that the CESL is aimed at the protection of consumers, the inclusion of the right of withdrawal as one of the specific duties to provide information in the acquisition of products and services will also be considered. Finally, the legal consequences of non-compliance of this obligation will also be addressed.

An overall consideration of all the parts of this contribution will lead the reader to gain a broad overview of the current regulation of the right of withdrawal, reflecting on the traditional view of this topic that has existed until now, while bearing in mind, at the same time, its future perspective under the forthcoming CESL.

4.2 Legal Antecedents: The Regulation in the DCFR

The Common Frame of Reference was conceived to bring the contract law of EU Member States closer together and form the starting point for the evaluation by the European Commission of whether it would be desirable to develop an "optional instrument" (Loos 2008), turning a combination of the "best solutions" in the domestic laws of the Member States and the existing *acquis communautaire* into a coherent whole (Twigg-Flesner 2008).

The current draft version of the Common Frame of Reference of 2008 (DCFR) provides rules designed to protect the vulnerable. The main example of this aspect of justice is the special protection afforded to consumers. It should be noted in this regard that for reasons of simplicity and legal certainty, withdrawal rights are granted to consumers, irrespective of whether individually they need protection, as a considerable number of consumers are considered to be in need of protection in such situations (Von Bar et al. 2009).

This special protection appears prominently: in the rules on marketing and pre-contractual duties in Book II, Chapter 3; on the right of withdrawal in Book II, Chapter 5; and on unfair contract terms in Book II, Chapter 9, Section 4. It also appears, notably, in the parts of Book IV dealing with sale, the lease of goods and personal security.

Focusing specifically on the subject of this chapter, the DCFR provides for general model rules on pre-contractual information duties and withdrawal rights, offering both the European and the national legislators a model set of sanctions for breach of information duties. These two aspects respond to the new developments existing in current markets, where consumers may feel "overwhelmed" by the ever-increasing choice of products, suppliers and methods of marketing such products (Twigg-Flesner and Schulze 2010).

In the first place, the regulation of the right to withdraw in the DCFR will be considered, followed by a brief reference to the information duties of businesses towards consumers and the remedies for breach of these information duties.

4.2.1 The Right of Withdrawal in the DCFR

The definition of this right under the DCFR is included in the Annex of this instrument, under which "A right to "withdraw" from a contract or other juridical act is a right, exercisable only within a limited period, to terminate the legal relationship arising from the contract or other juridical act, without having to give any reason for so doing and without incurring any liability for non-performance of the obligations arising from that contract or juridical act" (II.-5:101 to II.-5:105).

The main aspects regulated in the chapter devoted to the right of withdrawal (Chapter 5 of Book II of DCFR—"Contracts and other juridical acts") are the following: in Section 1—"Exercise and effect"—several aspects are dealt with: scope and mandatory nature; exercise of right to withdraw; withdrawal period; adequate information on the right to withdraw; and effects of withdrawal and linked contracts. In Section 2—"Particular rights of withdrawal"—this right is applied in two specific contracts: contracts negotiated away from business premises and timeshare contracts.

According to the first rule of Section 1, the provisions in this section apply where, under any rule in Books II–IV, a party has a right to withdraw from a contract within a certain period. In these situations, the parties may not, to the detriment of the entitled party, exclude the application of the rules in this chapter or derogate from or vary their effects (II.-5:101).

Under Article II.-5:102, the right to withdraw is exercised by notice to the other party and no reasons need to be given. But as well as an explicit notice, it can also be exercised implicitly through returning the subject matter of the contract, although the provision does not clarify when this returning must be accomplished. A possible solution to this lack of clarification may be to refer to art. I-1:109 which states how notice, for any purpose, must be given (Vaquer Aloy et al. 2012).

The right of withdrawal can be exercised at any time after the conclusion of the contract and before the end of the withdrawal period, i.e. 14 days after the latest of the following times: (a) the time of conclusion of the contract; (b) the time when the entitled party receives from the other party adequate information on the right to withdraw; or (c) if the subject matter of the contract is the delivery of goods, the time when the goods are received.

This period of 14 days must be understood as calendar days under art. I.-1:110 (5) because there is no explicit reference to working days.

Furthermore, the right of withdrawal cannot be exercised later than 1 year after the time of conclusion of the contract, a time limit that can be considered as a limitation period (Vaquer Aloy et al. 2012).

The DFCR (art. II.-5:201(4)) does not clarify whether this right can be exercised within the mentioned period when contracts have already been performed, because it only refers to financial services contracts concluded away from business premises (Diéguez Oliva 2009).

On the other hand, adequate information on the right to withdraw requires that the right is brought to the entitled party's attention appropriately, and that the information provides, in a textual form on a durable medium and in clear and comprehensible language, information about how the right may be exercised, the withdrawal period, and the name and address—both geographical and telematic—of the person to whom the withdrawal is to be communicated (art. II.-5:104).

If the above requirements are fulfilled, art. II.-5:105 provides for the effects of the withdrawal. Among them, "withdrawal terminates the contractual relationship and the obligations of both parties under the contract" and "where the withdrawing party has made a payment under the contract, the business has an obligation to return the payment without undue delay, and in any case not later than 30 days after the withdrawal becomes effective". It must be noted in this regard that the DCFR does not contemplate any sanction against the trader who does not return the payment within the said period.

As regards the costs associated with the right of withdrawal, art. II.-5:105(6) states that except where otherwise provided in art. II.-5:105 "the withdrawing party does not incur any liability". In particular paragraph (4) of this same provision establishes that "The withdrawing party is not liable to pay (a) for any diminution in the value of anything received under the contract caused by inspection and testing; (b) for any destruction or loss of, or damage to, anything received under the contract, provided the withdrawing party used reasonable care to prevent such destruction, loss or damage". By contrast, paragraph (5) states that "The withdrawing party is liable for any diminution in value caused by normal use unless that party had not received adequate notice of the right of withdrawal".

The DCFR also tackles the particular case of linked contracts, where the general rule under art. II.–5:106(1) states that the effects of withdrawal extend to any linked contract to a contract for the supply of goods, other assets or services by a business from which a consumer exercises a right of withdrawal.

Furthermore art. II.–5:106(1) establishes "where a contract is partially or exclusively financed by a credit contract, this forms linked contracts, in particular: (a) if the business supplying goods, other assets or services, finances the consumer's performance; (b) if a third party which finances the consumer's performance uses the services of the business for preparing or concluding the credit contract; (c) if the credit contract refers to specific goods, assets or services to be financed with this credit, and if this link between both contracts was suggested by the supplier of the goods, other assets or services, or by the supplier of credit; or (d) if there is a similar economic link".

This list must be deemed merely illustrative, meaning that other linked contracts may be included (Jiménez Muñoz 2011). Moreover, as regards linked contracts with similar economic links it is interesting to note that the ACQP refers to the "economic unit".

As stated above, Section 2 of Book II refers to particular rights of withdrawal, i.e. those exercised in the framework of contracts negotiated away from business premises (art. II.-5:201) and timeshare contracts (art. II.-5:202).

As regards the first category of contracts, a preliminary remark must be made regarding the broader definition of this type of contracts if compared with the one contemplated in the DCR. The DCFR establishes, in art. II.-5:201(1), a general rule that "a consumer is entitled to withdraw from a contract under which a business supplies goods, other assets or services, including financial services, to the consumer, or is granted a personal security by the consumer, if the consumer's offer or acceptance was expressed away from the business premises".

However, a long list of exceptions to this general rule is also contemplated, in line with the ACQP, save that in the latter instrument this right is only applied to contracts where the amount due by the consumer reaches a legally determined minimum (Diéguez Oliva 2009).

This rule does not apply under art. II.-5:201(2) to: "(a) a contract concluded by means of an automatic vending machine or automated commercial premises; (b) a contract concluded with telecommunications operators through the use of public payphones; (c) a contract for the construction and sale of immovable property or relating to other immovable property rights, except for rental; (d) a contract for the supply of foodstuffs, beverages or other goods intended for everyday consumption supplied to the home, residence or workplace of the consumer by regular roundsmen; (e) a contract concluded by means of distance communication, but outside of an organised distance sales or service-provision scheme run by the supplier; (f) a contract for the supply of goods, other assets or services whose price depends on fluctuations in the financial market outside the supplier's control, which may occur during the withdrawal period; (g) a contract concluded at an auction; (h) travel and baggage insurance policies or similar short-term insurance policies of less than 1 month's duration".

In addition to those exceptions, this rule does not apply either under art. II.-5:201(3) if "the business has exclusively used means of distance communication for concluding the contract, and the contract is for (a) the supply of accommodation, transport, catering or leisure services, where the business undertakes, when the contract is concluded, to supply these services on a specific date or within a specific period; (b) the supply of services other than financial services if performance has begun, at the consumer's express and informed request, before the end of the withdrawal period; (c) the supply of goods made to the consumer's specifications or clearly personalised or which, by reason of their nature, cannot be returned or are liable to deteriorate or expire rapidly; (d) the supply of audio or video recordings or computer software (i) which were unsealed by the consumer, or (ii) which can be downloaded or reproduced for permanent use, in case of supply by electronic means; (e) the supply of newspapers, periodicals and magazines; (f) gaming and lottery services".

In the second place, with regard to timeshare contracts, two preliminary remarks must be made. Firstly, the DCFR does not provide a definition for this type of contract; and secondly, other similar products such as the long-term holiday product—which is actually covered by Directive 2008/122/EC of the European Parliament and of the Council of 14 January 2009 on the protection of consumers in respect of certain aspects of timeshare, long-term holiday product, resale and exchange contracts—have not been contemplated (Feliú Rey 2009).

The DCFR only establishes in art. II.-5:202 that "a consumer who acquires a right to use immovable property under a timeshare contract with a business is entitled to withdraw from the contract".

The consumer is not obliged to reimburse any expenses when exercising the right of withdrawal in cases where the consumer has been put at a particular disadvantage in the sense of art. II.–3:103(1): consumers placed at a significant informational disadvantage because of the technical medium used for contracting, the physical distance between business and consumer, or the nature of the transaction. In other situations, if the consumer exercises this right, art. II.–5:202(2) states that "the contract may require the consumer to reimburse those expenses which (a) have been incurred as a result of the conclusion of and withdrawal from the contract; (b) correspond to legal formalities which must be completed before the end of the withdrawal period; (c) are reasonable and appropriate; (d) are expressly mentioned in the contract; and (e) are in conformity with any applicable rules on such expenses".

It should be noted in this regard that unlike the general regulation of the right of withdrawal and the particular rules devoted to the contracts negotiated away from business premises, the DCFR explicitly establishes for timeshare contracts in art. II.–5:202(3) that "The business must not demand or accept any advance payment by the consumer during the period in which the latter may exercise the right of withdrawal". If the trader does not comply with this obligation the same provision states that "the business is obliged to return any such payment received".

4.2.2 Information Duties in the DCFR

As mentioned above, after having dealt with the regime on the right of withdrawal, the information duties contemplated in Section 1 of Chapter 3 of Book II DCFR need to be considered. The aspects covered by this section are the following: the duty to disclose information about the goods, other assets and services; specific duties for businesses marketing to consumers; duty to provide information when concluding contract with a consumer who is at a particular disadvantage; information duties in real time distance communication; formation by electronic means; clarity and form of information; information about price and additional charges; information about address and identity of business; and remedies for breach of information duties.

Two of these aspects are particularly interesting: the information duties in real time distance communication (art. II.-3:104) and the remedies for breach of information duties (art. II.-3:109).

As regards the first issue, the DCFR provides a definition in art. II.-3:104(2). "Real time distance communication means direct and immediate distance communication of such a type that one party can interrupt the other in the course of the communication. It includes telephone and electronic means such as voice over internet protocol and internet related chat, but does not include communication by electronic mail".

Where these situations involve communication with a consumer, art. II.–3:104(1) states that "a business has a duty to provide at the outset explicit information on its name and the commercial purpose of the contract". If these pieces of information are not provided, paragraph (4) of this provision clarifies that the consumer has a right to withdraw from the contract within the general period of withdrawal mentioned above (14 days).

Finally it is also relevant to mention that "the business bears the burden of proof that the consumer has received the information required under paragraph (1)" in accordance with art. 3:104(3). The consumer is obviously the weakest party in the contractual relationship so he is benefited by the establishment of this burden of proof on the trader.

With regard to the general provision on remedies for breach of information duties, the first rule of art. II.–3:109 refers to contracts concluded with consumers who are at a particular disadvantage. In these situations a business must "provide information to a consumer before the conclusion of a contract from which he has the right to withdraw, the withdrawal period does not commence until all this information has been provided. Regardless of this, the right of withdrawal lapses after 1 year from the time of the conclusion of the contract". It should be noted, therefore, that this is the only consequence foreseen where there is a lack of information given about the right of withdrawal. Hence, the DCFR does not provide any explicit ineffectiveness sanction for breach of the duty to inform.

On the other hand, art. II.–3:109(2) establishes in a more general sense that where a business has failed to comply with any information duty previously mentioned and a contract has been concluded, "the business has such obligations under the contract as the other party has reasonably expected as a consequence of the absence or incorrectness of the information". Remedies for non-performance, provided under Book III, Chapter 3, also apply to non-performance of these obligations.

The next rule in art. II.–3:109(3) clarifies that "whether or not a contract is concluded, a business which has failed to comply with any duty imposed by the preceding Articles of this section is liable for any loss caused to the other party to the transaction by such failure". Although this provision does not go further, it is understood that the general theory of compensation for damages provided by the DCFR is applicable to the claim of any damages that may result from the failure of the duties of information.

However, art. II–3:109(4) states that "the remedies provided under this Article are without prejudice to any remedy which may be available under II.–7:201 (Mistake)". Although this provision establishes the possibility of referring to the defects of consent, it is submitted that it would have been preferable for the DCFR to have specifically contemplated a kind of inefficiency remedy following the breach of duties of information in order to avoid the necessity to prove, before the court, that the requirements for the cancellation of the contract due to mistake have been met.

And finally, art. II.–3:109(5) clarifies the mandatory nature of this regime: "In relations between a business and a consumer the parties may not, to the detriment of the consumer, exclude the application of this Article or derogate from or vary its effects".

4.3 Right of Withdrawal in the CESL[1]

This section will be devoted to the provisions on the right of withdrawal in the Proposal for a Regulation on a CESL, taking into account that, according to Recital 9 of the CESL, this instrument harmonises the contract laws of the Member States not by requiring amendments to the pre-existing national contract law, but by creating within each Member State's national law a second contract law regime for contracts within its scope (Illescas Ortiz and Viscasillas 2012). Therefore, it is conceived to operate as a directly applicable "second" regime within the legal systems of the Member States to be applied instead of the "first" national contract-law regime. This second regime would be identical throughout the Union and exist alongside the pre-existing rules of national contract law. The Common European Sales Law would apply on a voluntary basis to cross-border contracts upon an express agreement of the parties (Fernández Masiá 2012).

4.3.1 Beneficiaries and Mandatory Nature of the Right of Withdrawal

Section 1 of Chapter 2 CESL entitled "Pre-contractual information to be given by a trader dealing with a consumer" has a mandatory nature. Under Article 22 CESL "The parties may not, to the detriment of the consumer, exclude the application of this section or derogate from or vary its effects". This includes the obligation for the trader to provide particular pieces of information to the consumer such as the right of withdrawal.

By contrast, no reference to the right of withdrawal has been proposed in art. 23 CESL when stating the pre-contractual information to be given by a trader dealing with another trader.

[1] Please note that the Committee on Legal Affairs of the European Parliament launched a Report on the Proposal for a Regulation on the CESL on 24 September 2013 where a number of modifications of the current drafting of the Proposal have been suggested. The main suggestion refers to the modification of the material scope of application of the CESL: the limitation of its use to distance contracts, including online contracts (as shown in the amendments of arts. 1.1 and 5.1 CESL). More recently a European Parliament legislative resolution of 26 February 2014 has also been published. This research refers only to the wording of the Proposal for a Regulation dated 11 October 2011.

Therefore Chapter 4 CESL entitled "Right to withdraw in distance and off-premises contracts between traders and consumers" is exclusively applied to consumer contracts. Its rules are also mandatory under art. 47 CESL, which states that "the parties may not, to the detriment of the consumer, exclude the application of this chapter or derogate from or vary its effects".

This same feature ("*obligado cumplimiento*") is contained in art. 29(4) CESL as regards to the remedies for breach of information duties in contracts between traders and consumers.

4.3.2 Scope of Application of the Right of Withdrawal

The scope of application of the right of withdrawal is dealt with in art. 40 CESL. The function of this provision is the determination of the situations in which protection is to be afforded by means of a right of withdrawal (Schulze 2012).

Article 40.1 CESL states: "During the period provided for in Article 42 [which will be analysed later], the consumer has a right to withdraw from the contract without giving any reason, and at no cost to the consumer except as provided in Article 45 CESL, from (a) a distance contract; (b) off-premises contract, provided that the price, or where multiple contracts were concluded at the same time, the total price of the contracts exceeds € 50 or the equivalent sum in the currency agreed for the contract price at the time of the conclusion of the contract".

Several issues arise from this rule. In the first place, the right of withdrawal is only contemplated for some particular contracts: distance and off-premises contracts, which are defined in art. 2 of the preliminary section of the Proposal on "definitions".

Under paragraph (p), "distance contract means any contract between the trader and the consumer under an organised distance sales scheme concluded without the simultaneous physical presence of the trader or, in case the trader is a legal person, a natural person representing the trader and the consumer, with the exclusive use of one or more means of distance communication up to and including the time at which the contract is concluded".

Under paragraph (q), "off-premises contract means any contract between a trader and a consumer: (i) concluded in the simultaneous physical presence of the trader or, where the trader is a legal person, the natural person representing the trader and the consumer in a place which is not the trader's business premises, or concluded on the basis of an offer made by the consumer in the same circumstances; or (ii) concluded on the trader's business premises or through any means of distance communication immediately after the consumer was personally and individually addressed in a place which is not the trader's business premises in the simultaneous physical presence of the trader or, where the trader is a legal person, a natural person representing the trader and the consumer; or (iii) concluded during an excursion organised by the trader or, where the trader is a legal person, the natural person representing the trader with the aim or effect of promoting and selling goods or supplying digital content or related services to the consumer".

Furthermore, the CESL does not propose the right of withdrawal for a number of contracts listed in art. 40(2) CESL. This list of exceptions is similar to the one contained in art. 16 DCR. For instance, (a) contracts "concluded by means of an automatic vending machine or automated commercial premises"; (b) contracts "for the supply of foodstuffs, beverages or other goods which are intended for current consumption in the household and which are physically supplied by the trader on frequent and regular rounds to the consumer's home, residence or workplace"; or (c) contracts "for the supply of goods or related services for which the price depends on fluctuations in the financial market which cannot be controlled by the trader and which may occur within the withdrawal period".

In addition to these exclusions, the right of withdrawal as contemplated in the CESL does not apply either in certain other situations regulated in art. 40(3) CESL, such as: "(a) where the goods supplied were sealed, have been unsealed by the consumer and are not then suitable for return due to health protection or hygiene reasons; (b) where the goods supplied have, according to their nature, been inseparably mixed with other items after delivery; or (c) where the goods supplied were sealed audio or video recordings or computer software and have been unsealed after delivery; (…)".

Although attention could be drawn to the fact that the right of withdrawal is only provided for some types of contracts, i.e. distance and off-premises contracts, it must be understood that this legislative decision of the European legislator has to do with the special features of these contracts. In a distance contract, the consumer cannot see or inspect the goods before concluding it; and in an off-premises contract, he may be forced to acquire a product that he may not want or need. Also previous European instruments, such as the Directive on Consumer Rights, have followed this same rule (art. 9 DCR).

Therefore, the next question is to determine whether the right of withdrawal can be exercised in other cases that have not been contemplated in the Proposal, taking into account its scope of application in accordance with arts. 4 and 5 CESL. Some academics support the application of the relevant choice-of-law rules on contractual matters to determine the applicable State law which would resolve this issue (Roca Guillamón 2012). It should be noted in this regard that the CESL is actually available for the parties because the law governing the relevant contract is the law of a Member State under Regulation (EC) No 593/2008 of the European Parliament and of the Council on the law applicable to contractual obligations (Rome I) (Sánchez Lorenzo 2011).

Moreover, in this context it is also important to note the possible application of the United Nations Convention on Contracts for the International Sale of Goods of 1980 (CISG) adopted by UNCITRAL in cases where the law applicable to a particular case refers to the law of a contracting state to this Convention and provided that the application conditions of this instrument are met and the parties have not excluded it.

Finally, in case the substantive Spanish legislation is to be applied, it must be noted that the above mentioned TRLGDCU, covers relations between consumers and users and traders in accordance with art. 2 TRLGDCU and regulates the right of withdrawal for the cases provided for by law or regulation when so recognised in the offer, promotion, advertising or in the contract itself.

Hence, Spanish Law does not regulate this right in a broad sense, but limits it only to consumer contracts. Furthermore the TRLGDCU provides this right explicitly only for distance and off-premises contracts in arts. 101 and 110 respectively, but this does not prevent the parties from agreeing this right in other contracts under art. 1255 CC.

Besides, the Spanish legislation excludes this right for a number of distance and off-premises contracts. For instance (arts. 93 and 103 TRLGDCU), sales concluded by means of an automatic vending machine or automated commercial premises; contracts over financial services; contracts for the construction of immovable properties; or contracts for the supply of foodstuffs, beverages or other goods intended for everyday home consumption supplied by traders who make frequent and regular deliveries to this end.

4.3.3 Withdrawal Period

In accordance with art. 42 CESL: "The withdrawal period expires after 14 days from:(a) the day on which the consumer has taken delivery of the goods in the case of a sales contract, including a sales contract under which the seller also agrees to provide related services; (b) the day on which the consumer has taken delivery of the last item in the case of a contract for the sale of multiple goods ordered by the consumer in one order and delivered separately, including a contract under which the seller also agrees to provide related services; (c) the day on which the consumer has taken delivery of the last lot or piece in the case of a contract where the goods consist of multiple lots or pieces, including a contract under which the seller also agrees to provide related services; (d) the day on which the consumer has taken delivery of the first item where the contract is for regular delivery of goods during a defined period of time, including a contract under which the seller also agrees to provide related services; (e) the day of the conclusion of the contract in the case of a contract for related services concluded after the goods have been delivered; (f) the day when the consumer has taken delivery of the tangible medium in accordance with point (a) in the case of a contract for the supply of digital content where the digital content is supplied on a tangible medium; (g) the day of the conclusion of the contract in the case of a contract where the digital content is not supplied on a tangible medium".

However, a different rule is provided "where the trader has not provided the consumer with the information referred to in Article 17(1)". In this case art. 42(2) CESL states that "the withdrawal period expires:(a) after 1 year from the end of the initial withdrawal period, as determined in accordance with the previous paragraph; or (b) where the trader provides the consumer with the information required within 1 year from the end of the withdrawal period as determined in accordance with the previous paragraph, after 14 days from the day the consumer receives the information".

As will be seen later, the trader must provide the consumer with the relevant information about the right of withdrawal so that the period within which the consumer may withdraw is extended where the trader has not complied with this obligation.

Article 10 DCR follows the same line. It is important to stress with regard to this Directive that it has been adopted in terms of maximum harmonisation. It does not allow Member States to establish stricter standards in their national legal systems; thus the possibility to cancel the contract has disappeared (Tomás Martínez 2012).

Consequently, both the CESL and the DCR include the extension of the period to withdraw in cases of failure to provide information in line with the Acquis Principles and the DCFR. However, differences in the *dies a quo* can be ascertained. While the Acquis Principles and the DCFR establish a period of 1 year from the conclusion of the contract, the DCR and the CESL contemplate this same length of time but from the expiration of the 14 days. It is submitted that this last solution is more appropriate.

The failure to exercise the right of withdrawal within the period prescribed does not preclude the subsequent exercise of the action for annulment by mistake or fraud.

The Spanish legislation shares the same period as the CESL. In accordance with art. 71 TRLGDCU the consumer and user will have a minimum of 14 days to exercise the right of withdrawal from the reception of the goods which is the object of the contract, or from the conclusion of such a contract where it relates to a provision of services, provided that the trader had complied with the information and documentation duties. Before the amendment of March 2014 the period of withdrawal was 7 days. This same period of 7 days for returning the goods and receiving the amounts the consumer had paid is established in Catalonia under art. 23 Royal Legislative Decree of Internal Commerce of Catalonia (Bosch Capdevila 2009).

This period is extended to 12 months (3 months before the recent amendment) from the delivery of the goods, or the conclusion of the contract in case of a provision of services, if the trader had not complied with the information and documentation duty about the right of withdrawal. Where the trader fulfils the information and documentation duty within those 12 months, the period for exercising the right of withdrawal will start from that moment.

4.3.4 Form of Exercising the Right of Withdrawal

Firstly, it is important to stress that the CESL includes an Appendix 1 that contains the "Model instructions on withdrawal" which must be provided by the trader to the consumer before the conclusion of a distance or off-premises contract; and an Appendix 2 that sets out a "Model withdrawal form".

According to art. 41 CESL"(1) The consumer may exercise the right of withdrawal at any time before the end of the period of withdrawal provided for in Article 42. (2) The consumer exercises the right to withdraw by notice to the trader. For this purpose, the consumer may use either the Model withdrawal form set out in Appendix 2 or any other unequivocal statement setting out the decision to withdraw". Hence, the use of this second form is not mandatory for the consumer.

Secondly, the withdrawal by electronic means is also provided for. Under art. 41(3) CESL "Where the trader gives the consumer the option to withdraw electronically on its trading website, and the consumer does so, the trader has a duty to communicate to the consumer an acknowledgement of receipt of such a withdrawal on a durable medium without delay".

Article 41(5) CESL states: "The consumer bears the burden of proof that the right of withdrawal has been exercised in accordance with this Article". Given that the consumer is the person exercising this right, to require him to prove the exercise of the right seems coherent and appropriate.

With regard to the Spanish legislation on this point and similarly to the CESL, the Spanish legal system states, in art. 69 TRLGDCU, that it is the obligation of the trader to inform the consumer of the right of withdrawal in writing in the contract, including the requirements and consequences of its exercise, as well as the forms of restitution of the goods or the provided service, in a clear, understandable and accurate manner. Moreover, he must give him a withdrawal document, clearly identified as such, which will express the name and address of the person to whom the identification data of the contract and the parties must be submitted. The trader bears the burden of proving the fulfilment of this obligation.

However, despite the obligation of the trader to give the consumer a withdrawal document, art. 70 TRLGDCU states that the exercise of the right of withdrawal is not subject to any formal requirement. It can be evidenced through any form under the law and it can even be ascertained by returning the goods. The consumer bears the burden of proving the exercise of the right according to art. 72 TRLGDCU. Furthermore it must be noted that there is case-law of the Spanish Supreme Court as to the form in which the right of withdrawal must be included in a contract.

Taking into account that this right is contemplated as an exceptional rule in certain situations—the general rule under art. 1256 of the Spanish Civil Code (CC) states that the validity and the enforcement of contracts cannot be left to the sole will of one party—the Supreme Court ruled, as regards the inclusion of this right as a clause in a contract, that the parties must express their will in a clear, self-evident and unambiguous manner (STS 29 June 2009, RJ 2009/4762).

4.3.5 *Effects of Withdrawal: Restitution of Performances*

The right of withdrawal is a unilateral declaration of will that must be known to the trader in order to produce the relevant legal effects (Jiménez Muñoz 2011). In accordance with art. 43 CESL, "Withdrawal terminates the obligations of both parties under the contract". In accordance with this provision, the main effect of the exercise of this right is the termination of the relevant contract.

This entails the restitution of any performances that the parties had performed after the conclusion of the contract. Article 44(1) CESL establishes, in this regard, a first obligation that "The trader must reimburse all payments received from the consumer, including, where applicable, the costs of delivery without undue delay and in any event not later than 14 days from the day on which the trader is informed of the consumer's decision to withdraw from the contract…".

Regarding the way in which the reimbursement must be performed, the same provision clarifies that "The trader must carry out such reimbursement using the same means of payment as the consumer used for the initial transaction, unless the consumer has expressly agreed otherwise and provided that the consumer does not incur any fees as a result of such reimbursement".

Hence, as a general rule, the trader must provide the reimbursement through the same method used by the consumer in the transaction except that the consumer may agree to receive the reimbursement by an alternative method. However, it should be noted subsequently that art. 44(2) CESL states that "the trader is not required to reimburse the supplementary costs, if the consumer has expressly opted for a type of delivery other than the least expensive type of standard delivery offered by the trader".

Consequently, the consumer is given absolute freedom to choose the method of payment he prefers under the Proposal, but he will have to bear the extra costs derived from a choice of delivery method that has cost more than the least expensive one suggested by the trader.

Even though the trader has the obligation to reimburse, it must be noted that the trader does have the benefit of the right of withholding. In particular, art. 44(3) CESL establishes that "In the case of a contract for the sale of goods, the trader may withhold the reimbursement until it has received the goods back, or the consumer has supplied evidence of having sent back the goods, whichever is earlier, unless the trader has offered to collect the goods".

The first, and obvious, remark that can be drawn from this rule is its sole application to contracts for the sale of goods. Contracts for the provisions of services do not fall within its scope of application.

A second critical remark refers to the fact that this right is granted to the trader and not to the consumer. Given that the consumer is the person exercising the right of withdrawal, it could be understood that he is not interested anymore in keeping the goods, so the legislator could have assumed his good faith in returning such goods. Furthermore the consumer is the weakest party and where the trader does not reimburse the payment, he would be forced to cover the costs of a judicial claim. The establishment of a parallel sanction to the one contained in the Spanish legal system could have been proposed: the consumer who does not receive the due amount within the relevant period is granted the right to claim double this amount as well as compensation for damages.

It should be questioned why the European legislator has decided that the consumer should not be granted a right of withholding the goods until the trader reimburses the payment when it has provided for the trader's right to withhold, especially taking into consideration the fact that no consequences have been foreseen in the Proposal for case in which the trader takes more than 14 days to reimburse the money from the date he knows that the consumer has decided to withdraw from the contract.

A last obligation of the trader specifically devoted to off-premises contracts is regulated in art. 44(4)CESL: "In case of an off-premises contract where the goods have been delivered to the consumer's home at the time of the conclusion of the contract, the trader must collect the goods at its own cost if the goods by their nature cannot be normally returned by post".

From the authors' perspective, this rule may cause problems of interpretation. It refers to the "nature" of the goods to raise a situation where such goods cannot be normally returned by post. The meaning of this condition is unclear. The impossibility could refer to different difficulties: for instance, the size of the goods, their perishable nature, or the cost of the sending. The focus should have been established on the place of celebration of the contract such that the restitution of performances should have been done at the consumer's home.

On the other hand, the obligations of the consumer in the event of withdrawal must also be studied.

The main effect for the consumer is the sending back of the goods. Article 45(1) CESL states that "The consumer must sending back the goods or hand them over to the trader or to a person authorised by the trader without undue delay and in any event not later than 14 days from the day on which the consumer communicates the decision to withdraw from the contract to the trader (…)unless the trader has offered to collect the goods". Moreover "This deadline is met if the consumer returns the goods before the period of 14 days has expired", being regardless of the moment when the trader receives them.

It should be noted that the Proposal does not foresees the possibility of exercising the right of withdrawal in cases where the restitution is not possible due to loss, destruction or other reason.

With regard to the burden of paying the costs of returning the goods, art. 45(2) CESL states that "The consumer must bear the direct costs of returning the goods, unless the trader has agreed to bear those costs or the trader failed to inform the consumer that he had to bear them". It is then possible that the trader could agree to cover these costs. Nothing is said about the way in which he has to accept, but it is rather logical to assume that it can be included as a specific clause in the contract. This does not prevent the possibility of accepting this obligation verbally, but this option may cause problems of proof.

Furthermore it should be noted that the trader will have to bear these costs not only if he agreed to do it but also if "he failed to inform the consumer that he had to bear them". This could be interpreted as a sanction for not having complied with the duty of information properly.

In addition to these main obligations of the parties, other kind of obligations may also arise, such as compensation for damages or redress for misusing the goods.

In this respect, art. 45(3)CESL states that "The consumer is liable for any diminished value of the goods only where that results from handling of the goods in any way other than what is necessary to establish the nature, characteristics and functioning of the goods. The consumer is not liable for diminished value where the trader has not provided all the information about the right to withdraw (…)".

Again, a sanction has been provided against the trader following the lack of compliance of the duty to inform about the right of withdrawal. In this particular situation, the consumer will not be liable for the diminished value of the goods.

Furthermore, art. 45(4) CESL states explicitly that "(…) the consumer is not liable to pay any compensation for the use of the goods during the withdrawal period", unless the specific case mentioned in art. 45(5) arises: "Where the consumer exercises the right of withdrawal after having made an express request for the provision of related services to begin during the withdrawal period, the consumer must pay to the trader an amount which is in proportion to what has been provided before the consumer exercised the right of withdrawal, in comparison with the full coverage of the contract. The proportionate amount to be paid by the consumer to the trader must be calculated on the basis of the total price agreed in the contract. Where the total price is excessive, the proportionate amount must be calculated on the basis of the market value of what has been provided".

By contrast and consistent with the above, art. 45(6)CESL clarifies that "The consumer is not liable for the cost for (a) the provision of related services, in full or in part, during the withdrawal period, where (i) the trader has failed to provide information (…) or (ii) the consumer has not expressly requested performance to begin during the withdrawal period (…)".

Finally, art. 46 CESL refers to the effects of the right of withdrawal of ancillary contracts. Under this provision an ancillary contract means "a contract by which a consumer acquires goods, digital content or related services in connexion to a distance contract or an off-premises contract and these goods, digital content or related services are provided by the trader or a third party on the basis of an arrangement between that third party and the trader". Where this right of withdrawal is exercised by a consumer in a distance or an off-premises contract, then this article provides for the automatic termination of any ancillary contracts without cost to the consumer except the costs provided for in art. 46 paras. 2 and 3. Article 15 DCR follows the same line.

The application of this provision is directly related with the situation where the price to be paid by the consumer is fully or partially funded by a loan granted by the trader who is a party to the contract, or by a third party having agreed upon it with the trader. If this is the case, it can be understood that the exercise of the right of withdrawal would also lead to the termination of the finance contract without penalty to the consumer. This is actually the rule provided by the Spanish legislation, although the definition of ancillary contracts under the CESL is much broader and could contemplate other types of contracts such as insurance contracts, extended warranties, etc.

In the Spanish case, art. 74 TRLGDCU contains the reciprocal restitution of performances in accordance with art. 1303 and 1308 CC. Then, art. 75 TRLGDCU states that where the restitution of the performance is impossible due to loss, destruction or any other cause, these facts shall not prevent the consumer from exercising the right of withdrawal. If the cause that makes the restitution impossible is attributable to him, the consumer will be liable for the market value of the goods or services at the moment the right of withdrawal is exercised. Where this value exceeds the price of the acquisition, the consumer will be only liable of the price the goods had at the moment he bought them.

This provision does not make any reference to the consumer who has lost the goods despite having been diligent. If this is the case, it is submitted that the consumer could exercise his right of withdrawal without any responsibility. Therefore, the consumer would not be liable for either the market value of the goods or services at the moment the right of withdrawal is exercised, nor the price of the acquisition.

As regards the trader, he will have to reimburse the consumer for the amount the latter had paid without deduction of any costs as soon as possible and, in any case, within 14 days (30 days before the recent amendment of 2014) from the withdrawal. As already mentioned above, if the consumer has not received the due amount within that period, he will have the right to claim double the amount as well as being able to be compensated for damages.

Finally, the Spanish system provides for an explicit rule where the price to be paid by the consumer is fully or partially funded by a loan granted by the trader who is a party to the contract, or by a third party having agreed upon it with the trader. Art. 77 TRLGDCU states that the exercise of the right of withdrawal will involve the termination of the finance contract without any penalty to the consumer.

4.3.6 Duty to Provide Information

Pre-contractual information duties are conceived as one of the hallmarks of modern EU consumer law (Beale and Howells 2011),and thus these must necessarily be provided for in this instrument as well.

The right of withdrawal is set out in art. 13(1)(e) CESL as one of the aspects of the duty of the trader to provide information to the consumer in a clear and comprehensible manner before the contract is concluded or the consumer is bound by any offer of a distance contract or off-premises contract. (This duty is excluded in other contracts as mentioned above).

Article 13(2) CESL states that most of the information provided in paragraph 1 of that article, including the right of withdrawal, "forms an integral part of the contract and shall not be altered unless the parties expressly agree otherwise".

It can be understood that the intention of the European legislator with the above rule is to cover the situation where the parties have jointly agreed to alter the right of withdrawal. However, it must be noted that some aspects of this right cannot be altered by the parties due to their mandatory nature. By contrast, certain other aspects of this right are actually available for modification by the parties. For instance, the possibility that the trader may take on the costs of returning the goods, or the possible extension of the period in which it is possible to exercise the right of withdrawal.

As regards the form of providing this information, the CESL distinguishes between the two kinds of contracts.

Article 13(3) CESL states that "For a distance contract, the information required by this Article must (a) be given or made available to the consumer in a way that is appropriate to the means of distance communication used; (b) be in plain and intelligible language; and (c) insofar as it is provided on a durable medium, be legible". On the other hand, Article 13(4) CESL establishes for off-premises contracts that "the information required by this Article must: (a) be given on paper or, if the consumer agrees, on another durable medium; and (b) be legible and in plain, intelligible language".

The above rules are further developed in the subsequent provisions. Among them, the rules of art. 17 CESL are worth mentioning. First, the trader must provide not only the existence of the right of withdrawal but also "the conditions, time limit and procedures for exercising that right… as well as the model withdrawal form set out in Appendix 2" (art. 17(1) CESL).

Moreover, "Where applicable, the information… must include the fact that the consumer will have to bear the cost of returning the goods in case of withdrawal and, for distance contracts, that the consumer will have to bear the cost of returning the goods in the event of withdrawal if the goods by their nature cannot be normally returned by post." (art. 17(2) CESL).

Consistent with art. 45(5) CESL, where the consumer can exercise the right of withdrawal after having made a request for the provision of related services to begin during the withdrawal period, the information to be provided by the trader must include the fact that the consumer would be liable to pay the trader an amount which is in proportion to what has been provided before the consumer exercised the right of withdrawal (art. 17(3) CESL).

And finally, the consumer must also be informed of the fact that he is not entitled this right, or under which circumstances he can no longer exercise it (art. 17(5) CESL).

Every piece of information related to the right of withdrawal that must be provided to the consumer will be correctly made available if the trader gives the consumer the Model of Withdrawal contained in Appendix 1. In any case, in accordance with art. 21 CESL the trader bears the burden of proving that he has provided the required information.

In relation to the above, the breach of information duties is also provided for. In accordance with art. 28 CESL, "A party who supplies information before or at the time a contract is concluded, whether in order to comply with the duties imposed by this chapter or otherwise, has a duty to take reasonable care to ensure that the information supplied is correct and is not misleading".

In keeping with the above, a party who has failed to comply with any duty related to pre-contractual information is liable for any loss caused to the other party by such failure under arts. 28(2) and 29 CESL (Gómez Pomar and Gili Saldaña 2012).

One of the parties may receive incorrect or misleading information in breach of this duty. The remedies set out in art. 29 CESL are then available for those persons who reasonably rely on the information provided in concluding a contract with the party who supplied it. Moreover, in "relations between a trader and a consumer the parties may not, to the detriment of the consumer, exclude the application of this provision or derogate from or vary its effects" (art. 29(4) CESL).

However, the European Proposal has not established any penalty for contractual ineffectiveness following the breach of this duty except the extension of the period within which to exercise the right of withdrawal and some sanctions following the non-compliance of certain pieces of information related with the right of withdrawal, as previously explained.

Additionally, it is also important to note that under art. 29(3) CESL the consumer may allege the rule on annulment by mistake (art. 48 CESL) or fraud (art. 49 CESL) if the relevant facts are met.

In this same context, art. 24 DCR has established a general provision on the regime of penalties for breaches of the national rules adopted through the implementation of this Directive, providing that Member States are in charge of their determination. In this regard, a further harmonisation of the consequences of the duty to inform in the different EU Member States would have been preferred.

In the Spanish legal system, the right of withdrawal is also contemplated as a pre-contractual information duty of the trader under which he has to provide the consumer with the relevant information for him to be able to decide properly and freely whether he wants to conclude the contract or not (Serrano Fernández and Sánchez Lería 2013).

In accordance with art. 60 TRLGDCU, the trader must inform the consumer and user, in a clear and understandable manner adapted to the circumstances, of all the relevant, accurate and sufficient information about the essential features of the contract and, in particular under Section 2(h) of this provision, the existence of a right of withdrawal from the contract and the period and form of exercising it (art. 27 Royal Legislative Decree of Internal Commerce of Catalonia states that the trader must inform about the cooling-off period in offers of distance contracts; Bosch Capdevila 2009).

In case this information duty is not complied with correctly by the trader, either because he did not inform the consumer about this relevant information or because he did not do it correctly (Callejo Rodríguez 2003), Title III of TRLGDCU on distance and off-premises contracts does not establish any specific sanction for non-compliance of this duty.

However, this does not mean that the consumer is completely unprotected from the lack of information because where this lack of information refers to the object of the contract or the conditions that were essential to conclude it and the consumer has manifested his consent by mistake, there is the possibility of claiming under the general rules on the nullity of contracts (contract with no object, without consent or without a cause: art. 1261 CC) or on defects of consent (arts. 1265–1270 CC). In any of these situations a nullity action could be lodged under arts. 1300 *et seq.*CC.

4.4 Conclusions

Unlike other international instruments, the Proposal for a Regulation on a Common European Sales Law has been conceived as an optional instrument. It will only be applied if the law governing the contract is the legal system of an EU Member State and, furthermore, if the parties agree upon its application.

Nevertheless, once the parties have agreed upon this issue, some aspects of the instrument, such as the right of withdrawal, have a mandatory nature if the contract has been concluded between a consumer and a trader and, therefore, no modifications can be done by the parties to the detriment of the consumer.

This right may be exercised within 14 days either through an explicit declaration or by making use of the form provided in Appendix 2 of the Proposal; the period of exercise is extended to 1 year in those situations where the trader has not complied with the duty to inform the consumer about this issue.

The right of withdrawal is not provided in the Proposal for every kind of contract. As explained in this chapter, this is only foreseen for distance and off-premises contracts; and furthermore, this right can be excluded in some cases where the legislator has considered that this right is not suitable; for instance due to the special nature of certain goods and services, goods created under the orders of the consumer or clearly personalised, among others.

The direct consequences of the exercise of the right of withdrawal are, on the one hand, the obligation of the trader to reimburse the payments made by the consumer, including the possible costs the trader may have incurred; and, on the other hand, the obligation of the consumer to return the goods which were the object of the contract no later than 14 days after having notified the trader of his decision to withdraw from the contract.

Following the comparative analysis of the CESL and the Spanish TRLGDCU, a number of common aspects can be noted. For instance, the period of withdrawal (14 days, extendable to 1 year as a sanction of the lack of information); and the nature of the days mentioned (calendar days). They also share the duty of the trader to inform about the right of withdrawal; the moment from which the right can be exercised; the theory of the expedition as regards the exercise by the consumer of the notification within the relevant period of his right of withdrawal; or the establishment of the moment from which the withdrawal is effective and the performances must be restituted when the trader is fully aware of the exercise of the right.

Furthermore, it is submitted that the CESL should have included certain significant aspects that have been omitted, such as for instance: a sanction of ineffectiveness for those situations where the trader does not comply with his information duty; or a sanction where the trader does not reimburse the amounts paid by the consumer within the relevant period.

Moreover, from the authors' perspective, the new instrument should also have contained the right of withdrawal for every contract where consumers are involved, and not only in distance and off-premises contracts. With the aim of designing a whole framework of protection for consumers, it is suggested that this provision should extend to timeshare contracts, consumer credit contracts and financial services distance contracts.

To summarise, the right of withdrawal shares some common features in the different European instruments that have been adopted in this field so far, but, at the same time, its legal regime also contains certain divergences. Once the Proposal on the CESL enters into force, the parties will have the possibility of selecting the legal regime most suitable for them from among the available instruments dealing with contractual matters. In any case, it is important to remember that the current wording is still under debate and, thus, subject to possible future changes.

References

Arroyo i Amayuelas E (2008) Los principios de derecho contractual comunitario, Anuario de Derecho Civil, n. 1.

Beale H and Howells G (2011) Pre-contractual Information Duties in the Optional Instrument, in Schulze R and Stuyck J (ed.) Towards a European Contract Law, Sellier, Munich, pp. 49 *et seq*.

Bosch Capdevila E (2009) Derecho Contractual Europeo. Problemática, propuestas y perspectivas, Bosch, Barcelona.

Callejo Rodríguez C (2003) El deber precontractual de información: del esquema tradicional del Código Civil al régimen del derecho de consumo, Revista Jurídica del Notariado, n. 47.

Diéguez Oliva R (2009) El derecho de desistimiento en el marco común de referencia, Indret: Revista para el Análisis del Derecho, n. 2.

Ebers, M. and Arroyo i Amayuelas E (2006) Heininger y las sanciones a la infracción del deber de información sobre el derecho de desistimiento "ad nutum" (Sentencia TJCE de 13 de diciembre de 2001, Asunto C–481–99), Revista de la Facultad de Derecho de la Universidad de Granada, n. 6.

Feliú Rey M.I. (2009) "La nueva regulación europea de la figura del aprovechamiento por turno de bienes de uso turístico, de adquisición de productos vacacionales de larga duración, de reventa y de intercambio: la directiva 2008/122/CE", Derecho de los negocios, n. 222.

Fernández Masiá E (2012) "Optando por la normativa común de compraventa europea", Revista Electrónica de Estudios Internacionales, n. 23.

Gómez Pomar F and Gili Saldaña M (2012) "El futuro instrumento opcional del Derecho contractual europeo: una breve introducción a las cuestiones de formación, interpretación, contenido y efectos", Indret, n. 1.

Illescas Ortiz R and Perales Viscasillas P (2012) "El Reglamento opcional en materia de compraventa en el ámbito de la Unión Europea (CESL): crítica a su ámbito de aplicación", Revista Derecho de los Negocios, n. 265–266.

Jiménez Muñoz FJ (2011) "El derecho legal de desistimiento: presente y (posible) futuro", Actualidad civil, n. 7, 1- 15 April.

Klein M (1997) El desistimiento unilateral del contrato, Civitas, Madrid.

Loos M (2008) Review of the European Consumer Acquis, Sellier, Munich.

Roca Guillamón J (2012) "Armonización, unificación y modernización del derecho de obligaciones y contratos. Notas para una reflexión", XVI Jornadas de la asociación de profesores de derecho civil, Zaragoza, 16–17 octubre 2012. Available at: http://www.derechocivil.net/jornadas/APDC%202012%20Ponencia%20JROCA.pdf

Sánchez Lorenzo S (2011) "La propuesta de Reglamento relativo a una normativa común de compraventa europea y el Derecho internacional privado", Anuario Español de Derecho Internacional Privado, t. XI, pp. 35–61.

Schulze R (2012) Common European Sales Law (CESL) –Commentary-, Nomos Verlag, Baden-Baden.

Serrano Fernández M and Sánchez Lería R (2013) "Del Código Civil a las Directivas comunitarias sobre el derecho a la contratación: un recorrido sobre el deber de información precontractual al consumidor", Revista de Derecho patrimonial, n. 31.

Tomás Martínez G (2012) Derecho Privado Comunitario y evolución de las consecuencias del incumplimiento del deber de información del derecho de desistimiento: contratos celebrados fuera de establecimiento mercantil, Revista de Derecho Comunitario europeo, n. 42.

Twigg-Flesner C (2008) The Europeanisation of Contract Law, Routledge-Cavendish, New York.

Twigg-Flesner C and Schulze R (2010) Protecting rational choice: information and the right of withdrawal, in Howells G, Ramsay I, Wilhelmsson T and Kraft D (ed.), Edward Elgar, Cheltenham, pp. 130 *et seq*.

Vaquer Aloy A, Bosch Capdevila E and Sánchez González (2012) Derecho Europeo de Contratos, Libros II y IV del Marco Común de Referencia, Tomo I, Atelier, Barcelona.

Von Bar C, Clive E and Schulte-Nölke H (2009) Principles, Definitions and Model Rules of European Private Law. Draft Common Frame of Reference (DCFR), Sellier, Munich.

Chapter 5
The Integration of Advertising Statements into the Content of the Contract

Francisco Infante Ruiz

Abstract The ultimate goal of the advertising message is to promote, directly or indirectly, the contracting of goods, services, rights and obligations. Because of its great significance, most European systems contain rules for the integration of advertising into contracts. The European Community legal precedent is the Sales Directive. Currently, art. 69 CESL deals with the question of what are the necessary requirements of the professional supplier's pre-contractual statements, or the statements of a third party about the characteristics of the product to be incorporated into the content of the contract. This provision partially matches the corresponding text in the DCFR (II.-9:102 and IV.A-2:103). However, an analytical study of the rule contained in the CESL compared to some national laws reveals the existence of certain defects in it. For example, some national laws give greater protection to the consumer in the application of this rule than does the CESL. Moreover, it is submitted that a correct regulation of the subject is already provided by the DCFR. Therefore, future improvements of the CESL should take this regulation into account more closely.

Keywords Integration of advertising · Good faith · Offer · Pre-contractual information · Conformity of the goods · Liability to the consumer

5.1 Introduction

Following the antecedent of art. 2(2) Directive 1999/44/EC on certain aspects of the sale of consumer goods and associated guarantees, art. 69 CESL of the Proposal for a Regulation on a Common European Sales Law contains a rule covering the inte-

---

This part has been prepared within the framework of the Research Project DER2009-08705 ("The impact of EU directives on law of contract: critical analysis and proposals for reform"), funded by the Spanish Ministry of Science and Innovation.

F. Infante Ruiz (✉)
University Pablo Olavide Sevilla, Sevilla, Spain
e-mail: finfrui@upo.es

© Springer International Publishing Switzerland 2015
J. Plaza. Penadés, L. M. Martínez Velencoso (eds.), *European Perspectives on the Common European Sales Law,* Studies in European Economic Law and Regulation 4,
DOI 10.1007/978-3-319-10497-3_5

gration of advertising into contracts. In paragraph 1 of this article, it states that this rule is established for any contract, both B2C and B2B. The statement that the business makes to the other party, or makes *publicly*, on the characteristics of the goods in question is incorporated as contract term. This integration will not take place if either of the two exceptions mentioned is present: (a) ignorance of the inaccuracy of the statement by the seller at the time of concluding the contract, and (b) lack of influence of the statement on the buyer to conclude the contract. In paragraph 2 of art. 69 CESL, the application of this rule is also maintained in cases where the statement was made by a person engaged in advertising or marketing on behalf of the merchant. In paragraph 3, the application of this rule, in the B2C contracts, is extended when the statement has been made by a producer or any other person involved in the transaction chain. In these cases the statement is attributed to the trader, unless he did not know of such a statement or could not be expected to have known it at the time of the contract. The last paragraph of art. 69 CESL declares the character of these provisions as being a mandatory rule in B2C relationships. If the goods received by the purchaser do not comply with the characteristics stated in the advertising, there is a lack of conformity [art. 100(f) CESL]. This responsibility is not affected by any consideration of the conduct of anyone who advertises or makes the product or service available to the consumer (negligence or wilful misconduct). It is a strict liability.

The result of this regulation, from the point of view of consumer protection, has a special significance. The consumer may rely on the features announced in any advertising, regardless of whether the advertiser is his contracting party or not, when a mismatch with the contract document exists and the professional does not perform as promised according to the advertising. From a more general perspective where a consumer is not involved, any deviation from the content of advertising (publicity, brochures, advertisements in newspapers or on television, etc.) can also be relied on by any buyer because this must be integrated into the contract, but not when the statement was made by the producer or anyone else who have been involved in the transaction chain.

In this context, this chapter will first analyse the basis of the rule of integration of advertising into the contract; secondly, how such advertising should be treated in connection with the contract offer; thirdly, its regulation in certain national laws; and finally, the consequence of the application of this rule, and, in particular, the issue of the advertiser's liability 'per se'.

5.2 Basis for the Integration of Advertising into the Content of the Contract: Good Faith

Ever since the implementation of art. 2(1) of Council Directive 84/450/EEC of 10 September 1984 concerning misleading and comparative advertising, an advertising concept has been maintained in EU law, which continues today in Directive 2006/114/EC of the European Parliament and of the Council of 12 December 2006 concerning misleading and comparative advertising (codified version):

> 'advertising' means the making of a representation in any form in connection with a trade, business, craft or profession in order to promote the supply of goods or services, including immovable property, rights and obligations [art. 2(a)].

This concept of advertising, referred to as *any form of representation*, is independent of all media or devices used to externalise it. Therefore, all possible means of communication fall into it, no matter what their physical basis. This also includes every commercial and marketing communication transmitted through the new media of the so-called "information society" (Directive 2000/31/EC on Electronic Commerce), i.e. commercial communications via the Internet.

The ultimate goal of the advertising message is to promote, directly or indirectly, the contracting of goods, services, rights and obligations. Therefore, the significance of the social phenomenon of advertising for law can be viewed from two perspectives. The first is the competition between companies, where advertising is a powerful weapon in the coexistence of competitors, and where the rules established by the legislator tend to develop mechanisms to combat unfair competition. The other perspective, of which this chapter is concerned, is the protection of consumers from advertising that provides untruthful information.[1] An example of this, and of the reason why advertising is subject to criticism on many occasions, is that outside of its legitimate communication aspect of the business with potential consumers and facilitation or information on the essential characteristics of the products, it is often false or inaccurate, being *more suggestive and influential* than it really should be (a factual statement), and does not infrequently harm the rights of competition.[2]

According to the Directive 2006/114/EC (art. 2(b)) and previously to the Directive 84/450/EEC (art. 2(2)), advertising cannot mislead people by affecting their economic behaviour. Therefore, it is defined as misleading "any advertising which in any way, including its presentation, deceives or is likely to deceive the persons to whom it is addressed or whom it reaches and which, by reason of its deceptive nature, is likely to affect their economic behaviour or which, for those reasons, injures or is likely to injure a competitor". From these provisions the criterion of "veracity" can be extracted, under which advertising must respect the truth, avoiding the facts being deformed or misled.[3] *Misleading* basically means two things. First, a wrong advertising message encourages, if not causes, a party to enter into a contract; as if the recipient had known the truth, he probably would not have contracted. Secondly, the signed contract is a contract in which the interest of this subject is not satisfied. In the face of advertising, as in many other cases, the consumer is in a position of imbalance. This imbalance is manifested mainly by two facts: first, the information provided to the consumer through advertising that will not always be complete and adequate to inform its decision on the subject of the contract; and secondly, through the use of methods of incitement based more on the appeal, the appearance, and the exaggerations of improving life and social success than on the intrinsic quality of the product, and that attracts the consumer to the product as if it were an "object of desire".

[1] Morales Moreno (1988, p. 668).

[2] Von Hippel (1986, p. 94).

[3] In the Spanish doctrine, the rule of advertising integration is also based on the so-called "veracity principle" ("principio de veracidad"); cf., Pasquau Liaño (1992, p. 145).

The rule of integrating of advertising into the contract is founded on the general principle of good faith,[4] which is recognised in most European systems, and is part of the common core of the EU legal system.[5] Thus, advertising content hetero-integrates the content of contractual regulation—and is therefore enforceable—not by derivation of the presumed or implied intention of the parties, but by the objective requirements of the legal system.[6] Agreeing with Hesselink, it can be said that this would be a "concretisation" of good faith.[7] Article 69 CESL and art. II.-9:102 DCFR, as well as other equivalents, then concretise the principle of objective good faith. However, if the rule of integration of advertising can be deduced from the general principle of good faith, what is the need to expressly regulate it in law? The reasons are twofold. First, good faith is not expressed as a general principle in all European systems, as in the case of English law.[8] In addition, not in all systems it is possible to derive the rule of integration of advertising from the principle of good faith.[9] Secondly, according to the current expression of this rule in Community law, the range of application is larger. The integration of the contract by applying the principle of good faith can only be demanded by the contracting party as opposed to his counterparty, while in art. 69 CESL, art. II.-9: 102 DCFR and equivalent provisions, in the event that the advertiser and the professional supplier are not the same subject, the integration may also be required by the consumer face-to-face with the professional supplier who has contracted with him although not being responsible for advertising. In fact, it is not in accordance with good faith to take advantage of misleading advertising or publicity in order to achieve the conclusion of the contract without being responsible for its contents.

The protection afforded to the party under the rule of the integration of advertising into the contract is based on the appearance and confidence that the advertisement message arouses in him. According to the wording of art. 69 CESL and art. II.-9:102 DCFR, it is required that advertising has previously generated confidence in the recipient. The rule does not apply when the party knows or could be expected to know the inaccuracy of advertising (exception a), or when the statement could not have influenced his decision to contract (exception b).

---

[4] A preview of this idea is contained in the Judgment of the Spanish High Court (Tribunal Supremo) of 27 January 1977 (RJ 1977, 121), in which the benefits and characteristics stated in some advertising leaflets, which expressly said that they did not constitute any contractual document and were ultimately not included in the contract, were considered to be enforceable by a housing buyer. This judgment based its decision on the principle of good faith (art. 1258 Spanish Civil Code (CC)). For the significance of this judgment, see Lasarte Álvarez (1980, pp. 50–78).

[5] See Hesselink (2011, p. 619); Von Bar and Clive (2009), Art. II.-9:102 DCFR, Vol. I, Note I, p. 585.

[6] Pasquau Liaño (1992, p. 161).

[7] Hesselink (2011, pp. 635, 638).

[8] For further details, see Hesselink (2011, p. 620).

[9] In Clive's opinion, the general rule on good faith and fair dealing (in the CESL) "could not be used to create new rules" (Clive 2012, p. 130).

5.3 The Legal Consideration of Advertising in Connection with the Contract Offer

5.3.1 Advertising, Pre-contractual Information and Offer

False or misleading advertising also has an undeniable relationship to the subject of pre-contractual information when this is defective,[10] since it can also influence someone who trusts its content to enter into a contract for the advertised product. If advertising informs, it does so basically to promote the product, highlighting its features over the other products of the same nature that competitors offer on the market. The duty to inform the other party of the contract guarantees objectively ("truthful and sufficient information") in that the party knows the essential characteristics of the goods or services at the time of concluding the contract.[11] If the advertising is misleading by omission, because it does not announce the normal characteristics of products or services, these expected features could be demanded.

In this case, faulty pre-contractual information in contravention of duties incumbent on the professional will determine the application of its consequence under the law (e.g. art. 69 CESL and art. II.-9:102 DCFR): that is, the integration of the correct information with the contract so that the party may require the performance or characteristics of the product on which the professional should have informed correctly. Advertising also has an "informational" value.[12] This approach is evident in the new contract law texts, both in the PECL-DCFR system and the CESL.

When the essential elements of a future contract appear in the advertisement or public statement, there is a genuine offer; so its simple acceptance will give birth to the contract. In most jurisdictions a public statement made by a professional, that contains enough features to bind it, is considered a contractual offer. Italian law[13] clearly reflects this perspective, while in other systems it is reached by way of interpretation (e.g. German law), or the integration of the contract (e.g. Spanish law).[14] This view is prevalent in the new European contract law.[15]

This duty is especially relevant when the agent is a professional and makes a statement to the other party, or publicly, regarding the product characteristics before the conclusion of the contract. This statement must be integrated into the content of the contract, unless there are objective reasons to exclude it.

---

10 The reference to misleading information is clearly derived from art. 7 EC Directive 2005/29 on Unfair Commercial (Cravetto and Pasa 2011, p. 765).

11 See art. II.-3:101 DCFR.

12 Morales Moreno (1988, p. 668).

13 Article 1336(1) of *Codice Civile* (*offerta al pubblico*).

14 § 157 BGB (*ergänzende Vertragsauslegung, Treu und Glaube*); art. 61 Spanish Consumer Act (*integración de la oferta, promoción y publicidad en el contrato*) and art. 1258 Código Civil (*buena fe*).

15 See Von Bar and Clive (full ed., 2009), II.-4:201 DCFR, Vol. I, Note III, p. 295.

5.3.2 PECL-DCFR System

5.3.2.1 Framework of the General Regulation of Contract

The regulation of this issue is structured in the DCFR in this way: (a) general rule of integration of advertising for all business contracts (II.-9: 102(2)), (b) exceptions (II.-9: 102(2)(a) and (b)), (c) rule of liability for ancillary or dependent agents (II.-9: 102(3)), (d) extended liability rule in consumer contracts (II.-9: 102(4)), (e) right of indemnity against the advertiser in cases covered by paragraph (4)(II.-9: 102(5)), (f) mandatory rule for consumer contracts (II.-9:102(6)).

(a) General rule of Integration and (b) Exceptions Article II.-9:102 DCFR,[16] relating to "certain pre-contractual statements regarded as contract terms", establishes in paragraph (2):

> If one of the parties to a contract is a business and before the contract is concluded makes a statement, either to the other party or publicly, about the specific characteristics of what is to be supplied by that business under the contract, the statement is regarded as a term of the contract unless:
> (a) the other party was aware when the contract was concluded, or could reasonably be expected to have been so aware, that the statement was incorrect or could not otherwise be relied on as such a term; or
> (b) the other party's decision to conclude the contract was not influenced by the statement.

In this article a "special rule for professional suppliers" is established relating only to statements made to the other party or made *publicly* (e.g. in advertisements or in the course of marketing) by a professional supplier about specific characteristics of what is to be supplied under the contract. Under this rule any statements by a supplier becomes part of the contract unless one of the exceptions applies. The Comments on DCFR explain this as follows: The first exception applies if the other party was aware when the contract was concluded, or could reasonably be expected to have been so aware (e.g. public correction of a misleading advertising statement before the contract was concluded). The second exception applies if the other party's decision to conclude the contract was not influenced by the statement. The Comments clarify that this is essential in order to introduce a causal connection between the statement and the decision to conclude the contract.[17] It is submitted that this exception will not have any real application in the future. It requires very difficult proof as to the psychological status of the contracting party. At most, it may lead to a judgment about whether advertising or a declaration has not been enough to sway an average contracting person. However, this is not what is required in the article, at least on its wording.

(c) Rule of Responsibility for Ancillary or Dependent Agents Article II.-9:102 DCFR, in paragraph (3),[18] establishes a sort of liability rule for other third parties:

---

[16] Derivation from art.6:101(2) PECL.

[17] Von Bar and Clive (2009), Art. II.-9:102 DCFR, Vol. I Comment B, pp. 583–584.

[18] Derivation from art.6:101(3) PECL.

For the purpose of paragraph (2), a statement made by a person engaged in advertising or marketing on behalf of the business is treated as being made by the business.

This rule is no more than a specific precision of the general rule on the liability of the professional for the actions of its ancillary or dependent agents. This article seems to refer to cases where the professional has contracted out to a third party the embodiment of the advertising or marketing of his product or service. It can also be applied when advertising activity or marketing comes from an internal agent (a manager or other authorised agents), because the foundation of the rule is that the advertising is done "on behalf of the business".

(d) Extended Liability Rule in Consumer Contracts In B2C contracts an "extended liability" is established in paragraph (4);[19] this applies only to contracts between professional suppliers and consumers and extends the liability to public statements made by other relevant people such as the producer or any person in the business chain between the producer and the consumer. This paragraph provides:

Where the other party is a consumer then, for the purposes of paragraph (2), a public statement made by or on behalf of a producer or other person in earlier links of the business chain between the producer and the consumer is treated as being made by the business unless the business, at the time of conclusion of the contract, did not know and could not reasonably be expected to have known of it.

As the Comments to DCFR identify, this article is similar to that underlying art. 2(2) of the Consumer Sales Directive 99/44.[20] Nevertheless, it should not be forgotten that the scope is wider in the DCFR, extending not just to consumer purchases, but also to any consumer contracts.

This rule does not apply if, at the time of the conclusion of the contract, the professional supplier did not know and could not reasonably be expected to have known of the statement. This last requirement significantly reduces the number of cases in which the exception applies. The professional is not liable for third party advertising that is very disconnected from his activity, but in most cases it will be very difficult to prove that he could not reasonably be expected to know of the advertising statement.

(e) Right of Indemnity Paragraph (5) confers on the professional, who must respond to the consumer in accordance with the conditions mentioned above, a right to be compensated by the person who made the advertising statement, namely:

In the circumstances covered by paragraph (4) a business which at the time of conclusion of the contract did not know and could not reasonably be expected to have known that the statement was incorrect has a right to be indemnified by the person making the statement for any liability incurred as a result of that paragraph.

The application of this right of indemnity requires that the professional incurs liability for an incorrect statement made by the advertiser. It does not deal with a mismatch between the final contract and the contents of the statement. In this case

[19] From art. 6:101(3) PECL.

[20] Von Bar and Clive (full ed., 2009), Art. II.-9:102 DCFR, Vol. I, Comment D, p. 584.

there would be direct responsibility for the professional, generally resulting from the integration rule of para. (2).

This rule does not have an equivalent in the PECL; but it is similar, as Comment E recalls, to the underlying policy to Section 4 of the Consumer Sales Directive, which provides for an action when the final seller is liable to the consumer for a lack of conformity resulting from an act or omission by the producer or the previous intermediaries in the contracting chain.

(f) Mandatory Rule for Consumer Contracts Paragraph (6) provides as follows:

> In relations between a business and a consumer the parties may not, to the detriment of the consumer, exclude the application of this Article or derogate from or vary its effects.

The effect of this article cannot be displaced by a clause inserted into the contract concluded with a consumer. However, it can be displaced by a merger clause in B2B contracts stating that the terms of the contract are to be found exclusively in the contract document itself.[21]

5.3.2.2 Framework of the Particular Regulation of Sales

Under the rules governing the contract of sale, the integration rule of advertising can be found twice. On the one hand, in art. IV.A.-2: 303 DCFR (statements by third persons)[22] lays down that the statements concerning the features of the product made "by a person in earlier links of the business chain, the producer or producer's representative by virtue of II.-9:102" form part of the sales contract. This article contains a reference to art. II.-9:102 because it obviously establishes the same rule. It refers only to the statements made by others, but not to those made by the seller himself. However, in this latter case the result should be the same. On the other hand, in the definition of a consumer goods guarantee in art. IV.A.-6: 101 DCFR, in para. (2)(b), it is provided that "the goods will meet the specifications set out in the guarantee document or in associated advertising". The connection between this rule to the above mentioned, supposes, therefore, the integration of the guarantee within the advertising content. The possible discrepancies between the guarantee document and the associated advertising should be resolved through the interpretation that is the most favourable to the consumer in the given circumstances.[23]

---

[21] See Von Bar and Clive (full ed., 2009), Art. II.-9:102 DCFR, Comment E, Vol. I, p. 585.

[22] Derivation from art. 2:203 PEL S (Sales). The mentioned article applies in place of art. 6:101(3) PECL as it is more detailed. Cf. Hondius et al. (2008), *PEL S*, Comments A and D, p. 205. The same result should be appreciated in relation to the DCFR.

[23] See Von Bar and Clive (full ed., 2009), IV.A.-6:101 DCFR, Vol. III, Comment F, p. 1393.

5.3.3 Proposal for a Regulation on a Common European Sales Law (CESL)

5.3.3.1 Article 69 CESL: Which Public Statements Made by a Trader Should be Implied in the Terms of the Contract?

The regulation of this matter in the CESL is very similar to that of the DCFR, though obviously limited to sales contracts. Article 69 CESL deals with the question of what are the necessary requirements of the professional supplier's pre-contractual statements, or those of a third party, concerning the characteristics of the product under the contract that are to be incorporated into the content of it. The relevance of advertising, which was already covered in art. 2(2) of the Consumer Sales Directive, underlies this article.[24]

The legal formulation has a very similar structure to that seen earlier in the study of this matter in the DCFR: (a) general rule of integration of advertising for all business contracts (para. (1)), (b) exceptions (para. (1)), (c) rule of liability for statements from ancillary or dependent agents (para. (2)), (d) extended liability rule in consumer contracts (paragraph (3)), (e) mandatory rule for consumer contracts (para. (4)).

(a) General Rule of Integration and (b) Exceptions Paragraph (1) establishes:

> Where the trader makes a statement before the contract is concluded, either to the other party or publicly, about the characteristics of what is to be supplied by that trader under the contract, the statement is incorporated as a term of the contract unless:
> (a) the other party was aware, or could be expected to have been aware when the contract was concluded that the statement was incorrect or could not otherwise be relied on as such a term; or
> (b) the other party's decision to conclude the contract could not have been influenced by the statement.[25]

Here, there is no substantial difference with the regulation of art. II.-9: 102(2) DCFR, except with respect to its scope. Article II.-9: 102(2) DCFR provides a framework for general application to all parties to the contract, while art. 69 CESL

[24] Lorenz (2012, p. 728); Kieninger (2013, p. 338).

[25] The European Parliament's Amendments to the Proposal, 26 February 2014 [P7_TA-PROV(2014)0159], submit the following wording in the Amendment No. 140:

"1. Where the trader, **or a person engaged in advertising or marketing for the trader**, makes a statement before the contract is concluded, either to the other party or publicly, about the characteristics of what is to be supplied by that trader under the contract, the statement is incorporated as a term of the contract **unless the trader shows that**:

(a) the other party was aware, or could be expected to have been aware when the contract was concluded, that the statement was incorrect or could not otherwise be relied on as such a term;

(aa) the statement had been corrected by the time of conclusion of the contract; or

(b) the other party's decision to conclude the contract could not have been influenced by the statement".

is limited to the seller.[26] The general rule applies to both B2B and B2C contracts. Obviously, it corresponds to art. 2:203(2) PEL-Sales.

This article also applies to a contract concluded with another party where there exists a public statement (advertisement offer) or statement addressed to the other party (individual offer) prior to the conclusion of the contract; and it also requires that this statement is misleading, that the content of this statement refers to the characteristics of the product to be delivered, and that neither of the two exceptions mentioned is present. According to the Sales Directive and the national laws, the European Parliament's Amendment No. 140 proposes the inclusion of another exception: the correction of the statement by the time of conclusion of the contract[27]. With regard to the applicability of the exceptions, as compared to art. II.-9:102(2) DCFR, the burden of proof is reversed in the CESL: the statement is always binding unless the other party knew, or must have known, that the statement was wrong or unreliable, or the statement could not possibly have causally influenced the other party's decision to enter into the contract.[28] The European Parliament's Amendments introduce a new clearer wording about the burden of proof by expressing that the trader must show the existence of any contemplated exception[29]. All these Amendments seem to be necessary and match the existing European law.

(c) Rule of Liability for Ancillary and Dependent Agents Article 69(2) CESL provides a rule of attribution of responsibility for statements from ancillary or dependent agents:

> For the purposes of paragraph 1, a statement made by a person engaged in advertising or marketing for the trader is regarded as being made by the trader.

Here again a particular realisation is to be found of the general rule of assigning liability to the professional for the actions of its subsidiary or dependent. With the aim of improving the legal construction, the European Parliament's Amendment propose the suppression of this article, since its content should be included in paragraph 1.[30] This rule is applied only in consumer contracts.[31] In addition, this article can also be applied when the advertising or marketing come from the settler's internal sphere of operation; the essential question being that the advertising was made on behalf of the seller ("person engaged in advertising or marketing for the trader").

(d) Extended Liability Rule in Consumer Contracts In art. 69(3) CESL a rule of extension of liability to certain persons in consumer contracts is established, and this rule clearly comes from art. 2(2)(d) of the Consumer Sales Directive 99/44. Paragraph (3) provides:

---

[26] Kieninger (2013, pp. 339, 341).

[27] See above, note 24.

[28] Kieninger (2013, p. 340).

[29] See above, note 24.

[30] Amendment No. 141. For the wording see above, note 24.

[31] See a plea for the extension of this rule to B2B relationships in Lando (2011, p. 725), who considers that such an extension "would have a very sobering effect upon business".

> Where the other party is a consumer then, for the purposes of paragraph 1, a public statement made by or on behalf of a producer or other person in earlier links of the chain of transactions leading to the contract is regarded as being made by the trader unless the trader, at the time of conclusion of the contract, did not know and could not be expected to have known of it.

As with the equivalent rule in the DCFR, this rule does not apply if, at the time of conclusion of the contract, the trader did not know and could not reasonably be expected to have known of the statement. The European Parliament's Amendment intends to achieve the clarity of this paragraph by including an explicit reference to the burden of proof that the trader is expected to carry.[32] The situation is the same as discussed for the DCFR: the last requirement mentioned in this rule significantly reduces the number of cases in which the exemption is applied, because in most of them it will be extremely difficult to prove that the trader could reasonably be expected to know of the advertising statement.

(e) Mandatory Rule for Consumer Contracts The paragraph concludes with a mandatory rule for consumer contracts, namely:

> In relations between a trader and a consumer the parties may not, to the detriment of the consumer, exclude the application of this Article or derogate from or vary its effects.

This regulation does not exclude a merger clause in B2B contracts that states that all the terms are included in the document of the contract.

5.3.3.2 Article 100(f) CESL: Pre-contractual Statements (Qualities and Performance Capabilities) as Criteria for Conformity

Article 100 CESL indicates a number of different criteria that the goods and digital content must fulfil in order to comply with the contract (*criteria for conformity*).[33] In its letter (f) this regulation provides that "goods or digital content must possess the qualities and performance capabilities indicated in any pre-contractual statement which forms part of the contract terms by virtue of Article 69". Zoll considers, with good reason, that this Article is superfluous, because the qualities and capabilities of the goods promised in the pre-contractual statements by the seller or by a person engaged in advertising or marketing for the trader according to art. 69 become a part of the contract and are covered by art. 99(1).[34]

---

[32] European Parliament's Amendment, No. 142: "3. Where the other party is a consumer then, for the purposes of paragraph 1, a public statement made by or on behalf of a producer or other person in earlier links of the chain of transactions leading to the contract is regarded as being made by the trader unless the trader ***shows that***, at the time of conclusion of the contract, ***the trader*** did not know and could not be expected to have known of it".

[33] Zoll (2013, p. 471 et seq.); Eidenmüller et al.(2012, p. 280).

[34] Zoll (2013, p. 476).

5.3.3.3 Criticism

Article 69 CESL omits a general rule that is normally applicable to all pre-contractual statements made by either party (its rule only applies to sellers); while this omission is not found in its precursors such as the PECL and DCFR.[35] There is a glaring lack of an indemnity rule that allows the professional, who had to answer to the consumer for an incorrect or misleading advertisement by the producer or other person in the earlier chain of transactions, to proceed against the advertiser by demanding compensation for the damage. This should be taken into account in order to improve the final version of a future European regulation. It is also noteworthy that the CESL does not introduce any consideration of the inclusion of information on product features into the contract. This information should be part of the contract without being subject to the limits contained in art. 69 CESL. In this sense the criticism expressed by the Statement of the European Law Institute (ELI) on the Proposal for a Regulation on a CESL can be supported: "It is necessary to state that the information provided under Chap. 2 forms part of the contract terms and is not only implied by virtue of Article 69(ELI Art. 67) under the restrictive conditions mentioned therein. This is particular true of information concerning the characteristics of what is to be supplied".[36]

5.4 Overview in Certain National Laws

5.4.1 General Profiles

In most European jurisdictions there are legal provisions or court decisions that establish the rule of the binding nature of advertising and its subsequent incorporation into the contract. The regulations vary according to the extent of the rule; some jurisdictions apply it in all contracts, others only in consumer contracts. However, in English law this rule is not generally known. There are then, *grosso modo*, two opposing models, the English common law in which an integration rule is not expressed, and the civil law where particular manifestations of the principle of good faith generate different rules of advertising integration into the contract.

In this context, the treatment dispensed to '*offers to the public*' cannot be taken as a starting point. As outlined below, the offers to the public are considered in both English and German law generally as invitations to treat. However, English law does not formulate a rule of integration of advertising, while German law does so when its interpretation according to good faith (§ 157 BGB) is applicable. By contrast, in the PECL, the proposals containing prices, made by professional suppliers in public advertisements, catalogues, or displays of goods, are presumed to be offers

[35] See Kieninger (2013, pp. 342–343).

[36] ELI (2012, p. 212).

to sell at that price until the stock is exhausted.[37] Also the PECL, as seen above, includes a rule on the integration of public statements.[38] This same approach was also adopted by the DCFR, which is aimed to prevent businesses from misleading customers that goods or services are available at prices at which the businesses have no intention of supplying them.[39] Moreover, as we have seen above, there are two rules on the integration of advertising into the contract provided in the DCFR.[40] The CESL, however, returns to the traditional approach by establishing that a proposal made to the public is not an offer, unless the circumstances indicate otherwise.[41] However, at the same time, the CESL provides a rule, as seen above, on the integration of advertising statements into the contract.[42,43]

In respect of the conformity of the goods, the legal framework is similar in all European laws. Consumer Sales Directive (art. 2(2) and (4)) has provoked the introduction of special rules about the integration of advertising statements into the contract. This provision was new to many member states. The provision establishes, in substance, that any public statements on the specific characteristics of the goods made about them by the seller, the producer or his representative are relevant for the purpose of assessing the conformity to contract. Additionally, the liability of the seller for statements from third persons was not generally accepted in all European laws in the past. Currently, in this specific legal framework, the transposition of the Consumer Sales Directive has provoked the introduction of this special rule into all systems[44]. The transposition details and the problems deriving from it will not be assessed in this paper. We will focus on the assessment of the rule of integration of advertising from the point of view of comparative law, both in the general contract

[37] Art. 2:201(3) PECL.

[38] Art. 6:101 PECL.

[39] Art. II.-4:201(3) DCR. See Von Bar and Clive (2009), Vol. I, Comment D to this Article.

[40] Art. II.-9:102(2) and IV.A.- 2:303.

[41] Art. 31(3) CESL. For a criticism see Terryn (2012, pp. 187–188).

[42] Art. 69 CESL.

[43] For further details see the following notes. Up to 2008, see Twigg-Flesner (2007), "Comparative Analysis—H. Consumer Sales Directive (99/44)", pp. 671–672; and Hondius et al. (2008), *PEL S*, Notes, p. 207.

[44] See art. 1469ter *Belgium* CC (introduced by Act No. 38 of 01.09.2004); § 2161(1) new *Czech Republic* CC (Act No. 89/2012) (old art. 616(2)); art. 76(1) *Denmark* Sales Act (Act No. 237/28.3.2003); art. 14(2D)-(2F) *England and Scotland* Sale of Goods Act 1979 (amended by Statute No. 3045, The Sale and Supply of Goods to Consumers Regulations 2002); § 217(2)(No. 6) *Estonia* Law of Obligations Act (26.09.2001); Chap. 5-Sect. 13 *Finland* Consumer Protection Act (introduced by Act No. 1258/2001); art. L.211-5 and 6 *France* Consumer Code (inserted by Order No. 136/2005); § 434(1)(no. 3) *Germany* CC (amended by Act 26.11.2001; sec. 277(1)(b) and (2) *Hungary* CC; art. 129(2)(c) and (4) *Italy* Consumer Code; art. 7:18(1) *Netherlands* CC; § 17(3) *Norway* Consumer Sales Act; art. 4(4) and 5 *Poland* Consumer Sales Act (Act 27.7.2002); art. 37(3); *Slovenian* Consumer Protection Act (Act 13.03.1998, last amendment by Act No. 126/2007); art. 61 *Spanish* Consumer Protection Act (last amendment by Act 3/2014); § 19(2) *Sweden* Consumer Sales Act (Act No. 932/1990, last amendment 486/2008).

law and in the sales law. Only a few of the states contemplate general provisions which not restrict this liability exclusively to consumer sales[45].

5.4.2 English Law

English law approaches this issue from the perspective of contract formation by assessing whether advertising or a statement of fact is intended to be an offer or not. Generally speaking the answer is negative. Advertisements in newspapers or periodicals stating that the advertiser has goods for sale are not offers; neither are catalogues or price lists, etc.[46] This type of statements are merely *invitations to treat* since they do often lead to further bargaining, and since the advertiser may legitimately wish, before becoming bound, to assure himself that the other party is able to perform his part of any contract which may result.[47] Beatson explains this by saying that one reason given for this conclusion is that, otherwise, the advertiser would be obliged to sell to every person who accepted such an 'offer', even where supplies had run out.[48]

However, on the basis of the principle of the "objective test", the answer depends in each particular case on whether a reasonable person would infer, according to the terms of the advertising, that, on acceptance, it is intended that contract exists without the need to comply with any other condition.[49] This was so held in the case of *Carlill v. Carbolic Smoke Ball Co.*[50] in which advertising was sufficiently expressive and without reservations, as to it being an expression of an offer to contract.

From this perspective, in most cases advertising will not overstep the threshold of *representations* unless it reveals a genuine intention to contract that could be held to be an offer. This concept is defined in English law as follows: "a statement, o assertion, made by one party to the other, before or at the time of the contract, of some matter or circumstance relating to it. Though it is sometimes contained in the written instrument, it is not an integral part of the contract; and consequently the contract is not broken though the representation proves to be untrue".[51] Where an advertising statement is held to be an invitation to treat, it does not form part of the express terms of the contract.[52] Moreover, the issue of misinformation of the char-

---

[45] See § 92(2) *Austrian* CC; Chap. IV-Sect. 18 *Finland* Sales Act; § 434(1) *German* CC; § 18(2) *Norway* Consumer Sales Act and § 18(2) *Sweden* Consumer Sales Act.

[46] *Partridge v. Crittenden* [1968] 1 W. L. R. 1204; *Grainger & Son v. Gough* [1896] A. C. 325. See also *Harvey v. Facey* [1893] A. C. 552 (a statement of fact to supply information cannot be treated as an offer).

[47] Treitel (10th ed. 1999, p. 13).

[48] Beatson (27th ed. 1998, p. 33).

[49] Beale (4th ed. 2003, p. 122).

[50] [1893] 1 QB 256, CA.

[51] Williams J. in *Behn v. Burness* [1863] 3 B. & S. 751, at p. 753; *ad rem*, Beatson (27th ed. 1998, p. 126).

[52] But a statement by a party who is relatively expert is likely to be treated as a term of contract (Von Bar and Clive 2009, Vol. I., II.-9:102, Note II-11, p. 587).

acteristics or qualities of the normal object of the contract is fixed in the traditional category of *implied terms*.[53]

However, the integration rule of advertising is recognised in consumer sales, where new sections 14(2D)-(2F) of *England and Scotland* Sale of Goods Act 1979, amended by Statute No. 3045 to implement Directive 99/44[54], have to similar effect.[55] These provisions were transposed by making public statements a "relevant circumstance" for considering whether goods meet the statutory standard of "satisfactory quality".[56] Therefore, goods should be of "satisfactory quality" and this also means that they should comprise the content of any public statement made in advertising. The requirement of "satisfactory quality" is an implied term in English law and is in many respects, as very prominent authors express, the most important part of the law of sale of goods.[57] For the purpose of the integration rule any public statements on the specific characteristics of the goods made about them by the seller, the producer or his representative, particularly in advertising or on labelling, should be considered.[58] The "statutory standard" is the assessment by a "reasonable person", and the "relevant circumstances", as mentioned in subsection (2A), any description of the goods, the price (if relevant) and all the other relevant circumstances. Exceptions are provided in subsection (2E). Substantially, these are the same as in European Sales Directive. Formally, the words introduce certain improvements. According to them, a public statement is not a relevant circumstance if the seller shows that: (a) at the time the contract was made, he was not, and could not reasonably have been, aware of the statement, (b) before the contract was made, the statement had been withdrawn in public or, to the extent that it contained anything which was incorrect or misleading, it had been corrected in public, or (c) the decision to buy the goods could not have been influenced by the statement.

The control of misleading advertising is carried out through the administrative authority by administrative injunction. Thus, the Control of Misleading Advertisements Regulations 1988, implementing EC Directive 84/450 on Misleading Advertising, establishes a novel procedure for English law under which complaints about misleading business advertising should be made to a public official, the Director General of Fair Trading.[59]

---

[53] With regard to sale of goods, we must consider the implied terms regulated in Sections 12 and 13 of the Sale Goods Act 1979, Section 14(2) of the Sale and Supply of Goods Act 1994 and Sections 8–11 of the Supply of Goods (Implied Terms) Act 1973; for further references see Beatson (27th ed. 1998, pp. 150 et seq).

[54] The Sale and Supply of Goods to Consumers Regulations 2002.

[55] See Von Bar and Clive (2009), Vol. I., II.-9:102, Note II-11, p. 587.

[56] Twigg-Flesner (2007, p. 671).

[57] Atiyah et al. (2005, p. 164): "the implied term requiring goods to be of satisfactory quality is substituted for the former condition requiring goods to be of merchantable quality by the Sale and Supply of Goods Act 1994, and is in many respects the most important part of the law of sale of goods".

[58] In Scotland, as provided in subsection (2D), the integration rule is applied not only to sales but also to any consumer contract.

[59] See Beale (4th ed. 2003, p. 197).

5.4.3 German Law

German and English law coincide in the treatment accorded to offers to the public by contemplating them as an invitation to treat.[60] However, as regards the content of the contract, German law provides for the integration of advertising statements or public proposals into the terms of the contract. According to § 133 BGB (*Auslegung einer Willenserklärung*), in which the general rule on the interpretation of statements is provided, and § 157 BGB (*Auslegung von vertragen*) where the general rule of interpretation of contracts is supplied, as well as the § 434(1)(S. 2) BGB (*Sachmangel*) in which the lack of conformity in the purchase agreement is dealt with, the criterion established is that the public statement made by the professional forms part of the contract. The German regulation matches art. 69 CESL.[61]

Under German law the use of the criterion of good faith (*Treu und Glaube*) of § 157 is common in the interpretation of all kinds of statements. This section applies in conjunction with § 133, since it is considered that the two provisions should be applied for the purposes of interpretation.[62] From this section comes a genuine instrument of contract interpretation of German law, dating back to the nineteenth century and called *ergänzende Vertragsauslegung*. This concept aims to fill the gaps in the legal business (*Rechtsgeschäft*) by virtue of good faith and commercial usage, and expands its scope to all legal transactions of any class.[63] Under *ergänzende Vertragsaulegung*, and if good faith or traffic usage so require, the professional's public statements meant to catch the attention of the customer about the product or service can be integrated into the contract.

"An explicit expression of the integration rule is found in § 434(1) BGB, sentence 3.[64] Until the 2001 reform of the BGB (*Schuldrechtsmodernisierungsgesetz*), advertising was not considered in the BGB.[65] Following the mandate of European Sales Directive, Germany has transposed this provision as required, but it should be noted, as an exhaustive study states, that in German law "public statements" are ranking lower in priority than other factors in establishing conformity with the contract".[66] In § 434 the question of product defects (*Sachmängel*) is dealt with. Paragraph (1), sentence 3, states that the properties expressed by the seller in public statements, or by the producer or by its dependent, especially in advertising, or also when it comes to descriptions of certain product features that can be expected, form part of the contract. At the same time, some exceptions to the application of this rule are laid down. Statements are not part of the contract when the seller did not know and could not be expected to have known, or if they were rectified at the time of the

---

[60] Harvey and Schillig (2013, p. 269).

[61] Looschelders (2012, p. 649;) see also Eidenmüller et al. (2012, p. 280).

[62] Heinrichs and Palandt (66. Aufl. 2007), § 157, Rdn. 1; Busche (2006), § 133, Rdn. 17–18.

[63] See Heinrichs and Palandt (66. Aufl. 2007), § 157, Rdn. 2–3; Busche (5. Aufl. 2006), § 157, Rdn. 26–28; Vogenauer and Scmoeckel (2003), Bd. I, §§ 133, 157, Rdn. 89.

[64] For an overview of the new rules, Westermann (5. Aufl. 2008), § 434, Rdn. 1.

[65] Böttcher and Hucke (2003, p. 158).

[66] Twigg-Flesner (2007, p. 671).

contract conclusion in the same way as they were made, or in cases where they did not influence the decision to buy.

> Section 434 German Civil Code. Material defects: (1) The thing is free from material defects if, upon the passing of the risk, the thing has the agreed quality. To the extent that the quality has not been agreed, the thing is free of material defects:
> 1. if it is suitable for the use intended under the contract,
> 2. if it is suitable for the customary use and its quality is usual in things of the same kind and the buyer may expect this quality in view of the type of the thing.
> Quality under sentence 2 no. 2 above includes characteristics which the buyer can expect from the public statements on specific characteristics of the thing that are made by the seller, the producer (section 4(1) and (2) of the Product Liability Act [*Produkthaftungsgesetz*]) or his assistant, including without limitation in advertising or in identification, unless the seller was not aware of the statement and also had no duty to be aware of it, or at the time when the contract was entered into it had been corrected in a manner of equal value, or it did not influence the decision to purchase the thing.

The requirements for the application of this article are[67]: (1) Statements expressed in any form, oral, written, printed or electronically. The statements must be public. Publicity means any manifestation announcing to the customer that he may purchase the product. This can be any form of advertising: newspaper advertisements, commercials spots, flyers, etc. They must characterise the goods according to their status. (2) Influence on the buyer. The statement must have as a result that the buyer can expect certain qualities. This requirement is interpreted by the courts and the doctrine in the sense that expectations are not individual but that an average recipient could understand the statement as expressing the qualities of the product. (3) The statements must come from the seller, his dependent or the producer (according to the concept of product liability law), regardless of whether the sale is made directly or through other subjects. (4) Exceptions: (a) Ignorance by the seller of the existence of a public statement, which is possible in those cases where the origin of the statement is from an auxiliary or a producer. (b) That he does not have a duty to know, i.e., that the ignorance was not due to a fault of the seller. (c) Correction of the content of the false statement, which should be done in the same way in which the statement was made. (d) Lack of influence of the public statement on the decision to buy. Unlike art. 69(3) CESL, § 434(1)(3) BGB also excludes the liability of the seller if the statement was corrected at the time of entering the contract or it did not influence the buyer's decision to purchase the product.[68]

5.4.4 *Spanish Law*

Unlike English and German law, in Spanish law the public statements by the professional suppliers are considered to be a contractual offer and, therefore, have a binding character. Public statements produce contractual engagement provided they include specific content, capable enough of arousing specific expectations in the

[67] For further details see Westermann (5. Aufl. 2008), § 434, Rdn. 22–29.

[68] Schuller and Zenefels (2013, p. 601).

consumer.[69] Under Spanish law, the rule of advertising integration into the contract possesses a very rich legislative[70] and jurisprudential[71] history. The current provisions of reference are mainly art. 1258 of the Civil Code (general rules of integration of contract)[72] and art. 61 Spanish Consumer Act[73] (rule of integration of advertising into consumer contracts). To these provisions, the specific provisions for consumer sales contained in art. 116(1)(d)(part 1) and (part 2) of Consumer Act must be added.

The structure of the Spanish regulation can be explained through consideration of the following points: (a) general rules of integration for any contracts (art. 1258 CC), (b) integration rule of advertising for any consumer contracts (art. 61 Consumer Act), (c) special rule of conformity with public statements in consumer sales (art. 116(1)(d)(part 1) Consumer Act) and (d) exceptions in consumer sales (art. 116(1)(d)(part 2) Consumer Act).

(a) General Rules of Integration for any Contracts Article 1258 CC establishes:

> Contracts are perfected by mere consent, and since then bind the parties, not just to the performance of matters expressly agreed therein, but also to all consequences which, according to their nature, are in accordance with good faith, custom and the law.

This article sets out the general rules of contract.[74] It is applied to address any gaps in the contract. Although it does not refer to the treatment to be given to public statements of professionals and advertising, case law has long appealed to the criterion of good faith contained in this article as an instrument of integration of advertising into the terms of the contract.[75] The use of this article has been raised in all cases, decided by the Spanish courts, of contracts between businesses and consumers. Most cases have been real estate sales in which buyers were disappointed in their expectations because, in the contract documents, the qualities or features offered in the advertising were not included. For this reason, although the art. 1258

[69] Morales Moreno (1999, p. 269).

[70] This was first formulated in art. 8 of Consumer Act 1984 (Ley General para la defensa de consumidores y usuarios).

[71] See below, note 74.

[72] Additionally, art. 65 Consumers Act includes, for any consumer contract, a general rule of integration according to good faith which should be considered as an expression of the general rule of good faith contained in *Código Civil*: "Consumer contracts shall be drawn up in favour of the consumers and users, in accordance with the principle of objective good faith, including in circumstances in which the relevant pre-contract information is omitted".

[73] Royal Legislative Decree 1/2007, of 16 November 2007, approving the Revised Text of the General Law For the Protection of Consumers and Users and other supplementary Laws (Spanish Consumer Act).

[74] See recently García Rubio (2010, pp. 1373–1375); López y López (2011, pp. 613–617.

[75] Since the Judgments of Spanish High Court of June 14, 1976 and January 27, 1977, which stated in accordance with the principles of veracity and good faith (*per* art. 1258 CC) that the contract can be integrated with the content of the advertising message in which the consumers had reasonably relied. Many other subsequent judgments recognise the rule of integration of advertising into the contract: June 15, 2000; March 18, 2002; May 23, 2003; September 29, 2004; March 15, 2010; May 30, 2011; July 12, 2011.

CC is a general rule applicable to any type of contract, one (safe) general expansion of the criterion of good faith cannot be made to integrate other contracts. In theory this is possible,[76] but in reality the hypothesis has not been tested yet.

(b) General Rule of Integration of Advertising for any Consumer Contracts The article of reference here is art. 61 of the Spanish Consumer Act[77], which establishes:

> Inclusion of offer, promotion and advertising in the contract.
> 1. The offer, promotion and advertising of goods and services shall be in keeping with the nature, features, use or purpose thereof, and with the legal or financial terms of the contract.
> 2. The content of the offer, promotion or advertising, the features inherent to each of the goods and services, the legal and financial terms and the guarantees offered shall be enforceable by consumers and users, even when not appearing expressly in the signed contract or in the provided document or receipt, and must be taken into account when determining the principle of contractual compliance.
> 3. Notwithstanding the provision of the preceding paragraph, if the signed contract contains more beneficial clauses, these shall prevail over the content of the offer, promotion or advertising.

Article 61 Consumer Act provides, in its first two paragraphs, a rule of general application, applicable to any consumer contract, which substantially means that the advertising assertions integrate the contractual content and bind the entrepreneur or professional. For this to be binding, the requirements under this rule are[78]: (1) The advertisement must have an "informational content", since this is the only type that can create specific expectations in the consumer. (2) It is does not matter whether the advertisement can be considered as an offer of contract or not. (3) The promise usually covers any quality of the provision or of the legal and economic conditions. (4) If the contract contains more favourable terms than those laid down in the advertising, those will prevail as is expressly stated in art. 61(3) Consumer Act. (5) The integration rule is applied only if a contract exists and not if there is a loophole in it.

This article has more coverage than art. 69 CESL, because it applies to all consumer contracts; but less coverage than the article II.-9:102(2) DCFR since it does not apply to B2B contracts.

(c) Special Rule of Conformity with Public Statements in Consumer Sales Additionally, there is a special rule on contract compliance for consumer sales[79], in art. 116(1)(d)(part 1) Consumer Act[80]. This rule establishes, as the criterion for conformity of the contract, the preservation of the quality or characteristics of the product indicated by the seller, the producer or his assistants in their public statements.

---

[76] Especially if it is considered that art. 1258 CC is an "inflationary norm", which is used in a multitude of judicial decisions; see Carrasco Perera (2010, p. 485).

[77] Recently amended by Act No. 3/2014 (Consumer Act Reform 2014). Amendments let articles 61 and 65 unaltered.

[78] See García Vicente (2009, pp. 1487–1491); Pino Abad (2011, pp. 1114–1122).

[79] For further details on the regulation of conformity in Spanish law and compared to European law, see Fenoy Picón (2013, p. 731 *et seq.*

[80] Not amended by the recent Consumer Act Reform 2014.

> Article 116 Consumer Act: Conformity of products with the contract. (1) Save for evidence to the contrary, it shall be understood that products conform to the contract provided that they comply with all the requirements set forth hereafter, unless any of the requirements is not applicable due to the circumstances of the case:
> (d) They display the typical quality and features of a product of this type which consumers and users have good reason to expect, taking into account the nature of the product and, if any, the public statements made by the vendor, producer or representative thereof, regarding specific features of the product, especially in the advertising or labelling.

This rule agrees substantially with art. 100(f) CESL and as well as its preceding provisions in the Sales Directive; and, with regard to its purpose, with art. IV.A.-2:303 DCFR.

(d) Exceptions for Consumer Sales Article 116(1)(d)(part 2) Consumer Act establishes three exceptions to the general rule of enforceability of advertising statements as follows:

> Sellers shall not be bound as a result of public statements if they can prove that they were not aware or could not reasonably be expected to know of the statement in question, that the statement had been corrected by the time the contract was concluded, or that the statement could not have influenced the decision to purchase the product.

This exception relates to the lack of knowledge of the existence of advertising that exactly matches the European instruments already addressed (DCFR and CESL), and finds its origin in the Sales Directive. The same can be said about the exception relating to the lack of capacity of the advertising statement to influence the decision to enter into the contract.

By contrast, the exception providing for the possibility that the professional rectifies the advertising content by the time the contract was concluded, cannot be found here. However, this exception is found in other national laws, such as the German regime (§ 434(1)(3) BGB). The rationale for this exception is that the binding nature of advertising cannot have an absolute character and the professional should be allowed to correct the inaccurate contents or those that are misleading.[81] Most Spanish doctrine interprets this exception with caution and requires limits to its application, but admits that, by virtue of the autonomy of will, advertising can be modified provided that the reasonable consumer expectations are not disappointed.[82] Thus, the subsequent changes to the original advertising message only are possible when the entrepreneur or the professional honour the duty to communicate previously and explicitly to consumers that its contents must be corrected, provided there is a justification.[83]

---

[81] The case law supports this exception, but omits to outline its limits. See Judgments of the Spanish High Court of 15 April 2010 (*Fidel, Caridad and others v. Inmobiliaria del Sur, SA*), commented on by Camacho Pereira (2011), and 17 December 2010 (Buyers v. *Inmobiliria del Sur, SA*), commented on by Mas Badía (2012).

[82] Morales Moreno (1999) p. 275); Pasquau Liaño (1992, p. 27).

[83] Some authors require the additional requirement that a public communication exists to correct advertising (e.g. García Vicente 2009, p. 1490).

This author submits that, as it is not set in law, it is not necessary to add additional requirements; but that two objective limits deriving from the law itself should be appreciated. First, the modification of the advertisement is not possible when it is imposed on the consumer by a general clause that he needs to adhere to, because a clause of this type would be judged unfair (*per* arts. 82 and 85(3) Spanish Consumer Act), since it introduces an imbalance to the rights of consumers by defrauding their legitimate expectations.[84] Secondly, the professional cannot arbitrarily change the advertising, unless a time limit is set. There must be an objective justification; i.e. that the advertising is inaccurate or misleading. This consideration is implicit in the same art. 116(1)(d)(part 2), which allows the "correction" of advertising; and one can only correct what is inaccurate, incomplete or false.

The exceptions of art. 116(1)(d)(part 2) Spanish Consumer Act, unlike the DCFR, do not cover all B2C contracts, but only B2C sales. However, there is no obstacle in Spanish law to prevent its extension to all consumer contracts (by way of systematic interpretation).[85] The rationale for this exception is the same: the linking of advertising cannot be absolute, so the professional can always modify it as long as he respects legitimate consumer expectations. Good faith requires just the same solution.[86]

(e) Issues not Expressly Included in Spanish Legal Instruments In particular, two issues were not included in the Spanish law, namely, the extended liability rule and the right of indemnity.

On the one hand, an explicit formulation of the extended liability rule is missing. This rule is formulated, as already seen, both in the DCFR and CESL in order to make the professional responsible to the consumer for the public statements made by the producer or other professionals involved in the prior transaction chain. In Spanish law, this is not explicitly mentioned, but it is implicit in art. 116(1)(d)(part 2):[87] "Sellers shall be not bound as a result of public statements if they can prove that *they were not aware or could not reasonably be expected to know of the statement in question*". Obviously, the application of this exception makes sense when the seller is not the advertiser, but the producer or other professional in the chain. For a long time, Spanish doctrine has always held that the rule of integration of advertising also protects the consumer in this case, because its foundation is the protection of his trust in the truth of the advertising message, and because this rule is not built on the requirement of fault.[88]

On the other hand, the Spanish legislation does not foresee any right of indemnity as that regulated in art II.-9: 102(5) DCFR. This rule can be reached by way of damages (art. 1902 CC). According to most Spanish doctrine, in the interpretation

---

[84] Gómez Calle 1994, p. 76.

[85] For a similar approach, Font Galán (2010), p. 73.

[86] For further discussion, see Camacho Pereira (2012, pp. 14–16).

[87] In this sense, Note II-11 on art. II.-9:102 DCFR expressed in Von Bar and Clive (2009, Vol. I, p. 587), should be corrected, because it includes Spanish law among the laws without similar provisions.

[88] See, generally, Morales Moreno (1988, p. 687) and et seq.

of art. 61 Consumer Act, the liability for advertising is generally strict, so that the consumer does not have to prove the advertiser's negligence. However, the standard of liability cannot always be the same between professionals in this case, above all because a certain strict liability standard must be expressly established by law. Hence, the professional has to prove the advertiser's negligence for the success of this action. Furthermore, from the point of view of legal policy, it would be wise to include an express rule in Spanish law.

5.5 Consequences of the Inclusion of Advertising Statements in Contract

5.5.1 Remedies

From the point of view of private law, protection against misleading advertising offers several alternatives: the use of the liability *culpa in contrahendo*; the application of the remedy of terminating the contract; or nullity due to error or fraud. The rule of integration of advertising into the contract is the most satisfactory way to achieve this protection, because it provides for the possibility that the contracting party may want the features declared in the promotion and advertising of the products and services, even if they are not expressly mentioned in the signed contract document (art. II.-9: 102(2) DCFR, art. 69(1) CESL, and the equivalent provisions in national laws). This solution avoids the trick often used by professionals of offering features in the advertising that are later not included in the contracts, breaking the expectations raised in the parties. In consumer contracts, it is also possible to incorporate the content of advertising, even though it does not come from the entrepreneur that concludes the contract (art. II.-9:102(4)DCFR, art. 69(3) CESL, and the corresponding in national laws).

This ability to enforce the advertising content implies that its lack of inclusion in the terms of contract, or an amendment not negotiated individually, may constitute a breach of contract. Accordingly, pursuant to the rules of non-compliance,[89] the party may choose, depending on the circumstances, either the right to demand compliance, to terminate the contract, or to seek compensation for damages. In the case of the sale of consumer goods, according to the Sales Directive and the corresponding provisions in national law, the consumer may resort to remedies for lack of conformity as result of misleading advertising. This same idea is repeated in the CESL.

In the overall structure of the provisions governing the responsibility for advertising, the requirement of fault is not foreseen in any of the European provisions (art II.-9: 102(2) DCFR, art. 69(1) CESL) nor in any of the national laws studied. The responsibility is a manifestation of strict liability, justified because advertising creates confidence.

[89] See the chapter on Remedies in this book.

5.5.2 *Liability of the Advertiser to the Consumer: Issues Not Covered*

Those subjects who are passively responsible in this regard include: (a) the entrepreneur who contracts with the consumer and is the author of the advertising, even when the advertising is done by other persons on his behalf, to whom the integration of the contract shall be enforceable together with the content of the advertising, and who, consequently, is liable for the breach of contract in accordance with the general rules; and (b) the entrepreneur who enters into the contract but who is not the advertiser, against whom the contractual liability shall equally be enforceable.

However, neither the DCFR nor the CESL provide a rule establishing the advertiser's liability to the consumer, when the advertiser is not a party to the contract. Only the DCFR anticipates an action of reimbursement against the advertising entrepreneur to compensate the seller who has had to pay for misleading advertising. However, this is a rule of economic rebalancing between entrepreneurs, and outside the scope of this research.

Looking at this situation in a different way, it could be asked whether the consumer could seek redress from the advertiser, not through contractual liability, but for damages for misleading advertising? The answer is affirmative according to some European systems such as the Spanish one. The Spanish doctrine, starting from the fact that the responsibility for advertising is not built into Spanish Law with regard to the requirement of fault, allows the use of an action for damages against the advertiser who is not part of the contract. The wording of art. 8 of the previous Consumer Act 1984 and art. 61 of the current Consumer Act 2007 enable the adoption of this solution; as it is considered that this liability is based on an allocation of risk.[90]

5.6 Conclusions

In the Proposal for a CESL (art. 69) the integration rule of advertising into the content of the contract is only applied to sale contracts; but in some European systems (e.g. § 157 BGB, art. 1258 Spanish CC, and art. 61 Spanish Consumer Act) it can also be found in the framework of the general theory of contract. This situation must be taken into account, especially because in the DCFR the position is the same. In the DCFR, the integration rule of advertising is formulated generally, on the one hand, in the regulation of pre-contractual obligations (art. II.-9: 102) and in particular, on the other hand, by regulating the sales contract (art.IV.A.-2: 303). Compared to the DCFR and the national laws, the future art. 69 CESL suffers from flaws, both technical and substantive, which have been highlighted in this analysis. The main technical lacuna of art. 69 CESL is the lack of a specific provision covering an indemnity rule that allows the entrepreneur, who is liable for the advertising of a

[90] See, for example, Pasquau Liaño (1992, p. 168); Reyes López (1997, p. 75).

producer or of a person earlier in the chain, to obtain compensation for the liability that he had to deal with. It can also be emphasised that some national systems are more protective of consumers, because they limit the application of exemptions by the use of stricter requirements (for example, modification of advertising is submitted, in Spanish law, to conditions that protect consumer expectations). With regard to the substantive defects, two may be highlighted. On the one hand, art. 69 CESL only applies the integration of advertising to one of the parties to the contract: the seller. In the B2B contracts this is a defect. On the other hand, neither the CESL nor the DCFR lay down any rule for the responsibility held by the non-contracting advertiser to the consumer, which by contrast can be found in some other systems (e.g. the Spanish one). In conclusion, it is submitted that it is disappointing to identify that some national laws give greater protection to the consumer in the application of the integration rule of advertising than the Proposal on a future European Sales Law.

References

Atiyah P. S./Adams John N./MacQueen, Hector L. (11th ed. 2005), *Sale of Goods*, Pearson Education, London.

Beale, H. (2003), *Contract Law*, Hart Publishing, Oxford.

Busche (5. Aufl. 2006), in Säcker (ed.), *Münchener Kommentar zum BGB*, Bd. 1–1. Halbband, Beck, Munich, §§ 133, 157.

Beatson, J. (27th ed. 1998), *Anson's Law of Contract*, Oxford University Press, Oxford.

Böttcher, Eberhard/Hucke, Anja (2003), "Das Einstehenmüssen des Verkäufers für Werbeangaben", in Hucke (ed.), *Aktuelle Entwicklungen im Unternehmensrecht*, Gabler Verlag, München, pp. 157–177.

Camacho Pereira, Consuelo (2011), "Delimitación del contenido obligacional del contrato de compraventa de vivienda con consumidores, en caso de discrepancia entre documentación precontractual y contractual", *InDret* 2/2011, pp. 1–13.

Camacho Pereira, Consuelo (2012), "Comparativa de la regulación de la integración de la publicidad en el contrato con consumidores, en el TRLGDCU y en la Propuesta de Reglamento del Parlamento Europeo y del Consejo, relativo a una normativa común de compraventa europea", *InDret* 4/2012, pp. 1–28.

Carrasco Perera, Ángel (2010), *Derecho de contratos*, Thomson-Reuters, Cizur Menor (Navarra).

Clive, Eric (2012), "Recent Legal Developments: A Common European Sales Law. A General Perspective on the European Commission's Proposal for Regulation on a CESL", 19 MJ 1 (2012), pp. 120–131.

Cravetto, Chiara/Pasa, Barbara (2011), "The 'Non-sense' of Pre-contractual Information Duties in Case of Non-concluded Contracts", *ERPL* (No. 6, 2011), pp. 759–785.

Eidenmüller, Horst/Jansen, Nils/Kieninger, Eva-Maria/Wagner, Gerhard/Zimmermann, Reinhard (2012), "Der Vorschlag für eine Verordnung über ein Gemeinsames Europäisches Kaufrecht", *Juristen Zeitung* (No. 67), 269–320.

ELI (European Law Institute) (2012), *Statement of the European Law Institute on the Proposal for a Regulation on a Common European Sales Law*, Vienna.

European Parliament (2014), TEXTS ADOPTED PART III at the sitting of Wednesday 26 February 2014, P7_TA-PROV (2014) 0159 *Common European Sales Law—Amendments*, p. 83 ff.

Fenoy Picón, Nieves (2013), "La compraventa del Texto Refundido de consumidores de 2007 tras la Directiva 2011/83/UE sobre los derechos de los consumidores", *ADC* (Vol. LXVI, No. II), pp. 717–836.

Font Galán, Juan Ignacio (2010), "Publicidad comercial y contrato con consumidores. Conexiones funcionales y normativas: sustantivación obligacional e integración contractual de las ofertas promocionales y publicitarias", *Revista Derecho Patrimonial* (No. 25), pp. 47–79.
García Rubio, Mª Paz (2010), "Art. 1258 CC", in Domínguez Luelmo, A. (ed.), *Comentarios al Código Civil*, Lex Nova, Valladolid, pp. 1373–1375.
García Vicente, José Ramón (2009), "Integración contractual de las declaraciones publicitarias", en Bercovitz Rodríguez-Cano, R. (ed.) *Tratado de contratos*, Vol. 2, Tirant lo Blanch, Valencia, pp. 1484–1493.
Gómez Calle, Esther (1994), *Los deberes precontractuales de información*, La Ley, Madrid.
Harvey, Caroline/Schillig, Michael (2013), "Conclusion of contract", in Gerhard Dannemann and Stefan Vogenauer (eds.), *The Common European Sales Law in Context Interactions with English and German Law*, Oxford University Press, Oxford, pp. 248–293.
Hesselink, Martijn W. (2011), "The Concept of Good Faith", in Arthur S. Hartkamp, Martijn Hesselink et al., *Towards a European Civil Code*, 4th ed., Kluwer International, The Netherlands, pp. 619–649.
Hondius, Ewoud/Heutger, Vola/Jeloscheck, Christoph/Sivesand, Hanna/Wiewiorowska, Aneta (2008), *Principles of European Law—Sales (PEL S)*, Oxford University Press, Oxford.
Kieninger, Eva-Maria (2013), "Art. 69 CESL", in Schulze (ed.), *Common European Sales Law (CESL). Commentary*, C.H. Beck-Hart-Nomos, Baden-Baden, pp. 337–343.
Lando, Ole (2011), "Comments and Questions Relating to the European's Commission's Proposal for a Regulation on a Common European Sales Law", *ERPL* (No. 6, 2011), pp. 717–728.
Lasarte Álvarez, Carlos (1980), "Sobre la integración del contrato: la buena fe en la contratación", *Revista de Derecho Privado* (No. 64, 1), pp. 50–78.
Looschelders, Dirk (2012), "Das allgemeine Vertragsrecht des Common European Sales Law", *AcP* (No. 212), pp. 581–693.
López y López, Ángel M. (2011), "Art. 1258 CC", en, Cañizares, Laso/Orduña, Moreno/Valpuesta, Fernández (eds.), *Código Civil Comentado*, Vol. II, Aranzadi, Madrid, pp. 613–617.
Lorenz, Stephan (2012), "Das Kaufrecht und die damit verbundenen Dienstverträge in *Common European Sales Law*", *AcP* (No. 212), pp. 702–847.
Mas Badía, Mª Dolores (2012), "Sentencia de 17 de diciembre de 2010. Compraventa de vivienda sobre plano", *CCJC* (No. 88), pp. 131–145.
Morales Moreno, Manuel (1988), "Información publicitaria y protección del consumidor (Reflexiones sobre el art. 8º de la LGCU)", in *Homenaje a Juan Berchmans Vallet de Goytisolo*, Vol. VIII, Madrid, pp. 667–693.
Morales Moreno, Manuel (1999), "Declaraciones públicas y vinculación contractual (reflexiones sobre una Propuesta de Directiva)", *ADC* (Vol. LII, No. I), pp. 265–287.
Heirinchs/Palandt (66. Aufl., 2007), *Bürgerliches Gesetzbuch*, C. H. Beck, München, § 434.
Pasquau Liaño, Miguel (1992), "Art. 8.1 LGDCU", in Bercovitz/Salas (eds.), *Comentarios a la Ley General para la defensa de los consumidores y usuarios*, Madrid, pp. 139–175.
Pino Abad, Manuel (2011), "Comentarios a los artículos 61 y 65. La relevancia negocial de la publicidad comercial: integración publicitaria del contrato celebrado con consumidores", in Rebollo Puig/Izquierdo Carrasco (eds.), *La defensa de los consumidores y usuarios: (comentario sistemático del Texto Refundido aprobado por Real Decreto Legislativo 1/2007)*, pp. 1106–1131.
Reyes López, María José (1997), "El carácter vinculante de la oferta y de la publicidad en el art. 8 de la LGDCU", *EC*, 43/1997, pp. 63–81.
Schuller, Christopher/Zenefels, Alexander (2013), "Obligations of Sellers and Buyers", in Gerhard Dannemann and Stefan Vogenauer (eds.), *The Common European Sales Law in Context Interactions with English and German Law*, Oxford University Press, Oxford, pp. 581–611.
Terryn, Evelyne (2012), "Art. 31 CESL", in Schulze (ed.), *Common European Sales Law (CESL). Commentary*, C.H. Beck-Hart-Nomos, Baden-Baden, pp. 184–187.
Treitel, Guenter (1999), *The Law of Contract*, Sweet & Maxwell, London.

Twigg-Flesner, Christian (2007), "Comparative Analysis—H. Consumer Sales Directive (99/44)", in Hans Schulte-Nölke (ed.), *EC Consumer Law Compendium—Comparative Analysis* -, Universität Bielefeld, pp. 646–713.

Vogenauer, Stefan (2003), in *Münchener Kommentar zum BGB*, Bd. I (Redaktion: Mathias Schmoeckel), Mohr Siebeck, München, §§ 133, 157.

Von Bar, Christian/Clive, Eric (eds.) (2009, full ed.), *Principles, Definitions and Model Rules. Draft Common Frame of Reference (DCFR)*, Sellier, Munich, Vol. I.

Von Bar, Christian/Clive, Eric (eds.) (2009, full ed.), *Principles, Definitions and Model Rules. Draft Common Frame of Reference (DCFR)*, Sellier, Munich, Vol. III.

Von Hippel, Eike, *Verbraucherschutz*, 3. Aufl., Tübingen, 1986.

Westermann, H. P. (5. Aufl. 2008), in Wetermann, H. P. (ed.), *Münchener Kommentar zum BGB*, Bd. 3, Beck, Munich, § 434.

Zoll, Fryderik (2013), "Art. 100 CESL", in Schulze (ed.), *Common European Sales Law (CESL). Commentary*, C.H. Beck-Hart-Nomos, Baden-Baden, pp. 471–476.

Chapter 6
Unfair Contract Terms

Hans Fredrik Marthinussen

Abstract Europe has a long standing tradition of law demanding good faith and fair dealing in contractual relationships. Such provisions have in many traditions been subject to harsh interpretation and "stretching" in order to deal with contract terms that are considered unfair. With time, many of these provisions have also been supplied with some form of regulation of standard terms.

In this chapter the Nordic regulations will then be compared with the CESL and the Draft Common Frame of Reference, and, through this comparative analysis, the author also hopes to contribute towards a further understanding of pan-European unfair contract terms regulations. In light of the differences, certain challenges for European businesses selling to Nordic countries under the CESL will be highlighted. Finally, this chapter will conclude with some comments on the possible development of common European legislation on unfair contract terms in the future.

Keywords Unfair contract terms · Good faith and fair dealing · Consumer protection · Directive on unfair terms · No binding effect of the unfair contract term

6.1 Introduction

Europe has a long standing tradition of law demanding good faith and fair dealing in contractual relationships. Such provisions have in many traditions been subject to harsh interpretation and "stretching" in order to deal with contract terms that are considered unfair.[1] With time, many of these provisions have also been supplied with some form of regulation of standard terms.

The Nordic contract acts from the 1910s also contained provisions stating, roughly put, that a contract could not be enforced if it would be against good faith and fair

[1] The most common referred to example might be "treu und glauben" in BGB § 242, famous, together with the introduction to the law of obligations, for filling an entire band of the Staudinger commentary to the BGB.

H. F. Marthinussen (✉)
University of Bergen, Bergen, Norway
e-mail: hans.marthinussen@jur.uib.no

© Springer International Publishing Switzerland 2015

J. Plaza Penadés, L. M. Martínez Velencoso (eds.), *European Perspectives on the Common European Sales Law*, Studies in European Economic Law and Regulation 4,
DOI 10.1007/978-3-319-10497-3_6

dealing (§ 33). The Nordic contract acts were a result of joint Nordic legislative co-operation, and thus of common wording.[2] Although dynamic in character through the use of adaptable terms such as good faith and fair dealing, these provisions were traditionally interpreted not to be applicable on the content of the agreement as such. According to the preparatory works, a distinct interpretation feature of the Nordic legal systems, their scope was limited to the circumstances at the conclusion of the contract. A general rule allowing scrutinising of unfair contract terms did not, therefore, exist.

During the 1970s and early 1980s all the Nordic countries, Denmark (1975), Sweden (1976), Finland (1983), Norway (1983) and Iceland (1986), introduced a general provision dealing with unfair contracts or unfair contract terms.[3] This was a result of a decade of evolving consumer protection legislation first and foremost within the area of sales law. The provisions on unfair contracts were all introduced into the general statute on contracts § 36, and are broadly the same in design. The uniqueness of these legal provisions is the lack of limitations: they simply give the courts discretion to review unfair contract terms in general.[4]

This chapter will begin by presenting the basic features of these particular Nordic provisions, including a brief presentation of important or illustrative Supreme Court rulings. The Nordic regulations will then be compared with the CESL and the Draft Common Frame of Reference (DCFR), and, through this comparative analysis, the author also hopes to contribute towards a further understanding of pan-European unfair contract terms regulations. In light of the differences, certain challenges for European businesses selling to Nordic countries under the CESL will be highlighted. Finally, this chapter will conclude with some comments on the possible development of common European legislation on unfair contract terms in the future.

6.2 The Nordic Contract Acts, § 36

6.2.1 Structure and Wording of the Legislative Text

The Provisions[5] State:

Denmark:

1. A contract may be modified or set aside, in whole or in part, if it would be unfair or in violation of honest dealing to enforce it. The same applies to other legally binding acts.

[2] Up until Sweden and Finland joined the EU in the early 1990s, the Nordic countries, and especially the Scandinavian ones, Sweden, Norway and Denmark, cooperated closely on a large amount of legislation, over an extensive period of time.

[3] The Icelandic provision will not be considered further, since the author's Icelandic is rather limited.

[4] The effect of the passing of the new provision in § 36 on the use of § 33 has been different in each of the Nordic countries. While § 33 is invoked and applied relatively often in Norway, it has, to a large extent, been replaced by § 36 in Sweden and Finland, cf. Sisula-Tulokas (2005, pp. 324–325).

[5] Official translations do not exist; the translations are a combination of unofficial translations from various publications together with the author's own.

2. When making a decision under subsection (1), regard shall be taken to the circumstances existing at the time the contract was concluded, the terms of the contract and subsequent circumstances.

Norway:

A contract may be modified or set aside, in whole or in part, if it is unfair or contrary to good business practice to enforce it. The same applies to unilateral binding acts.

Any decision to this effect should take into account not only the content of the agreement, the relationship between the parties and the circumstances at the conclusion of the contract, but also any subsequent developments and other circumstances.

The rules in the first and second paragraphs apply equally when it would be unfair to enforce commercial practice or other contractual customs.

Sweden:

A contract term may be adjusted or held unenforceable if the term is unfair with respect to the contract's content, circumstances at the formation of the contract, subsequent events or other circumstances. If the condition is of such importance to the contract that it cannot reasonably be demanded that the rest of it should prevail unaltered, the contract may be altered, even in other respects, or be set aside completely.

When taking a decision under the first paragraph, special consideration is to be given to the need for protection of those who by virtue of being a consumer, or in any other way, hold an inferior position in the contract.

The first and second paragraphs apply equally to questions of the terms in other legal acts than contracts.

In questions of adjustment of certain contract terms in consumer relations, § 11 of the statute (1994:1512) about contract terms in consumer relations also apply.

Finland:

If a contract term is unfair, or its application would lead to an unfair result, the term may be adjusted or set aside. In determining what is unfair, regard shall be had to the entire content of the contract, the positions of the parties, the circumstances prevailing at and after the conclusion of the contract, and to other factors.

If a term referred to in paragraph one is such that it would be unfair to enforce the rest of the contract after the adjustment of the term, the rest of the contract may also be adjusted or declared terminated.

A provision relating to the amount of consideration shall also be deemed a contract term.

The provisions of the Consumer Protection Act (38/1978) apply to the adjustment of consumer contracts.

Although all Nordic countries introduced a § 36 provision in their contract acts within a decade, this provision was not a result of joint legislative cooperation. However, it is evident that inspiration was sought from the other Nordic countries when drafting the individual provisions. The most thorough preparatory report, from Sweden[6], clearly shows how Danish and Norwegian law was taken into

[6] SOU 1974:83, pp. 83–84.

consideration; and the other nations' preparatory works are also clear on this point. This is also completely in accordance with Nordic legal culture.

Nevertheless, there are differences in the wording and construction of the different national provisions which are significant. One major difference is that while the Norwegian and Danish § 36 speak of unfair contracts in general, the Swedish and Finnish § 36 are limited to unfair contract *terms*. According to the Swedish and Finnish § 36, unfair contract terms may be set aside or changed; while according to the Norwegian and Danish § 36 unfair *contracts* may be set aside or altered.

Even though the Swedish and Finnish provisions are narrower in scope, covering only unfair contract terms, there is a possibility to set aside or alter the entire contract. Both provisions do state that in cases where the term in question is of such importance that it would be unreasonable to uphold the contract without it; the entire contract may be altered or left ineffective.

It is worth pointing out explicitly that the provisions in the contract acts § 36 do not only provide for setting contracts or contract terms aside if they are found unfair, they also provide their *alteration*.[7] In practice, one must clearly assume that there will be limits as to how far a court will go with regard to rewriting or creating a new contract, but legally this is completely left to the discretion of the courts.

All provisions expressly point to a broad basis for the judgement of unfairness. They all mention the contents of the contract, circumstances at the time the contract was entered into, later developments, and even simply "other relevant circumstances". A contract that would have been considered fair at the time it was entered into may, therefore, *become* unfair with the passing of time and changing circumstances. It is sufficient that the contract is unfair at the time it is scrutinised by the courts.

Another important factor is the relationship between the contracting parties, in particular if there is a mismatch in strength between them. In the Swedish provision it is expressly stated that particular concern is to be paid to the position of a weaker consumer party. In the Norwegian and Finnish texts, there is a reference to the consideration of the relationship in between the parties, which must obviously be interpreted similar to the Swedish text; and even though there is no explicit reference to this in the Danish text itself, it is evident that this factor is an important one also under Danish law.

The scope of § 36 is not limited to contracts between businesses and consumers, in contrast to the Directive on unfair terms in consumer contracts (EC 93/13). It is, however, undoubtedly of vast significance whether there is a contractual relationship where one party can be considered strong, and one weak, for the provision to be applied by the courts. This is expressly pointed out in several of the Nordic statutory texts and, in addition, the preparatory works clearly point to consumer protection and protection of the weaker party as a main purpose of the regulation, while, at the same time, pointing out that the threshold for setting aside or adjusting contracts is generally high. This may quickly lead to the conclusion that it is mainly in strong-weak party relationships that § 36 may be used.

---

[7] Originally this was not the case for the Danish provision. It was brought into line with the other Nordic provisions in 1994.

It may, in addition, be noted that the Norwegian and Danish provisions include an alternative condition for the application of § 36: not only may the contract be set aside or altered if it is found to be unfair, it is also subject to judicial review if it is either found to be contrary to good business conduct (Norway) or contrary to honest dealing (Denmark). These alternatives are relatively close to the standard of good faith and fair dealing in § 33, but they differ in the way that they open up the broader revision process of § 36 (including alteration, not only invalidity). These standards are seldom used, or even referred to, and it has been claimed that they do not really make up an independent category in practice (Gomard 2005, p. 210).

6.2.2 *§ 36 in the Supreme Courts*

The presentation of Supreme Court rulings can, of course, be done either by working forward from the first rulings after the passing of § 36, or by working backwards from the newest rulings. Due to the discretionary nature of § 36, this chapter will look at some current cases, giving a fairly good picture of how § 36 is perceived and applied in current Nordic jurisprudence.[8]

During 2012 and 2013, the Norwegian Supreme Court handled not less than three cases ("Lognvik", "Fokus bank" and "Røeggen")[9] concerning consumers having invested in so-called "structured savings products"; ending with a Grand Chamber decision in the case called "Røeggen". All cases concerned consumers' purchases of rather speculative financial products, and they show how the Norwegian Supreme Court undertakes a broad analysis of the entire contract and circumstances related to it.

The starting point for all three cases was (to a somewhat different extent in each case) high risk financial products, which were bought before the financial crisis hit in 2008. In the Lognvik case, two consumers had loaned money to invest in financial products (indexed bonds). The consumers were guaranteed to have their investment back at the end of the 4 year investment period, after the deduction of underwriting fees by the bank, and thus the bank marketed the products as "guaranteed" savings products. Including interest on the loan (that was taken out to purchase these bonds), the total cost of these products amounted to 11 % of the sum invested. In other words, even though marketed as "guaranteed", they contained a potential loss of 11 %. So in order for the investment to be profitable, the yields would have to exceed these costs.

The majority of the Supreme Court, four out of five judges, came to the conclusion that the agreement was not unfair, and thus upheld it. They stated that if one

[8] Due to the amount of material, the limited space available, and trying to balance the text to some extent, another fairly well known option used in legal texts will also have to be invoked in this chapter: a somewhat random selection of illustrative court decisions based on the author's discretion.

[9] Published in Norsk Retstidende (Rt.) 2012, p. 355 (Lognvik), Rt. 2012, p. 1926 (Fokus bank) and Rt. 2013, p. 388 (Røeggen).

looked solely at the price paid for the possibility of an uncertain yield, the price would seem unfair. Even though the investment was a package presented by the bank, the majority of the Court stated that how the investment was financed, by loan or other ways, should not be taken into account—a statement later heavily criticised in legal literature. The majority of the Supreme Court also stated that the investor had to bear the risk of his own investment decisions, unless there were "qualified defects" in the information given by the bank. One judge found that the product's main function was to promote a marketing strategy without proper foundation, that the information given to the consumer had been misleading and that the bank's financial "adviser's" advice to invest in the product was not a reasonable one.

The Fokus bank case involved more experienced consumers, who were more aware of the risks involved in the product they had purchased, which was a highly geared investment. After the ruling in the Lognvik case, it was no surprise that the consumers lost in the Supreme Court. Then, the Supreme Court had to consider yet another case very similar to Lognvik, where there were inexperienced consumers that had been persuaded to buy similar bonds to the ones in Logvik, the so-called Røeggen-case. The Supreme Court decided to deal with the case in the Grand Chamber, which is provided for in cases of utmost importance.[10]

In Røeggen, 11 judges unanimously found that the agreement had to be set aside as unfair, in accordance with the Contract Act § 36. This ruling provides a representative picture of a Nordic contract revision under § 36, at least under the Norwegian-Danish regime where the provision opens up the possibility of finding the contract as a whole to be unfair.

The Supreme Court started by stating that contracts containing elements of speculation or risk cannot be set aside solely on the grounds that the risk materialises. An investor has to bear the risk of his own expectations of the development of the market, as long as these are not based on misleading information from the other contracting party. The last part of the sentence is as important as it should be obvious in consumer contracts, and hopefully in accordance with most European legislation. It was, however, an important correction after the slip in the Lognvik ruling, where the Supreme Court demanded that there be a *qualified* defect in the information given. The Supreme Court further stated that Røeggen was a non-professional investor, being approached by his bank with an investment proposal. The bank's duty of care when providing information, therefore, had to meet a high standard; and when selling risky, complex financial products to a non-professional investor, a bank has to make sure the customer understands the content of the contract he enters into, and not give misleading or false information about important factors with regard to the decision whether to invest or not. The Supreme Court concluded that the information given in the Røeggen case, where the bank had focused almost solely on potential gains with classic "small print-warnings", was insufficient. Moreover, given the total picture—the cost of the product, the risk involved, the lack of proper informa-

[10] One of the factors in a decision to treat a case in Grand Chamber is whether the Supreme Court might deviate from a prior ruling, see the Act on the Courts of Justice § 5.

tion about these risks, and the relationship between the parties—the Supreme Court concluded that the entire agreement had to be set aside.[11]

The Røeggen ruling is representative of the broad approach taken to setting aside or adjusting contracts in accordance with § 36. In the lower courts in the Lognvik-case, Lognvik's counsel had also argued along the lines of § 33 with its standard for good faith and fair dealing, but that seemed to lead the case into a narrower judgment of the information provided; while § 36 clearly opened up the possibility of taking all relevant circumstances into consideration. It can be pointed out that the distinction may not be a sharp one, but it was clearly of importance in these cases.

The Røeggen ruling fits well into a tradition where consumer cases make up the core of § 36 disputes. The "professional" party must not necessarily be a medium sized or large corporation. In the Supreme Court case published in Rt. 1991, p. 147, a tenant's complaint was heard that a time limitation in her rental contract was unfair, and it was set aside. The apartment building was a set up as a single purpose company, owned by one person. He was clearly the professional party to the rental contract, and the result would probably have been the same if he had also owned the building himself instead of through a corporation.

This last ruling leads on to a point that does not stand out quite so clearly from the Røeggen ruling: ordinarily, also in cases regarding the Norwegian and Danish § 36, the question will be whether a *contract term* in question is to be found unfair.[12]

The strong consumer element of the provision in the Contract Act § 36 is quite evident if one looks at cases where professionals have invoked it. Wilhelmsson (2008, p. 124) points to a total of seven Finnish Supreme Court cases where adjustment of the contract has been denied because the parties where found to be of equal strength. Giertsen (2012, p. 211) points out a total of 11 Norwegian Supreme Court decisions where a professional party invoked § 36, and none of them led to the revision of the contract. In Sweden, the famous Bergman and Beving case published in Nytt Juridiskt Arkiv (NJA) 1979, p. 483 shows the same restraint with regard to using § 36 for commercial contracts: even though it was a large company against a small one, including standard terms and a far reaching exclusion of liability clause, the Swedish Supreme Court did not find grounds for its revision under § 36.

There is, however, a clear example of the application of § 36 in one commercial contract in Sweden in the Supreme Court's ruling published in NJA 1989, p. 346. A seller of fur coats had fur coats valuing more than 50,000 € stolen from a locked room. The insurance terms stated that theft was covered in cases of forced entry, picking of locks or stolen keys, which were obtained through robbery or forced entry into other buildings. In this case, a copy of the proper key had been used, and it was assumed it had been obtained though the security agency that the insurance company had recommended, since the owner himself possessed the only other key. The Supreme Court stated that the security arrangements had been extraordinary, and that if the owner had understood the insurance terms' distinction between a

[11] In practical terms, this leads to a restitution of the performance of the contract; i.e. that in this case, the consumer was compensated for the loss caused by the investment.

[12] Cf. Giertsen (2012, p. 212).

picked lock and a "false key" (albeit an illegally obtained copy), he would not have deposited a key with the security company. This led the Supreme Court to the conclusion that the insurance contract had to be adjusted so that the theft in question was covered. The court came to this conclusion even though the term itself could hardly be considered generally unfair—the difference between forced entry and lock picking on one side, and illegally obtained copies on the other, was based on a fairly reasonable assumption of which risks it would be possible for the insured to avoid himself.

It may, however, be noted that in a subsequent insurance case in the Swedish Supreme Court, NJA 1992, p. 782, the court refused to adjust insurance terms, which led to the termination of the insurance coverage when the premium was not paid on time, even though it was an ordinary slip of mind by the insured, and a subsequent fire damaged the hotel in question amounting to around 2.5 million Euros.

One arbitration case attracted quite heavy attention in Nordic doctrine in the mid and late 1980s: the so-called "Mascot-case", published in Nordiske Domme i Sjøfartsanliggender (Nordic collection of shipping related court decisions) 1985 p. 234. The Court of Arbitration, led by one of Norway's leading professors in private and commercial law, Sjur Brækhus, revised a bare boat charter freights currency conversion calculation clause with reference to the Contract Act § 36. The decision was based on the fact that the clause in the contract had not been written by any of the parties, and led to results neither of the parties to the contract had foreseen, or even wanted.

One type of case stands out as independent from the position of the parties and their relative strength: long term leases. These cases have been brought in all Nordic countries, on the basis of inflation making the rents close to worthless. In Norway, the question of whether the rent could be adjusted was decided in favour of the lessor by the Supreme Court in the famous joint plenary decisions in "Røstad" (Rt. 1988, p. 276) and "Skjelsvik" (Rt. 1988, p. 295). In Norway, such cases have even been brought by corporations against consumer tenants; "Periscopus" (Rt. 1990, p. 500). It was held that, in the course of time, the rents had deviated substantially from the market price. The Supreme Court did, however, note that the tenants had also paid a substantial sum for their originally-priced favourable rental agreements, and that these contracts were known to the lessor when acquiring the property in question. Similarly, the Finnish Supreme Court in HD 1994:88 stated that a mere comparison of the rent with local market rent was not sufficient; one had to look at the agreement as a whole and scrutinise the premises on which the parties entered into the contract.[13] As for Denmark, the rent in a long lease contract from 1847 was adjusted from 10 Kroner a year (just under 1.50 €) to 8000 kroner (a little more than 1000 €) in a Court of Appeal decision published in Ugeskrift for Retsvæsen (UfR) 2004, p. 2518 (Vestre landsret).

In Sect. 2.1 of this chapter, it was pointed out that the courts will ordinarily refrain from actually re-writing contracts under the alternative option in § 36. This has, however, happened in the Finnish Supreme Court in HD 1992:42. A redemp-

[13] Similarly, also in HD 1988:24; see Wilhelmsson (2008, p. 121).

tion clause in a limited company was found to be unfair; and the Supreme Court did not simply set aside the clause, but formulated a new redemption clause. The flexibility offered by the Nordic contract acts' § 36 is, in other words, extensive.

6.2.3 *The Relationship with the Directive on Unfair Terms in Consumer Contracts*

When the Directive on unfair terms in consumer contracts was passed, it necessitated adjustments to the Nordic legislation. All Nordic legislators concluded that the current Contract Act § 36 covered the main part of the Directive. However, to fulfil all the requirements of the Directive, some provisions regulating particular consumer non-negotiated contract terms were added. Norway and Denmark added these provisions in the Contract Acts (§ 37 for Norway, § 38a, b and c for Denmark), while Sweden passed a separate act on consumer contracts, and Finland introduced provisions in its Consumer Protection Act.

The "grey list" of the Directive is not explicitly incorporated into legislation in the Nordic countries. Instead, the tradition of elaborating the details of the content of the legislative text in the preparatory works was used. There is not much doubt that Nordic courts will find these lists an important factor in considering fairness, and this technique of incorporation was accepted by the ECJ in Commission v Sweden, C-478/99.

The details that had to be included following the passing of the Directive were: firstly, a rule stating that the interpretation of unclear terms shall be to the advantage of the consumer (a rule that quite clearly already had plenty of support in the case law). Second, a rule was passed stating that subsequent events, after the conclusion of the contract, could not "fix" an originally unfair term to the detriment of the consumer. This is due to the fact that fairness, according to the Directive, is to be assessed at the time of the conclusion of the contract. Since it was a minimum standards Directive, Nordic courts were still allowed to consider subsequent events in favour of the consumer. Third, a rule stating that if a term is unfair, the consumer has a right to demand that term be considered as if it had not been written, while the rest of the contract is upheld. As pointed out above, broad Nordic assessment, according to the contract acts' § 36, allows for setting the entire contract aside if the term is central to the agreement as such. Such a revision would be contrary to the Directive. Finally, the business party has the burden of proof when claiming that a term has been individually negotiated—another rule that, nevertheless, would have been deduced from current case-law.

After the passing of the Directive, it is hard to find any shift whatsoever in the way the courts handle questions of unfair terms in consumer contracts. Consumers still point to § 36, and the courts do not seem to invoke the Directive *ex officio* as presupposed by the EJC in *Oceano*, C-240/98. Giertsen (2012, pp. 216–217), has investigated Norwegian case-law and not found a single case where the Directive has been actively used since its introduction into Norwegian law. The reason might well be that the protection granted by § 36 is at least as strong as that of the Directive, and that Nordic lawyers prefer to use the well-known and well tested provision in § 36. In the above mentioned Røeggen case, the Norwegian Supreme Court stated that the Directive together with the Contract Act § 37 was not of independent value in the case, as the standard required for revision under § 37 and the Directive was higher than that of § 36. At least in Denmark, one case has been tried on the grounds of the Directive-based legislation in the Supreme Court, and decided in favour of the consumer. In the ruling published in UfR 2006, p. 706, the Danish Supreme Court set aside a term stating that the consumer had to pay a fine of 10% of the contract price if he withdrew from the agreement to buy a used car without just cause. This clause was common in the Danish car sellers' standard terms, but was found, by the Supreme Court, to violate the rule in appendix 1(e) to the Directive concerning terms "requiring any consumer who fails to fulfil his obligation to pay a disproportionately high sum in compensation". The Supreme Court did, however, also find that it violated the Contract Act § 36. The result was upheld in a later case: UfR 2004, p. 2876, where the seller claimed to have sustained a heavier loss because of the consumer's withdrawal from the contract.[14]

The fact that the financial crisis hit Iceland especially hard, has led to a heavy debate over the prior and current regulation of mortgage loans for the acquisition of real property. (One of the main problems was Icelanders having their residential loans in Euros, when the Icelandic krone plunged.) This has again led to one of the Icelandic courts requesting an opinion from the EFTA-court on several matters relating to the Directive on unfair consumer contracts; see case E-25/13 (case pending as of December 2013).

6.3 A Brief Presentation of the Regulation of Unfair Terms in the CESL in Light of DCFR and PECL, and Some Comparative Remarks on the Nordic Contract Acts' § 36

The main rule, the "general clause" on unfair contract terms, is contained in CESL art. 79, which states that "a contract term which is supplied by one party and which is unfair under sections 2 and 3 of this chapter is not binding on the other party". The main rule in art. 79 clearly points to Sects. 2 and 3, and can hardly be seen as itself containing a standard of unfairness.[15] To find the actual conditions for holding a term unfair, one has to go to the provisions in section 2 for consumer sales and section 3 for sales between traders.

One important general rule can, however, be found already in the introductory art. 79. In its second paragraph, it is stated that "where the contract can be main-

[14] See further Gomard (2005, pp. 214–215).

[15] Cf. Schultze et al. (2012, p. 378).

tained without the unfair contract term, the other contract terms remain binding". This is a similar wording to that of the Directive on unfair terms in consumer contracts art. 6, where it is laid down that "the contract shall continue to bind the parties upon those terms if it is capable of continuing in existence without the unfair terms". Thus, this seems to be a clear punitive element in the regulation of unfair contract terms: the one who imposes an unfair term, risks having the contract upheld without it, even though that may cause an imbalance in the opposite direction. It is, in this regard, worth noting that the second paragraph of art. 79 also applies to contracts between traders.

One might ask whether the wording in art. 79 CESL is slightly "softer" than that of the unfair terms Directive. It is possible to argue that "can be maintained" is less absolute than "capable of continuing". A comparison with the DCFR does not, however, leave much room for a softer interpretation of the CESL than of the Directive. Article II.-9:408 DCFR states that the contract remains binding upon the parties if it "can reasonably be maintained without the unfair term". In light of the wording of the DCFR, it is hard to understand art. 79 CESL otherwise than that it has been a desire to preserve the strict and partly punitive element introduced into the unfair terms Directive, by excluding the word "reasonably". Moreover, even with the condition "reasonably" included, the standard of the DCFR is fairly strict: in the commentaries on art. II.-9:408 DCFR, it is duly noted that the exception for not reasonably being maintained refers to terms "essential for the contract", and which "cannot be supplied by reference to default rules or background provisions".[16]

The DCFR (and clearly then the CESL) is stricter here than the Principles of European Contract Law (PECL), where art. 4:116 states that the contract as such will be upheld without the term unless this is "unreasonable", given due consideration to all the circumstances of the case. It is explicitly stated in the comments to the article on unfair terms (PECL 4:110) that the effect on the rest of the contract from finding a term unfair is regulated by art. 4:116.[17] The Nordic regulation is definitely along the lines of art. 4:116 PECL. The advantage of the regulation in the DCFR, and even more so for that in the CESL, is legal certainty, in particular with regard to consumer cases, where litigation is often disproportionately expensive and risky in terms of the sums involved. On the other hand, the rule is rather harsh, and may simply lead to just another unfair contract, at least in commercial relationships. In this perspective, it is interesting to note that the UNIDROIT Principles of International Commercial Contracts (PICC) art. 3.2.7, concerning avoidance due to gross disparity, in subparagraphs (2) and (3) states that a court may also adapt the contract "in order to make it accord with reasonable standards of fair dealing". This clearly means that there is room to go beyond simply setting terms aside. Then again, with the threshold for use on commercial contracts, this author's objection might not be of critical importance to the choice of regulation here.

Article 80 CESL removes certain clauses from the scope of the fairness test. In the first paragraph it is stated that the fairness test is not applicable on "terms which

[16] DCFR Volume I (2010, p. 656).

[17] Lando and Beale (2000, p. 270).

reflect rules of the Common European Sales Law". When the revision is only carried out on the level of evaluating individual terms, it is in any case hard to picture that these terms themselves could be considered unfair; not least when taken into consideration that the CESL is to be interpreted as independent of national law, cf. art. 4.[18] It does, however, have a narrower scope on this point than the DCFR article II-9:406, which not only excludes the draft rules themselves, but also provisions on applicable law and international conventions to which the Member States of the EU are parties. It is interesting to point out that a debate that has been raised from time to time in the Nordic countries, is whether a contract based on legislative provision, nevertheless may be revised through the contract acts § 36. There are some key factors that make this a more realistic problem and option in comparison with the CESL and the DCFR: subsequent events, after the time of the conclusion of the contract, may be taken into account, and in Norwegian and Danish law there is also the possibility to evaluate the contract as a whole. There is, as of now, no clear example that a Nordic Supreme Court has revised a contract based on non-mandatory statutory law. But already the above mentioned Swedish case concerning the theft of furs (NJA 1989, p. 346) shows how these problems could possibly arise: it is reasonable to assume it was not the term itself, at the time of the conclusion of the contract, which was unfair, but when subsequent events were regarded and viewed in light of the entire factual situation, the term was nevertheless found unfair. This could clearly also possibly happen with terms based on "background law".

Another sharp difference between the Nordic provisions on the one hand, and the CESL, DCFR and PECL on the other, is the question of fairness of the main contract performance. The CESL clearly states in art. 80 para. 2 and 3 that the fairness test is not applicable on "the definition of the main subject matter of the contract, or to the appropriateness of the price to be paid". This is in accordance with the unfair terms Directive art. 4 para. 2, DCFR art. II.-9:406 para. 2, and PECL art. 4:110 para. 2.[19] It is, in other words, a provision with a solid base. The DCFR explains that such control is not suitable in a market economy, where the choice of the parties to enter into an exchange of goods and money is made individually. It is also pointed out that it would be difficult to find good criteria for such an evaluation.[20] In the commentaries to art. 4:110 PECL, it is emphasised that the scope of this exception has to be interpreted strictly, and that *inter alia* terms which allow a party to raise the price are covered by the ordinary fairness test in the first paragraph.[21] It would be in accordance with general principles of consumer protection to apply the same interpretation to art. 80 CESL.

In the Nordic § 36 it is just as clear that the scope extends also to the main subject matter and the price. This underlines the discretionary character of these provisions.

[18] Cf. Schultze et al. (2012, p. 379).

[19] For an outline of policy considerations (or lack thereof) behind this rule, see Hellwege and Miller (2013, pp. 453–455).

[20] DCFR Volume I (2010, p. 646).

[21] Lando and Beale (2000, p. 269).

The difficult part of this is, of course, finding the proper legal criteria for an unfair price. Usually, there is a broad evaluation of the price, the strength of the parties, possible poor information and other circumstances. The basis for revision is definitively broader in the Nordic § 36, but at least the limitation of the exception in the CESL, DCFR and PECL to cases where the terms are drafted "in plain and intelligible language" (CESL art. 82 together with art. 80, DCFR article II-9:406 para. 2, and PECL art. 4:110), narrows the gap. At this point at least the art. 3.2.7 PICC on gross disparity seems to be more in line with the Nordic regulation than that of the CESL, DCFR and PECL, allowing the courts to look at the contract as a whole, without excluding the price or main subject matter. In any case, it is hard to picture the revision of a contract being conducted solely on the grounds of a high price; it must at least be combined with some form of lack of information on the side of the contracting party accepting the price in question.

As stated above, "unfair" is not the relevant legal condition, since its content is defined in Sects. 2 and 3 in the CESL. In contracts between traders and consumers, according to Sect. 2, a term is considered unfair "if it causes a significant imbalance in the parties' rights and obligations arising under the contract, to the detriment of the consumer, contrary to good faith and fair dealing". The condition "significant imbalance" is the same as in the unfair terms Directive and art. 4:110 PECL. It does, however, deviate from the solution in the DCFR. Article II.-9:403 DCFR instead uses the condition "significantly disadvantages the consumer". The reason for the wording of the DCFR was "to avoid the possible misunderstanding that the price-performance ratio of the contract could be a measure to determine unfairness".[22] Content-wise, in other words, it is not meant to be an alteration. One may criticise the choice of "significant imbalance" in the CESL for permitting this possible misunderstanding[23]; but the content of the condition does seem clear enough in light of the provision's history: a comparison of the contents of the term in question with what would have followed from basic non-mandatory law.[24] In the comments accompanying the PECL, it states that the imbalance may be of either economic or legal nature: "In the first case, the economic consequences are significantly abusive to the other party. In the latter case, a term may be deemed imbalanced if it confers rights upon one party and not upon the other (mirror image rule)."[25]

It can be argued that what is more unfortunate is that the significant imbalance is not itself enough to provide for setting aside the term; in addition to providing for a significant imbalance, it must be "contrary to good faith and fair dealing".[26] In light of all the provisions already existing, demanding parties to a contract to act in accordance with good faith and fair dealing, one might then ask if these provisions on unfair terms are superfluous. One must naturally assume that the intent has not

---

22 DCFR Volume I (2010, pp. 634–635).

23 See e.g. Hellwege and Miller (2010, p. 440).

24 Cf. DCFR Volume I (2010, p. 635).

25 Lando and Beale (2000, p. 269).

26 Also critical at this point, Schultze et al. (2012, p. 385).

been to invoke the general European standard of good faith and fair dealing; after all, one has gone to the trouble of formulating rules against unfair contract terms. In addition, the blacklist and the grey list do point in the direction that the "significant imbalance" is by far the most important part of the unfairness regulation as such. The closest thing to an explanation for the "contrary to good faith and fair dealing" might be the short comment found in the DCFR. Here, it is asked whether there is a justification for the significant disadvantage, bearing in mind that the good faith and fair dealing criterion allows a flexible test: "The more significant the disadvantage, the better the justification must be."[27] In the PECL, good faith and fair dealing is not commented on at all; it may seem that it is not considered to have much independent value. In this author's opinion, an open acknowledgement of a fairness assessment, such as in the Nordic § 36, would have been clearer and better. It is submitted that support for this view can be found in the notes to the DCFR, where it is stated that the criterion of good faith is lacking in many national regimes, which tends to result in lowering the burden of proof for consumers.[28] Interestingly, the French legislator also refrained from using the term "good faith" in Code Civil art. 1134 para. 3, as it was held that a business that gains a significant imbalance cannot by definition be acting in good faith.[29]

Article 83 para. 2 CESL contains a list of circumstances that are to be regarded when evaluating fairness. There is no equivalent list in the DCFR. Article 83 states that regard is to be taken as to "whether the trader complied with the duty of transparency set out in Article 82; the nature of what is to be provided under the contract; the circumstances prevailing during the conclusion of the contract; to the other contract terms; and to the terms of any other contract on which the contract depends". The PECL provides for this more briefly by: "taking into account the nature of the performance to be rendered under the contract, all the other terms of the contract and the circumstances at the time the contract was concluded." Both provisions show a broad approach to the evaluation of fairness and imbalance. At the same time, they exhibit one significant difference with the Nordic contract acts § 36 that has already been pointed out: they do not allow for the consideration of subsequent development when assessing fairness.

It is interesting to note that in art. II.-9:403 para. 2 DCFR, it is stated that breach of the duty of transparency (using plain intelligible language) alone may lead to a term being considered unfair. Such a consequence is neither stated in the unfair terms Directive or in the CESL. As far as the Directive is concerned, this has been a disputed question; and it is unfortunate that this is also left open in the CESL.[30]

[27] DCFR Volume I (2010, p. 635).

[28] On the possible effects of this criterion in the CESL on the burden of proof, see Schultze et al. (2012, p. 385).

[29] See DCFR Volume I (2010, p. 637). An outline of the discussion of the equal worded provision in the English Unfair Terms in Consumer Contracts Regulations 1999 is provided by Hellwege and Miller (2013, pp. 443–444).

[30] Cf. also Schultze et al. (2012, pp. 381–382). For a broader discussion over the consequences of lack of transparency, see DCFR Volume I (2010, pp. 632–633).

From the system in the CESL, one must at least assume that if the duty of transparency is breached, it does not take much of an imbalance before it will be considered significant and thus unfair.[31]

The CESL and DCFR both also regulate business to business contracts. The threshold for revision is significantly higher for commercial contracts than for those entered into with a consumer. According to art. 86 CESL, a term in a contract between traders is unfair if it is of "such a nature that its use grossly deviates from good commercial practice, contrary to good faith and fair dealing".[32] The wording of the condition in art. II.-9:405 DCFR is identical to that of the CESL. From a comparative perspective, it is interesting to compare the legislative technique of the DCFR and the CESL with that of art. 4:110 PECL and the Nordic § 36. The latter ones have just one joint provision for consumers and businesses. However, for both the PECL and the Nordic § 36, it is, of course, of significance whether it is a consumer or commercial contract. For information purposes, one might prefer the regulation in the CESL and DCFR. On the other hand, the distinction between consumers and traders could become unnecessary sharp.[33] A person running his own business might be just as weak a party when he is dealing with a large company as a business owner is when he contracts as a private individual. Some flexibility would obviously be lost with the sharp distinctions in the CESL and the DCFR, while the flexibility of the PECL and the Nordic § 36 may pose a challenge for legal certainty. The latest thorough book on the validity of contracts in the Nordic countries, Hauge (2009), goes so far as to question whether § 36, after 20 years of practice, has become something more than a "lottery ticket in the reasonableness lottery", and struggles to conclude otherwise (pp. 262–263). What, however, is clear for both categories is that setting aside contract terms as unfair in commercial contracts between traders of rather equal strength, will be reserved for exceptional cases.

For businesses, the "hardship" article, art. 89 CESL on change of circumstances, may be a more important and useful development, not least as it carries with it proper consequences if the parties do not reach an agreement through re-negotiations. It must, nevertheless, be pointed out that here also the threshold for revision is very high: performance must become "excessively onerous because of an exceptional change of circumstances".

[31] Cf. Schultze et al. (2012, p. 382). An interesting middle way can be found in art. 2.1.20 PICC, which states that standard terms that are "of such a character that the other party could not reasonably have expected it" are ineffective unless expressly brought to the other party's intention and accepted.

[32] For the origin of the expression "grossly deviates from good commercial practice", see Schultze et al. (2012, p. 394).

[33] A similar opinion is expressed in Schultze et al. (2012, p. 395).

6.4 Some Challenges for European Traders Selling to the Nordic Countries

As of now, the text of the CESL poses certain challenges with regard to the scope of its application. It is clearly stated in art. 4 that the CESL is to be interpreted independently of national law, a clear progress from the Freiburger kommunalbauten case (C-237/02) where the ECJ left the content of unfairness in the unfair terms Directive to the national courts, under an influence of national legal culture and interpretation. It is also clear that the CESL, as a regulation of an optional instrument, has to be incorporated without alteration into national law. What is not so clear, however, is to what extent it regulates subjects of which it does not speak.

Paragraph 27 of the Preamble states that "all the matters of a contractual or non-contractual nature that are not addressed in the Common European Sales Law are governed by the pre-existing rules of the national law outside the Common European Sales Law that is applicable under Regulations (EC) No 593/2008 and (EC) No 864/2007 or any other relevant conflict of law rule". One could ask whether terms that have been negotiated individually, could be subject to revision in a Nordic court, on the grounds that this subject is not regulated in the CESL.[34] Or would it be possible to even go so far as to say that only the question of unfair *terms* is regulated, not the question of whether the contract as a whole is unfair? At least the latter seems rather far-fetched, as the list of legal issues mentioned as examples of what has to be decided according to national law in paragraph 27 ("legal personality, the invalidity of a contract arising from lack ofcapacity, illegality or immorality, the determination of the language of the contract, matters of non-discrimination, representation, plurality of debtors and creditors, change of parties including assignment, set-off and merger, property law including thetransfer of ownership, intellectual property law and the law of torts") quite clearly indicates that it is legal questions of a somewhat different character that have to be decided according to national law. What, however, does seem a possibility is the use of the Contract Act § 36 in cases of possible invalidity based on e.g. a broad assessment of a situation with a contract party with weakened mental capacity, taking into account whether the contract had been properly understood, with some degree of substantial imbalance as well—if it is then all in all reasonable to enforce it. The boarders here do not seem very sharp, and give rise to some difficult demarcation questions.

---

[34] For a European seller trading with Nordic consumers, jurisdiction will be in the consumer's domicile according to the Brussels I Regulation, EC 44/2001 (Sweden, Finland and, although having opted out of the area of freedom, security and justice, also Denmark, by special agreement) and the Lugano Convention (Norway). As for choice of law, the Rome I Regulation leads to the law of the consumer's habitual residence. This means that such a case could most likely come before a Nordic court and be decided according to the relevant Nordic law (except for Norway, as Norway is not bound by the Rome I Regulation, EC 593/2008, as it is not considered EEA relevant, and has legislation stating that the seller's place of business is the main connecting factor for the choice of law).

6.5 A Few Closing Remarks

Since the passing of the Directive on unfair terms in consumer contracts, the standard for unfair contract terms seems to have been set: there are only minor differences between the regulations in the Directive, the CESL, DCFR and PECL. Whether using the term significant "imbalance" or "disadvantage" also seems simply a matter of terminology.[35]

What is an interesting point for the future is whether this development over time will spread to the contract as a whole. The Study Group on a European Civil Code wanted to extend the unfairness control also to individually negotiated terms, which has led to the condition "which has not been individually negotiated" being put in brackets in art. II.-9:403 DCFR.[36] The experience with the Contract Acts § 36 in the Nordic countries does not contradict such a development: these countries have managed fairly well with a broader clause, although the broad, discretionary assessment causes some legal certainty issues. Moreover, given the level of legal knowledge of most consumers, it is submitted that it is hard to accept the upholding of terms that create a significant imbalance, simply because they have been subject to individual negotiation. That may seem more like accepting an abuse of freedom of contract than protecting it.

The change of circumstances regulation in art. 89 CESL is also an interesting development for the regulation of unfairness. In the future, should it also not be possible to have regard to subsequent developments in judging if terms in consumer contracts are fair? For a Nordic lawyer, being educated and practicing in a legal culture where the revision of contracts is always a possibility at some point (although the threshold may be high even here), it seems artificial to undertake an evaluation of fairness that cannot take into consideration all the circumstances known at the time of this assessment. It may also be asked why one should not be able to assess the entire contract as such; and if not, whether the possibility to adjust the rest of the contract is too narrow, at least in non-consumer contracts, in cases where one condition is found to be unfair. On the other hand, the main challenge when permitting further judiciary discretion is to safeguard the foreseeability for the weaker party, so that the risk of litigation does not impose too large a practical obstacle for the enforcement of the rules of unfairness.

References

DCFR Volume I: von Bar C, Clive E (ed.), Principles, Definitions and Model Rules of European Private Law. Draft Common Frame of Reference (DCFR). Full edition. Oxford University Press, Oxford (2010).

Giertsen J (2012): Avtaler, Universitetsforlaget, Oslo.

[35] Cf. Hellwege and Miller (2013, p. 440).

[36] See further Hellwege and Miller (2013, p. 441).

Gomard B (2005): "Rimelighed og god skik. Bunden eller fri retsdannelse og fortolkning?", pp. 205–225, in Flodgren B et. al. (red), Avtalslagen 90 år, NorstedtsJuridik, Stockholm.
Hauge H (2009): Ugyldighet, Universitetsforlaget, Oslo.
Hellwege P, Miller L (2013): "Control of Standard Contract Terms", pp. 423–468 in Dannemann G, Vogenauer S (ed.), The Common European Sales Law in Context. Interactions with English and German Law, Oxford University Press, Oxford.
Lando O, Beale H (2000) (ed.): Principles of European Contract Law, Parts I and II, prepared by the Commission on European Contract Law, 2000.
Schultze R (ed.), Mazeaud D, Sauphanor-Brouillaud N (2012): Common European Sales Law (CESL). Commentary. C. H. Beck/Hart/Nomos, München 2012.
Sisula-Tulokas L (2005): "Skumma affärsmetoder, tvångochohederlighet" pp. 317–328, in Flodgren B et. al. (ed.), Avtalslagen 90 år, NorstedtsJuridik, Stockholm.
Wilhelmsson T (2008): Standardavtalochoskäligaavtalsvivillkor, Talentum, Helsingfors.

Chapter 7
Breach of Contract

Martin Schmidt-Kessel and Eva Silkens

Abstract Historically, the notion of breach of contract was by no means clear and coherent within European Private Law and even less so in the field of sales law in Europe. In this area of law many European national legal systems are influenced by the legacy of Roman sales law, in particular the claims regarding defective goods (*actio redhibitoria* and *actio quanti minoris*). For most continental legal systems this Roman heritage led to a diffuse structure of legal rules for breach of contract. Starting with the Hague Sales Law and the CISG, on which Art. 1:301(4), 8:101 PECL were based, the notion of non-performance has become foremost the term used when describing breach of contract in European Private Law. Today the standard is set by Art. III.–1:102(3) DCFR as complemented by Art. III.–3:101 DCFR. It was adopted by the European Commission in Art. 87 CESL. Art. III.–1:102(3) DCFR reads: "Non-performance of an obligation is any failure to perform the obligation, whether or not excused, and includes delayed performance and any other performance which is not in accordance with the terms regulating the obligation."

Furthermore, the law of defences and excuses for breach of contract is by no means coherent, neither on most national levels nor on the European level, and that includes notions of force majeure and change of circumstances; of impossibility and frustration; of hardship and *imprévision*; of fault, *culpa* and *Verschulden*. Here, a general solution is established in Art. III.–3:104 DCFR, containing a kind of *force majeure* clause, which was derived from Art. 79 CISG and Art. 8:108 PECL and has now been used by the European Commission in Art. 88 CESL.

The same holds true for remedies for breach of contract: Neither the kind nor the system of remedies is agreed upon among European Member States nor is the answer to the question whether specific performance is a remedy or a kind of self-evident element of the concept of obligation, in the sense of the famous saying by *Ernst Rabel,* referring to the "Rückgrat der Obligation" (spinal column of the obligation); (Rabel 1936). The right to cure, first formulated as a separate defence in Art. III.–3:201 to Art. III.–3:205 DCFR, was adopted by the European Commission in Art. 109 CESL.

M. Schmidt-Kessel (✉) · E. Silkens
University of Bayreuth, Bayreuth, Germany
e-mail: martin.schmidt-kessel@uni-bayreuth.de

E. Silkens
e-mail: silkenseva@aol.com

© Springer International Publishing Switzerland 2015

J. Plaza Penadés, L. M. Martínez Velencoso (eds.), *European Perspectives on the Common European Sales Law,* Studies in European Economic Law and Regulation 4,
DOI 10.1007/978-3-319-10497-3_7

All these incoherences and uncertainties regarding concepts, notions and structures as well as to basic policy decisions are—as mentioned earlier—reflected in the Commission's proposal for a Common European Sales Law. One could and should read this proposal and its predecessors in the Draft Common Frame of Reference on the Principles of European Contract Law as a mirror of the development of contract law, and sales law in particular, in Europe.

Keywords Breach of contract · Fault · Force majeure · Hardship · Change of circumstances · Fault · Specific performance · Right to withhold performance · Termination of the contract · Price reduction · Damages

7.1 Breach of Contract

The Commission's draft proposal for a Common European Sales Law now contains in Art. 87 general definitions of the notions of "non-performance" and "fundamental non-performance". Art. 87(1) CESL reads: "Non-performance of an obligation is any failure to perform that obligation, whether or not the failure is excused …". This constitutes a unitary concept of breach of contract and, therefore, sticks to the European standard based on CISG, PECL and DCFR.

A non-exhaustive list of six cases of breach of contract is added to this definition, symptomatic of the not particularly concise drafting style of the whole proposal, which is strongly influenced by the plain and clear language movement.[1] This list again reflects the diverging approaches of national legal systems of the European Member States to the notion and the concept of breach of contract. Furthermore, it has to be analysed as the result of a development of uniform law starting with the Hague Sales Law and ending so far with the notion of breach of contract in the Draft Common Frame of Reference. The solution proposed now for the Common European Sales Law by the European Commission has to be analysed by the light of both the diverging approaches of the national legal orders and the history of emergence of what now becomes a common European notion of breach of contract in a legal sense.

7.1.1 The Different Approaches to Breach of Contract in National Legal Orders

By its attempt to bring forward a uniform notion of breach of contract, called "non-performance", the proposal clearly abandons every idea of a cause approach. Such a cause approach distinguishes between different types of breaching contractual

[1] See also *Kossak* The Remedial System under the Proposed Common European Sales Law (CESL). In: EJCCL (1/2013), 7.

duties and obligations—like impossibility of performance, delay of the debtor, non-conformity, breach of a kind of *obligation de sécurité* and so forth—and connects these types with diverging remedies and prerequisites for those remedies.[2] Until the end of 2001 the former German law could be seen as paradigm for such a cause approach and today it may be found in the Greek civil code. Therefore, the first question under the cause approach is: what kind of breach has happened? Under such a cause approach, for example, the impossibility of performance of contractual obligation becomes the basis of a separate system of remedies, because the impossibility as such is seen as a breach of obligations. The consequences of such a type of breach may result in a claim for damages or termination of the contract or other consequences. These consequences are dealt with by the legal system separately from the same kind of consequences of other types of breach. Thus the kinds of remedies of the types of breach are kept separate.

A more subtle approach is presented by the majority view of French law and legal systems within the French legal family by distinguishing only between the types of duties; (Demogue 1925). However, the French concept of an *inexécution* is not a uniform one either: The difference between the various types of duties lies in the diverging prerequisites to fulfil the duty or to become excused in case of non-performance. Moreover, French law usually draws a line between cases of non-performance and the breach of a security duty (*obligation de sécurité*) for which a separate set of remedies applies.

The English common law is characterized by a uniform notion of breach of contract. Such a breach occurs where a person fails to perform his or her side of the contract. Under the English concept of breach of contract the reason for that non-performance is not decisive.[3] The most general consequence of such a kind of breach is that it provides the party aggrieved with a claim for damages regardless of the severity of the breach. Therefore, the English concept is usually described as being a unitary rule of breach of contract. This description is correct apart from one rather important exception: The English notion of breach of contract usually does not include the breach of a duty to care for the security of the other contractual party. Such cases of misbehaviour besides the core obligations of the contract are usually dealt with under the auspices of tort law; contract, where similar duties might be implied by law, is usually not argued. Therefore, it is not entirely clear, whether the unitary notion of breach of contract in the English law is restricted to cases of non-performance in a narrower sense or covers ancillary duties protecting parties' integrity as well.

The latest reform of the German law of obligations went a step further: In some of the articles—§§ 280, 314 BGB, at least—the legislator brought together the concepts of non-performance and of breach of a duty to care for the integrity of the other party in one concept. This happened by introducing one single notion for breach of contract which was not called *Nichterfüllung* (non-performance) but rather

[2] See also *Schmidt-Kessel* Remedies for Breach of Contract in European Private Law. In: Schulze (ed.), New features in Contract Law (2007), 183, 184.

[3] See *Schmidt-Kessel* Standards vertraglicher Haftung nach englischem Recht (2003), 32.

Pflichtverletzung, which should be translated as "breach of a contractual duty".[4] The German legislator, thereby, merged the two concepts and contractualised large areas of tort law duties emerging in the surroundings of a contract. This merger of the two concepts was heavily discussed when the German law of obligations was reformed and led to diverging models for how to interpret the new system.

7.1.2 The Solution Proposed for the European Common Sales Law

On earlier stages of International Uniform Law several instruments followed the U.S. and the English Common Law by establishing a uniform notion of breach of contract.[5] However, this CISG did not contain a true uniform rule, but in Artt. 45, 61 CISG distinguished between breaches by the buyer and breaches by the seller; only for the defences of impediment beyond control (Art. 79 CISG) and the creditor causing the breach (Art. 80 CISG) and in the general definition of fundamental breach in Art. 25 CISG did a more general approach also became visible in the text of the Convention.

The Principles of European Contract Law and the Draft Common Frame of Reference consolidated the different concepts in one article respectively. However, Art. 8:101 PECL and Art. III.-3:101 DCFR established another distinction instead: Both articles distinguish between "excused" and "not-excused" non-performance.[6] Both texts thereby established the excused non-performance as a separate category or a separate type of breach. This type of breach differs from the non-performance not-excused, as the debtor is able to "excuse" him- or herself by proving an impediment, which is beyond their control in the sense of Art. 8:108 PECL or Art. III.-3:104 DCFR. This dogmatic category is connected with the exclusion of the remedies of specific performance and damages.[7]

The draft Common European Sales Law now goes an important step further: Art. 87(1) CESL only defines a uniform notion of non-performance, without referring to any excuse either for impediment beyond control or for the creditor's misbehaviour.[8] The consequences of an excuse under Art. 88 CESL are only dealt with in the rules on remedies, Artt. 106(4), 131(2), 167(1), 168(1) CESL. Therefore, there is a significant dogmatical shift between the DCFR and the Commission's proposal for a Common European Sales Law: Whereas the DCFR (as the PECL) establishes two separate categories of excused non-performance and non-performance

[4] Illustration of the notion *Pflichtverletzung*: Diskussionsentwurf eines Schuldrechtsmodernisierungsgesetzes. In: ZRP (2000), 454.

[5] See also *Schmidt-Kessel* Standards vertraglicher Haftung nach englischem Recht (2003), 33.

[6] See especially *Jud* Die Principles of European Contract Law als Basis des Draft Common Frame of Reference. In: Schmidt-Kessel (ed.), Der gemeinsame Referenzrahmen (2009), 71, 91.

[7] See *Jud* Die Principles of European Contract Law als Basis des Draft Common Frame of Reference. In: Schmidt-Kessel (ed.), Der gemeinsame Referenzrahmen (2009), 71 (91).

[8] See also *Kossak* The Remedial System under the Proposed Common European Sales Law (CESL). In: EJCCL (1/2013), 7, 8.

not-excused, the CESL simply proposes a uniform category of non-performance and is distinguishing between excused and not-excused non-performance only on the level of remedies.[9] From a pragmatic point of view this difference may be seen as minor, however, for dogmatically trained continental lawyers this shift is of an importance which should not be underestimated. The text and the structure of the Commission's proposal prevents or, at least, should help to prevent dogmatic national lawyers from raising systematical arguments based on two different types of breach. Coming from a legal system with a bad experience with cause approaches and their necessities to draw lines between the types of breach, this solution proposed by the Commission to us seems an important and innovative progression in the formulation and structuring of European Contract Law.

7.1.3 The Undecided Case: Duties to Protect the Other Party's Integrity

As seen earlier, Member States provide for diverging answers to the question of whether the contract does protect the other party's integrity beyond the main obligations of the parties. Whereas, English law—having the technical possibility to employ tort law duties of care into the contract as contractual duties—usually does not work with such a concept of contractual protection of other parties' integrity, French law rather early developed the concept of contractual *obligations de sécurité* obligating the contractual party to look after the personal integrity of the other party and after the integrity of its property and assets. In German law in 2002 the legislator in § 241(2) *Bürgerliches Gesetzbuch* approved a long line of court decisions establishing a general concept of contractual duties protecting the other parties' integrity and property. Both concepts, the French and the German one, are identical only at first sight: While the German approach of *Schutzpflichten* was developed to fill gaps in the field of tort law (vicarious liability in particular) the French approach on the other hand was developed to limit tort law, with its famous general clause of Art. 1382 Code Civil, by applying the *principe de non cumul*.[10]

Neither the uniform sales law nor the Principles of European Contract Law nor the Draft Common Frame of Reference comes up with a clear solution concerning duties to protect the other parties' integrity. The Vienna Convention in Art. 5 CISG explicitly excludes personal damage from the scope of application of the convention and thereby tries to avoid the issue all together. In contrast, the Principles of European Contract Law do not even mention cases of damages to the other parties' integrity which are not a consequence of a breach of the main obligations of the contract.

---

[9] See especially *Zoll* in: Schulze (ed.), CESL Commentary (2012), Art. 87 no. 3, 16 and 18; *Faber* in: Wendehorst/Zöchling-Jud (eds.), Am Vorabend eines Gemeinsamen Europäischen Kaufrechts (2012), 147, 210.

[10] From a comparative perspective see *Schlechtriem* Vertragsordnung und außervertragliche Haftung (1972).

Whether the Commission's proposal for the CESL also contains rules for ancillary duties to care for the integrity of the other party as part of the contractual regime is still an open question; and this openness also includes the question of which remedies for breach of such duties are applicable under the CESL.[11] The proposal does not mention such duties in Artt. 2, 3 CESL—which is not so surprising, given the aforementioned development of European Private Law texts. The only general basis for duties to take care for the other parties' integrity within the instrument would be the definition of good faith by Art. 2 lit. b CESL-Reg., which refers to "honesty, openness and consideration for the interests of the other party to the transaction or relationship in question"; this definition should include that other party's personal integrity. At the very least, CESL includes the concept of protection of the other party's integrity in the concretisation of the quality of goods or digital content owed by the seller or supplier per Art. 99-101 CESL. For the duties of the service provider in the sense of Art. 148 CESL it is impossible to even clearly distinguish between the performance interest of the other party and their interests regarding personal or proprietary integrity—for example, in the case of an agreement for continued maintenance of machinery being sold, the obligation also aims to protect the machinery as part of buyer's property. And finally, Art. 107 CESL explicitly acknowledges the "donee's" interests in not suffering loss or damage to property by way of a lack of conformity. Taking all this evidence, the result should be that the Commission's proposal for the CESL covers all kinds of duties to protect the other party's integrity as to the person and its property.[12]

7.2 Defences and Excuses

Within the last four decades European Private Law not only developed a unitarian concept of breach of contract, but additionally a set of defences and excuses has been distilled from the rich stock of solutions in the national legal systems. The decision for the unitarian notion of breach of contract enabled the promoters of the discipline of European Private Law to develop a particular standard of liability and to distinguish that standard from particular defences against the claim for specific performance, like impossibility or impracticability, and from rules of hardship or change of circumstances. This new standard of liability was then amended by a general defence for the misbehaviour of the creditor. What is even more important, however, is the development of a so-called "right to cure" as the second standard defence of the debtor. All these developments now are reflected in the Commission's proposal for a Common European Sales Law where the Commission took over the dogmatical state of the art of European Private Law for its own proposal.

[11] See *Schmidt-Kessel/Kramme* in: Schmidt-Kessel (ed.), GEK-E (2014), Art. 87 no. 21–22.

[12] Contra *Faust* Leistungsstörungsrecht. In: Remien/Herrler/Limmer (eds.), Gemeinsames Europäisches Kaufrecht für die EU? (2012), 161, 162.

7.2.1 *Fault, Force Majeure and Change of Circumstances*

The first success of the discipline of European Private (or Contract) Law has been the rationalisation of prerequisites and effects of impediments excusing the debtor's non-performance. In this process it has become most helpful to accept that a claim for specific performance is by no means a self-evident consequence of a non-performance, but only one of the whole set of remedies. This dogmatical progress was connected to the recognition that the scope of application of the claim for the damages for non-performance is usually broader than the scope of claims for performance in kind. These two developments made it possible to bring the several topics concerning defences into a new systematical order.

7.2.1.1 "Unmöglichkeit", Force Majeure and Frustration

The topics or notions of *Unmöglichkeit*, force majeure and frustration all have in common, that they refer to impediments preventing the debtor from the fulfilment of the obligation. However, the function of the three topics within their respective legal systems differs from one system to the other. The German *Unmöglichkeit*, dealt with in § 275(1) BGB was originally seen as a type of breach of contract. This breach, if excused, brought the contract to an end or, if not excused, gave the creditor a right to terminate the contract and claim for damages. The effects on the claim for specific performance were much debated in theory while the text of the BGB was quite clear in saying that only an excused *Unmöglichkeit* would free the debtor from the claim for specific performance. In 2002 the legislator tried to unwind the bundle of legal consequences of *Unmöglichkeit* by reducing it to a defence against the claim for specific performance with some consequences as to the counter-performance and right to terminate the contract. However, the difficult drafting of the new texts invited German lawyers to underlie the new rules with the old concepts and, therefore, the significance of *Unmöglichkeit* for German contract law is heavily debated even today.

The French concept of *force majeure* may be found in Artt. 1147, 1148, 1722 Code Civil. The concept shows its effects mainly where the debtor owes an obligation to reach a specific result (*obligation de résultat*). Where one party owes such a duty to achieve a specific result, it may evade its liability only by successfully pleading *force majeure* (or *cas fortuit*). The core elements of force majeure have been developed by French jurisprudence and legal writers as being a fact which is *imprévisible* and *irresistible* and which is a kind of *exterritorial.* The classical consequence of *force majeure* under the French law is the exclusion of the claims for specific performance and damages. Moreover, the creditor may ask the court to declare the contract as being terminated under Art. 1184 Code Civil.[13]

[13] See for the French concept of force majeure *Schmidt-Kessel/Meyer* Supervening events and force majeure. In: Smits (ed.), Elgar Encyclopedia of Comparative Law (2006), 689.

English law on the other hand developed its doctrine of frustration only in the second half of the nineteenth century.[14] Starting from the idea of absolute contracts and a most strict liability (*Paradine v. Jane* [1647] EWHC KB J5) the English courts developed a general doctrine of frustration of contract starting with the famous decision of *Taylor v. Caldwell* from 1860. It was continued in the coronation cases of 1902 and 1903 of which (*Krell v. Henry* [1903] 2 KB 740) is the leading case. The later so-called "doctrine of frustration" was then developed mainly with cases of the two world wars and other cases of international crises after the Second World War. The core element of frustration is the impossibility of performance which may be a factual or a legal impossibility. The event bringing about such impossibility must be supervening, unforeseeable and external. As a consequence the courts decided to discharge both parties from the whole contract and this discharge was amended later on by a limited right to get restitution under the Law Reform (Frustrated Contracts) Act 1943. This rather radical doctrine was amended by some limits of frustration referring to a diverging contractual distribution of risks and cases of frustration self-induced by the debtor (or the creditor). However, this doctrine has always been restricted to cases of distortions of the contract which are so serious that the contract has to fall away all together. Only in some cases of liability for breach of covenant (which strictly speaking does belong to contract) English courts also accepted an excuse of one or more duties of one party without cancelling the whole relationship. The answer of practicing lawyers has been the development of so-called force majeure clauses which until today are a standard element of contracts under English law. These force majeure clauses usually work like the *force majeure* defence under French law.

Uniform sales law and the Principles of European Contract Law and the Draft Common Frame of Reference have taken over this idea of *force majeure* as a defence restricted to obligations. Therefore, force majeure in this international and European sense does not necessarily bring the contract to an end, but only excludes the claim for damages and, following the majority view, the claim for specific performance. The topic of impossibility on the other hand remained important as a defence against the claim for specific performance, however, restricted to such claims and without any necessary consequences concerning counter-performance. Therefore, the force majeure defence against claims for specific performance or damages has been, as a standard, been separated from impossibility as a pure defence against claims for specific performance. Moreover, with Art. 79 CISG, which has been more or less copied in Art. 8:108 PECL and Art. III.–3:104 DCFR international and European uniform law developed a standard formulation for the force majeure defence referring to an impediment beyond control which is unforeseeable and may not be overcome by alternative means.[15]

[14] See for the English doctrine of frustration *Treitel* Frustration and Force Majeure (1994).

[15] *Atamer* in: Kröll/Mistelis/Perales Viscasillas (eds.), CISG (2011), Art. 79 no. 43.

7.2.1.2 Hardship and "Imprévision"

Sanctity of contract is one of the basic principles in contract law throughout the western world. The binding force of contracts is, therefore, the starting point for all considerations regarding every instrument to enable contracts to react flexibly to cases of change of the circumstances under which the contract was originally concluded. In this sense Art. 6:111(1) PECL and Art. III.–1:110(1) DCFR emphasise the binding effect of the contract prior to formulate exceptional cases in which the general principle does not apply. Both articles refer to the onerosity of performance caused by the increase of the cost of performance or the diminishment of the value of the price. However, the criteria for the relevance of such onerosity differ: Under Art. 6:111(2) PECL the onerosity needs to be excessive, while Art. III.–1:110(2) DCFR refers to the consequence of the onerosity, which has to be that holding the debtor to the contract would be manifestly unjust. On the contrary, the CISG does not provide for a kind hardship clause (as opposed to the force majeure clause in Art. 79 CISG). However, many German authors have argued, that Art. 79 CISG also provides for a kind of *Opfergrenze* ("limit of sacrifice"), which is politically reasonable.[16]

The findings in uniform law reflect the situation under the national laws: Whereas all Member States to a certain extent provide for such exceptions to the binding force of the contract, most of them do not accept an aggregation of such exceptions under one general principle. French law traditionally refuses any general rule providing the judge with a possibility to intervene a binding contract. However, this general refusal by the civil courts is not shared by the administrative courts deciding on long term contracts with public utilities like contracts for the supply of gas or electricity.[17] English courts refused to adapt the contract in case of change of circumstances; moreover, the doctrine of frustration does usually not apply to simple cases of change of circumstances.[18] On the other hand, Italy codified the principles of *eccessiva onerosità* (excessive onerosity) in Art. 1467 Civil Code and German law even broader refers to change of circumstances in § 313 BGB, which is even not restricted to economic onerosity. Other Member States, e.g. Spain, absorbed this general idea.

German law also demonstrates that it is necessary to separate ideas of hardship, change of circumstances and *imprévision* from all cases of non-performance: While non-performance and the reasons for such non-performance only refers to the level of performance of an existing contract and sanctions in case of breach, the instruments here under consideration intervene one important step earlier in modifying or ending the contractual duties and obligations. Between such a modification of the contract and the legal reactions to breaches of contract a significant and even

16 See the references in *Schwenzer* in: Schechtriem, CISG (2013), Art. 79 no. 30 and *Magnus* in: Staudinger, CISG (2012), Art. 79 no. 24. Much more restrictive *Saenger* in: Ferrari/Kieninger, Internationales Vertragsrecht (2012).

17 See the case *Gaz de Bordeaux* [1916], D.P. 1916 3, 25.

18 See the case *Davis Contractors Ltd. vs. Fareham U.D.C.* [1956] A.C. 696 (H.L.).

categorical difference has to be stated. Moreover, the idea of a duty to renegotiate the contract—however useful it may be in practice—should be analyzed under this more basic approach going to the root of the contract and not being restricted to the realm of remedies for non-performance of a contractual obligation (may it be excused or not excused).

7.2.1.3 Fault, "Faute" and "Verschulden"

As to the topics, fault, *faute* and *Verschulden* the general principles of European contract law have emerged in a spectrum between the English idea of an absolute obligation and the Germanic fault principle in its subjective version advocated in the past by a minority of writers. The German idea of fault analyses the topic as a separate prerequisite to rules providing for remedies for breach of contract. Today the relevance of this principle has mainly being reduced to the remedy of damages for breach of contract while in the past other remedies and the right to terminate the contract in particular was also dependent on the fault of the debtor. This fault principle in its German or Germanic version presupposes an ethical responsibility of the party in breach. Coming from this rather extreme starting point, the principle has been made workable by the reference to objective standards of care combined with the explanation that the party, which is not able to meet such a standard of care, is responsible for taking over an obligation which he or she could not fulfil (so-called *Übernahmeverschulden*). Moreover, a basic capacity to act responsibly forms a (theoretically) important element of fault; this element is missing in case of minors below 7 years and restricted for the older group of minors up to 18.

On the other hand, the English starting point is the obligation of the debtor, and nothing else. The simple breach of contract is sufficient to give way to a claim for damages for breach of contract. No fault-based additional prerequisite needs to be fulfilled. Functionally, the only exception consists of the line of case law which lead to the doctrine of frustration of the whole contract. In this world of a rather strict liability, most parties agree on force majeure clauses which are a kind of common element of contracts and continental lawyers might even ask why such clauses are not implied by law into every English contract. With such clauses a non-performance of contractual obligation may be excused because of an impediment beyond control. For relationships of bailment, which are not necessarily qualified as contracts, such kind of rule even applies by law with a classical formula that the bailee is not responsible for the "acts of God and the Queen's enemies". This legal excuse in bailment as well as the contractual force majeure clauses in the formulations and effects comes very close to general rules of French law.

The French approach to the standard of contractual liability is somewhat in between the German fault principle and the English solution and might be qualified as the French version of the continental fault principle. This French version is based on essential division between *obligations de moyens* and *obligations de résultat*. In the first case the debtor providing for the necessary care is simply not in breach of the contract but in line with its contractual obligation, whereas, in cases of *obligations de résultat* an excuse by an external impediment is necessary for the debtor not to be liable in damages. This excuse is constituted by some sorts of impediment beyond control (*force majeure* and *cas fortuit*) which the debtor is not able to overcome or to avoid the consequences thereof.

It is this French solution, which has become the standard of international uniform law and European contract law: Art. 79(1) CISG has established the famous formula of impediments beyond control, which was taken over by Art. 8:108 PECL and Art. III.–3:104 DCFR. One could formulate, that European contract law has taken over the French approach. Compared to English law it establishes a force majeure clause implied by law and thereby absolved the lawyers from formulation an express term in the contract. In comparison with German law, internal impediments (mainly errors but also failures of servants or agents) may not excuse the debtor's non-performance. This analysis of the European standard of liability is reflected in Art. IV.H.–3:204 DCFR, where the words "beyond control" are missing in the description of the standard of the donor's liability.

7.2.2 *Wrongful Conduct of Creditor*

European Contract Law after all tends to become or remain a strict contractual liability regime. Under such a regime the misbehaviour of wrongful conduct of the creditor has to provide an additional defence of the debtor. By contrast, within the realm of the fault principle such an additional defence is superfluous insofar as the misbehaviour of the creditor excludes the fault for the debtor, which it usually does. While most Member States do not formulate an explicit defence for misbehaviour of the creditor Art. 80 CISG and Art. 8:101 (3) PECL do: In the case where a non-performance is attributable to the creditor because it was caused by his act or omission the debtor is excused from all the consequences of his non-performance.[19]

Therefore, the defence for wrongful conduct of the creditor goes significantly further than the force majeure defence described above: Not only claims for damages and specific performance are precluded, but also termination and price reduction. This fact shows that the liability of the debtor is not the only point to which such misbehavior of the creditor raises effects: Excluding termination for non-performance and price reduction signifies that the interest of the debtor to obtain the counter-performance (i.e. the price) also has to be protected in such a case. However, in this particular aspect no general line of compromise is found until now: While some of the Member States only protect the performance interest of the debtor by way of the damages claim, other Member States even confer a claim for the price which—as the case may be—has to be reduced. While the CISG is silent on this point, Art. 9:101(2) PECL proposed a kind of intermediate solution: The debtor may claim for the counter-performance unless he could have made a reasonable substitute transaction without significant effort or expense or performance would have been unreasonable in the circumstances.

[19] See also *Schmidt-Kessel/Meyer* Supervening events and force majeure. In: Smits (ed.), Elgar Encyclopedia of Comparative Law (2006), 689, 695.

7.2.3 The Right to Cure

The most innovative step in the process of Europeanization of contract law has been the development of a "right to cure" of the debtor as an additional defence against the remedies of the creditor in case of non-performance. The law confers on the debtor the option to avoid negative consequences of a first non-performance by using a kind of second chance for performance. Continental legal systems have enshrined such cure-defence in technical solutions like the German *Nachfristlösung*. Rules like Art. 1512(2) Italian Civil Code or §§ 281(1), 314(2), 323(1) BGB enshrine the protection of a presupposed right to cure in the normative programme; the other purpose on that programme is the determination of the weight of non-performance, i.e. whether it has become a fundamental non-performance giving way to termination of the contract. The authors of the Vienna convention did not entirely succeed in separating these two purposes from another; accordingly, Artt. 47-49 CISG are extremely difficult to understand. Within the general emergence of a common European Contract Law the right to cure has become separated from the *Nachfristlösung:* Starting with Art. 8:104 PECL the authors of these uniform texts started to formulate a separate "right" to cure a performance, which does not meet the contractual obligations completely. Later on, Artt. III.–3:301 to III.–3:205 DCFR developed this rather short article of PECL and its rather unclear legal consequences further to a separate defence for the debtor in breach: If the debtor manages to make a new and conforming tender which is not legitimately refused by the creditor, the debtor has a good defence against any remedy of the creditor apart from his liability for damages for any loss caused by the debtor's initial or subsequent non-performance or by the process of effecting cure.[20]

For the time being, in the DCFR the defence is restricted to cases of lack of conformity (without defining what is meant by this notion), Art. III.–3:201 DCFR. Furthermore, the right to cure is excluded in cases of fundamental non-performance or where the creditor has reason to believe that the debtor's performance was made with knowledge of the non-conformity or that the debtor will be unable to effect cure within a reasonable time or, lastly, that cure would be inappropriate in the circumstances. On the other hand, if the creditor sets an additional period for curing the defect, the creditor may within that period not resort to any remedy apart from withholding its own performance of the counter-obligations.

One could discuss whether such a "right" to cure is really a right in a legal sense or should be qualified rather as an onus of the creditor. This usually would be the case under national laws which have adopted the German version of the concept of *mora creditoris*. However, within the process of Europeanization of contract law this "right" results in a real obligation to accept cure, if no legitimate reason to refuse is at hand. As European Contract Law has not yet adopted the differentiating model of duty and onus as an instrument to organise the system of breach of contract law remedies, this qualification seems to be reasonable.

[20] See especially *Jud* Die Principles of European Contract Law als Basis des Draft Common Frame of Reference. In: Schmidt-Kessel (ed.), Der gemeinsame Referenzrahmen (2009), 71, 89.

7.2.4 The Concept(s) of CESL

The European Commission's proposal for a Common European Sales Law mainly carries forward the solutions developed in international sales law and in the European Private Law instruments. This is particularly true as to the standard of liability: The CESL neither provides for an absolute liability, under which the parties need to provide for their own standards by agreeing on force majeure and similar clauses, nor proposes to establish a general fault principle in the German sense. What is established is a general force majeure defence in Art. 88 CESL, which has its main effects in the realm of *obligations de résultat*, where the impediment explains, why the debtor did not reach the promised result. On the other hand, Art. 148(2) CESL clearly shows that in some cases—the *obligation de moyens*—the performance of reasonable skill and care is sufficient to avoid non-performance, even if the original purpose of the contract (the result not promised) is not fulfilled. In such a case, the defence under Art. 88 CESL remains without practical effect. Art. 148 CESL therefore clarifies that the general force majeure defence has its factual constraints.[21] This general standard decides on the availability of damages and specific performance; the latter may also be excluded when it becomes excessively burdensome, Art. 110(3)(b) CESL.[22]

By contrast, the defence of misbehaviour of the creditor excludes all remedies altogether as far as non-performance is caused by that misbehaviour. However, this general rule is not formulated in a general way, but may be found only in Art. 105(5) CESL for the remedies of the buyer and Art. 131(3) for the remedies of the seller. One should see in these two rules the basis for a general principle of the whole instrument; which may be supported also by the fact that both, Art. 155 for the remedies of the client and Art. 157 for the remedies of the service provider, refer to the two aforementioned articles.

Unfortunately, the Commission's proposal complicated the rules on cure significantly. In fact, cure remained dealt with in a long separate article; however, cure under Art. 109 CESL has been changed in many respects compared to the DCFR: First, the Commission dropped the general exclusion of cure, when this would be inappropriate in the circumstances, and only proposed an exhaustive list in Art. 109(4) CESL, which does not even contain the particular exclusion of cure if a first performance is made with knowledge of non-conformity. Second, after the time agreed for performance it is not entirely clear when the debtor has to effect a cure: The debtor first has to notify "without undue delay" his offer to cure (Art. 109(2) CESL) and has then a "reasonable period of time" to effect that cure (Art. 109(5) CESL), whereas the buyer may refuse such an offer if cure cannot be effected "promptly" (Art. 109(4)(a) CESL). Moreover, Art. 109(3) CESL now

---

[21] Whether this is also the case under the CISG has been discussed recently: See *Schwenzer* in: Schlechtriem/Schwenzer, CISG (2008) (for a majority view) and on the other hand *Schmidt-Kessel* Festschrift (2011).

[22] See also *Unberath/McKendrick* Supervening Events. In: Dannemann/Vogenauer (eds.), The Common European Sales Law in Context (2013), 579.

clarifies that an offer to cure is not precluded by notice of termination, which would otherwise effect termination of the contract. On the other hand, Art. 109(4)(c) CESL would exclude cure if a delay in performance would amount to fundamental non-performance. One could read this system as a deviation from the general rule that fundamental performed as such does not legitimize a refusal of an offer to cure which seems to be a difficult policy decision as such.

What is even more problematic, is the rule of Art. 106(3)(a) CESL excluding the seller's right to cure if the buyer is a consumer. This leads to the somewhat absurd situation that the consumer may require cure by way of repair or replacement of the goods, but is then not forced to accept it in the sense of the defence of cure. Moreover, the consequences of cure effected by the seller on the rights of the consumer are not clear. Without such rules a seller curing would always be under the risk that the necessary agreement, which allows the seller to cure would be subject to the right to withdraw under the rules of distance selling or door-step selling contracts, because this construction makes it necessary to construe the acceptance of cure by the consumer as being a separate contract to which the particular rules of consumer protection apply. This solution does not only exaggerate consumer protection but also leads to rather strange consequences as far as environment and sustainability aspects are concerned: It could be too risky for the trader to offer cure.[23]

On the other hand, the Commission's proposal kept the distinction between force majeure and impediments beyond control on the one hand and the more general rule on change of circumstances. The Commission also stuck to the much broader function of change of circumstances including the right of the judge to adapt the contract if prior negotiations had failed. In that respect, the proposal reflects the state of the art of European Contract Law.

7.3 Remedies for Breach of Contract

Thinking of remedies for breach of contract does not only mean thinking of the separate remedies and their prerequisites and consequences. Rather, it also includes thinking about questions of the relationship between remedies: Is there a kind of hierarchy of remedies? And how far the remedies to be found in the law may be combined? A complete picture of remedies includes these topics also.

7.3.1 Types of Remedies

European Private Law has developed five main types of remedies which today may be found in every Member State. One should, however, keep in mind that the

[23] For more disadvantages of the rule of Art. 106(3)(a) CESL see *Kossak* The Remedial System under the Proposed Common European Sales Law (CESL). In: EJCCL (1/2013), 7, 13.

five remedies of specific performance, withholding performance, termination of the contract, price reduction and damages do not constitute the complete picture, e.g. rules on a self-help sale or a right to deposit goods illegitimately not accepted are only two further examples. However, the five "main" aforementioned remedies constitute a kind of core of the remedial aspect of breach of contract in European Private Law and this paper henceforth is restricted to these five types.

7.3.1.1 Right to Specific Performance

From a comparative perspective the main difference between national rules on specific performance lays in the systematic position: For continental lawyers in general and the German lawyer in particular specific performance forms part of the obligation, which includes the right to enforce it in kind. In terms of remedies, i.e. functionally, one could speak of the obvious remedy; (Lando 2004). In contrast, for a common lawyer an order to specific performance is obviously restricted to a small number of cases and therefore—systematically—the exception.[24] It is quite clear that from a non-dogmatic, functional perspective these extreme positions have their weaknesses. The law of the European Union does not necessarily ask for specific performance and its enforcement by courts in all cases of contractual duties established under EU-law; however, it is self-evident that some provisions—mainly in the field of consumer protection—ask for performance in kind, like the obligations of replacement and repair in Art. 3(2) and (3) Consumer Sales Directive 1999/44/EC and their equivalence in Art. 4(6) and (7) Package Travel Directive 90/314/EEC.[25]

It is not too astonishing that uniform sales law and the several instruments of European Private Law attempt to find a line of compromise between these extreme systematically divergent positions.[26] While Art. 28 CISG abstained from deciding the case by referring to national law Art. 9:102 PECL and Art. III.-3:302 DCFR both try to follow a line of compromise which is based on the perception that, functionally speaking, the differences between the separate solutions are restricted to one single situation which consists of the case in which the creditor could have made a reasonable substitute transaction without significant effort or expense (including the idea of a rather strong liability in damages). However, all three approaches, the CISG as well as the European instruments, take the remedy approach to specific performance as a starting point and, at least, the two European instruments see the scope of obligation of such remedy closer than the scope of obligation of the claim

[24] See also *Schmidt-Kessel* Remedies for Breach of Contract in European Private Law. In: Schulze (ed.), New features in Contract Law (2007), 183, 187.

[25] See also *Remien* Folgen von Leistungsstörungen. In: Schulte-Nölke/Schulze (eds.), Europäisches Vertragsrecht im Gemeinschaftsrecht (2002), 139, 141 et seq.

[26] See generally *Weller* Die Struktur des Erfüllungsanspruchs im BGB, common law und DCFR—ein kritischer Vergleich, JZ (2008), 765.

for damages. One could therefore say that that classical idea of an obligation including the competence of enforcement in kind loses one of its legs.

The legal systems of the Member States agree on most limits of a right to specific performance while differing in their formal organisation. Impossibility (today) always excludes the remedy, Art. 9:102(2)(a) PECL, Art. III.-3:302(3)(a) DCFR. Even where specific performance is not impossible but unreasonable in the circumstances, most legal systems under consideration concur in excluding specific performance; however, the formulations of the thresholds differ significantly from unreasonable effort or expense (Art. 9:102(2)(b) PECL) to unreasonable burdensome or expensive (Art. III-3:302(3)(b) DCFR) and to yardsticks of disproportionality (Art. 3(3) Consumer Sales Directive 1999/44/EC[27], § 275(2) BGB). Functionally, the European legal systems also agree on the general exclusion of an enforcement of *obligation de faire* services or performances of such a personal character that it would be unreasonable to enforce it (Art. 1144 French Code Civil, Art. 9:102(2)(c) PECL, Art. 3.-3:302(3)(c) DCFR), which in German law may be found in the rules on the enforcement of a judgement which orders specific performance but will not be enforced in kind by the responsible institutions, §§ 887, 888 *Zivilprozessordnung* (Act of Civil Procedure).

The true functional difference between the several solutions is connected to generic obligations or more generally formulated to cases where the aggrieved party may reasonably obtain performance from another source by a substitute transaction. While it is quite self-evident for English law that specific performance would be excluded in such a case, on the German law only a small minority of authors denies the possibility of enforcement in kind.[28] The authors of the DCFR tried to solve the policy issue not by excluding specific performance but by applying the principle of mitigation to reduce damage in such cases, if the creditor had unreasonably insisted on specific performance, Art. III-3:302(5) DCFR.

The Commission's proposal for the Common European Sales Law sticks to the general approach developed for European Private Law: Specific performance is organized as a remedy which is distinct from the obligation and the notion of obligation. However, what is surprising is the reduced number of exclusions of the remedy in cases of impossibility and unreasonableness, Art. 110(3) CESL. The famous services-exception was dropped altogether and may not even be found in the particular rules on connected services, see Art. 155 CESL. Also the—rather complicated—compromise of broadening the mitigation principle to solve the policy issue in cases of a reasonably possible substitute transaction does not appear in the Commission's proposal. This is clearly a step backwards.

[27] See the restrictive interpretation by ECJ, Judgment of 16 June 2011 in joined cases C-65/09 and C-87/09—*Weber and Putz*.

[28] See *Schmidt-Kessel* in: Prütting/Wegen/Weinreich (eds.), § 275 BGB (2013) no. 20 and 25.

7.3.1.2 Right to Withhold Performance

The right to withhold performance is of a twofold character: On the one hand it identifies the time of performance depending on the creditor's rendering counter-performance; this is the approach in Art. 58 CISG and § 273 BGB. On the other hand the right to withhold performance works as a remedy against the creditor who is in breach regarding counter-performance; in this respect the right to withhold performance may rearrange the content of the contractual duties.[29]

Rights to withhold performance are well known as an element of the general rules of the law of contract of the Member States, whereas, it is unusual in Community Law so far.[30] Within the instruments of European Private Law the authors opted for establishing a kind of modern *exceptio non adimpleti contractus* first in Art. 9:201(1) PECL and then in Art. III.-3:401(1) DCFR, thereby reflecting the traditional idea of the functional synallagma.

Particular rules apply to cases where one party is obliged to render advanced performance: Such an agreement includes taking the risk of insolvency of the other part. This risk is somewhat balanced in the texts under consideration by an additional right to withhold performance based on foreseeable future non-performance of the other party. Such rules—on the national level generalized in § 321 BGB—has led to Art. 71 CISG on which Artt. 8:101(1) and 9:201(2) PECL have been based. The authors of the DCFR reduced these rules to Art. III:401(2) and (3) DCFR and included a separate duty to give notice of the fact that the creditor withholds performance.

The Commission proposes to take over the basic structure of the DCFR provision by establishing in Art. 113(1) CESL the general right to withhold performance in the sense of an *exceptio non adimpleti contractus* in the classical sense. Moreover, the aforementioned insecurity defence construed as another right to withhold performance was included in paragraph (2) of the provision. However, under Art. 113 CESL the buyer is proposed not to have the duty to inform the seller.[31]

7.3.1.3 Termination of the Contract

Compared to the binding force of the contract the remedy of termination seems to be somewhat contradictory. Therefore, it is difficult to find an entirely common ground for the remedy of termination in Europe. However, some elements are—at least functionally—beyond discussion: Modern rules on termination are based on a non-performance of some significant weight, which usually is enshrined in the

---

[29] See *Schmidt-Kessel* Remedies for Breach of Contract in European Private Law. In: Schulze (ed.), New Features in Contract Law (2007), 183, 188.

[30] See *Schmidt-Kessel* above.

[31] See also *Schopper* Verpflichtungen und Abhilfen der Parteien eines Kaufvertrages oder eines Vertrages über die Bereitstellung digitaler Inhalte. In: Wendehorst/Zöchling-Jud (eds.), Am Vorabend eines Gemeinsamen Europäischen Kaufrechts (2012), 131.

notion of fundamental non-performance. Moreover, it is most common to combine the idea of a fundamental non-performance with a kind of *Nachfristlösung* in one way or the other: In some legal systems the *Nachfrist* is the rule and this *Nachfrist* is dispensable in case of a fundamental breach; this, e.g., is the case in the younger German law of obligations, cf. § 323(1) and (2) BGB. The alternative is the idea of making time of the essence by giving notice in setting a further period, while fundamental breach applies as a kind of general rule; this is the concept of Art. 49 CISG, taken over by Art. 9:301 PECL and Art. III-3:502, 503 DCFR.

The general concept of the reference to a fundamental breach was taken over also by European Commission when proposing Art. 134 CESL. In adaption of the solutions developed under the CISG, PECL and the DCFR Art. 135 CESL amends the general rule by a *Nachfrist*-solution for cases of delay of performance. The purpose of the restriction of this *Nachfrist*-solution to cases of delay is not to open the door to termination in cases of non-conformity which does not amount to a fundamental non-performance. However—as *Faust* has pointed out for the DCFR—Art. 135 CESL would also cover the case of delay in replacement or repair of a non-conformity which is not fundamental.[32] One could avoid this consequence by interpreting the term delay as deliberately excluding all situations of non-conformity. However, this is not self-evident. From a policy point of view the answer is also not entirely clear: On the one hand a seller disputing the non-conformity always risks to run into termination even where he is acting in *bona fide*. On the other hand it seems to be necessary to provide for cases where the seller repudiates his obligation to provide for replacement or repair and a substitute transaction of the buyer is not reasonable or even possible. A solution would probably be the introduction of a general concept of supervening fundamentality of the breach, which is originally non-fundamental simply by referring to the behaviour of the party in breach.

The party aggrieved by non-performance usually brings about termination by a (constitutive) unilateral declaration. An ipso facto-avoidance of the contract for fundamental breach does not belong the common core of European Contract Law anymore, nor is a court decision presupposed for bringing the contract to an end in case of fundamental non-performance or equivalent situations. Therefore, European instruments including Art. 137 CESL opted for a notice of termination as the instrument to bring the termination about.

European Contract Law does not distinguish between sorts of termination with retroactive active effects or *ex nunc*-effect only. The German remedies of *Rücktritt* and *Kündigung* are integrated in one single remedy of termination. The Vienna Convention answers to this policy issue by establishing a kind of partial termination in case of instalment sales contracts, see Art 73 CISG. By contrast, the Principles of European Contract Law—following English ideas of partial failure of consideration—only modified the rules on restitution with the effect, that restitution was excluded, as far as performances of both parties were rendered under the contract and as far as they correspond. The DCFR then combined both instruments

[32] See *Faust* Leistungsstörungsrecht. In Remien/Herrler/Limmer (eds.), Gemeinsames Europäisches Kaufrecht für die EU? (2012), 161.

in Art. III.-3:506 DCFR establishing the possibility of partial termination, where the obligations are sufficiently divisible, and the exclusion of restitution to the extent that a conforming performance by one party has been met by performance by the other in Art. III-3:511(1) DCFR. The relationship between both instruments never became clear in the considerations of the Study Group on the European Civil Code responsible for this part of the DCFR. The European Commission for the CESL now has taken over approach: On the one hand, Art. 137 CESL refers to divisible obligations under the contract enabling the parties to a partial termination and, on the other hand, the proposal restricts the retroactive effect of termination by Art. 172(3) CESL. The provision excludes the necessity to return of, what is received, to any instalment or parts of performance, where the obligations on both sides have been fully performed or where the price of what has been done remains payable under the instrument, c.f. Art. 8(2) CESL. This mixed solution now seems to become the new standard of European Contract Law.

7.3.1.4 Price Reduction

Price reduction is the remedy where the traditional divide between Common Law and Civil Law maybe stays even today: While continental legal systems provide for some sorts of price reduction at least for sales contracts following the antique idea of *actio quanti* minoris, English law originally refused ideas of a price reduction, which is not construed by way of damages for the lack of quality; cf. *Attorney General v. Blake*; *Birse Construction Ltd. v. Eastern Telegraphical Ltd.* However, price reduction is also well known to the European Common Law countries, today, because of the transposition of the Consumer Sales Directive 1999/44/EC, which explicitly provides for remedy of price reduction.[33]

This English and Irish development is in line with the emergence of price reduction as a general remedy in European Contract Law: Starting with Art. 50 CISG price reduction nowadays forms part of the common core of European Contract Law.[34] The amount of reduction usually is calculated following the proportionality test which leads to a reduction of the price which is proportional to the loss in value.

The European Commission has proposed to integrate a right to reduce the price in Art. 120 CESL following what is now the leading idea of price reduction in European Contract Law: The remedy refers to cases of non-performance by non-conformity and the reduction of the price is proportional to the decrease in the value. The main difference to the traditional English approach lays in the consequence that the price is reduced even if the non-performance did not cause any loss.[35]

---

[33] See also *Chen-Wishart/Magnus* Termination, Price Reduction and Damages. In: Dannemann/Vogenauer (eds.), The Common European Sales Law in Context (2013), 671.

[34] See *Schmidt-Kessel* Remedies for Breach of Contract in European Private Law. In: Schulze (ed.), New Features in Contract Law (2007), 183, 191.

[35] See *Chen-Wishart/Magnus* above.

7.3.1.5 Damages

A strict liability for non-performance combined with a force majeure-defence has emerged as being the common core of European Contract Law related to damages. Apart from non-performance and the force majeure-defence the loss to be compensated and causation of that loss by non-performance are the other two main prerequisites of contractual liability in damages in Europe. For causation, the classical *conditio sine qua non*-formula is usually used as the starting point. Further considerations take into account ideas of adequacy of imputation, foreseeability of the loss and other normative considerations. Member States' legal systems here differ as to the standard of how far decisions by first instance judges are controlled in the appellate courts: While some Member States have developed a large number of legal rules how to determine causation, others simply refer to the competence of the first instance judge in fact finding.

Damages for non-performance mainly refer to the performance interest, which means that the creditor has to be put into the position which he would have been if the obligation had been duly performed or, at least, as nearly as possible in that position. Following the majority view of legal authors and legal systems in Europe Art. 160 CESL clarifies that damages be calculated under this basic rule also include loss suffered and gain of which the creditor has been deprived. Therefore, damages for non-performance in European Private Law do not only cover performance interests, but also protect by way of monetary compensation the integrity of the creditor and his assets. As the Vienna Convention and the Principles of European Contract Law did not cover any pre-contractual misbehaviour of the parties, there was no need to determine which rules would apply in case of the breach of a pre-contractual obligation under these instruments. This status changed under the DCFR, however, without any consequences for the black letter rules on damages. Also the proposal of the European Commission for a Common European Sales Law does not clarify, whether the general rule in Art. 160 CESL also applies to damages for breach of pre-contractual duties, which in many cases only protect the reliance interest of the party aggrieved

A particular policy problem derives from the question whether also non-economic loss may be compensated. English and German law follow a rather restrictive line mainly including non-economic loss in the form of pain and suffering, but excluding other forms of non-economic loss such like loss of enjoyment. Other legal systems are much less restrictive in this point. The DCFR intentionally broadened the scope of losses covered by damages for non-performance and included non-economic loss without any restriction to the definition of loss. Pain and suffering and impairment of the quality of life have been explicitly included in the notion of loss as examples and therefore were able to be compensated, Art. III.-3:701(3) DCFR, without excluding other immaterial losses from being recoverable. This broad approach under the DCFR would have included also immaterial losses due to the breach of duties under data protection and privacy laws included in the contractual relationship. The European Commission in its proposal on a Common European Sales law was much more reluctant by explicitly confining the notion of loss to only some forms of non-economic loss (plus all sorts of economic losses) in Art. 2(c) CESL-Reg. Other forms of non-economic losses such as impairment of the quality of life or loss of enjoyment are explicitly excluded and therefore may not be compensated in case of breach. This raises the question as to the relationship to—mostly EU-law-based—remedies for contractual or quasi-contractual losses like immaterial loss for breach of duties in the field of data protection or privacy.

Not every loss caused by the non-performance is covered by the remedy of damages: This is quite self-evident where the creditor has contributed to the loss in one way or the other. Loss which is as such attributable to the creditor needs not be compensated by the debtor even in case of non-performance and the same holds true where the creditor could have reduced the loss by taking reasonable steps, but did not fulfil this duty to mitigate. These rules belong to the general standard of European Sales Law and are taken over by the European Commission in Artt. 162, 163 CESL. From the German perspective not self-evident is the restriction of the damages to foreseeable losses. However, this foreseeability test or contemplation rule is found in most European legal systems and was taken over also by Art. 74 CISG, Art. 9:503 PECL and Art. III-3:703 DCFR. The reason behind these rules is the calibration of the damages to the mechanisms of contract interpretation: The basic idea is that a debtor should be liable for non-performance only in so far as he could reasonably be expected to have foreseen the loss as a likely result of the non-performance when the contract was concluded. The foreseeability or contemplation rule, therefore, is a functional equivalent to ideas of adequacy and purpose of the contractual or legal duty or obligation.

A rather difficult topic is touched upon with the rules on substitute transactions and the calculation of damages on the bases of a current price. First, one has to make clear the perspective of the respective rules which have been passed down generations of uniform and European instruments: Artt. 75, 76 CISG had been more or less copied by Artt. 9:506, 507 PECL and Artt. III.-3:706, 707 DCFR, from which they have been taken over by the European Commission for the preparation of Artt. 164, 165 CESL. German lawyers which are trained in drawing lines between the overarching idea of specific performance and the changeover to damages under headlines like *Schadensersatz statt der Leistung, kleiner* and *großer Schadensersatz* as well as *Differenz-* and *Surrogationsmethode* will usually see in those articles and particular in Art. 164 CESL and its predecessors a rule which solves the concurrency of specific performance and damages. Those authors must see in the termination requirement, which is found in Art. 164 CESL as in all predecessors, an instrument ordering a kind of priority of specific performance and they are encouraged in this way of thinking by the fact, that the CISG originally had been very reluctant towards termination and attempted to keep the contract alive wherever possible. Looking at the original purpose of both rules encapsulated in Artt. 164, 165 CESL they have to be read as particular instances of the litigation principle and have nothing to do with the idea of concurrency of remedies. The main problem of substitute transactions and calculation of damages on the basis of current prices is to prevent the party aggrieved from dealing in a reckless manner and causing additional loss which should not be compensated. The reference to termination from this perspective only has the function to avoid speculative behaviour of the party aggrieved by the non-performance. It would be not in line with such purpose to exclude the calculation on the basis of a substitute transaction in cases, where that substitute transaction has taken place before termination had been declared. And the same holds true in cases, where the substitute transaction does not replace the whole performance of the party in breach but only part of it as the case may be where a buyer organizes repair himself by a substitute transaction and then asks only for the costs of this substitute transaction. Sticking to termination as a decisive criterion would clearly be a legislative fault. The significant change in the importance of specific performance, which had taken place in the CESL compared to the CISG, leads to the need to adapt that criterion. An alternative criterion could be e.g. the reference to the prerequisites of termination on the one hand and the relevance of partial termination on the other. This would presuppose that the possibility to speculate for the party aggrieved ends in the moment, when the substitute transaction has taken place at latest. Here will be much to do in the forthcoming legislative process.

7.3.2 A Hierarchy of Remedies?

Rules on the relationship of remedies usually contain hidden policy choices. Sometimes these policy choices are laid open as it is the case with the general rule of priority of specific performance under German law, the consequences of which are not entirely clear until today. European Contract Law as the international instruments usually abstain from policy choices in such rules of hierarchy or other rules concerning to the relationship of different remedies.[36] Rules on the relationship or combination of remedies usually do not indicate elements of hierarchy. By contrast, the proposal of the European Commission for a Common European Sales Law includes two rules which simply indicate that generally no remedy prevails the other. Artt. 106(6) and 131(3) CESL order that remedies which are not incompatible may be cumulated. Therefore, the proposal sticks to the general tendency of European Contract Law aforementioned. This general approach is supported by the split of the buyer's remedy of specific performance dealing with non-conformity issues by replacement or repair on the one hand and the seller's right to cure on the other. While many national legal orders and German law in particular integrated the idea of the defence by curing in the rules of remedies by establishing a priority of replacement or repair, the split of the two distinct ideas now enables the legislator to avoid any idea of hierarchy of remedies. Moreover, as seen above the termination requirement for substitute transactions and the calculation of damages on the basis of current price does not represent ideas of hierarchy either, but only attempt to prevent the party aggrieved from speculation to the detriment of the party in breach.

[36] See also *Schmidt-Kessel* Remedies for Breach of Contract in European Private Law. In: Schulze (ed.), New Features in Contract Law (2007), 183, 193.

The only hint remaining to some sorts of hierarchy is the idea of a possible incompatibility of remedies, which could exclude one remedy because the other was brought forward. However, such a rule would not lead to a kind of fixed hierarchy, but only aims to protect the legitimate reliance of the party in breach in the binding nature of the declarations of the party aggrieved by the non-performance. Moreover, the prevention of double recovery is an important aim of such incompatibility. The overall approach of the CESL therefore remains.

7.3.3 Combination of Remedies

The aforementioned rules of Artt. 106(6) and 131(4) CESL represent the general approach of European Contract Law to questions relating to the combination of remedies: Every combination is possible as far as not incompatible. This general rule had its first general predecessor in Art 8:102 PECL, whereas, the CISG only ordered that the party aggrieved is not deprived of any claim for damages by exercising any other remedies, Artt. 45(2) and 61(2) CISG. The PECL rule was simply copied into the DCFR in Artt. III-3:102 which then provided the model for the aforementioned rules in the European Commission's proposal.

European Contract Law strengthens this general position by a set of particular rules dealing with the combination of remedies, which usually are incompatible in part: E.g., Art. 120(3) CESL concretises the incompatibility of prize reduction and damages to the loss compensated by the price reduction and enables the buyer to ask for damages for any further loss suffered. A similar example is found in Art. 166(3) CESL, which declares any further loss recoverable beyond the interest the debtor has to pay. Today the general rules of a free cumulation of remedies as far as not incompatible seems to be so self-evident that the European Commission even abstained to propose a clarifying rule that damages are not precluded by the fact that the right to specific performance is excluded, cf. Art. 9:103 PECL and Art. III.-3:303 DCFR.

Based on its predecessors the CESL as proposed by the European Commission brings forward a rather pragmatic system of remedies: The general idea to compensate the party aggrieved by non-performance is managed in a rather flexible way in which policy decisions have been laid open.

7.4 Conclusion

Contracts are working unless breached or otherwise disturbed. Contract law, therefore, has to provide for the situations of such breaches. The first policy issue concerning rules for breach of contract, therefore, is to provide for a pragmatic structure helping parties and courts out of the situation. Path dependencies in dogmatics and notions are not helpful in this respect, but they keep an enormous amount of practical and theoretical experience which without good reason should not get lost in a process of legislation in the field of breach of contract and its consequences.

On the other hand, legislation in European Contract Law inevitably leads to different *façons de parler* and dogmatic codes in the field of breach of contract, in particular. This also has something to do with the fact that the general binding nature of contract as well as its limits, and particularly in the field of termination were not developed completely, when the tendency of nationalisation overcame the *use commune* approach in European universities in the nineteenth century.

The proposal of the European Commission for a Common European Sales Law as to breach of contract and its consequences is certainly based on what could today be named the common core of European Contract Law. This does not prevent the Commission from copying old mistakes or from the omission to adapt rules taken over from earlier instruments like the CISG, the PECL or the DCFR without consciousness of the changes in the system altogether. Main directions of these changes are the strengthening of the specific performance, the introduction of a separate idea of a right to cure and, finally, the lowering of the threshold for termination of the contract compared to CISG and PECL. Legal theory and legal practise will have to cope with these developments and they will be able to do so.

References

Journals and Articles

Diskussionsentwurf eines Schuldrechtsmodernisierungsgesetzes. In: ZRP (2000), p 454–456

Kossak M The Remedial System under the Proposed Common European Sales Law (CESL). In: European Journal of Commercial Contract Law (1/2013), p 7–18

Weller M-P Die Struktur des Erfüllungsanspruchs im BGB, common law und DCFR—ein kritischer Vergleich. In: JZ (2008), p 765–773

Books and chapters

Chen-Wishart M/Magnus U Termination, Price Reduction and Damages. In: Dannemann G/Vogenauer S (eds.), The Common European Sales Law in Context, Oxford (2013), p 647–686

Demogue R Traité des obligations, Bd.V. Paris (1925)

Faber W Dienstleistungsverträge. In: Wendehorst C/Zöchling-Jud B (eds.), Am Vorabend eines Gemeinsamen Europäischen Kaufrechts, Wien (2012), p 147–224

Faust F Leistungsstörungsrecht. In: Remien O/Herrler S/Limmer P (eds.), Gemeinsames Europäisches Kaufrecht für die EU?, Munich (2012), p 161–188

Jud B Die Principles of European Contract Law als Basis des Draft Common Frame of Reference. In: Schmidt-Kessel M (ed.), Der gemeinsame Referenzrahmen, Munich (2009), p 71–92

Lando O Non-Performance (Breach) of Contracts. In: Hartkamp A et al. (eds.), Towards a European Civil Code, Nijmegen (2004), p 505–515

Rabel E Das Recht des Warenkaufs, Bd.I. Berlin (1936)

Remien O Folgen von Leistungsstörungen. In: Schulte-Nölke H/Schulze R (eds.), Europäisches Vertragsrecht im Gemeinschaftsrecht, Bonn (2002), p 139–150

Schlechtriem P Vertragsordnung und außervertragliche Haftung. Frankfurt am Main (1972)

Schmidt-Kessel M Standards vertraglicher Haftung nach englischem Recht. Munich (2003)

Schmidt-Kessel M Remedies for Breach of Contract in European Private Law—Principles of European Contract Law, Aquis Communautaire and Common Frame of Reference. In: Schulze R (ed.), New features in Contract Law, Munich (2007), p 183–196

Schmidt-Kessel M Festschrift für Ingeborg Schwenzer zum 60. Geburtstag. Zurich (2011), p 1513–1527

Schmidt-Kessel M/Meyer K Supervening events and force majeure. In: Smits JM (ed.), Elgar Encyclopedia of Comparative Law, Cheltenham (2006), p 689–698

Schopper A Verpflichtungen und Abhilfen der Parteien eines Kaufvertrages oder eines Vertrages über die Bereitstellung digitaler Inhalte. In: Wendehorst C/Zöchling-Jud B (eds.), Am Vorabend eines Gemeinsamen Europäischen Kaufrechts, Wien (2012), p 107–145

Treitel G Frustration and Force Majeure. London (1994)

Unberath H/McKendrick E Supervening Events. In: Dannemann G/Vogenauer S (eds.), The Common European Sales Law in Context, Oxford (2013), p 62–580

Commentaries

Atamer YM in: Kröll S/Mistelis L/Perales Viscasillas P (eds.), UN Convention on Contracts for the International Sale of Goods (CISG), Munich (2011), Art. 79

Magnus U in: Staudinger J, Wiener UN-Kaufrecht (CISG), Munich (2012), Art. 79

Saenger I in: Ferrari F/Kieninger M, Internationales Vertragsrecht, Munich (2012), Art. 79

Schmidt-Kessel M in: Prütting H/Wegen G/Weinreich G (eds.), BGB Kommentar, Munich (2013), § 275 BGB

Schmidt-Kessel M/Kramme M in: Schmidt-Kessel M (ed.), Entwurf eines Gemeinsamen Europäischen Kaufrechts, Munich (2014), Art. 87

Schwenzer I in: Schlechtriem P/Schwenzer I (eds.), Kommentar zum Einheitlichen UN-Kaufrecht, Munich (2008), Art. 79

Zoll F in: Schulze R (ed.), CESL Commentary, Munich (2012), Art. 87

Chapter 8
Change of Circumstances

Luz M. Martínez Velencoso

Abstract In many legal systems a fundamental change to the circumstances of a contract can serve to loosen the binding nature of that contract. The legal doctrine that provides this effect is called by various names in the different European countries. In previous European instruments, such as the PECL and the DCFR, the term used has been "change of circumstances", and this is also the term settled on for the CESL, specifically in Article 89 CESL. When the exact fulfillment of a contract becomes disproportionate due to an unexpected change of circumstances, Article 89 contains a duty to renegotiate. If, within a reasonable period of time, the parties do not reach an agreement, they may request the assistance of the court or arbitrator. The judge may decide to adapt the contract taking into account the hypothetical will of the parties, or declare the dissolution of the contract and lay down the conditions for so doing.

The application of Article 89 CESL should not be problematic in the different European countries as there are a lot of similarities between the various European legal systems in this field, both in the terms used and the results achieved, as well as in its treatment by legal scholars.

Keywords Change of circumstances · Unforeseen circumstances · Imprévision · Geschäftsgrundlage · Eccessiva onerosità sopravvenuta · Hardship, clause "rebus sic stantibus" · Frustration · Adaptation of the contract · Termination

8.1 Change of Circumstances in the CESL

8.1.1 Legal Precedents

8.1.1.1 Regulation in the PECL

The principle of "pacta sunt servanda" is universally recognised. Contracts are binding because individuals are willing to fulfill them and they also trust that their

L. M. Martínez Velencoso (✉)
LL.M. Humboldt Universität Berlin, University of Valencia, Valencia, Spain
e-mail: luz.martinez@uv.es

© Springer International Publishing Switzerland 2015

J. Plaza Penadés, L. M. Martínez Velencoso (eds.), *European Perspectives on the Common European Sales Law*, Studies in European Economic Law and Regulation 4,
DOI 10.1007/978-3-319-10497-3_8

counterparts will do the same. If all contracts were generally reviewable, the confidence of the economic agents would vanish, and it is confidence that is fundamental in any economic system. In any case, the idea that, as a general rule, contracts are binding and, therefore, in the case of non-performance there would be some kind of responsibility, is a necessary condition for the efficient functioning of the economic system.

However, in many legal systems a fundamental change to the circumstances of a contract can serve to loosen the binding nature of that contract. The legal doctrine that provides this effect is called by various names in the different European countries. In previous European instruments, such as the Principles of European Contract Law (PECL) and the Draft Common Frame of Reference (DCFR), the term used has been "change of circumstances", and this is also the term settled on for the Common European Sales Law (CESL). Although their rules are very similar, these instruments will be discussed separately, and then compared.

In the PECL the doctrine of change of circumstances is regulated in art. 6:111, which establishes that:

(1) A party is bound to fulfill its obligations even if performance has become more onerous, whether because the cost of performance has increased or because the value of the performance it receives has diminished.
(2) If, however, performance of the contract becomes excessively onerous because of a change of circumstances, the parties are bound to enter into negotiations with a view to adapting the contract or terminating it, provided that:

    (a) the change of circumstances occurred after the time of conclusion of the contract,
    (b) the possibility of a change of circumstances was not one which could reasonably have been taken into account at the time of conclusion of the contract, and
    (c) the risk of the change of circumstances is not one which, according to the contract, the party affected should be required to bear.

(3) If the parties fail to reach agreement within a reasonable period, the court may:

    (a) terminate the contract at a date and on terms to be determined by the court; or
    (b) adapt the contract in order to distribute between the parties in a just and equitable manner the losses and gains resulting from the change of circumstances.

In either case, the court may award damages for the loss suffered through a party refusing to negotiate or breaking off negotiations contrary to good faith and fair dealing.

The aim of this article is to prevent that an increase of costs incurred as a result of unforeseen circumstances should be born entirely by one of the parties. In this sense, the article reflects the modern tendency to confer on the court the power to moderate the rigor of the principle "pacta sunt servanda".

In the opinion of Lando and Beale (2000), an argument against the inclusion of a provision of this type could be made in that the defence of the principle "pacta sunt servanda" is an incentive for the parties to introduce appropriate clauses in the contract preventing them from such a risk. However, in their opinion, experience shows that the parties do not have adequate means or often do not pay attention to possible future contingencies, or even include clauses that do not cover all eventualities.

Consequently, it is not useful to rely on the parties' ability to protect themselves from these kinds of contingences.

Nevertheless it has to be taken into account that the Principles are designed as default rules, so that the parties may adopt, in the contract, any other mechanism as to how the benefits may be adapted, or how any negotiation may be carried out. They can even provide that in the case of certain specific change of circumstances, this will not affect the contract.

The application of art. 6:111 requires that:

1. Compliance has become excessively burdensome, in the sense that it must have caused a serious imbalance in the contract, not only that it has become more onerous. As the precept states, this imbalance may be due to an increase in the cost of compliance, or a devaluation of the value of the service (for example, in the case of a work execution contract, the value of the performance of the contractor is devalued when it is determined according to a price index that unexpectedly depreciates).
2. The change of circumstances must occur after the conclusion of the contract; but it could also be that such circumstances already existed at that time without any of the parties having realised. In such cases, the rules on mistake would be applicable.
3. The change of circumstances should not have been foreseen at the time of the conclusion of the contract. In other words, that change should be unpredictable, since the law cannot protect irresponsible conduct. This requirement should be interpreted in the same way as in the case of non-performance, taking into account the parameter of the reasonable man. Consequently, any event is unforeseeable when a reasonable man in the same situation as the parties could not have anticipated it. (For example, if traffic is interrupted regularly in a particular region as a result of a strike, a reasonable person would not choose a route through the region with the hope that on that day in question he could move freely, but would opt for another route).
4. Finally, it must be decided whether the party affected by the change of circumstances should bear the risk associated with such a change, either because he expressly assumed it, or because it is a speculative contract. In these cases, the party may not invoke the application of art. 6:111.

As for the consequences, a duty to renegotiate is established. According to art. 6.111(2), the party that suffers the effects of the supervening hardship must start the renegotiation process within a reasonable time, specifying the effects that the change of circumstances has had on the contract.

The negotiation process should be carried out in accordance with the requirements of good faith; for example, there is bad faith if a party enters into a contract with a third party that is incompatible with the contract in the process of renegotiation. Usually the principle of good faith requires that every aspect of the dispute between the parties is addressed in the negotiations. The consequences of the breach of the duty to renegotiate is compensation for losses suffered as a result of the refusal to bargain for one party, or the breakdown of negotiations in a way that is contrary to good faith. This sanction is not contemplated for instance, in art. 6.2.1 of the UNIDROIT principles that regulates the "hardship", a term that is similar to the "change of circumstances".

The immediate consequence of change of circumstances is the renegotiation of the contract. It is intended that the parties reach an agreement that is the same that they would have reached if the new circumstances had been known at the moment of the conclusion of the contract. This preference for the renegotiation has its explanation in the fact that the parties to the contract are those best placed to recover the equilibrium of the contract.

Both art. 6.2.3 UNIDROIT principles and art. 6.111(3) PECL provide for judicial intervention in the event of the failure of the renegotiation process. The court's intervention is seen as the last resort; however, the judge is granted great discretionary powers. In this sense, the court could terminate or modify the contract; or they could even require the parties to make a final effort to renegotiate if they consider that there is still a chance to save the contract. Also they would be entitled, if permitted by their national law, to appoint a mediator to assist the parties.

If negotiations end unsuccessfully, the court can adapt the contract to the new circumstances, restoring the initial equilibrium and making sure that the extra costs arising from the unforeseen circumstances are shared equally between the parties. Unlike the risks arising from impossibility of performance, in cases of change of circumstances the parties must share the risks of unforeseen events.

The judicial resolution could involve, or not, depending on the nature of the change of circumstances in the case, a price adjustment or an extension of the period established to fulfill the contract. However, the variation would not necessarily reflect the total loss suffered by the changed circumstances since the court has to consider, for example, the extent to which a party has assumed the risk and the extent that the party entitled to require performance can still take advantage of such compliance (so in adapting the contract the court cannot impute just one of the parties with the risk represented by the change of circumstances).

On the other hand, according to Lando and Beale (2000), courts have wide powers in terms to adapt the contract, but there is a limit to this, which is that they cannot write contracts for the parties. Consequently, the court may modify some clauses, but cannot rewrite the entire contract. In this case, the only option remaining to the court is to terminate the contract (the court will fix the date from which it is understood that the contract is terminated, and the consequences of it).

8.1.1.2 Regulation in the DCFR

It is stated in the Introduction to the Draft Common Framework of Reference that many European legal systems have recognised that where, after the conclusion of the contract there is a relevant change of circumstances, this can affect the fulfillment of the contractual obligations. As already noted, this was reflected in the PECL. The DCFR also recognises this doctrine; and, as in the PECL, this rule is non mandatory so that the parties are free, if they prefer, to exclude any possibility of modifying the contract without their consent.

Moreover, in the opinion of the editors of the Draft, the recognition of the legal effects brought about by the change of circumstances is a derivation of a supreme principle of the Draft according to which the parties are obliged to act in accordance with the standards imposed by good faith ("good faith and fair dealing") in fulfilling their obligations, in the exercise of their rights, in determining a remedy in case of non-performance, or in exercising the right to terminate the contractual relationship (cf. I.-1:103 DCFR).

This legal institution is regulated inside the Book III, art. 1:110. According to this article:

(1) An obligation must be performed even if performance has become more onerous, whether because the cost of performance has increased or because the value of what is to be received in return has diminished.
(2) If, however, performance of a contractual obligation or of an obligation arising from a unilateral juridical act becomes so onerous because of an exceptional change of circumstances that it would be manifestly unjust to hold the debtor to the obligation a court may:

  (a) vary the obligation in order to make it reasonable and equitable in the new circumstances; or
  (b) terminate the obligation at a date and on terms to be determined by the court.

(3) Paragraph (2) applies only if:

  (a) the change of circumstances occurred after the time when the obligation was incurred;
  (b) the debtor did not at that time take into account, and could not reasonably be expected to have taken into account, the possibility or scale of that change of circumstances;
  (c) the debtor did not assume, and cannot reasonably be regarded as having assumed, the risk of that change of circumstances; and
  (d) the debtor has attempted, reasonably and in good faith, to achieve by negotiation a reasonable and equitable adjustment of the terms regulating the obligation.

As for the legal consequences, it is the judge who should decide on the modification of the contract or on its termination. In both cases, the decision as to how the contract should be modified or the effects of termination is a matter for judicial discretion.

Here, an additional criterion has been introduced for the application of judicial intervention due to change of circumstances. As well as the traditional criteria of an unexpected supervening change of circumstance, and the unforeseeability of any legal or contractual risk that could have been contemplated previously, there is the requirement that the debtor attempted in good faith to renegotiate the contract.

8.1.2 Regulation in the CESL

The Proposal for a Regulation on a Common European Sales Law regulates the effect that a change of circumstances could have in a contract (art. 89 CESL).

1. A party must perform its obligations even if performance has become more onerous, whether because the cost of performance has increased or because the value of what is to be received in return has diminished.

Where performance becomes excessively onerous because of an exceptional change of circumstances, the parties have a duty to enter into negotiations with a view to adapting or terminating the contract.

Consequently, as a general rule, the parties must fulfill their obligations even if performance has become more onerous, either because the cost of compliance has increased or because the value of what is going to be received has decreased.

Where compliance has become excessively onerous because there has been an exceptional change in circumstances, the parties have a duty to negotiate in order to adapt or terminate the contract.

2. If the parties fail to reach an agreement within a reasonable time, then, upon request by either party a court may:

   (a) adapt the contract in order to bring it into accordance with what the parties would reasonably have agreed at the time of contracting if they had taken the change of circumstances into account; or
   (b) terminate the contract within the meaning of Article 8 at a date and on terms to be determined by the court.

For this rule to apply, it is necessary that (according to paragraph 3):

(a) the change of circumstances occurred after the time when the contract was concluded;
(b) the party relying on the change of circumstances did not at that time take into account, and could not be expected to have taken into account, the possibility or scale of that change of circumstances; and
(c) the aggrieved party did not assume, and cannot reasonably be regarded as having assumed, the risk of that change of circumstances[1].

4. For the purpose of paragraphs 2 and 3 a 'court' includes an arbitral tribunal.

This article begins by recognising the general principle "pacta sunt servanda", so that the contract should be fulfilled even though it is more onerous because costs have increased or the value of the consideration is less than expected. However, when this is disproportionate, art. 89 contains a duty to renegotiate.

If, within a reasonable period, the parties do not reach an agreement, they may request the assistance of the court or arbitrator. The judge may decide to vary the contract taking into account the hypothetical will of the parties or declare the termination of the contract and lay down the conditions of that termination. Thus, the court is bound by the parties' request; but there is no provision for a case in which there is a total absence of an express request in this sense. This situation should be resolved, according to Schmidt-Kessel (2013), by taking account of the laws of the States involved.

---

[1] Amendment 177 of the European Parliament legislative resolution of 26 February 2014 on the proposal for a regulation of the European Parliament and of the Council on a Common European Sales Law (COM(2011)0635-C7-0329/2011-2011/0284(COD)) has changed Article 89—paragraph 3—point c in this sense: "(c) the aggrieved party*, relying on the change of circumstances,* did not assume, and cannot reasonably be regarded as having assumed, the risk of that change of circumstances".

Article 89 is not applicable in cases of initial error as to the economical basis of the contract; in such cases arts. 48 et seq., relating to mistake, would be applicable.

It is also necessary that the change of circumstances is unexpected, so art. 89 should not be applied in cases where a risk has been assumed by the contracting parties.

In comparing art. 89 CESL with its precedents in the PECL and the DCFR, we can conclude that there are no great differences in their respective rules. In all of them, at the very beginning, there is an explicit recognition of the principle "pacta sunt servanda". Nevertheless this principle can be moderated in cases where there is a change of circumstances that makes the contract more onerous, either because it has increased the value of the performance or because it has devalued the value of the consideration. The impact that the exceptional change of circumstances would have on the contract is described in different words: "performance of the contract becomes excessively onerous" in the PECL; the contract "becomes so onerous (…) that it would be manifestly unjust to hold the debtor to the obligation" in the DCFR; and "performance becomes excessively onerous" in the CESL. On the other hand, there is no hierarchy established between variation of the contract or its termination; the decision in each case is left to the judge. The remedy of termination does not present a huge problem: the judge will determine its consequences. As for variation, the terminology changes, "adapt the contract in order to distribute between the parties in a just and equitable manner the losses and gains" in the PECL; "vary the obligation in order to make it reasonable and equitable in the new circumstances" in the DCFR; and "adapt the contract in order to bring it into accordance with what the parties would reasonably have agreed at the time of contracting if they had taken the change of circumstances into account" in the CESL.

Both the CESL and PECL, as a consequence, first establish the duty to renegotiate. The Draft refers directly to the judge's intervention, but the renegotiation is a prerequisite for application of that intervention. Apart from that, the requirements for the application of this intervention almost totally coincide, except that art. III.-1:110 of the DCFR is applicable to contractual obligations and obligations arising from a unilateral juridical act. The inclusion of the latter category is not a common feature of national jurisdictions or international instruments. Its inclusion in the Draft has its justification in the protection of a debtor in cases of unilateral contracts that, in most cases, are gratuitous in nature.

On the other hand, it is only in the PECL that the court may award damages for the loss suffered through a party refusing to negotiate or breaking off negotiations contrary to good faith and fair dealing.

This rule of 'unexpected change of circumstances' does not have an equivalent in every legal system of the Member States, but there are some that recognise this legal doctrine.

8.2 Change of Circumstances in certain European Legal Systems

After the conclusion of the contract the parties are obliged to fulfill their obligations even when a change of circumstances makes the contract more onerous (according to the principle "pacta sunt servanda"). Nevertheless, there might be circumstances beyond the reasonable expectations of the contracting parties that could create doubts as to whether the contractual obligations should remain unchanged. In this sense, it is important to take into consideration the financial crisis that is taking place nowadays as that will definitely be affecting many contractual relations.

These issues have been addressed by the courts in many Western legal systems, in such a way that the event of unforeseen circumstances may, under certain conditions, influence the rights and duties arising from the contract. In fact, in many legal systems there are doctrines (statutory or case law) that identify certain circumstances as an exception to the binding nature of the contract. The essence of such doctrines goes beyond the contract itself giving a solution for the effects that this contract should have according to equity. Therefore, the basis for the termination of the contract is equity. These are doctrines that operate by way of exception to the general rule. The name is different in the different legal systems such as: "Wegfall der Geschäftsgrundlage" in Germany; "Frustration of contract" in England; "eccessiva onerosità sopravvenuta" in Italy; and a "rebus sic stantibus" clause in Spain; and the effects also differ as regards to termination of the contract, variation and renegotiation.

8.2.1 *The Theory of "imprévision" in French Law*

In France, where the effects of the two World Wars did not produce the amount of unforeseen circumstances with regard to existing contracts as in other countries, these types of doctrines are not widely accepted. Nevertheless, there has been a development of the so-called theory of "imprévision". This doctrine refers to cases where unforeseen economic circumstances become apparent after the conclusion of the contract and compliance is extremely difficult or much more expensive, but not impossible.

This doctrine is not regulated in the French Civil Code, which was influenced to a large extent by a liberal conception of the economy (art. 1134 contains the principle "pacta sunt servanda"). It has its origin in case law, in particular the famous French court decision of "*Canal de Craponne*". This case concerns a judgment by the Court of Aix, 1874, whereby it resolved the dispute between the owners of a canal built by the engineer Craponne in the seventeenth century and the owners of a farm who were the beneficiaries of the concession for the irrigation of the canal. In this case, agreements concluded in 1560 and 1567 fixed the price of a watering fee that the beneficiary had to pay to the owner of the irrigation canal. But in the middle of the nineteenth century, the firm in charge of the exploitation of the canal asked for an increase of the fee, considering that it no longer corresponded to the maintenance cost. The French Court of appeal of Aix-en-Provence, taking into account the imbalance of the agreements, held on the 31st of December 1873 that the price should from then on increase up to the price of a similar contract concluded at the date of the judgment, and so fixed the amount of this new price.

However, in 1876 the Cour de Cassation (France's highest civil law court), taking into account the legal uncertainty which in the opinion of many scholars this thesis generated, overruled this solution and decided the case in favour of the specific performance of the contract.

Larenz (1957), commenting on this case, states that the Cour de Cassation maintained the negative argument against the "rebus sic stantibus" even when many lower courts were inclined to deviate somewhat from the rigor of the "pacta sunt servanda" during the First World War. Thus it can be seen that they were not reluctant to undertake an extensive interpretation of the concept of "force majeure".

Nevertheless after the *Canal de Craponne* case, French case law developed the so called theory of "imprévision" within the context of the economic situation after the First World War. This was in another case, where the city of Bordeaux had granted the "Compagnie générale d'éclairage of Bordeaux" a concession to supply gas to the city. The contract contained a fixed price, but also provided for an adjustment mechanism in the case of certain price fluctuations. After the war, the price of coal used by the company tripled, exceeding the price that had been set in the concession. The Conseil d'Etat decided that the adjustment mechanism fixed in the concession agreement was not enough in the context of the new circumstances, so that the economic viability of the contract was frustrated. "Gaz de Bordeaux" could not be obliged to fulfill the contract according to the original conditions. In order for the application of the theory of "imprévision" it was necessary that the event be unforeseen and external to the parties; also that it exceeded their reasonable expectations and provoked a serious imbalance in the contractual equilibrium. The solution had to be temporary to preserve the viability of the contract. This doctrine became known as the "théorie de l'imprévision" because of the emphasis on the unforeseeability of the event.

8.2.2 The "Geschäftsgrundlage" in German Law

8.2.2.1 Introduction

The German doctrine "Geschäftsgrundlage" (the literal translation being "the basis of the contract"), which lacked legal regulation until recently, was developed by case law on the basis of § 242 BGB (referring to good faith).

Nevertheless, the doctrine of "Geschäftsgrundlage" is today a real legal doctrine in Germany introduced in the German Civil Code (BGB) by the Law Reform of Obligations Act which came into force in January 2002 (in § 313 BGB). The reason for the inclusion of this provision was, in the opinion of the Commission responsible for the reform, that the "Geschäftsgrundlage" was a very important doctrine in German law, and the fact that there were legal principles, which had been applied by the courts for several decades, left out of the Civil Code should be viewed negatively.

According to § 313 BGB:

> (1) If circumstances which became the basis of a contract have significantly changed since the contract was entered into and if the parties would not have entered into the contract or would have entered into it with different contents if they had foreseen this change, adaptation of the contract may be demanded to the extent that, taking account of all the circumstances of the specific case, in particular the contractual or statutory distribution of risk, one of the parties cannot reasonably be expected to uphold the contract without alteration.
> (2) It is equivalent to a change of circumstances if material conceptions that have become the basis of the contract are found to be incorrect.
> (3) If adaptation of the contract is not possible or one party cannot reasonably be expected to accept it, the disadvantaged party may revoke the contract. In the case of continuing obligations, the right to terminate takes the place of the right to revoke.

The new § 313 BGB mainly reflects the definition of the "Geschäftsgrundlage" developed by the case law. However, among the requirements set out in paragraph 1 of the § 313 for the application of the doctrine the unforeseeability ("Unvorsehrbarkeit") required by the courts is not to be found. However, it can be understood that it is included in § 313 BGB in as much as the article refers to those changes of circumstance that, if they had been anticipated by the parties, would mean that they would not have concluded the contract or would have concluded it with different content. Furthermore, when the rule talks about the legal or contractual assumption of the risk, it is assumed that the change of circumstances has not been foreseen because otherwise it would be a risk that would have been assumed by the party that should have been able to anticipate it. The same is true for cases where there are risks that a party can control—those risks should be assumed by that party.

8.2.2.2 Requirement for its application

The requirements for the application of § 313 BGB are the following:

1. A change in any circumstance that forms part of the content of the contract has occurred.
2. There should be no express provision in the contract concerning the distribution of risks; and also that this could not be determined by a comprehensive interpretation of the contract or by applying statutory rules.
3. There should also be a considerable alteration of the equilibrium of the obligations of the parties within the contract, provided that none of the parties is obliged to undertake a more onerous compliance. Proof of this requirement forces the court to an assessment of the interests involved in each particular contract.
4. The change of circumstances should not be attributable to any of the parties. Also, the doctrine of "Geschäftsgrundlage" should not be applied when one party is in late in its performance of the contract.

8.2.2.3 Consequences

With regard to the legal consequences, there is a distinction between variation of the contract in order to adapt to the new circumstances and the termination of the contract. Legal scholars and case law have argued that the first solution is possible in the event of a disruption of the equilibrium of the contract, but not in cases of frustration of the contract, so that in cases of late performance it would be better to terminate the contract.

The variation of the contract should take into account the original contractual aim as an objective criterion. For that purpose, a consistent interpretation of the contract is helpful. However, § 313 BGB does not provide criteria for the variation of the contract; in some instances the courts take into account the behaviour of the parties in an economic sense to find the best solution that fits the particular case.

According to Peer (2001), the text of § 313 BGB departs significantly from the traditional construction as to its consequences, since it was affirmed that variation could occur only *ipso jure* and must be laid down in every case by the judge.

In this sense, Cashin-Ritane (2001) asserts that although § 313 BGB does not answer the question of how to vary the contract, one must accept that this should be arranged jointly by the parties, overriding the role of the judge. Only when variation is not possible or when one party cannot be held to it, should the contract be terminated with consequent damage compensation, if applicable. In his sense, according to the new German law, parties have great freedom, so they should renegotiate the contract and when this is not possible, request its termination. This interpretation is consistent with the text of the Principles of European Contract Law.

On the other hand, variation must take into account the distribution of contractual or legal risks, since variation of the contract is also an aspect of risk sharing (i.e. it should be determined who should bear the risk of that change). Consequently, if the contract provides for that eventuality, it must be respected. The same is true in a case where the change is predictable or the law determines who should bear the risk.

Secondly, in accordance with an economic analysis of the law, variation is not possible when one party is insured against such a risk or when the contract represents only a small percentage of the total assets of the parties. Nor would it be possible when the creditor is in a position to satisfy his interest elsewhere at a lower cost; in this case it would be better to terminate the contract with or without compensation for the damages caused in each individual case.

The German Supreme Court has recently ruled what consequences the failure of the basis of the contract should have in a particular case (cf. Judgment of September 30, 2011 (NJW 2012, 373)). In the opinion of the court, in such cases, the claim of the party aggrieved by the change of circumstances to adapt the contract obliges the other party to carry out the variation. Otherwise, that party could sue the other in order to obtain this effect. The breach of this duty would lead to compensation for damages in accordance with § 280 I BGB. For the termination of the contract by the injured party it is necessary that the circumstances required by § 313 III BGB are fulfilled (i.e., that variation of the contract is not possible or is not accepted by that party).

8.2.3 *"Eccessiva onerosità sopravvenuta" in Italian Law*

8.2.3.1 Concept of "eccessiva onerosità sopravvenuta"

In Italian law the principle concerning the change of circumstances is contained in arts. 1467 et seq. Codice Civile. According to art. 1467 Codice Civile, in the case of contracts whose execution is deferred, if the performance of one of the parties has become excessively onerous as a result of extraordinary and unforeseeable events, the party that is obliged to fulfill such an obligation may seek the termination of the contract, the effects of which are contained in Article 1458 Codice Civile. Termination cannot be required if the excessive hardship falls within the normal distribution of risks according to the contract. The other party can prevent termination by offering a modification of the terms of the contract.

Excessive hardship can be defined as the effect of the contractual obligations of the parties (or one of them) becoming more onerous due to certain events that occur between the time of conclusion of the agreement and its fulfillment, where they could not have been anticipated by the parties despite applying due diligence (as to the event in question, its harshness or duration). These events mean that the performance of one of the parties requires disproportionate expense and effort or, conversely, the obligation of the other party is depreciated significantly.

8.2.3.2 Requirements for its application

a) Alteration of the equilibrium of the contract: The application of Article 1467 Codice Civile requires proof that the extraordinary and unforeseeable events have altered the contractual balance between the parties, demanding a higher economic sacrifice than expected according to the contract. This assessment requires an objective criterion; i.e. it is necessary to find a quantitatively significant aggravation of the cost of fulfillment of one obligation at the time of execution of the contract in relation to the expected value at the time of its conclusion, taking into account the type of contract, and also the ordinary market fluctuations or conventionally assumed risk by the inclusion of specific clauses in the contract. In case of a disagreement between the parties on this point, the case will be solved at the discretion of the court.

b) The event should be foreseeable: Foreseeability requires a normal level of care. Moreover, this must take into account the situation at the time of contracting, as well as the market situation in which the particular contract is to be found. Therefore, foreseeable events are those that a reasonable contracting party in this position could have anticipated within the circumstances in which the contract was concluded.

Legal scholars have discussed the issue as to whether devaluation could be considered an unforeseeable event that produces supervening hardship. For some authors, currency devaluation could lead to the termination of the contract provided that it arises suddenly severely effects the contract. Thus, during the war, devaluation of the currency may not have been foreseeable, and therefore, much less so the terrible state that it produced. Nevertheless once currency devaluation materialises, it would be considered arguable whether its rapid aggravation was unforeseen.

c) Normal distribution of risks within the contract: This requirement contributes to the definition of the risk that the parties may assume (by the agreement or by the nature of the legal transaction) at the time of conclusion of the contract and thereby excluding, in this case, the application of the remedy of hardship.

8.2.3.3 Consequences

When all the requirements of art. 1467 Codice Civile are satisfied, the obligated party may claim for the termination of the contract. Nevertheless it is necessary that the debtor affected by the hardship has not previously breached the contract or is late in its performance.

a) Termination of the contract: This power to terminate the contract should be exercised judicially and where the court orders its termination, the effects are "*ex tunc*". This is considered to be a constitutive judgment.

Article 1467 Codice Civile states that the other party can prevent the termination by offering to modify the terms of the contract. This is a remedy in accordance with the principle of the conservation of the contract. According to Bianca (1994), the other party rectifies the content of the contract so that the party affected is released from the effects of the hardship.

The exercise of the power to modify of the contract requires a unilateral declaration of will similar to the cases of mistake (art. 1432 Codice Civile where the party that makes the mistake cannot ask for the contract to be annulled if the other party offers to fulfill the contract in accordance with the content of what was intended).

It also has to be born in mind that this is a judicial remedy, which may be claimed only by the party who has an interest in avoiding the effects of the termination. Thus, the party that makes the offer is the one that has to fulfill the terms of the modification. The judge cannot formulate the contract; he can only assess the correctness of the offer.

The aim of this modification should be to eliminate any hardship that goes beyond the distribution of risks according to the contract. This could be achieved by reducing or increasing the consideration.

8.2.4 Supervening Hardship in Dutch Civil Code

The modification of the Dutch Civil Code in 1992 introduced arts. 6:258 and 6:260, which contain specific rules for the doctrine of unexpected circumstances.

Article 6:258 BW states:

1. Upon the demand of one of the parties, the judge may modify the effects of a contract, or he may set it aside in whole or in part on the basis of unforeseen circumstances which are of such a nature that the contracting party, according to criteria of reasonableness and equity, may not expect that the contract be maintained in an unmodified form. The modification or the setting aside of the contract may be given retroactive force.
2. The modification or the setting aside of the contract is not pronounced to the extent that the person invoking the circumstances should be accountable for them according to the nature of the contract or common opinion.
3. For the purposes of this article, a person to whom a contractual right or obligation has been transferred is assimilated to a contracting party.

According to art. 6:258, the court may vary the contract or terminate it on the basis of unforeseen hardship if the circumstances have changed in such a way that the contracting parties, according to the criteria of reasonableness and fairness, could not be expected to comply with the unchanged contract. Before the reform of the Civil Code, the Dutch Supreme Court ("Hoge Raad") had already applied this rule as a derivation of the principle of good faith. Article 6:258 is considered a "*lex specialis*" derived from the general principle of good faith, codified in art. 6:248 BW.[2]

Article 6:260 BW

1. The judge may pronounce a modification of the contract or set it aside, as referred to in articles 258 and 259, subject to conditions to be determined by him.
2. If, pursuant to these articles, the judge modifies, or partially sets the contract aside, he may determine that one or more of the contracting parties may totally set aside the contract by a written declaration within a period specified in the decision. The modification or partial setting aside of the contract does not take effect before this period has expired.
3. Where the contract which is modified, or wholly or partially set aside pursuant to articles 258 and 259, is entered in the public registers, the decision modifying or setting aside the contract can also be registered, provided that it has become final or is provisionally enforceable.
4. Where in this respect a person is summoned at the domicile which he has elected according to article 252 paragraph 2, first sentence, all his successors who have not made a new registration have thereby also been summoned. Article 29 paragraph 2 and paragraph 3, second-fifth sentence of Book 3 apply mutatis mutandis.
5. Other juridical facts which modify or terminate a registered contract may also be registered to the extent that judicial decisions are concerned, provided that they have become final or are provisionally enforceable.

The new Code gives the judge wide discretion. Thus, the court decision may contain certain conditions, such as the payment of compensation (art. 6:260, paragraph 1) and may vary or terminate the contract with retroactive effect (art. 6:258, paragraph 1). The remedies contained in art. 6:258 are not subject to any hierarchy. In general, the way in which a contract can be modified falls into the sphere of the discretion of the judge[3]. According to the Civil Code, the variation (modification) or the termination of the contract should be considered as an exceptional remedy, and, therefore, it should be applied restrictively. This interpretation has been also approved of by the Dutch Supreme Court[4]. This is reflected in Arts. 6:258 and 6:260. It is also nec-

[2] Judgment of the Supreme Court 25 June 1999, *NJ* 1999, 602.

[3] Judgment Supreme Court 18 January 2002, *NJ* 2002, 106.

[4] Judgment Supreme Court 20 February 1998, *NJ* 1998, 493.

essary for the interested party invoke this rule, and not to leave the subject to the courts own motion (art. 6:258, p. 1).

Secondly, the change of circumstances is only applicable if it was unexpected by both parties (art. 6:258, p. 1). That is, the change of circumstances should not be part of the risk contractually assumed by the parties. In this sense, the contract should be interpreted to determine if the change of circumstances falls into one of the parties' sphere of risk.

Thirdly, the party that invokes the change of circumstances cannot be the party responsible for that change, according to the nature of the contract or "common opinion" (art. 6:258, p. 2). This criterion can be seen as a special feature of the general principle according to which, given the unforeseen circumstances, the other party cannot expect that the contract remains unchanged (art. 6:258, p. 1). Consequently, if a party is a professional in the field of activity of the contract, then that change of circumstances must be borne by him; i.e., it is a contractual risk.

Fourthly, if the court finds variation of the contract inappropriate, the other party could be required to terminate the contract within a specified period of time laid down in the decision (art. 6:260, p. 2).

These criteria appear, *de facto*, to have a preventive effect. In recent years since the new version of the Civil Code entered into force, the courts have not often had to apply arts. 6:258 and 6:260.

Article 6:258 does not, expressly address the issue of renegotiation. However, following the example of the so-called "hardship clauses" in international commercial contracts, the Dutch doctrine assumes that in certain cases the parties would be obliged to renegotiate, even if they had not expressly stipulated this in the contract. This duty is based on the general clause of good faith contained in art. 6:248, so the judge who has to decide a dispute on the basis of art. 6:258 should take into account any breach of this obligation.

8.2.5 Clause "rebus sic stantibus" in Swiss Law

In Swiss law there is no express provision of the clause "rebus sic stantibus". However, the Swiss Supreme Court has admitted that some long-term contracts can be terminated if there is an unexpected and fundamental change of circumstances on the basis of art. 2 Civil Code, which contains the general duty of good faith (Van Houtte 1993).

Only changes that could unjustly enrich one party can lead to this effect, since the clause "rebus sic stantibus" has a restrictive application. Moreover, the change of circumstances must be substantial, unusual and excessive. It should be obvious to any impartial third party that an imbalance in the contractual obligations of the parties has been produced. Also the change of circumstances should be valued according to objective criteria meaning that the particular circumstances would affect any contracting party, not only those in the subjective situation of the actual parties to the contract.

Moreover, the party affected by the change of circumstances must prove the disproportion between the promise and the consideration. Finally, the affected party should not be an expert in the field of economic activity in which the contract falls.

For the application of the "clause rebus sic stantibus" Swiss courts require the following assumptions:

- The changes should not have been foreseeable or anticipated by the parties.
- The party obliged to fulfill the obligation in question should not have recognised either "expressly" or in any previous negotiations, that he would also be liable in the case of the compliance becoming even more onerous.
- Changes must be extraordinary; and this requirement should be interpreted objectively.
- Changes must have caused extraordinary disproportionality between the obligations of the parties so that performance is considered objectively unacceptable.
- The court's intervention should not lead to unacceptable results for the creditor, in the sense that the excessive hardship should not be transferred entirely from the debtor to the creditor.

For the application of the clause it is also necessary that changes are substantial. Judicial practice shows that judges have a strict approach in deciding whether to accept that a particular change of circumstances, such as currency depreciation or a change in legal regulation, substantially affects the contract.

8.2.6 "Frustration" in English Law

8.2.6.1 General remarks and requirements

In English law, frustration of the contract is one of the causes by which the debtor is discharged from performance.

This doctrine of "frustration of contract" has its origin in the so-called "Coronation Cases". One of the most relevant is the case "*Krell v. Henry*"[5]: the plaintiff was the owner of some rooms in Pall Mall from where the coronation procession could be seen that was going to take place on 26 and 27 June 1902. The complainant agreed that the defendant could use the rooms to see the coronation at a price of £ 75, £ 25 of which was paid as a deposit at the time of the conclusion of the contract. The coronation did not take place as a result of the king's illness. The court held that the defendant was entitled to the return of the £ 25 paid by way of deposit. The plaintiff appealed.

In order to solve this case, the Court of Appeal considered not only the terms of the contract, but also the circumstances surrounding both contracting parties, which went to the substance of the contract, and then considered the question of whether the foundation of the contract required the existence of a particular state of affairs. If

[5] [1903] 2 KB 740

not, then there would not have been a breach of contract. The court concluded that, in this case, the use of the rooms was agreed for a particular purpose, which was to see the coronation and not for anything else. In addition, the parties had not considered the possibility that the coronation may not take place. Here, the contract was frustrated and all future obligations were discharged, although any obligations already carried out—such as the payment of the deposit—were not recoverable. However, the House of Lords, in *Fibrosa Spolka Ackyjna v Fairbairn Lawson Combe Barbour Ltd*,[6] held that, in certain circumstances where there was a total failure of consideration, money already paid could be reclaimed.

Despite its English origin, this doctrine is also recognised in American law, where the courts have developed the doctrine of "commercial impracticability".

The main purpose of the doctrine of frustration is to create an appropriate way to distribute the risks of unforeseen events amongst the contracting parties in cases where they have not done this explicitly by introducing express or implied contractual terms in the contract.

Therefore, one of the requirements for the application of the doctrine of "frustration" is the unforeseeability of the changed circumstances. In addition, for such a remedy to be available, it is necessary that the party invoking it has no control over the change of circumstances, and that it has not been produced by the negligent behaviour of one of the parties.

These requirements can be illustrated with two examples from the case law.

The Hong Kong case of "*Wong Lai Ying and Investment v. Chinachem Investment Ltd*"[7] illustrates the requirement of unforeseeability. The parties had entered into a contract of sale for flats under construction. Under the terms of the contract "Chinachem", as developer and builder, was obliged to finish the work in a period of 18 months after taking possession of the property. The buyer paid in the full purchase price in advance as a deposit. Seven months after obtaining the building licences and beginning the work, a change of circumstances occurred that hindered performance. It took about a year and a half to get a new licence. In fact, due to the instability of the area, work did not continue until three and a half years later. The contract had included a clause that allowed for a delay in the building of up to 365 days should one of a number of factors take place. Clause 22 of the contract was fundamental to the resolution of the case: "It is further agreed that notwithstanding anything herein contained should any dispute arise between the parties … or should any unforeseen circumstances beyond the Vendor's control arise … the Vendor shall be at liberty to rescind this Agreement forthwith …". The buyers demanded performance of the contract while the seller claimed that the contract was frustrated. The court at first instance decided that the contract should be terminated as a result of frustration. However, the Court of Appeal considered whether or not clause 22 in the contract provided for such a result, and held that this was not a case of frustration. With regard to this case, it should be noted that this was a contract for

[6] [1943] AC 32. The allocation of loss is now covered by the Law Reform (Frustrated Contracts) Act 1943—see below.

[7] [1979] B.L.R. 81.

the execution of building works and that the seller bore the risk until the completion of the work. Furthermore, it should be noted that the place of performance was Hong Kong where it was reasonable to assume a change in the socio-political circumstances, and so it was not an unforeseeable event, according to the court. This case, however, went on appeal to the Judicial Committee of the Privy Council in London (Hong Kong's highest appeal court at that time), where it was decided that the landslip was an unforeseeable natural disaster leading to the frustration of the contract, and that the words of clause 22 could not be construed as covering the possibility of a landslip.

On the other hand, the requirement that the parties lack responsibility for the change of circumstances is illustrated by the case of "*J. Lauritzen AS v. Wijsmuller BN (The Super Servant Two)*"[8]. In July 1980 the parties entered into a purchase agreement under which the defendants agreed to transport a drilling rig ("the Dan King") purchased by the plaintiffs, from Japan to a place on the peripheries of Rotterdam. The defendants provided two semi-submersible trailers that could be used for transportation. Delivery had to done between 20 June and 20 August 1981. On 29 June 1981 one of the boats belonging to the defendant ("Super Servant Two") sank while being used in the performance of the contract, so that on 16 February 1981 the defendants decided that they could not fulfill the contract with the other boat, and claimed frustration of contract. Alternatively they argued that the loss of the ship was included within the clause "*force majeure*", which permits the cancelation of the contract if certain events occurred. The lower court ruled in favour of the plaintiffs, so the defendants appealed. The Court of Appeal rejected the application of the doctrine of frustration to cases such as this one, because the application of the doctrine of the frustration of contract required that there be no fault of the party claiming the frustration. In this case, for the doctrine of frustration to apply, it would have been necessary to stipulate that the transportation should be carried out by "Super Servant Two" without any other alternative, and that the ship had been lost due to no fault of the debtor. However, this was not the case, since transportation could have been effected on any ship that would serve for this purpose.

8.2.6.2 Consequences of "frustration of the contract"

In cases of frustration both parties are discharged of their obligations. The discharge is complete and automatic, but, at common law, could cause problems where the parties have begun to fulfill their obligations. The Law Reform (Frustrated Contracts) Act 1943 attempted to resolve these issues.

In accordance with section 1 of the Law Reform (Frustrated Contracts) Act 1943:

> (1) Where a contract governed by English law has become impossible of performance or been otherwise frustrated, and the parties thereto have for that reason been discharged from the further performance of the contract, the following provisions of this section shall, subject to the provisions of section two of this Act, have effect in relation thereto.

[8] [1990] 1 Lloyds Rep. 1

(2) All sums paid or payable to any party in pursuance of the contract before the time when the parties were so discharged (in this Act referred to as "*the time of discharge*") shall, in the case of sums so paid, be recoverable from him as money received by him for the use of the party by whom the sums were paid, and, in the case of sums so payable, cease to be so payable:

Provided that, if the party to whom the sums were so paid or payable incurred expenses before the time of discharge in, or for the purpose of, the performance of the contract, the court may, if it considers it just to do so having regard to all the circumstances of the case, allow him to retain or, as the case may be, recover the whole or any part of the sums so paid or payable, not being an amount in excess of the expenses so incurred.

However, this rule has not solved all the problems related to the consequences of the "frustration". The 1943 Act was designed to prevent one party from being unjustly enriched at the expense of the other, but not to distribute losses under the contract. Section I (2) of the 1943 Act raises a ńumber of problems: first, it refers to amounts paid, or that should have been paid, before the time of discharge (before the event resulting in the frustration took place). So what would happen with the amounts paid after that? It has been argued that in these cases an action of "*quantum meruit*" could be brought, although the courts would accept this only in limited circumstances. There are also issues regarding the determination of the amount to be restored. Another issue raised was whether the party that received the money can claim compensation for damages, as this option is granted to the party that paid. Finally, it is possible that no payment was made but the debtor had incurred some expenses necessary for compliance.

Consequently, it has been argued that the doctrine of frustration should be more flexible to prevent the burden of the consequences falling exclusively on one party.

On the other hand, frustration, unlike termination, can be invoked by any of the parties to the contract and not just the party affected by the event. Another difference is that in the case of frustration there is no obligation to compensate for damages, otherwise than in the case of breach of the contract. Furthermore, breach of contract requires the party who breached the contract to be at fault, whereas in the case of frustration both parties are equally victims of an event for which neither party is responsible.

The general effect of frustration is, therefore, the total liberation of the parties from their pending obligations; but it does not affect the obligations already carried out. In English law, there is no possibility of modifying the contract to adapt it to the new circumstances, since this would affect legal certainty, and also would empower the courts to conclude contracts instead of the parties, both being circumstances that are not considered desirable.

8.2.7 *The Clause "Rebus Sic Stantibus" in Spanish Law*

The legal doctrine used to solve problems arising from unexpected circumstances in Spanish Law is the so-called clause "rebus sic stantibus". This remedy seeks to restore the equilibrium of the contract, which has been destroyed as a result of an unforeseeable change of circumstances.

There is no regulation of the clause in the Spanish Civil Code; instead it has been developed by the case law.

According to the case law, the requirements for the application of the clause are the following:

a. First of all, the clause is only applicable to deferred execution contracts or contracts that should be performed at successive intervals.
b. Secondly, the change of circumstances should be unforeseeable.

There must be a change in the basis of the contract due to the fact that the equilibrium of the contract is destroyed or because the aim of the contract is frustrated.

The change in the basis of the contract must be considered extraordinary and unforeseeable at the time of conclusion of the contract. For that reason it is possible to apply the clause when the change of circumstances concern a contractual risk that has been assumed by the parties.

In many judgments, the application of the clause has been dismissed because there was an express assumption of the risk of changed circumstances in the contract, or that the change of circumstances formed part of the normal distribution of risks (contractually or statutory). For example, in the Judgment of the Spanish Supreme Court 16 June 1983 (RJ 1983, 3632) a case of a contract for the execution of building works, there was a clause excluding justification for late delivery of the building in the event that the workers went on strike. For that reason, the High Court did not apply the clause "rebus sic stantibus" where the work became more expensive than initially expected because of the strike. There was also another clause that the price should not be increased.

In addition, the change in circumstances must be unforeseeable. This requirement is a difficult one, because in the modern society certain risks are not natural but artificial, in the sense that they arise as a social product, and it is very difficult in some cases to anticipate and to insure against them. Thus, unforeseeability should be assessed in relation to the type of contract and the amount of information to which the contracting parties have access.

For that reason, depreciation of currency is not considered an unforeseeable circumstance according to the case law[9].

Case law has also held that the alteration of the value of the assets in the period between the time of conclusion of the contract and its performance is not an unforeseeable circumstance[10].

On the other hand, none of the parties must be responsible for the change of circumstances. It is considered unfair to grant a defence mechanism to that party

[9] Judgment of the Supreme Court 14 December 1940 (RJ 1940, 1135) involving a contract for the sale of a mine; Judgment of the Supreme Court 26 March 1963 (RJ 1963, 2120) on the use of water by a community; Judgment of the Supreme Court 31 November 1963 (RJ 1963, 4264).

[10] Judgment of the Supreme Court 5 June 1945; Judgment of the Supreme Court 6 October 1987 (RJ 1987, 6720); Judgment of the Supreme Court 29 May 1996 (RJ 1996, 3862); Judgment of the Supreme Court 27 April 2012 (RJ 2012, 4714).

who being held to account because he has violated the duty of care that was required according to the good faith to avoid the risk[11].

As for the effects arising from the change of circumstances of the contract, although only a few judgments have accepted the application of the clause to the case under consideration, some of them have allowed the termination the contract, while others have opted for its modification. The modification of the contract is done by the court through an integrated interpretation of the content of the contract. The legal basis for this integrated interpretation is art. 1258 CC, which states that, apart from the agreed obligations, parties should also respect the obligations arising from the principle of good faith[12].

8.3 Common features of the Change of Circumstances in the different European Legal Systems and in Harmonised Texts

We can conclude that in many European countries there is a recognition of some kind of exception to the principle "pacta sunt servanda" that is called by different names in the different legal texts, such as: "Wegfall der Geschäftsgrundlage", "frustration of contract", "eccessiva onerosità sopravvenuta", cláusula "rebus sic stantibus", etc. However, in the text of the UNIDROIT principles, the widely recognised term "hardship" was chosen for international commerce, due to the inclusion of the so-called "hardship clauses" in many international contracts.

There are some countries, such as Austria, Germany, Greece, Italy, Netherlands, Portugal and Sweden, where there is a special regulation for the doctrine of the change of circumstances. Others, like England, France, Denmark and Spain, do not regulate it, but this does not mean that a solution to these problems has not been granted by case law.

In general, we can say that it is necessary for there to be a fundamental change in the equilibrium of the contract; the assessment of which will depend on the circumstances. In practice, a fundamental change in the balance of the benefit to each party can be revealed in two ways:

a. By a substantial increase in the cost of compliance for one party. This substantial increase in the cost could be due, for example, to a dramatic increase in the price of raw materials necessary for the production of the goods or performance of the services.

---

11 Judgment of the Supreme Court 19 April 1985 (RJ 1985, 1804); Judgment of the Supreme Court 19 November 1994 (RJ 1994, 8539); Judgment of the Supreme Court 15 November 2000 (RJ 2000, 9214).

12 In the Judgment of the Supreme Court 23 November 1962 (RJ 1962, 5005) the effects of the clause is to modify the contract. However, the Judgments of the Supreme Court 28 January 1970 and 23 March 1988 (RJ 1988, 2228) declared that it terminated the contract. In the Judgments of the Supreme Court 9 July 1984 (RJ 1984, 3803), 6 November 1992 (RJ 1992, 9226) and 21 July 2010 (RJ 2010, 3897) the effect was the modification of the contract.

b. By a substantial decrease in the value of the performance of one of the parties, including cases in which the performance has no value. This reduction in value could be due to a considerable change in the market conditions, but also to a frustration of purpose required by the performance This decrease in value must be considered in an objective sense, not based on the change of the personal opinion of the creditor. Frustration of the contract can only be taken into account in cases where the purpose in question was known or at least should have been known by both parties.

Furthermore, it is necessary for the changed circumstances that affect the equilibrium of the contract not to have been anticipated by the disadvantaged party at the time of concluding the contract, because if this is the case, it shall be deemed to form part of his sphere of risk. Regarding the possibility to foresee the change, the specific circumstances at the time of conclusion of the contract will be taken into account.

This requirement of unforeseeability is very complex, because modern risks are not natural but artificial, in the sense that they arise as a social product, and the ability to anticipate and insure against them is increasing. Thus, predictability should be assessed in relation to the type of contract involved and the amount of information available to the contracting parties. For example, in international contracts the occurrence of a certain event may not be anticipated by one of the parties, even though this would not be the same for the other party, since it is possible that this could be a very common phenomenon in the latter's country or environment.

The definition of unforeseeability as a requirement for the change of circumstances could be construed from an objective point of view so that the nature of the change of circumstances is linked to objective standards capable of external and neutral assessment. This would be the case where an event affects the whole society or affects all contractual parties in the same situation (requiring, for instance, statistical classification; this interpretation has been followed by Italian case law in the application of art. 1467 Codice Civile). This would mean a restrictive application of the doctrine. On the other hand, a more flexible interpretation could be to consider whether the particular affected party could not reasonably have taken into account the change (as in the case law that applies § 313 BGB and art. 6:258 Dutch BW). This "reasonable foreseeability" would facilitate the application of the legal doctrine in situations where it would not otherwise be invoked in practice.

The issue of unpredictability is related to the distribution of risks within the contract. Thus, it is necessary that the party invoking the application of this doctrine has not expressly or impliedly assumed the risk. It can be seen, therefore, that a tacit assumption of risk exists in all cases in which a change has been foreseen and its effects not prevented in the contract.

For instance, A buys shares in a company (B) and after the conclusion of the contract but before paying the price, the company becomes insolvent and the price of the shares diminish considerably. In this case it could be argued that the risks of fluctuations in the price of the shares should be assumed by the buyer (taking into account the special nature of the goods).

There will be no effect for the contracting parties if the change of circumstances falls within the sphere of control of one of the parties, especially the disadvantaged party. This is actually a logical requirement derived from the general principle according to which no one can take advantage of his own negligence.

On the other hand, according to the principle of freedom of contract, it is possible that one of the parties assume the risk of the new circumstances supervening. In these cases, the doctrine of "change of circumstances" or its equivalents cannot be applied, even though the adverse economic consequences are greater than anticipated. Nevertheless, in this type of case this clause should be subject to good faith, so that the clause could not be applied in cases in which the change of circumstances is due, either completely or partially, to the party in whose benefit the clause operates.

On the other hand, the doctrine of "change of circumstances" (or its equivalents) applies only in those cases where performance has not yet taken place. Once it is completed, a substantial increase in performance costs or a significant decrease in the value of the benefit can no longer be invoked. If the performance has been only partially fulfilled, the "change of circumstances" may be relevant only with respect to the part of the benefit not yet delivered.

To sum up, we can conclude that although there exists different legal terminology for this concept as well as different regulation, the requirements for its application are similar in the different legal systems:

1. The contract must have been fundamentally affected by an exceptional event.
2. This event must not have been regulated in the contract or not contemplated (as it was not foreseeable) by the parties at the time of the conclusion of the contract.
3. The risk of the supervening event should not have been attributed to either party under a statute or contractual provision.

According to Hondius and Grigoleit (2011), following the approach of case law to this legal concept in Europe in cases of long-term contracts, these usually can be terminated if the price initially agreed has been increased disproportionately. In many systems, the right to terminate the contract in these cases is an essential principle of contract law (e.g. German law in § 313 BGB).

However, where excessive hardship results from an extraordinary inflation, it is not generally considered as an unforeseeable event, since inflation is a common phenomenon in the economy. In these cases, one can observe the dominance of the nominalist principle, so that the amount of a monetary debt is based on its nominal value and not on its real value.

On the other hand, where government action has caused the imbalance between the benefits, it is usually considered as unpredictable, since it is beyond the control of the contracting parties.

In European legal texts such as the PECL, DCFR or CESL, in cases where there is a change of circumstances, parties are required to renegotiate the contract as they cannot go to the courts until renegotiation has failed.

Renegotiation has to be reasonable and in good faith, which means that renegotiation should be requested without delay and indicating the grounds relied on. That the renegotiation should be done according to good faith means that the proposals have to be serious, providing all the information necessary for the other party and also undertaken in a reasonable period of time. The aim of the renegotiation would be to make the contract reasonable and equitable in the new circumstances (according to the DCFR), or to distribute between the parties in a just and equitable manner the losses and gains (according to the PECL), or to adapt the contract in order to bring it into accordance with what the parties would reasonably have agreed (according to the CESL). That is, to restore the initial economy of the contract that was destroyed because of the change of circumstances.

Nevertheless drafters of the European texts are aware of the difficulties implied in renegotiation. For that reason the DCFR and also CESL, in contrast to the PECL, do not impose an obligation to renegotiate, but instead, in order to encourage negotiated solutions, the debtor has to insist on renegotiation if he wants to rely on the remedies provided by the article.

As far as the remedies are concerned, the European texts refer both to the variation and to the termination of the contract, leaving that decision to the court. In this sense, the courts are given wide powers. In the case of termination, the courts can also determine its terms (with regard to retroactivity, questions about restitution, etc.).

Nevertheless according to the widely accepted principle of "*favor contractus*" courts first have to explore the eventual variation of the contract by way of solution. The aim should be to make the obligations of the parties reasonable and equitable under the new circumstances, by reestablishing the contractual equilibrium. There is one limit to this: that is the prohibition of the court redrafting the whole contract, as there is the danger that the will of the court can be placed above the hypothetical will of the parties. Also it should be born in mind that the remedy of variation of the contract is accepted in certain European countries, such as Germany, the Netherlands or Spain, but not in others such as England, where the effect of frustration is always the termination of the contract.

However, a certain level of uncertainty can be observed in the different European legal texts with regard to the legal consequences of the change of circumstances. As stated above, one of the consequences—the most drastic—is represented by the termination of the contract. The application of this remedy is relatively simple and does not require much judicial discretion. Nonetheless, in order to mitigate the adverse effects of the termination of the contract upon the parties and third parties, the judge should be provided with broad powers to determine the conditions of the termination in relation to its date, retroactive effects, obligations pending or partially fulfilled and damages, amongst others, as is stated in the UNIDROIT Principles, PECL, DCFR and also the CESL.

However, in many cases termination of the contract does not achieve a fair result as the whole risk represented by the changed circumstances is attributed to just one of the parties. Therefore, equity is better respected in these cases by undertaking a variation of the contract. This consequence is contemplated in some legal systems such as Germany in its BGB.

Even in those legal systems that do not recognise an doctrine equivalent to the clause "rebus sic stantibus", it is clear that the courts try to find a mechanism for adjusting the contract on the basis of some legally regulated precepts, such as by implying terms into the contract according to good faith or equity.

On the other hand, in the UK, as has been analysed, the development of the doctrine of frustration of contract shows that the choice of whether to terminate the contract, in terms of all or nothing, is not adequate to confront the problem of the change of contractual circumstances.

Even so, the variation of the contract implies a large number of unresolved issues, e.g. the relationship between the termination of the contract and its variation (in the sense of determining the conditions in which termination or variation of the contract is the best solution). Neither is the question resolved as to whether the party not affected by the event in question is entitled to object the variation and claim termination of the contract instead.

The way in which variation should take place also remains to be clarified: if it should be a specific modification of the terms of the contract or if only economic compensation should be imposed (Momberg Uribe 2011).

Moreover, another issue in need of resolution is the standard to be applied in determining the extent of the variation; that is, if the injured party has to bear the losses arising from the change of circumstances to a reasonable level, or, alternatively, the losses are to be divided equally between the parties.

Then again, the technical implementation of the adjustment needs to be considered; i.e., if it becomes effective by law (as laid down by the courts), or if the injured party is entitled to specify its conditions. Additionally, it must be decided if the variation must be preceded by a negotiation process, and whether, and to what extent, such renegotiation can be regulated by law.

Despite these technical problems, in the author's opinion, the application of art. 89 CESL would not be problematic in the various European countries as there are a lot of similarities between the different European legal systems in this field both in the terms used and the results achieved, as well as in its treatment by the legal scholars.

References

Bianca GM (1994) Diritto civile, t. V, Giuffrè Editore, Milano.

Cashin-Ritaine E (2001) Imprévision, Hardship und Störung der Geschäftsgrundlage: Pacta sunt servanda und die Wege zur Anpassung des Vertrages im deutsch-französischen Rechtsverkehr, in Helms T Neumann D Caspers G Sailer, R Schmidt-Kessel M (ed), Jahrbuch Junger Zivilrechtwissenschaftler. Das neue Schuldrecht, Freiburg, pp. 85 ff.

Grigoleit C, Hondius E (2011) Unexpected circumstances in European Contract Law, Cambridge University Press, New York.

Lando O, Beale H (2000) Principles of European Contract Law, Parts I and II, prepared by the Commission on European Contract Law, 2000.

Larenz K (1957) Geschäftsgrundlage und Vertragserfüllung: die Bedeutung "veränderter Umständen" im Zivilrecht. C.H. Beck, München.

Momberg Uribe R (2011) Change of Circumstances in International Instruments of Contract Law. The Approach of The CISG, PICC, PECL and DCFR, 15(2) VJ, pp. 233 ff. http://www.cisg.law.pace.edu/cisg/biblio/uribe.pdf

Peer GM (2001) Die Rechtsfolgen von Störungen der Geschäftsgrundlage. Ein Vergleich zwischen § 313 RegE eines Schuldrechtsmodernisierungsgesetzes und dem geltenden deutschen und österreichischen Recht sowie modernen Regelwerken, in Helms T Neumann D Caspers G Sailer, R Schmidt-Kessel M (ed), Jahrbuch Junger Zivilrechtwissenschaftler. Das neue Schuldrecht, Freiburg, pp. 61 ff.

Schmidt-Kessel M (2013) Der Entwurf für ein Gemeinsames Europäisches Kaufrecht Kommentar, Sellier, Munich.

Van Houtte H (1993) Changed Circumstances and Pacta Sunt Servanda, in: Gaillard E (ed), Transnational Rules in International Commercial Arbitration, ICC Publ. Nr. 480,4, Paris, pp. 105 ff.

Chapter 9
Non Conformity of Goods and Digital Content and its Remedies

María Paz García Rubio

Abstract The concept of conformity is one of the most important topics in modern Contract Law, especially concerning the sale, as well as other types of contracts of goods and services. This is also true for the CESL, where the lack of conformity constitutes a case of non-performance, which may be down to both contractual parties, although it is more often that a non-performance is the responsibility of the seller. A situation of non-performance opens up the possibility of recourse to the panoply of remedies. The analysis of the general rules laid down in the CESL for the lack of conformity and the remedies available to the buyer, is the subject of this contribution.

Keywords Principle of conformity · Criteria for conformity · Remedies for lack of conformity · Requiring performance · Right to withhold performance · Termination · Price reduction · Damages and interest

9.1 The Principle of Conformity

9.1.1 Scope of Application

The rules concerning the non-performance and conformity of the contract included in CESL are a direct inheritance from the United Nations Convention on Contracts for the International Sale of Goods (CSIG), refined by Directive 1999/44/EC of the European Parliament and of the Council of 25 May 1999 on certain aspects of the sale of consumer goods and associated guarantees, the case-law of the ECJ that interprets the afore-mentioned Directive, and the Draft Common Framework of Reference (DCFR). In all of these instruments the issue of conformity is one of the most significant topics.

First of all it is important to remember that, according to the text originally proposed by the Commission, art. 1.1 CESL specified that the rules of this text "can

M. P. García Rubio (✉)
University Santiago de Compostela, Santiago de Compostela, Spain
e-mail: mpaz.garcia@usc.es

© Springer International Publishing Switzerland 2015
J. Plaza Penadés, L. M. Martínez Velencoso (eds.), *European Perspectives on the Common European Sales Law,* Studies in European Economic Law and Regulation 4,
DOI 10.1007/978-3-319-10497-3_9

be used for cross-border transactions for the sale of goods, for the supply of digital content and for related services where the parties to a contract agree to do so". However, in the text of the European Parliament (Report of the Committee on Legal Affairs–JURI-, of 24 September 2013), the objective matter is restricted to the same cross-border contracts, but only those "which are conducted at a distance, in particular online". According to the Working Group of the European Law Institute, this restriction of distance contracts brings with it a stronger focus on digital content, including a desire to use the CESL as a tool for further unleashing the potentials of cloud computing; (in this sense, *vid.* 1st Supplement: Reactions to the Draft Report of 18 February 2013 of the EP Committee on Legal Affairs).

Furthermore, following the criteria of the European Law Institute (ELI, Statement on the Proposal for a Regulation on a Common European Sales Law of 2012), the Parliament has also merged the "chapeau" regulation with Annex I, because this division of the Regulation in two different parts seems to have created unnecessary confusion.

The Proposal of the Commission and the Report of the European Parliament affects both contracts between traders (B2B), and those agreed by traders and consumers (B2C). This has drawn criticism by some authors who believe that the CESL should only be for consumer protection, and take the form of a Directive. This is the opinion given by the Committee on the Internal Market and Consumer Protection (IMCO), for the Committee of Legal Affairs (JURI), released on 11 July 2013.

According to this pedigree and following the trends of modern Contract Law, art. 87.1 of Annex I of the text proposed by the Commission provides us with a concept of non-performance of large amplitude and maximum neutrality with regard to its causes; (in relation to this modern concept of non-performance, see, in the Spanish literature, Morales Moreno 2010, pp. 29–30). Furthermore the concept of non-performance relates equally to the two subjects of the obligation. In this way, art. 87.1 establishes "Non-performance of an obligation is any failure to perform that obligation, whether or not the failure is excused";and in paragraph 2 of the same article, a definition of "fundamental non-performance", which is of great important for opening up the possibility of using the remedy of termination, is added. This article, which is essential to the construction of the system providing the remedies (Zoll 2012, p. 397), has not been amended by the Parliament, although it would have been desirable to also introduce a definition of "the insignificant lack of conformity", because under art. 114.2, in a B2C contract, the consumer may not terminate de contract if the lack of conformity is insignificant.

In a general, it can be said that a non-conforming performance is a specific, and very accurate, type of non-performance for sales contracts (Shelhaas 2009, p. 734), which seems to reflect a general principle of Contract Law: i.e. that contracts have to be performed in accordance with the terms of the agreement (Principles of European Sales Law 2006). The broad concept of non-performance includes, in the text of the CESL, three situations that refer specifically to the lack of conformity contained in the sub-paragraphs (c), (d) and (f) of the non-exhaustive list of article 87.1. Cases of non-performance are, among others: "(c) delivery of goods which are not in conformity with the contract; (d) supply of digital content which is not in conformity with the contract; (f) any other purported performance which is not in conformity with the contract." Therefore, sub-paragraph (f) contains any alleged breach of contract which in turn assumes a lack of conformity with the contract, consequently also including the situation of *aliud pro alio*, as in § 434 (3) BGB, in art. 7:13.3 Dutch Code, or in art. III-1:102 (3) DCFR. This sub-paragraph (f) can affect both the buyer and the seller; while sub-paragraphs (c) and (d) only relate to the benefits payable by the seller. In any case, the concept of conformity is flexible enough to take into account very different situations.

Although the proposed Regulation is intended to rule three types of contractual arrangements: i.e. the sale of goods, supply of digital content and other services contracts, in principle it seems that the "not in conformity" is an idea applicable to goods and digital content, and should not be applied to "related services". In fact the heading of Section 3, Chapter 10 of Part IV of Annex I is "Conformity of goods and digital content." Similarly, art. 91 (c) includes, among the main obligations of the seller, the obligation to "ensure that the goods or the digital content are in conformity with the contract", but does not mention 'related services'.

At first glance, this restriction is not consistent with the general tenor of art. 87.1 (f) CESL. However, those who think that services should be excluded from the idea of conformity, do so because they believe that in the contracts of services, the debtor's diligence represents a role that is not in accordance with the notion of conformity (*cf. ad. ex.*, art. 148 Annex I), which is a purely objective concept. This review is in line with those authors who think that the idea of "conformity" only fits with the obligations to achieve a result and never with the obligations of care and skill (Zamir 1991: *passim*; vid, however, Vaquer Aloy 2011, pp. 31–32, advocating overcoming the duality result versus care and skill, and supporting the general application of the concept of conformity). However, it should be noted that in related service contracts a reference to conformity is also included. Generally speaking, this is because art. 147 CESL determines the application of the rules of Chapter 9 to related services contracts, including art. 87 where both concepts, non-performance and conformity, are to be found. Specifically, this is because under art. 148.4 CESL "Where in a contract between a trader and a consumer the related service includes installation of the goods, the installation must be such that the installed goods conform to the contract as required by Article 101". Certainly, if the distinction between the obligations of result and the obligations of care and skill is accepted, the installation obligation included in a contract is configured as a result and, therefore, in those contracts the idea of "conformity" could fit, even for the more restrictive doctrine. Furthermore, art. 156 CESL governs the requirement of notification of lack of conformity in related service contracts between traders (B2B contracts), which means that related services contracts are also affected by the rule of the conformity (Vaquer Aloy 2012, p. 442).

The concept of conformity under the CESL resolves some of the problems that it had in Directive 1999/44. So, contrary to what happened in this Directive or in Spanish Law (arts. 114-127 TRLGDCU), where there have been some doubts expressed, and in accordance with the BGB (§ 453) (Schuller and Zebefels 2013, p. 588), in the CESL the concept of conformity clearly applies to digital content, regardless of whether it is incorporated in a material form or not, because, for example, they have been downloaded either online or offline(*cf.* art. 5 b Proposal and Parliament Amendment Number 62). Thus, in the CESL, the corporeality of the contract object is irrelevant. For the European Law Institute (ELI) (1st Supplement, 2013) it would be unrealistic in the twenty-first Century to treat these transactions as conceptually different, the first governed by the law of sales and the second governed by intellectual property law. Actually, they are simply different ways of supplying the product to the purchaser and should be treated both as sales contracts and within the scope of the CESL.

However, it is considered by some authors (Spindler 2012, p. 461; Yanguas 2012, p. 479) that all digital content that is not transferred to the client in a way that he holds it as if he were its owner, such as the streaming of a broadcast that can be used only at the specific time or that cannot be used offline (cloud computing) must be excluded. In a similar way, the ELI (1st Supplement, 2013) takes the view that a Sales Law regime is an appropriate legal regime only where the customer has the right to request the download of a usable copy of the digital content to a suitable storage facility within the customer's control at no further cost. Where, by contrast, the digital content has to remain in the seller's cloud, or where it can be downloaded but is usable only while the customer's device is connected to the seller's cloud, the contract resembles a service contract more than a sales contract.

In principle, the Regulation will be applied to digital content acquired through the payment of a price as well as those acquired without such payment. Indeed, art. 5(b) CESL governs this type of contract "irrespective of whether the digital content is supplied in exchange for the payment of a price". In the Commission's Proposal for the contracts that are not supplied in exchange for a price, there was an important limitation to the remedies available (*cf.* art. 107 Appendix I), and a special rule about conformity (art. 100 g) that reduced the legitimate expectations of the buyer in those cases. However, the absence of a price does not necessarily mean that they are gratuitous contracts, because the digital content can be delivered without paying a price but in exchange for things other than money that can be very valuable for the purchaser, such as the personal data (Loos et al. 2011, p. 750). For this reason, Amendment 62 of the Parliament (also ELI, 2012) no longer distinguishes between digital content contracts with or without price, but between digital content supplied in exchange for the payment of a price or in exchange for a counter-performance other than the payment of a price on the one hand, and those that are not supplied in exchange for any other counter-performance on the other hand. Only in the last category are contracts really free and, therefore, a limitation of the remedies available can be justifiable. Moreover, following the stronger focus on distance contracts (and in particular electronic contracts) taken by the Parliament, the storage and use of the buyer's personal data should receive more attention and more protection (ELI, 1st Supplement, 2013).

Furthermore, the concept refers to conformity, or lack of it, both physically and legal, although there is a difference between the two types since the latter is expressly provided for in art. 102 under the heading "Third party rights or claims".

As stated above, among the primary obligations of the seller, art. 91 (c) includes the power to "ensure that the goods or the digital content are in conformity with the contract". In order to measure if such conformity exists, arts. 99–105 CESL contain the rules that establish the concept, the criteria and the relevant time to gauge the performance. As reported in the Commission's Proposal, in B2C contracts many of these rules are mandatory in favour of the consumer (*vid., ad ex.*, arts. 99.4, 101.2, 102.5 and 105.5).

Article 99.1 contains the general rule concerning the meaning of 'conformity with the contract'. According to this precept "In order to conform with the contract, the goods or digital content must: (a) be of the quantity, quality and description required by the contract, (b) be contained or packaged in the manner required by the contract, and (c) be supplied along with any accessories, installation instructions or other instructions required by the contract."

In relation to the quantity mentioned in sub-paragraph (a), it should be noted that when this is lower than that required by the contract, art. 130.2 recognises "If the seller delivers a quantity of goods or digital content less than that provided for in the contract the buyer must take delivery unless the buyer has a legitimate interest in refusing to do so", which according some authors means that the only quantity that can imply lack of conformity is there is a concealed delivery (Zoll 2012, p. 467). By contrast, when the quantity is greater than that promised by the contract, in principle this situation is one of non-conformity, because according to art. 130.3. "If the seller delivers a quantity of goods or digital content greater than that provided for by the contract, the buyer may retain or refuse the excess quantity", although the article adds in para. 4 "If the buyer retains the excess quantity it is treated as having been supplied under the contract and must be paid for at the contractual rate". In a consumer sale (B2C), this last paragraph does not apply if the buyer reasonably believes that the seller has delivered the excess quantity intentionally and without error, knowing that it had not been ordered (art. 130.5).

In this context, conformity is not limited to goods as such. Article 99 sets out that the goods must be of the quality and description required by the contract, and be contained or packaged in the manner required by the contract; in this text 'contained' and 'packaged' seem to be synonyms (Zoll 2012, p. 468). Finally, the failure to deliver any accessories and instructions required by the contract also falls under the category of lack of conformity.

9.1.2 Conformity and Consent of the Contracting Parties

The concept of conformity gives priority to the contractual specifications, according to the principles of party autonomy and *pacta sunt servanda* (Feltkamp and Vanbossele 2011, p. 886).

Article 99.3, interpreted "*a contrario*", implies that in B2B contracts the criteria of conformity can be excluded by the parties. For these same contracts, art. 104 establishes a self-liability rule for the trader-buyer, by providing "In a contract between traders, the seller is not liable for any lack of conformity of the goods if, at the time of the conclusion of the contract, the buyer knew or could not have been unaware of the lack of conformity". The wording of this provision has been restricted to the case of lack of conformity of the goods (digital content not being mentioned), not any lack of conformity with the contract under art. 87.1 f, as would be the delivery of an *aliud pro alio.*

Article 99.3 provides "In a consumer sales contract, any agreement derogating from the requirements of articles 100, 102 and 103 to the detriment of the consumer is valid only if, at the time of the conclusion of the contract, the consumer knew of the specific condition of the goods or the digital content and accepted the goods or the digital content as being in conformity with the contract when concluding it". This rule has to be combined with the rules on protection against unfair terms, including the issue of whether these may or may not affect the main object of the contract. It should be noted that following the submissions of certain doctrine (Zoll 2012, p. 470), Amendment 184 European Parliament has replaced the reference to arts.100, 102 and 103, with arts. 100, 101 and 102.

Furthermore it is necessary to interpret art. 100 sub-para. (f) in relation to other provisions of the CESL, because this rule establishes a criterion for conformity that is: that the goods or the digital content "possess the qualities and performance capabilities indicated in any pre-contractual statement which forms part of the contract terms by virtue of article 69". Article 69 governs the contract terms derived from certain pre-contractual statements and according its para. 4 "In relations between a trader and a consumer the parties may not, to the detriment of the consumer, exclude the application of this article or derogate from or vary its effects". This means that art. 99.3 lacks utility in the case provided for by art. 100.f, as highlighted by Zoll (2012, p. 476). In fact the same author notes that art. 100.f is superfluous, because its content is already contained in art. 69, which shows that these pre-contractual statements promised by the seller or by a person engaged in advertising or marketing become part of the contract, and also that this rule cannot be deviated from in the case of B2C contracts.

9.1.3 Criteria for Conformity

Article 100 specifies the criteria for conformity of the goods and digital content, extracted from different sources. In this case, they are positively formulated, unlike its predecessors, art. 35.2 CISG (Schuller and Zenefels 2013, p. 597) and IV.A.-2:301 DCFR, that approached the criteria negatively, that is, as so-called non-conformity. Moreover, the DCFR and CESL, following the words of the Principles of European Sales Law (2006), seem slightly more straight-forward than the CISG, although, in the end, the result remains more or less the same.

Under art. 100 CESL, the "goods or digital content must:

a. be fit for any particular purpose made known to the seller at the time of the conclusion of the contract, except where the circumstances show that the buyer did not rely, or that it was unreasonable for the buyer to rely, on the seller's skill and judgement;

b. befit for the purposes for which goods or digital content of the same description would ordinarily be used;
c. possess the qualities of goods or digital content that the seller held out to the buyer as a sample or model.
d. be contained or packaged in the manner usual for such goods or, where there is no such manner, in a manner adequate to preserve and protect the goods;
e. be supplied along with such accessories, installation instructions or other instructions as the buyer may expect to receive;
f. possess the qualities and performance capabilities indicated in any pre-contractual statement which forms part of the contract terms by virtue of Article 69; and
g. possess such qualities and performance capabilities as the buyer may expect. When determining what the consumer may expect of the digital content regard is to be had to whether or not the digital content was supplied in exchange for the payment of a price."

All these criteria, which are very similar to those of art. IV.A-2:302 DCFR, can be applied in a cumulative manner.

In the case of sub-paragraph (a), the criteria is laid down for situations where a specific use is required by the buyer and communicated to the seller. This is deemed applicable if the seller either said that the goods or the digital content were suitable for that use or he remained silent when the buyer had made known his or her particular expectation (Zoll 2012, p. 473).

It has been said that the ordinary purposes or normal use criterion, referred to in sub-para. (b), that seems completely objective, is not very useful in the case of digital content, because in this type of content a permanent standard of quality often does not exist (Loos et al. 2011, pp. 102–108; Yanguas 2012, p. 482).

Furthermore, in almost all of these sections the criterion of reasonable expectations is present, being expressly mentioned in art. 100 (g) and, to some extent, implicit in all the others. This criterion of the legitimate or reasonable expectations of the creditor, to which the debtor is entitled, is one of the most characteristic features of the modern Contract Law (Zoll 2012, p. 406). It is an open concept that needs to be completed case-by-case. The "legitimate expectations" test is particularly difficult in digital content contracts, because in this kind of agreement it is often uncertain what the buyer may reasonably expect from the digital content; and also because the standard of the "ordinary purpose" ordinarily does not (yet) exist, (in this context, Loos et al. 2011, p. 741 consider that the conformity test is somewhat subject to manipulation by the trader).

Moreover, in the original Proposal, art. 100 (g) refers to the relevance of whether or not, in the case of digital content, a price has been paid, because in the latter case, the expectations are lower. This position is not shared by the Legal Affairs Committee of the European Parliament approved in the Report on 17 September 2013, which has amended the provision in the following sense (Amendment 185): "When determining what the buyer may expect of the digital content, regard is to be had to whether or not the digital content was supplied in exchange for the payment of a price or any counter-performance"

In connection with 'reasonable expectations', it is necessary to ask whether the lack of security could constitute a case of non-conformity, because this is a question that is not clear in the text of the CESL (Zoll 2012, p. 398). In the case of digital content contracts, it seems that security problems such as flaws, bugs, and defects, leaving the consumer's hardware or software open to viruses and trojan horses, may also constitute non-conformity of that digital content (Loos et al. 2011, p. 747). Clearly, the buyer may reasonably expect that the digital content does not cause physical or material damage to other hardware or software. Where such damage occurs as a result of a flaw, bug, or defect in the digital content, the trader is without doubt liable for non-conformity, as the buyer would always expect that use of the digital content is safe (Loos et al. 2011, p. 747).

On the other hand, incorrect installation is a special case of lack of conformity in terms of art. 101 that covers two different scenarios: "a) the goods or the digital content were installed by the seller or under the seller's responsibility; or b) the goods or the digital content were intended to be installed by the consumer and the incorrect installation was due to a shortcoming in the installation instructions". The aim of the first paragraph is to protect the buyer against the situation where the goods are damaged during the installation or simply do not function properly as a result of the installation. In a case covered by the second paragraph, it does not matter whether the buyer himself actually performed the wrong installation, as long as these two criteria are met.

As already mentioned, it should be noted that incorrect installation is also considered to be non-conformity in the related service contracts, because the art. 148.4 stipulates that "Where in a contract between a trader and a consumer the related service includes installation of the goods, the installation must be such that the installed goods conform to the contract as required by article 101".

Moreover, there is also the rule that third parties' rights or claims (which are not manifestly unfounded) constitute non-performance for lack of conformity, which would also cover the situation previously known as 'legal defects'. For example, the transfer of ownership of the property lacks conformity with the contract where it has already been transmitted to a third party, or where its transfer was subject to certain encumbrances when the ownership was declared to be free from them (article 102.1).

Article 102.2 governs the case of third party claims involving intellectual property, which will be especially important in the contracts of digital content; and this also supposes a case of lack of conformity (Feltkamp and Vanbosselе 2011, p. 888). The rule applies only if the seller knew or should have known of the claim by a third party, which is an exception to the usually strict standard of liability by the seller for non-conformity. However, if, in addition, the buyer knew or ought to have known it, art. 102.3 has to be considered, because it states that the previous rule does not apply to B2B contracts. In the case of B2C contracts, the rule does not apply if the buyer knew of the rights or claims of third parties at the time of conclusion of the contract (art. 102.4). In B2C contracts, these provisions are compulsory (art. 104.5).

It should be emphasised here that there is some contradiction between art. 102.4 (the consumer knew) and art. 99.3 (the consumer knew and accepted). Indeed, this last provision allows the non-performance to be excused by the knowledge and of the consumer purchaser of goods and digital content, and his acceptance as conforming to the contract; although, according to art. 102.4, knowledge is enough on its own without the requirement of acceptance. In addition, it seems clear that there is a reiteration by art. 104, which, in general, says "In a contract between traders, the seller is not liable for any lack of conformity of the goods if, at the time of the conclusion of the contract, the buyer knew or could not have been unaware of the lack of conformity", of art. 102.4, which in the case of non-performance because of third party rights or claims states "in contracts between a trader and a consumer, paragraph 2 does not apply where the consumer knew of the rights or claims based on intellectual property at the time of the conclusion of the contract".

Under art. 103, the risk of the obsolescence of digital content does not constitute a case of lack of conformity. This provision reflects art. 6.2 Council Directive 85/374/EEC of 25 July 1985 on the approximation of the laws, regulations and administrative provisions of the Member States concerning liability for defective products; and it is a logical consequence of the continuous technological advancement in this type of products. Some authors are of the opinion that this rule in the CESL has an informative meaning and not a normative content; which is most likely reason for which Parliament Amendment number 187 deletes this article. However, it can be considered that a rule like this could be useful, especially for digital content contracts, because it may well be that a newer version of the same digital content (for example, standard software), rectifies certain existing problems in older versions of that digital content. If this is so, the older digital content may very well be considered to be substandard if sold to the consumer when the new digital content has been put on the market and, at that time, the trader does not mention that these known defects have been remedied in the newer version of the digital content (Loos et al. 2011, p. 746; Yanguas 2012, p. 498).

Article 105 refers to the relevant point in time for establishing conformity. The first paragraph sets out that: "The seller is liable for any lack of conformity which exists at the time when the risk passes to the buyer under Chapter 14".

In B2C contracts, the presumption of lack of conformity contained in art. 105.2 is very important, in that it prescribes that: in a consumer sales contract (contract between a trader and a consumer, according Parliament Amendment 189), "any lack of conformity which becomes apparent within 6 months of the time when risk passes to the buyer is presumed to have existed at that time unless this is incompatible with the nature of the goods or digital content or with the nature of the lack of conformity".

Finally, art. 105.4 lays down that the trader must ensure that the digital content remains in conformity with the contract throughout the duration of the contract, "where the digital content must be subsequently updated by the trader", although in order to avoid loopholes, Parliament Amendment number 190 has also added to this the situation where the trader supplies its components (of the digital content) separately.

9.2 Remedies FOR Lack of Conformity

9.2.1 General Overview

According, more or less, to the Vienna (CISG) model, the CESL contains a system of remedies for non-performance that distinguishes between the remedies for the buyer (Chapter 11 arts. 106 et seq.), and the remedies for the seller (Chapter 13, arts. 131 et seq). On the other hand, the remedies established for the service contracts listed in Chap. 15, arts. 155–158 must also be considered, as well as the general remedy consisting of damages and interest payable, grouped together in Chap. 16 for both parties, the buyer and the seller.

In this chapter, an overview of the system of remedies for non-conformity is presented, without looking in detail at most of them, which will be the subject of separate chapters in this book. Attention will be paid to the remedies available to the buyer, as the contracting party who is most frequently affected by the lack of conformity.

In reality, the buyer is the party who will commonly use the lack of conformity as a contractual non-performance entitling him to seek different types of remedies. These remedies, which are inextricably linked to the issue of conformity, are imperative in the B2C contracts, as recognised by art. 108, which contains a "mandatory rule". This provision states that "In a contract between a trader and a consumer, the parties may not, to the detriment of the consumer, exclude the application of this chapter, or derogate from or vary its effect before the lack of conformity is brought to the trader's attention by the consumer".

However, it is submitted that some of the assumptions contained in art. 85 CESL, which is one of the provisions relating to "unfair contract terms in a contract between a trader and a consumer", gathered under the general rubric "Contract terms which are presumed to be unfair", are not consistent with the already mentioned mandatory rule of art. 108. Article 85 (b) states that a term is presumed to be an unfair contract term where it "inappropriately exclude[s] or limit[s] the remedies available to the consumer against the trader or a third party for non-performance by the trader of obligations under the contract". Actually, there is no possibility of any presumption here because when the breach amounts to a lack of conformity, such a clause is not allowed, according to the aforementioned art. 108. Thus art. 85.(b) should be deleted, as it has done by the European Parliament Amendment number 166. For the same reason, it is also submitted that other sections of art. 85 should be removed, such as that contained in sub-para. (g), which qualifies as a presumed unfair contract term when it enables a trader to terminate a contract of indeterminate duration without reasonable notice, except where there are serious grounds for doing so. It would seem that the only "serious grounds" are those established in Chapter 11.

Article 106 CESL begins the chapter concerning buyer's remedies with the case of the seller's non-performance, setting out the array of remedies already known in the CISG, the Lando Principles, UNIDROIT Principles, Directive 1999/44,and in

DCFR. The different remedies are: requiring performance, which includes specific performance; repair or replacement of the goods or digital content; withholding of the buyer's own performance; termination of the contract together with claiming the return of any price already paid; reduction of the price; and, finally, the claiming of damages.

It is important to note that, unlike its closest precedent, the various remedies in the CESL are not in any order of priority, and there is no preference for specific performance; i.e. the CESL chooses not to regulate the system of remedies hierarchically. Furthermore, according to the text proposed by the Commission, in B2C contracts the consumer can freely choose any remedy without being subject to any specific solution proposed by the seller (art. 106.3. a). This means that, generally, the consumer may immediately require the return of the price paid for the goods or digital content. This is, therefore, an improvement on the position in relation with that of most legal systems of the European countries that do not recognise the possibility of immediate termination (Schulte-Nölke 2012, p. 69). However, Amendment 192 of the Parliament recognises the seller's right to remedy the situation where the buyer's rights relate to goods or digital content which are manufactured, produced or modified in accordance with the consumer's specifications, or which are clearly personalised.

Unlike what happens in the other texts of the modern Law of Contracts, there are some differences between B2B and B2C contracts. In the contracts between traders the rule "*pacta sunt servanda*" is reinforced much more; for example, through the 'seller's right to cure' provision (art. 109), or the duties of examination and notification of the buyer included in arts.121 and 122 (vid. also arts.106.2 and 106.3 CESL). Article 106 also contains limitations to the use of certain remedies: where a seller's non-performance is excused, the buyer may resort to any of the remedies except for requiring performance and seeking damages (art. 106.4); and the buyer may not resort to any of the remedies if he had caused the seller's non-performance (art. 106.5). Additional limitations are:

1. The exclusion of the remedy of termination where the non-performance does not represent an essential or fundamental breach (art. 114.1 that complies with art. 87); or that in B2C contracts such non-performance is insignificant (art. 114.2), except in the case of art. 115, which permits termination for the delay in delivery after additional time for performance has been allowed.
2. Limitation of remedies for digital content not supplied in exchange for a price (even though they are not free), a case in which the art. 107 only provides a limited right to damages. It should be noted that Amendment 193 of the European Parliament seeks the change of this rule and it distinguishes, in line with what has been said above, between digital content supplied in exchange for payment of a price or any other counter-performance, and digital content not supplied in exchange for any counter-performance. The rule that limits the remedies in this sense would be only for cases where there is absence of any counter-performance. If the counter-performance were other than the payment of a price, the only excluded remedy would be the right to reduce the price, which is logical

> since no money had been paid. With the new rule, the limitation of the liability should not apply to the contracts in which the reciprocity of obligations exists, even though the obligation of the consumer is not expressed in money (Zoll 2012, p. 493).

In any case, and in relation to the issue already raised, the provision included in art. 107 CESL demonstrates that defects of security that can cause damage, are involved in the concept of non-conformity. As stated above, contrary to the opinion of Yanguas (2012, pp. 491 and 501), it is submitted that such security defects do not fall outside the scope of the contract and they must not be reserved to the field of the liability for defective products. In the CESL, lack of security is also a lack of conformity; and the CESL system should not replicate the difference that exists, for example, in the product liability system. However, certain authors such as Zoll (2012, p. 398) believes that the text of the Proposal is not clear and that art. 88 does not clarify that the breach of security duties by the debtor (the duty to perform the obligation in a way that does not endanger the other interests of the creditor) should be qualified as non-performance.

Before mentioning the different types of buyer's remedies, it is important to say that under art. 106.6, remedies that are not incompatible may be applied cumulatively (vid. also art. 8 Annex I).

9.2.2 Requiring Performance

Article 100 CESL provides that the buyer is entitled to require performance of the seller's obligations.

This is a remedy that does not fall into any primary remedy category, unlike what happens, for example, in the case of Directive 1999/44. It includes the remedying, free of charge, of a performance which is not in conformity with the contract. In B2C contracts, this right is accomplished by the provision concerning the consumer's right to repair and replacement (art. 111). In the B2B contracts, this remedy normally will be achieved through the seller's right to a remedy, and, therefore, the seller's right to insist on the use of this mechanism.

Under art. 106.4, the possibility of requiring performance (like damages) is excluded if the seller's non-performance is excused. This remedy is also excluded in the event of impossible performance (both initial and supervening); or if it has become unlawful, or the burden or expense of performance would be disproportionate to the benefit that the buyer would obtain (art. 110). That means that B2C contracts are also affected by absolute disproportion, and not only by the relative disproportion that is set down in art. 111. This means that the consumer's right to require performance has to be economically efficient. Therefore, in this context, it is not possible to use a solution, such as "that the European Union legislature intended to give the seller the right to refuse repair or replacement of the defective goods only if this is impossible or relatively disproportionate", derived from the ECJ Judgment in *Weber* and *Putz* Cases, of 16 June 2011.On the contrary, in the

CESL, if the remedies of damages or price reduction are more suitable and cause less inconvenience to the seller, without damaging the purchaser, then these should be preferred (García Rubio 2013, p. 336). Nonetheless, it must be said that, unlike what happens in Directive 1999/44 that did not include the reference to damages, in the CESL, the remedy of the performance can be completed with compensation for damages if the requirements are fulfilled.

In B2C contracts, art. 111 grants the consumer the right to choose between repair and replacement; Zoll believes that consumer protection here prevails over economic efficiency. However, the provision also regulates the limits on consumer choice because this choice is not possible where the option chosen would be unlawful or impossible or, compared to the other options available, would impose costs on the seller that would be disproportionate. The question here is whether the absolute disproportion is not mentioned because it is irrelevant and does not limit the rights of the consumer purchaser to choose any of the modes of requiring performance, or rather it is not mentioned because any remedy disproportionately burdensome and disproportionate *ex ante* is excluded under the previous rule. It is submitted that this second option is the most plausible and most consistent with the fact that, unlike what happens in Directive 1999/44, in the CESL the remedies for non-performance are all treated equally and are not organised into a hierarchy (García Rubio 2013, p. 337). Furthermore, this second option ensures that a proportionate relationship between the value of a given remedy to the buyer and the cost incurred by the seller is preserved.

Under art. 111.2, if the consumer has required the lack of conformity is remedied by repair or replacement, the consumer may resort to other remedies only if the trader has not completed that repair or replacement within a reasonable time, not exceeding 30 days. However, the consumer has the right to suspend his performance while the seller is undertaking the repair or the replacement.

Article 112 regulates the return of a replacement item stipulating that where the seller has remedied the lack of conformity by replacement, the seller has a right and an obligation to take back the replaced item at the seller's expense. At first glance there appears to be no limitation on the scope of the costs that must be borne by the seller as a result of the process of replacing the goods not in conformity. However, if this is interpreted in the context of the preceding article, the replacement process would never have occurred if the estimated costs for the seller would have been disproportionately burdensome and expensive relative to other possible remedies, and consequently such expenses, if any, would be always proportionate (García Rubio 2013, p. 337). Moreover, compensation is only due for costs that are reasonable and directly linked to the remedies in question.

The second part of art. 112 prescribes that the buyer is not liable to pay for any use made of the replaced item in the period prior to the replacement. This rule is applied in the B2B contracts if the parties do not agree with each other; but in B2C contracts the rule is mandatory under art. 108.This is a consequence of the ECJ, (Judgment of 17 April 2008, the *Quelle* Case) which was based on desire of the Community legislature in Directive 1999/44 to make the 'free of charge conformity of the goods by the seller an essential element of the protection that the Directive gives consumers. It seems that the CESL follows the same criteria; but it should be understood that the reference to the use of the object refers to its proper and normal use and not any misuse that has spoiled the replaced item (García Rubio 2013, p. 337). In this sense, it should be remembered that in the *Messner* Case (ECJ Judgment of 3 September 2009), the provisions of Directive 97/7 do not prevent the consumer from being required to pay compensation for the use of the goods where he has made use of those goods in a manner incompatible with the principles of civil law, such as those of good faith or unjust enrichment; on condition that the purpose of that Directive and, in particular, the efficiency, effectiveness and efficacy of the right of withdrawal are not adversely affected; this being a matter for the national court to determine, (see Zoll 2012, p. 513, who contends that although the *Messer* Case concerned the right of withdrawal, this consideration has broader relevance and that it is also essential in the context of replacement).

9.2.3 Right to Withhold Performance

Article 113 CESL contains this remedy, which is typical of the reciprocal contracts, and which is, despite its importance, poorly regulated and poorly studied. This remedy goes beyond mutual contractual benefits and can even have preventive effects: for example, the seller may decide not to replace the defective goods until he has them returned, or vice versa. The main effect of the use of this remedy is the temporary suspension of the buyer's own performance. It temporarily neutralises the right of the seller, but does not extinguished it. This mechanism sometimes works as a prelude to termination, minimising the restitutional effect.

Anticipatory retention is possible, when the buyer who is going to perform before the seller performs, reasonably believes that there will be a non- performance by the seller; this situation can remain for as long as the reasonable belief continues (art. 113.2).

This remedy also applies to cases of lack of conformity (art. 113.3 a). In this case, the original provision, enhanced by the Commission, provided that the performance that may be withheld, would be the whole or part of the performance to the extent justified by the non-performance. However, the difficulties in harmonising this provision with art. 130 relating to early delivery and delivery of the wrong quantity (Zoll 2012, p. 516), explains the need for Amendment 200 of the Parliament that proposes a new text stipulating that, in a B2C contract, the entire performance may be withheld, unless such withholding is disproportionate to the significance of the lack of conformity.

Partial retention is also possible. In the case of lack of conformity, the buyer may withhold performance to the extent (total o partial) that it is justified by the level of non-performance.

It is interesting to consider that after the last version of the CESL was enhanced by the Parliament with a stronger focus on distance contracts (and in particular electronic contracts), the ELI believes that the storage and use of the buyer's personal data should receive more attention. It is important to consider to what extent issues relating to the use of personal data (such as pre-contractual information), and to the buyer's consent to the use of the data, should be included in the CESL. The ELI considers that, in general, Sales Law and Data Protection Law should be kept apart in order to avoid inconsistencies. However, Sales Law can play an important role in underpinning the buyer's right to withdraw consent to the use of personal data; in particular, by making sure that the seller no longer uses the buyer's personal data after the buyer has exercised a right of withdrawal, avoidance or termination (Explanation Number 19, ELI First Supplement, 2013).

9.2.4 Termination

Termination is a powerful remedy that, because of its importance, will be treated in extensively in another chapter of this book. This chapter contains only a brief commentary.

Termination is defined in art. 8 CESL (Annex I), where the main principles governing its effects are also to be found. These are mainly the possibility of cumulative damages, and the rights concerning return after termination under Chap. 17 (Restitution). According this provision, "to terminate a contract" means to bring to an end to the rights and obligations of the parties under the contract with the exception of those arising under any contract term providing for the settlement of disputes or any other contract term which is to operate even after termination (art. 8.1 Annex I, CESL).

The right of the buyer to terminate the contract is governed by Sect. 5 of Chap. 11 (arts. 114–119). Pursuant to the first of these provisions, a buyer may terminate the contract if the seller's non-performance is fundamental within the meaning of art. 87; but in B2C contracts where the goods are not in conformity with the contract, the consumer may terminate the contract "unless the lack of conformity is insignificant" (art. 87.2). That means that for B2C, in cases of lack of conformity of the goods or digital content, the requirements of the termination are relaxed by reducing the concept of the 'fundamental non-performance' to only 'not insignificant non-performance'.

Termination for the seller's anticipated non-performance (including lack of conformity; art. 116), and partial termination (art. 117) are also possible. As happens in Spanish Law, the right to terminate is exercised by giving notice to the seller (art. 118). The only amendment introduced by the Parliament with regard to this issue has been to art. 119. Under the text proposed by the Commission, in B2B contracts a buyer loses his right to terminate the contract if the notice of termination had not been given within reasonable time; but this rule did not apply to B2C contracts, so that a consumer may terminate the contract without limitation until the end of the prescribed period. Nevertheless, according to Amendment 201 of the Parliament "The buyer loses the right to terminate under this Section if notice of termination is not given within two months from when the right arose or the buyer became, or, if the buyer is a trader that buyer could be expected to have become, aware of the non-performance, whichever is later".

It is important to remember that, as a consequence of the termination, the parties to the contract would have to return the benefits from the performance of an obligation that usually has already taken place (Part VII, Chap. 17). Such restitution, although in theory possible, poses important problems in the case of digital content. For this reason, Amendment 230 of the Parliament introduces a new paragraph in art. 172 specifying the cases where the digital content should be considered as returnable and the buyer should not have to pay the monetary value.

9.2.5 Price Reduction

The right to reduce the price in cases of lack of conformity is an economic choice. This is the traditional *quanti minoris* action that facilitates partial resolution and compensation.

This is a right of the buyer that does not require the seller's consent. Although there is not a specified provision, by analogy with termination, all that is required for this remedy is for the buyer to notify the seller that he intends to assert his right to this option.

Article 120.3 provides for the relationship of this remedy to the payment of damages and interest, stipulating that a buyer who reduces the price cannot also recover damages for the loss thereby compensated, but remains entitled to damages for any further loss suffered. In the latter case, the buyer will get the difference between the price paid and the real price of the goods subject to a lack of conformity; (this is also so in art. 45.2 CISG and 9:401 PECL, *vid.* Morales Moreno 2010, pp. 44 and 192).

At this point, it is interesting to consider the Judgment of the ECJ in the *Soledad Duarte* Case, of 3 October 2013, where it was said that Spanish procedural legislation does not guarantee the effectiveness of Directive 1999/44. The Court of Justice found that, under the Spanish procedural system, a consumer who brings proceedings seeking solely the termination of the contract for the sale of goods is definitively deprived of the possibility of benefiting from the right to seek an appropriate reduction in the price of those goods in the event that the court dealing with the dispute should find that, in fact, the lack of conformity in those goods is minor. Only in the event that the consumer had made an application containing an alternative claim seeking such a price reduction would that outcome not occur. However the European Court understood that there was a significant risk that the consumer would not put forward an alternative claim requesting a reduction in the price either by reason of the particularly rigid requirement that the two claims must be presented at the same time or because the consumer is unaware of, or does not appreciate, the extent of his rights.

The Court of Justice found that such procedural rules are liable to undermine the effectiveness of the consumer protection intended by the European Union legislature in so far as they do not allow the national court to recognise of its own motion the consumer's right to obtain an appropriate reduction in the price of the goods, even though that consumer is not entitled to refine his initial application or to bring a fresh action to that end. Consequently, the ECJ declared that the Spanish procedural legislation does not appear to comply with the principle of effectiveness, in so far as, in proceedings brought by consumers in cases where the goods delivered are not in conformity with the contract of sale, it makes the enforcement of the protection which the Directive seeks to confer on them excessively difficult, if not impossible.

However, the Court of Justice makes it clear that it is for the Spanish Court to do whatever lies within its power, taking the whole body of domestic law into consideration and applying the interpretative methods recognised by domestic law, with a view to ensuring that the Directive is fully effective and to achieving an outcome which is consistent with its objective of guaranteeing a high level of consumer protection. It must be said that according to the Spanish authors, the interpretation given to art. 400 of the Civil Procedure Act by the European Court Of Justice is neither the only one, nor the best. In fact, the particularly rigid requirement that the two claims (termination and price reduction) must be presented at the same time in the same procedure is not required by the legal text (Ormazábal 2013).

9.3 Damages and Interest

The right to claim damages is a classic remedy in Contract Law, and is included in all the texts that have been a model for the CESL, with the exception of Directive 1999/44.

In the CESL, this is the only remedy that is provided jointly to both contractual parties. Part VI (Chap. 16) is dedicated to it, without making any distinction between the buyer and the seller. Furthermore there are other provisions in the Regulation relating to damages, such as art. 2.2. Annex I, where the liability is established for any loss caused to the other party in the case of breach of the duty of good faith.

This remedy is applicable to all cases of non-performance, and, therefore, also cases of lack of conformity.

According the art. 159.1 "A creditor is entitled to damages for loss caused by the non-performance of an obligation by the debtor, unless the non-performance is excused". Consequently, there must be a loss (actually as defined in art. 2 c of the Proposal) and a causal relationship between the breach of contract and the loss. Negligence on the part of the debtor is not required; but under the art. 106.4 CESL, the debtor only avoids the payment of damages if he can justify the breach in the terms of art. 88. Under that provision the non-performance will be excusable if there occurs "an impediment beyond that party's control and if that party could not be expected to have taken the impediment into account at the time of the conclusion of the contract, or to have avoided or overcome the impediment or its consequences". However, in this case art. 88.3 entitles the other party to claim compensation damages for any loss resulting from the breach of the duty to give notice of the impediment.

It is important to determine the meaning of the term "impediment beyond that party's control". It seems that it attempts to state that is not enough that the debtor proves that he has been sufficiently diligent. This raises the problem of non-performance due to the actions of an independent auxiliary (e.g. the post or other consignment providers). It is submitted that the authors who think that this kind of situation, as occurs in the CISG system, should be considered in the field of control of the debtor (Zoll 2012, p. 411) are correct. The CESL contains a limited notion of damage or loss: under art. 2 (c) "loss" means economic loss and non-economic loss in the form of pain and suffering, excluding other forms of non-economic loss such as impairment of the quality of life and loss of enjoyment. Therefore, the so-called "moral harm" is not considered compensable, perhaps because of the type of contracts governed in the proposed Regulation. Nonetheless, it is possible that the item purchases is, for example, a wedding dress that is delivered broken or burned, or a digital gaming content whose lack of conformity spoils a Christmas gift. However, the Parliament has not introduced any change in this narrow concept of loss.

Article 159.2 includes future losses and provides that "The loss for which damages are recoverable includes future loss which the debtor could expect to occur".

Pursuant to art. 160, "the general measure of damages for loss caused by non-performance of an obligation is such sum as will put the creditor into the position in which the creditor would have been if the obligation had been duly performed, or, where that is not possible, as nearly as possible into that position. Such damages cover loss which the creditor has suffered and gain of which the creditor has been deprived". This is the so-called positive interest (*restitutio in integrum*) that is also appropriate in cases of termination.

The foreseeability of loss is provided for in art. 161, which states that "the debtor is liable only for loss which the debtor foresaw or could be expected to have foreseen at the time when the contract was concluded as a result of the non-performance".

The CESL does not include penalty clauses regulating compensation alternatives, and nor does it mention the clauses limiting liability, except in the unfair contracts terms' provisions. However, this last regime is not totally consistent with art. 108, which stipulates that in B2C contracts all remedies are mandatory.

It is interesting to consider that, although financial compensation is the common type of compensation for damage, the digital environment offers traders other means to redress the damage, such as free downloads, free extensions of contracts, and discounts on future purchases (Loos et al. 2011, p. 749).

References

Feltkamp R/Vanbosselle F. (2011) "The Optional Common European Sales Law: Better Buyer's Remedies for Seller's Non-performance in Sales of Goods" *ERPL* 6 pp. 873 et seq.

García Rubio M.P (2013) "Las obligaciones del vendedor de retirar el bien defectuoso y de instalar el bien de sustitución en caso de saneamiento en una compraventa de bienes de consumo (comentario a la STJUE de 16 de junio de 2011 en los asuntos acumulados Weber y Putz)" *Anuario de Derecho Civil* pp. 323–337.

Loos M/Helberger N/Guibault L/MakCh (2011) "The Regulation of Digital Content Contracts in the Optional Instrument of Contract Law" *ERPL* 6 pp. 729–758.

Morales Moreno A.M. (2010) Incumplimiento del contrato y lucro cesante Madrid.

Ormazábal G. (2013) "Comentario a la STJUE de 3 octubre 2013 caso Soledad Duarte" *La Ley Unión Europea* diciembre.

Principles of European Sales Law (2006) Draft 6 October. Utrecht Working Team on Sales Law.

Schulte-Nölke H (2012) "El Derecho de consumo en la Propuesta de Reglamento sobre un Derecho común europeo de la compraventa" in *La revisión de las normas europeas y nacionales de protección de los consumidores* S. Cámara Lapuente (Dir.) E. Arroyo Amayelas (Coord) Cizur Menor Civitas-Thomson Reuter pp. 63–80.

Schuller Ch/Zenefels A. (2013) "Obligations of Sellers and Buyers" in *The Common European Sales Law in Context. Interactions with English and German Law* G. Dannemann/Stefan Vogenauer Oxford.

Shelhaas H. (2009) "Non-Performance" in *Commentary on the Unidroit Principles of International Commercial Contracts (PICC)* ed. By S. Vogenauer/J. Keinheisterkamp Oxford pp. 726 et seq.

Spindler G (2012) "Implicaciones para los servicios de contenidos digitales de la Propuesta de Reglamento sobre un Derecho común de compraventa" in *La revisión de las normas europeas y nacionales de protección de los consumidores* S. Cámara Lapuente (Dir.) E. Arroyo Amayelas (Coord) Cizur Menor Civitas-Thomson Reuter pp. 457–470.

Vaquer Aloy A. (2011) "El principio de conformidad: ¿supraconcepto en el Derecho de obligaciones?) *Anuario Derecho Civil* pp. 4–39.

Vaquer Aloy A. (2012) "Contratos de servicios: entre el Derecho del consumo y el Derecho contractual general" en *La revisión de las normas europeas y nacionales de protección de los consumidores* S. Cámara Lapuente (Dir.) E. Arroyo Amayelas (Coord) Cizur Menor Civitas-Thomson Reuter pp. 421–456.

Yanguas Gómez R. (2012) "El principio de conformidad y su aplicación a los contenidos digitales" en *La revisión de las normas europeas y nacionales de protección de los consumidores* S. Cámara Lapuente (Dir.) E. Arroyo Amayelas (Coord) Cizur Menor Civitas-Thomson Reuter pp. 471–508.

Zamir E. (1991) "Toward a General Concept of Conformity in the Performance of Contracts" *Louisiana Law Review* vol. 52–1 pp. 4–90.

Zoll F (2012) *Common European Sales Law (CESL). Commentary* Schulze (ed.) Baden-Baden C.H. Beck. Hart. Nomos pp. 396 et seq.

Chapter 10
Passing of Risk

Francisco Oliva Blázquez

Abstract The theory of passing of risk is one of the most problematic topics regarding contract sales law. Indeed, when the sold goods are lost or damaged by accident, the buyer does not receive what he bought because the seller is discharged from its obligation of delivering (art. 88.1 CESL). However, there remains an unsolved question: does the buyer's obligation to pay the price subsist? If the answer is positive, it is maintained that the buyer bears the risk. Hence, it is very important to determine clearly at what stage in the life of the contract does the risk pass to the buyer.

National laws usually link the passing of risk to abstract and general concepts, such as the conclusion of the contract, the transfer of ownership or the transfer of the physical possession of the goods. However, these "key concepts" are rigid and unsuited to international commercial practice. For these reasons, the CESL has opted to follow the "analytical approach" set out in the CISG. In short, this legal technique seeks to determine the moment of the passing of risk in the various situations that may arise in commercial reality. So, Chapter 14 of CESL regulates the passing of risk in sales involving carriage of goods, when the goods are sold in transit or when the goods are placed at buyer's disposal. Each of these situations has its own rule governing the passing of risk. Moreover, the CESL expressly distinguishes between B2B and B2C contracts, thus ensuring a high level of consumer protection.

Keywords Passing of risk · Identification of goods or digital content · Delivery · Carriage of the goods · Goods sold in transit · Retaining of documents · Physical possession of the goods · Obligation to pay the price

---

F. Oliva Blázquez (✉)
University Pablo de Olavide, Sevilla, Spain
e-mail: folibla@upo.es

© Springer International Publishing Switzerland 2015
J. Plaza Penadés, L. M. Martínez Velencoso (eds.), *European Perspectives on the Common European Sales Law,* Studies in European Economic Law and Regulation 4,
DOI 10.1007/978-3-319-10497-3_10

10.1 Introduction

10.1.1 The Problem of Passing of Risk in Sale of Goods Contracts

The passing of risk is one of the most complex legal issues related to sales law. In fact, it can be said that the wording "risk" has become a cult concept in the contract law world.[1] Nonetheless, it is intrinsically versatile, and hence the main problem is that of determining what is the exact meaning of "passing of risk".

When goods or digital content suffer any kind of loss or damage by accident (or due to no fault of either party) in the period in between the time of the conclusion of the contract and its performance, the seller is discharged from its obligation to deliver the goods that have been lost or destroyed. This is called "delivery risk" (*Leistungsgefahr*) or "risk of performance".[2] However, when we talk about the passing of risk in sales contracts we refer to the "price risk" (*Preisgefahr*), the "risk of counter-performance" or the "risk of payment". Therefore, the following question must be answered: does the buyer's obligation to pay the price remain in the above-mentioned situation?[3]

If the answer to this question is affirmative, the buyer shall bear the risk of the loss or damage (*periculum est emptoris*). In this situation, the buyer does not receive the goods if they are accidentally lost or, in the event of partial damage, he will only take over damaged goods, because, as we have seen, the seller is normally excused from the obligation to deliver other conforming goods. In addition, he must fulfil the obligation of paying the full price under the contract, provided of course, that the risk has passed, as we will see below.

On the contrary, the seller shall bear the risk of loss or damage (*periculum est venditoris*) when he loses the right to obtain the agreed price of the goods that have perished or become completely or partially damaged. Given the extraordinary significance that both solutions have for the parties, determining the exact time when the risk passes is deemed to be the key element in this problem.[4]

---

[1] Lilleholt (2011), Passing of Risk and the Risk of Mystification: Some Drafting Issues, *European Review of Private Law*, 19, 6, p. 928.

[2] Indeed, according to art. 88.1 CESL, "a party's non-performance of an obligation is excused if it is due to an impediment beyond that party's control and if that party could not be expected to have taken the impediment into account at the time of the conclusion of the contract, or to have avoided or overcome the impediment or its consequences". See, likewise, art. III.-3:104 DCFR (Excuse due to an impediment).

[3] "In other words, is the buyer obliged to perform even if the goods are not received at all, or only in a damaged state?" Von Bar and Clive (2011), *Draft Common Frame of Reference, Full Edition,* vol. 2, München, Sellier. Art. IV.A.-5:101 DCFR. Comment A.

[4] *Vid.,* Fiorillo and Bodin (1992), A., International Sale of Goods. In Barbero, L., *International Trade Law Post-Graduate Course. Participant's Review. Turín, 3 April–26 June 1992.* Turin. University Institute of European Studies Turín, International Training Centre of the ILO-Turín, p. 359. Kahn (1996). Vente Commerciale Internationale. In *Juris-Classeur de Droit International.* 9, Fascicule 565-A-5, París. Éditions du Juris-Classeur, p. 19.

10.1.2 Passing of Risk in Private Comparative Law: Different Solutions for the Same Problem

The issue of passing of risk is a well-known subject in the national legal systems around the world and, in the course of its immemorial history,[5] has raised uncountable doctrinal problems. In a nutshell, we can distinguish at least three different criterions normally invoked to solve the problem:

1) *The conclusion of the contract*
   The criterion of the conclusion of the contract appears in various legal systems[6] as a reflection of the powerful Roman rule: *periculum est emptoris.*[7] However, this rule poses several problems. Firstly, the task of determining the exact time of the conclusion of a contract between parties located in different places is not easy.[8] It could also provoke unjust outcomes. Thus, it makes no sense to allocate the risk of loss or damage to the buyer from the moment of the conclusion of the contract because he usually has no access or control over the goods. Moreover, international sales normally involve bulk goods that have not been manufactured or specified, and in that situation the buyer bears the risk solely from the time of identification, not from the conclusion of the contract.[9]

2) *Transfer of ownership*
   According to this second criterion, the risks are borne by the party having the ownership of the goods.[10] This principle finds support in the legal proverb *res perit domino.*[11] But, in the point of view of most of the scholars, this is a legal

[5] This history began with Roman Law: the risk passed to the purchaser as soon as the contract was *perfecta* (Inst. 3,23.3). See, Nicholas (1962), *An Introduction to Roman Law, Oxford,* Clarendon Law Series, p. 171.

[6] Article 185 Swiss Code of Obligations; art. 1452 Spanish Civil Code. See, Alonso Pérez (1972), *El riesgo en el contrato de compraventa*, Madrid, Montecorvo, pp. 291–311; López y López (1993), Artículo 1452, in *Comentario del Código Civil*, Tomo II, Madrid, Ministerio de Justicia, pp. 895–898.

[7] Adame Goddard (1984), La regla periculum est emptoris aplicada a la compraventa internacional de mercaderías, *Anuario Jurídico* (México D.F.), pp. 248 and 249. Seymour (2008), The Passing of Risk in Contracts for Sale in Roman Law and Australian Law: A Comparative Perspective, *Queensland Law Student Review*, Number 1, Volume 1.

[8] Audit (1990), *La vente internationale de marchandises*, Convention des Nations-Unies du 11 avril 1980, Paris, L.G.D.J., p. 87.

[9] Enderlein and Maskow (1992), International Sales Law. United Nations Convention on Contracts for the International Sale of Goods—Convention on the Limitation Period in the International Sale of Goods. Commentary. New York/London/Rome, 1992, p. 255.

[10] This system has been the fruit of a progressive spiritualisation of the "*traditio*" made by the French scholars under the influence of the School of Natural Law, and has been adopted by many systems, such as the French (arts. 1138 and 1538 *Code Civil*), the Italian (arts. 1376 and 1465.1 *Codice Civile*) or the English (*The Sale of Goods Act*, 1893, s. 20).

[11] See, Von Hoffmann (1986), Passing of Risk in International Sales of Goods, in Sarcevic, P. & Volken, P. *International Sale of Goods: Dubrovnik Lectures*, Oceana, p. 268.

criterion that ignores the needs of modern international sale of goods contracts.[12] Linking the passing of risk to ownership may cause many problems because of the variety of systems regulating the question of the transfer of ownership under current comparative law.[13] Moreover, it seems clear that the passing of risk is a problem that must be dealt with on a purely obligational plane (*obligationis periculum*). In other words, it can be misleading to try to solve the risk problem through the adage "*periculum rei*".

3) *Transfer of Physical Possession (Delivery)*
The "delivery" criterion is found in German Law (*Übergabeprinzip*)[14] and in the Uniform Law of International Sales of 1967 (art. 97 ULIS): "the risk shall pass to the buyer when delivery of the goods is effected in accordance with the provisions of the contract and the present Law". This latter rule was subject to hard criticism on the ground that the concepts of "delivery" and "handing over" were too generic and, as a consequence, were used in many different legal contexts. However, at first glance, this could be a reasonable solution, because the party in physical possession of the goods is always in the better position to take measures for the prevention of risks of loss and damage.

10.1.3 The Typological Approach of CISG and its Influence in CESL

We have just seen how the national laws usually resort to abstract and general concepts (key concepts) to regulate the passing of risk. But these criteria, because of their limited flexibility, face highly important difficulties in adapting to the changing conditions of commercial life.

Mainly for this reason, the United Nations Convention on the International Sale of Goods (CISG) abandoned the legislative technique known as the "lump concept",[15] provided by civil law countries[16] and, instead, adopted a new technique called the "typological approach", whose origin is located in the common law sys-

[12] As Professor Rabel said in 1938, "to make the passing of property and risk coincide is surprisingly primitive", Rabel (1938), A Draft of an International Law of Sales, *The University of Chicago Law Review*, 1938, p. 551; Thieffry (1988), Sale of Goods between French and U.S. Merchants: Choice of Law considerations under the U.N. Convention on Contracts for the International Sale of Goods, *The International Lawyer*, p. 1024.

[13] Angelici (1981), La disciplina del passaggio dei rischi in *La Vendita Internazionale. Convegno S. Margherita Lugure, 26- 28.8.80*, Milano, Giuffrè, p. 222. Ionasco and Nestor (1966), *Le risque de perte en transit: existe-t-il des differences quant aux effects de certaines clauses similaires concernant le risqué*, in Honnold, J., *Unification of the Law Governing International Sale of Goods, The Comparison and Possible Harmonization of National and Regional Unifications*, Paris, Librairie Dalloz, p. 151.

[14] § 446 BGB.

[15] Angelici (1979), *"Consegna" e "proprietà" nella vendita internazionale*, Milano, Giuffrè, pp. 50–51.

[16] Vid., Roth (1979), The Passing of Risk, *The American Journal of Comparative Law*, p. 294.

tem. This analytical technique tries to determine the passing of risk in each of the different situations that can be found in commercial reality. In other words, instead of establishing an all-encompassing legal standard (such as the transfer of ownership or the conclusion of the contract), the new rules describe in detail most of the situations that take place in the legal dealings, determining in each case the exact time in which the buyer begins to bear the risk.[17] Thus, each of the situations that may appear in international sales will have a consistent and appropriate solution, adapted to commercial reality. This formula underlies the wording of the American Uniform Commercial Code[18] and the Incoterms of the International Chamber of Commerce.[19]

Under this author's opinion, this methodological approach meets in the main the objective requirements of legal dealings, i.e. it serves to "*mirror commercial reality*".[20] However, although this technique has been well received by legal scholars and practitioners as an important legal improvement,[21] its problems should not be forgotten:

First, it is virtually impossible for a set of legal rules, no matter how detailed and complete they are, to capture the richness of forms and situations in which the international sale unfolds.[22] In fact, it has been argued that the absence of specific rules

---

17 "The Convention establishes clear rules specifying the allocation of the risk or damage to the goods. Risk passes from seller to buyer at clearly definable moments in the transaction". Burke (1981), International Trade: Uniform Law of Sales, *Harvard International Law Journal*, p. 477.

18 "These provisions of risk of loss deal with the problem in much the same way as the equivalent provisions of the Uniform Commercial Code (UCC 2-509, 2-510)." American Bar Association (1984), Report to the House of Delegates. Section of International Law and Practice. Symposium Atlanta 1.8.1983, *The International Lawyer*, p. 48.

19 "The result concerning risk of loss under the UCC and the combination of CISG and INCOTERMS would appear to be almost exactly the same", Hancock (1986), *The Convention on Contracts for the International Sale of Goods compared with the Uniform Commercial Code,* in Hancock, W.A., *Guide to the International Sale of Goods Convention*, Chesterland, OH, Business Laws, Inc., p. 106.19.

20 Stocks (1993), *Risk of loss under the Uniform Commercial Code and the United Nations Convention on Contracts for the International Sale of Goods: a comparative analysis and proposed revision of UCC Sections 2-509 and 2 510*, Northwestern University Law Review, p. 1420. Honnold (1984a), The new Uniform Law for International Sale of Goods and the UCC: a comparison, in Symposium on International Sale of Goods, *The International Lawyer*, p. 27.

21 "To the extent that these physical events rather than metaphysical concepts of passage of title determine the substantive rights of the parties, a great improvement in achieving predictability and certainty of results has been made", Del Duca and Del Duca (1996), Practice under the Convention on International Sale of Goods (CISG): a primer for attorneys and international traders, (Part II), *Uniform Commercial Code Journal*, p. 130.

22 "Demands for simplicity contending with claims for delicate adjustment to meet the wide range of settings for international trade", Honnold (1984b), Risk of Loss. Chapter 8, in Galston, N. & Smit, H., *International Sales: The United Nations Convention on Contracts for the International Sale of Goods; Conference held by the Parker School of Foreign and Comparative Law, Columbia University, October 1983*, New York, Matthew Bender, p. 8–2.

for the passing of risk in the case of multiple sales of goods during transit ("daisy chain sales") is the "Achilles heel" of the Vienna Convention.[23]

Furthermore, the emergence of new forms or variants of international sales contracts can lead to the obsolescence of any one law. As a consequence, the legislator has to review the rules continuously in order to guarantee their perfect suitability to reality, and, obviously, this situation is not to be recommended.[24]

In any case, we can assert, without any doubt, that the rules governing the passing of risk in the CESL are clearly inspired by the CISG[25]. Hence, it is essential to this study to take into consideration this important international Convention at every stage.

10.2 Passing of Risk in CESL: General Rules

10.2.1 Effect of Passing of Risk

The CESL regulates the passing of risk in Chapter 14,[26] and distinguishes expressly between business to consumer (B2C) and business to business contracts (B2B). Since consumers deserve specific protection, the CESL opts, as does the DCFR, for setting two different regimes governing the problem of the passing of risk. However, the first section of Chapter 14 establishes two general rules governing any type of sale: effect of passing of risk (art. 140) and identification of goods or digital content to contract (art. 141).

Article 140 CESL lays down the legal effect of the transfer of risk as follows: "Loss of, or damage to, the goods or the digital content after the risk has passed to the buyer does not discharge the buyer from the obligation to pay the price, unless the loss or damage is due to an act or omission of the seller". This rule is fully coherent with art. 105 CESL (*Relevant time for establishing conformity*), according to which the seller is liable for any lack of conformity existing at the time when the risk passes to the buyer under Chapter 14.

It should be noted, firstly, that the rule clearly regulates the "price risk" (or "the risk of counter-performance"), and, therefore, implies that the buyer has to pay the price of the goods once the risk has passed. The time of passing of risk depends on the kind of contract of sale concluded (B2B or B2C), but the legal effect is always

[23] Grewal (1991), Risk of Loss in Goods Sold During Transit: a comparative study of the U.N. Convention on Contracts for the International Sale of Goods, The U.C.C. and the British Sale of Goods Act, *Loyola of Los Angeles International and Comparative Law Journal*, p. 94.

[24] Rosset (1997), *Improving the Uniform Commercial Code*, Centro di studi e ricerche di diritto comparato e straniero, Saggi, Conferenze e Seminari, Roma, p. 2.

[25] "Articles 140–146 CESL rely heavily on Articles 66–69 CISG", De Wit (2013), Duties of buyer and seller. Transfer of risk, in Claeys, I. Feltkamp, R., *The Draft Common European Sales Law: Towards and Alternative Sales Law? A Belgian Perspective,* Cambridge (UK), Intersentia, p. 178.

[26] Nonetheless, Lilleholt, for different reasons, stated he was against the regulation of the passing of risk in the Feasibility Study, Lilleholt, p. 929.

the same: the buyer has to pay the price of the goods and the digital content even though they have been lost or damaged.

On the other hand, if the loss or damage is due to an act or omission of the seller, the buyer does not remain bound to pay the price. The rule does not require the act or omission of the seller to amount to a breach of contract, but normally the seller shall be responsible for loss or damage due to the total or partial breach of its obligation to deliver, if he has packed the goods in an insufficient or incorrect manner. The seller will be also liable for acts and omissions by persons for whom the seller is responsible (e.g. employees). It is very important to point out that, in both these cases, there is a breach of contract (non-performance) and, therefore, the buyer may invoke all the remedies provided by the CESL (art. 106). In other words, the rules governing the passing of risk in the CESL are not applicable in these situations. However, it must be noted that if the loss or damage has occurred as a result of a legal act by the seller, such as the legitimate exercise of a legally granted right,[27] the rule would not come into play. In fact, in this case, the potential damage to the goods would have actually been caused by "*a fait de l'acheteur*".[28]

Article 2(c) CESL defines 'loss' as "economic loss and non-economic loss in the form of pain and suffering, excluding other forms of non-economic loss such as impairment of the quality of life and loss of enjoyment."[29] Nevertheless, under art. 140 CESL, the concepts of "loss" (*periculum interitus*) and "deterioration" (*periculum deteriorationis*) must be interpreted according to their literal meaning, including both physical damage and any case in which the buyer is unable to receive the goods. Therefore, these situations could include theft, fire, shipwreck, shrinkage of the goods, emergency unloading or other transport risks.[30]

However, it is unclear whether the concept of "loss" also covers "acts of State" (e.g. confiscation of the goods, export or import bans, embargo, etc.) because, strictly speaking, these acts do not involve an impairment or loss of the goods. In other words, the key question is whether the "legal risks" are included, or not, in the concept of passing of risk. Günter Hager maintains that the acts of State have nothing to do with risk, and hence are a matter governed by international trade law.[31] How-

[27] E.g. when the seller exercises his right of stoppage in transit, Oliva Blázquez (2000), *La transmisión del riesgo en la compraventa internacional de mercaderías*, Valencia, Tirant lo Blanch, p. 70.

[28] Neumayer and Ming (1993), *Convention de Vienne sur les contrats de vente internationale de marchandises. Commentaire,* Lausanne, CEDIDAC, p. 424.

[29] See the new Article 2—point f g, according to the European Parliament legislative resolution of 26 February 2014 on the proposal for a regulation of the European Parliament and of the Council on a Common European Sales Law (COM(2011)0635-C7-0329/2011-2011/0284(COD)). Hereinafter EPLR of 26 February 2014.

[30] "A figure of speech which covers both "acts of God" and the acts of mortal third parties (thieves, vandals)", Bernstein and Lookofsky (1997), *Understanding the CISG in Europe. A Compact Guide to the 1980 United Nations Convention on Contracts for the International Sale of Goods*, The Hague/London/Boston, Kluwer Law International, p. 74.

[31] Hager (2005), G., Art. 66, in Schlechtriem, P. & Schwenzer, I., *Commentary on the UN Convention on the International Sale of goods (CISG)*, 2ª ed, Oxford, Oxford University Press, p. 677.

ever, this author is in complete agreement with Johan Erauw, who points out that if the parties have not adopted a trade term (Incoterms) to deal with these risks, they might be treated under the risk-of-loss rules (in our case, the CESL).[32] In this sense, an arbitration court, attached to the Hungarian Chamber of Commerce and Industry, considered the United Nations embargo against Yugoslavia as an act of *force majeure* that had to be borne by the party to whom the risk had passed, according to art. 67 CISG.[33] On the contrary, the so-called "economic risk" (fluctuation of the value of goods on the market or, equally, exchange-rate fluctuation) is not covered by the rules governing passing of risk. Finally, however, it has to be remembered that it does not matter whether the goods have been lost or damaged completely or merely partially, because, in any case, the buyer has to pay the overall price of the goods.

10.2.2 Identification of Goods or Digital Content to Contract

It must also be borne in mind that the risk does not pass to the buyer until the goods or the digital content are clearly identified as the goods or digital content that are to be supplied under the contract (art. 141 CESL). Indeed, it must be remembered that if the goods are not properly identified, delivery still remains a possible option because "*genus nunquam perit*". So, when the goods are generic in nature, there is not an issue regarding allocation of risk ("obligationis periculum").

In addition, it can be said that proper identification of the goods protects both parties. On one side, the buyer is protected against unjustified claims brought by an "unscrupulous" seller.[34] On the other side, the seller is also protected because "the identification of the goods sets limits for the potential liability in the case of failure on delivery of the good (or digital content) which has been specified in the contract only by its genus".[35] In fact, the requirement of identification is of particular importance for the passing of risk in sales involving carriage, because if the carrier has not identified the goods sent to several clients, the seller has to bear the risk of loss or damage.

Therefore, art. 141 CESL links the passing of risk to the specification of the goods or the digital content.[36] Whether the goods had, or not, been duly identified in the contract before they were lost or damaged will often be a question of proof. In any case, the identification of the goods may be done in three different ways:

---

[32] Erauw (2005–2006), "The Risk of Loss and Passing It", *Journal of Law and Commerce*, 25, p. 204.

[33] CLOUT. Case 163. Arbitral award in case No. VB/96074 of 10 December 1996.

[34] Gabriel (1994), H.D. *Practitioner's Guide to the Convention on Contracts for the International Sale of Goods (CISG) and the Uniform Commercial Code (UCC)*, New York/London/Rome, Oceana, p. 208.

[35] Zoll and Watson (2012), "Article 141", in Shulze, R., (ed.), *Common European Sales Law (CESL). Commentary*, Baden-Baden, C.H. Beck, Hart, Nomos, p. 604.

[36] Article 1585 French Civil Code; arts. 1378 and 1465.3° Italian Civil Code; § 279 BGB; art. 1452.3° Spanish Civil Code.

- This can be done "by the initial agreement", i.e., at the precise moment of the conclusion of the contract of sale of goods or supply of digital content.
- The seller can identify the goods by way of a simple notice given to the buyer. The notice "becomes effective when it reaches the addressee" (art. 10.3 CESL) and, therefore, has only prospective effects (*ex nunc*)[37]: the buyer bears the risk when he receives the notice regarding the specification of the goods (art. 10.4.(a) CESL).
- Finally, the identification may take place "otherwise": by markings or by the packaging of the goods, by shipping documents, by separation of the goods, etc. [see, arts. 67.2 CISG and IV.A.-5:102(2) DCFR].[38]

10.3 Passing of Risk in Contracts Between Traders

10.3.1 General Rule

The passing of risk in B2B contracts is regulated separately in Section 3 of Chapter 15. This section consists of four articles (143–146 CESL)[39] that are not of a mandatory nature.[40] Hence, the parties may deviate from these rules in order to determine the exact moment in which the risk has passed to the buyer. However, in the opinion of Zoll and Watson, the essential deviation from the standards set out in these provisions may sometimes appear abusive within the meaning of Chapter 9 (*Unfair contract terms*).[41]

Article 143 CESL contains the general rule applicable to all B2B contracts: "In a contract between traders the risk passes when the buyer takes delivery of the goods or digital content or the documents representing the goods". Thus, the criterion used to determine the passing of risk is linked to the concept of "taking delivery", and, therefore, the interpretation of this rule must be made in coordination with the provisions of art. 94 CESL (*Method of delivery*)[42] and art. 129 (*Taking delivery*).

As can be seen, the article distinguishes two different situations: on the one hand, where the buyer takes delivery of the goods or the digital content; and, on the other hand, where the buyer takes delivery of documents representing the goods. In the first case, the buyer bears the risk when he takes physical control of the goods;

[37] Feltham (1981), The United Nations Convention on Contracts for the International Sale of Goods, *The Journal of Business Law*, p. 357.

[38] Enderlein and Maskow (1992, p. 268).

[39] It should be noted that the EPLR of 26 February 2014 has deleted the articles 144–146 CESL. The different situations covered by these rules are now regulated by the new article 143.

[40] Cf., Art. 142 CESL.

[41] Zoll and Watson (2012, p. 608).

[42] It has been pointed out that the formulation of paragraph 1 is not sufficiently coordinated with the rules governing delivery (art. 94(1)(b) and (c) CESL), "because names the delivery of the documents as it would be the case not covered by the notion of delivery", Zoll and Watson (2012, p. 609).

while in the second case, the risk passes at the moment in which the buyer takes delivery of certain documents, such as a bill of landing or a warehouse receipt.[43] In almost identical wording, the CESL considers that the buyer has fulfilled his obligation to take delivery when (a) he has done all the acts which could be expected in order to enable the seller to perform the obligation to deliver; and (b) he has taken over the goods, or the documents representing the goods or the digital content, as required by the contract (art. 129 CESL).

Surprisingly, the rule makes no reference to the passing of risk in a contract for the supply of digital content not supplied in a tangible medium. As we will see below, art. 142(2) links the passing of risk to the moment in which the consumer has obtained the control of the digital content. However, art. 142 CESL does not take into consideration the situation concerning intangible digital content. This is a gap in the proposed law that may provoke uncertainty among the traders involved in these contracts. Perhaps the best solution to overcome this interpretative problem is to deem both concepts ("taking delivery" and "obtained the control") as one and the same.[44]

Finally, it should be noted that the general rule linking the passing of risk to the time when the buyer "takes delivery" of the goods is subject to the specific rules provided by the CESL for three different types of sale: Goods placed at buyer's disposal (art. 144 CESL), Carriage of the goods (art. 145 CESL) and Goods sold in transit (art. 146 CESL)[45].

10.3.2 Goods Placed at Buyer's Disposal

10.3.2.1 Types of Sales

In international trade, the seller often undertakes personally to deliver the goods at a particular place determined in the contract. This place may be the seller's own place of business (EW: Ex Works), a terminal for loading and unloading (DAT: Delivered At Terminal), a warehouse, the buyer's habitual residence, etc. Article 144 CESL governs these situations distinguishing between two broad categories: disposal at the seller's place of business (art. 144.1 CESL) and disposal at other locations (art. 144.2 CESL).

Both models of contracts are characterised by the obligation of the buyer to take delivery of the goods at the seller's place of business or at other locations. Hence, the buyer must do all the acts that could be expected in order to enable the seller to perform the obligation to deliver, such as taking over the goods on time or paying

[43] Dannemann (2012) Article 129. In Shulze, R., (ed.), *Common European Sales Law (CESL). Commentary*, Baden-Baden, C.H. Beck, Hart, Nomos, 567.

[44] Wiese (2012), Gefahrübergang nach Artt. 140 ff. GEKR, in Schmidt-Kessel, M. *Ein einheitliches europäisches Kaufrecht? Eine Analyse des Vorschlags der Kommission*, Munich, Sellier, p. 496.

[45] Arts. 143.2, 143 2(a) and 143 2(b) of the EPLR of 26 February 2014.

the price. The seller, likewise, must do all the acts necessary to place the goods at the buyer's disposal, such as identifying the goods and informing the buyer.[46]

Nevertheless, the passing of risk is not strictly linked to the general concept of "taking delivery" laid down in art. 141 CESL, but to other criteria that are explained below.

10.3.2.2 Seller's Place of Business

When the goods have been placed at the buyer's disposal at the place of business of the seller, the former bears the risk when the goods are made available but he fails to fulfil his duty to take over the goods according to the contract. Thus, the rule lays down the following requirements for the allocation of the risk to the buyer:

Firstly, the goods or the digital content must be placed at the buyer's disposal. Therefore, the seller must fulfil his obligation to deliver the goods or supply the digital content [art. 91(a) CESL] by making the goods or the digital content—or where it is agreed that the seller need only deliver documents representing the goods, the documents—available to the buyer [art. 94.1(c) CESL].[47]

Secondly, the seller must fulfil his obligation to place the goods at the buyer's disposal. This means that the seller must have complied with his duty to deliver according to the terms required by the contract, i.e., at the time and place agreed upon. In addition, the goods have to be clearly identified *per* art. 141 CESL.

The buyer must be aware that the goods are available. This requirement seems quite rational, since otherwise it would be too difficult for the buyer to take delivery of the goods placed at his disposal at the seller's place of business. Normally, the correct way to fulfil this requirement requires the seller to notify that the goods are available to the buyer. It can be possible that the buyer is aware of this from other sources other than the seller (e.g. a third person), but, in any case, the seller carries the burden of proving the fact that the buyer was aware that the goods were available at the seller's place of business.[48]

If the buyer is aware of the fact that the goods or the digital content are placed at his disposal at the seller's place of business, the buyer then bears the risk "at the time when the goods or digital content should have been taken over".[49] Thus, it is clear that is not necessary, for the allocation of the risk, that the buyer takes physical possession of the goods: he bears the risk at the time when the goods "should have been taken over". It has be to borne in mind that, where the time of delivery cannot be otherwise determined, the goods or the digital content must be delivered without undue delay after the conclusion of the contract (art. 95.1 CESL)[50]; and the de-

[46] Hager (2005), pp. 691–692.

[47] Zoll and Watson (2012, p. 610).

[48] Zoll and Watson (2012, p. 610).

[49] Article 144 CESL.

[50] "Within a reasonable time after the contract was concluded", according to the new wording of art. 95.1 (EPLR of 26 February 2014).

layed delivery of the goods is considered a type of non-performance *per* art. 87.1(a) CESL. Furthermore, as seen above, the buyer must take delivery of the goods or the digital content (art. 123.1b CESL), by doing all the acts which could be expected in order to enable the seller to perform the obligation to deliver, by taking over the goods or the documents representing the goods or digital content, as required by the contract (art. 129 CESL).

The approach adopted by the CESL is entirely consistent and coherent with the principles of "control and accessibility of the goods" governing the determination of the exact time of the passing of risk in this type of sales. It is assumed that the risk passes to the buyer when, after being made aware that the goods are available to him, he takes delivery of them.

However, if the buyer does not fulfil his obligation to take delivery of the goods without undue delay, he will bear the risk from the time when the goods or the digital content should have been taken over. In this sense, the spirit of the rule seems to be punishing the buyer's breach of his obligation to take delivery, forcing him to bear the risk of loss and destruction from the moment he should have taken over the goods or the digital content.[51] In short, art. 144.1 CESL prevents the buyer from postponing the passing of the risk by not taking delivery of the goods from the seller (the so-called *mora creditoris*), and, at the same time, incentivises the buyer to take over the goods, since he will bear the risk of paying the full price in case of loss or damage taking place during the period of the delay.[52]

Nevertheless, there is an exception to this specific regime. The buyer does not bear the risk if he is entitled to withhold taking of delivery pursuant to art. 113 CESL. Therefore, if the buyer has the right to withhold performance,[53] the seller bears the risk of loss or damage of the goods or the digital content, even if all the above requirements are met[54].

---

[51] "When the entire batch perishes, the risk burdens the buyer that has accepted delivery too late". Court of Appeals of 's-Hertogenbosch No. C0300064/HE, 20 December 2005, Dutch appellant v Pflanzen König GMBH (Germany), CLOUT Case 943.

[52] "In fact, the buyer may suffer a triple detriment upon the failure to take over goods that are subsequently accidentally lost or damaged: loss of the goods; payment of the price; and a possible liability in damages for breach of contract (if non-performance of the obligation to take delivery has caused the seller any incidental loss)". Von Bar & Clive, IV.A.-Art. 5:201 DCFR. Comment B.

[53] The general rule is that a buyer, who is to perform at the same time as, or after, the seller performs, has a right to withhold performance until the seller has tendered performance or has performed (art. 113.1 CESL). Likewise, a buyer who is to perform before the seller performs and who reasonably believes that there will be non-performance by the seller when the seller's performance becomes due may withhold performance for as long as the reasonable belief continues (art. 113.2 CESL).

[54] It has been pointed out that there is no express reference to the right to suspend performance in the second paragraph of Article 144. This omission is regrettable, because the buyer is equally entitled to withhold taking of delivery when is obliged to take over the goods at a place other than the place of business of the seller. Other interpretation would be contrary to the general intention of Article 113 CESL, De Wit, p. 182.

10.3.2.3 Taking Delivery at Other Places

Article 144.2 CESL applies to cases in which the buyer is obliged to take over the goods at a place other than the place of business of the seller. This article is a "catch-all provision"[55] and covers a wide range of situations:[56] where the buyer takes delivery of the goods at the warehouse of a third party (bailment contracts); the seller, acting as an international carrier, sends the goods to the premises of the buyer, using his own transport; or, finally, the seller concludes a contract of transport with an international carrier to deliver the goods at a particular place (destination contracts).[57]

In these cases, the risk passes to the buyer when the following requirements are met: firstly, the goods or the digital content are placed at the buyer's disposal at a place other than the place of business of the seller; secondly, the seller hands over the goods; and thirdly, the buyer is aware of the fact that the goods are available to him at that place.

The goods or the digital content are placed at the buyer's disposal when the seller gives the depositary an order to keep the goods available for the buyer (delivery order) or when he delivers to the buyer a title authorising him to take over the goods (warehouse certificate). If all these requirements are met, the risk is transferred to the buyer at the very moment when the delivery is due.

This rule does not take into account the "*mora creditoris*", and hence the non-performance by the seller of an obligation stated in the contract is not required for the passing of risk. However, what if the seller delivers the goods before the agreed time? The literal meaning of the provision considered above could suggest that the risk passes only when the expected delivery date is met. Therefore, if the seller decides to fulfil his obligation to deliver before that moment, he shall bear the risk during the period of time remaining until "delivery is due". Nevertheless, this solution appears rather inconsistent and, in this author's opinion, it should to be understood that the buyer bears the risk whenever he decides to accept the goods.[58] Moreover, it should be noted that if the seller delivers the goods or supplies the digital content before the time agreed upon, the buyer must take delivery unless he has a legitimate interest in refusing to do so (art. 130.1 CESL).

---

[55] Stocks (1993), Risk of loss under the Uniform Commercial Code and the United Nations Convention on Contracts for the International Sale of Goods: a comparative analysis and proposed revision of UCC Sections 2-509 and 2-510, *Northwestern University Law Review*, p. 1433.

[56] See Incoterms 2010: DAT—Delivered At Terminal, DAP—Delivered At Place, DDP—Delivered Duty Paid.

[57] Honnold (1991), *Uniform Law for International Sales under the 1980 United Nations Convention*, Deventer/Boston, Kluwer, Second Edition, p. 461. But see, Bernstein and Lookofsky (1997, p. 76).

[58] Gabriel, p. 214; Heuzé (1992), *La vente internationale de marchandises*. Droit uniforme, París, GLN JOLY Éditions, footnote n. 319.

10.3.3 Carriage of the Goods

10.3.3.1 Sphere of Application: Contracts of Sale Involving Carriage of Goods

Article 145 CESL applies to contracts of sale that involve carriage of goods. At first glance, this statement may be deemed an unnecessary tautology, as every international sale contract requires the transport of the goods from the seller's place of business to another place usually determined in the contract.[59] Therefore, it is important to clarify that this rule applies provided that the contract of sale authorises one of the parties to arrange the international transport of goods.

In other words, to qualify the type of contract of sale, it is not enough to take into account the simple transit of goods from one country to another, because it is necessary for one of the parties to conclude a contract for international carriage. Under this contract, the carrier undertakes the duty to move the goods to a particular place. The mere presence of this contract and the involvement of an independent carrier[60] is enough to bring Article 145 CESL into play.[61]

These types of contracts, involving carriage of the goods, are the most common in international trade; and the passing of risk depends on whether or not the seller is bound to hand over the goods at a particular place. Therefore, each of these assumptions must be considered separately.

10.3.3.2 The Passing of Risk when the Seller is not Bound to Hand Over the Goods at a Particular Place

If the seller is not bound to hand over the goods at a particular place, the risk passes to the buyer when the goods are handed over to the first carrier for transmission to the buyer in accordance with the contract (art. 145.2 CESL). This rule is fully coherent with art. 94.1(b) CESL, which states that, in contracts involving carriage of the goods by a carrier, the seller fulfils the obligation to deliver "by handing over the goods to the first carrier for transmission to the buyer and by handing over to the buyer any document necessary to enable the buyer to take over the goods from the carrier holding the goods".

Therefore, the risk passes to the buyer when the goods are handed over to the first carrier. Furthermore, it is deemed that the goods have been handed over for transportation when have been placed in the carrier's area of control.[62]

---

[59] Nicholas (1989), The Vienna Convention on International Sales Law, *The Law Quarterly Review,* p. 238.

[60] Vid., Fouchard (1990), *Rapport de synthèse*. In Derains, Y. & Ghestin, J., *La Convention de Vienne sur la Vente Internationale et les Incoterms. Actes du Colloque des 1er et 2 décembre 1989*, París, L.G.D.J., p. 168.

[61] Zoll and Watson (2012, p. 612). Neumayer and Ming (1993, p. 430). Enderlein and Maskow (1992, p. 264).

[62] Von Bar & Clive, Art. IV. A.-5:202. Comment B.

Since the risk does not pass with the physical delivery of the goods to the buyer, the rule implies that the buyer bears all the risks of the international transport.[63] Hence, if the goods or the digital content are lost or damaged accidentally during the transport, the buyer is obliged to pay the full price in spite of not receiving the agreed goods.[64] In this regard, it is important to clarify that the first carrier has to be independent,[65] because if he reports directly to the seller (as an auxiliary or dependent), it makes no sense to allocate the risks to the buyer.

The historical justification for this rule might be found in the development of the modern forms of international transport. Currently, a typical international "door-to-door" sale begins when the goods are packed and placed in a container at the seller's place of business. Subsequently, a truck picks up the container and moves it to a dock where a ship will transport it to the port of destination. There, the goods will be picked up by another truck that will transport it to the buyer's place of business. This operation can be further complicated by the implication of other ways of transport, such as rail, air or the so-called "roll-on roll-off" sea transportation. It is easy to understand that this complex web of successive deliveries, and loading and unloading operations, directly affects the problem of determining the exact time of the passing of risk. Article 145 CESL reflects almost literally the provisions of arts. 67.1 CISG and IV.A.-5:202 DCFR and, as a consequence, links the passing of risk to the delivery of the goods to the first carrier.[66] Briefly, the reasons for choosing this critical point are:

- When the seller hands over the goods to the first carrier, he fulfils his obligation to deliver according to the contract (art. 94 CESL). In addition, when the goods

[63] The owner of a pizzeria in Germany, ordered 90 stacks of pizza cartons from an Italian manufacturer. The defendant buyer paid the price in advance; but when the cartons were delivered he noticed they had been damaged by the carrier. The Court held that the seller was only obliged to hand over the goods to the carrier and, according to article 67(1) CISG, the risk of damage passed to the buyer at that moment. Therefore, the seller could not be held responsible for the subsequent damage caused by the carrier. Amtsgericht Duisburg, 49 C 502/00. 13 April 2000. Clout Case 360.

[64] The parties, an Italian seller and a Spanish buyer, had concluded a contract of sale of steel, and the buyer, after discovering that the steel had oxidized, commenced a legal action against the seller, because the damage had occurred before they were loaded aboard the ship. The Appellate Court, according to arts. 31 and 67 CISG, held that the seller was not liable because the risk had passed on to the buyer when the goods were handed over to the carrier for shipment, Audiencia Provincial de Córdoba. 31 octubre 1997. CLOUT Case 247. *Vid.,* Oliva Blázquez, p. 120 et seq.

[65] Von Bar & Clive, Art. IV. A.-5:202. Comment C. Nicholas, p. 238; De Vries (1982), The Passing of Risk in International Sales under the Vienna Convention 1980 as compared with Traditional Trade Terms, *European Transport Law*, p. 500.

[66] "The rule stating that handing the sold commodities over to the first carrier is considered as delivery, as long as there is no other agreement among the parties, makes the CISG a suitable legal system for multimodal and container transport". Alazemi (2012). Passing of Risk in International Contracts of Sale of Goods; A Comparative Study Between the United Nations Convention on Contracts for Sale of Goods 1980 and the English Sale of Goods Act 1979, http://www.cisg.law.pace.edu/cisg/biblio/alazemi.html#chIII. *Vid., Section 2-509(1)* UCC. § 447 BGB. Art. 1378 *Codice civile italiano.*

have been transferred into the carrier's custody, the seller loses control over the goods.[67]

- The goods are usually covered by a transport insurance policy endorsed in favour of the buyer. Furthermore, the buyer is the party in the better situation to claim against the insurance company, because he will usually examine the goods on arrival pursuant to art. 121.1 CESL.[68]
- In the case of multimodal transport, it is advisable to avoid dividing the risks during the transport ("transit risk splitting").[69]
- This rule prevents the buyer from using minor damages as a pretext for rejecting the goods when, for instance, the market has declined and he is anxious to back out from a bad bargain.[70]
- It is also customary in international trade to consider the carrier as an "extension" of the buyer.

Finally, paragraph 2 of art. 145 CESL contains an express limitation: namely that the goods are handed over "in accordance with the contract". If the seller does not deliver the goods as provided for in the contract, then the buyer will not bear the risk when the goods are handed over to the first carrier, but when delivery is due and he is aware that the goods are placed at his disposal (art. 144.2 CESL). Thus, the rule penalises the seller that has breached his obligation to deliver the goods in accordance with the contract, by bearing all the risks throughout transport.

10.3.3.3 The Passing of Risk When the Seller is Bound to Hand Over the Goods to a Particular Place

It is usual in international commercial practice that the parties include in their contracts specific terms aimed at postponing the passing of risk to a point in time other than that of the delivery to the first carrier. Thus, under certain commercial terms, the risk does not pass to the buyer until the goods have passed the ship's rail (FOB, CIF or CFR), or until the goods have been placed alongside the ship at the named port (FAS).

Paragraph 3 of art. 145 governs this type of situations in which the seller is bound to hand over the goods at a particular place, and determines that the risk does not pass to the buyer until the goods are handed over to the carrier at that place; i.e., the buyer bears the risk from the moment in which the goods are delivered to the carrier at the place fixed in the contract. Therefore, this rule only applies when the

---

[67] Caffarena Laporta, p. 528.

[68] "In a contract between traders the buyer is expected to examine the goods, or cause them to be examined, within as short a period as is reasonable not exceeding 14 days from the date of delivery of the goods, supply of digital content or provision of related services" (art. 121.1 CESL). *Vid.* Art. 38.1 CISG.

[69] Schlechtriem (1986), Uniform Sales Law: The UN-Convention on Contracts for the International Sale of Goods, Wien, Manz, p. 87.

[70] Roth (1979, p. 296).

contracting parties have expressly set out in the contract the seller's obligation to deliver the goods to a particular place other than the seller's place of business or the final destination. This usually means that the buyer will arrange for the transportation of the goods.

10.3.3.4 Risk and Property: the Retaining of Documents

Finally, art. 145.4 CESL expressly states that "the fact that the seller is authorised to retain documents controlling the disposition of the goods does not affect the passing of the risk" (*cf.* Art. 67.1 CISG).[71]

This rule applies to the two types of sales contracts studied in this section, and its meaning is loud and clear: if the parties conclude a sale contract involving transport, the buyer bears the risk from when the goods are handed over to the carrier, irrespective of the fact that the seller retains the documents representing the goods as security for payment of the price.

This article is consistent with the modern forms of international financing and payment, such as the letters of credit.[72] In addition, retention of documents does not amount to possession or physical control of the goods;[73] it only seeks to ensure the payment of the price.[74] Finally, as seen above, it has to be borne in mind that the problem of the allocation of risks should not be linked to abstract criteria, such as the transfer of ownership.[75]

10.3.4 Goods Sold in Transit

The sale of goods in transit (in *cours de voyage*)[76] is very common in modern international commercial traffic. These are contracts of sale related to goods that are

---

[71] "Regardless of whether the seller is authorised to retain documents controlling the disposition of the goods", Art. 143. 2 a (new) EPLR of 26 February 2014. "La précision est néanmoins apparue nécessaire du fait que divers droits internes associent le transfert des risques à celui de la propriété", Audit, pp. 88 y 89.

[72] "In documentary credit operations all parties concerned deal in documents and not goods", *Problems and Materials On Sales Under the Uniform Commercial Code and the Convention on International Sale of Goods*, Commercial Transactions, Volume two, Cincinnati, Ohio, Anderson Publishing, pp. 382 y 383.

[73] Neumayer and Ming (1993, pp. 434 and 435).

[74] Enderlein and Maskow (1992, p. 268); Gabriel, p. 207; Honnold, p. 463.

[75] "Risk and ownership are two different institutions", Rabel (1958), *Das Recht des Warenkaufs*, Berlin, Tübigen, p. 296. "Moreover, according to Article 67(1), the passage of risk and transfer of title need not occur at the same time, as the seller's retention of documents controlling the disposition of the goods does not affect the passage of risk", U.S. District Court, S.D., New York, 26.03.2002, St. Paul Guardian Insurance Co., et al. v. Neuromed Medical Systems & Support, et al. http://www.unilex.info/case.cfm?id=730.

[76] Ionasco and Nestor (1966, p. 150).

already travelling (via sea, air or land) from the point of departure to their original destination. Raw materials are usually the object of such sales, mainly because they may be sold during international transport on several occasions, acting as speculative securities. Along this chain of purchases and sales (known as "daisy chain sales")[77], the goods are exposed to several dangers that can prevent the delivery to the final buyer. In that case, it must be asked: who should bear the risks of loss and damage, and when? Article 146 is inspired by art. IV.A.-5:203 DCFR and art. 68 CISG, and establishes three different rules:

a. The risk passes to the buyer at the time the goods are handed over to the first carrier. This rule implies that the buyer bears the risk retroactively, because the goods had been handed over to the first carrier before the contract was concluded. Although this may seem surprising, the "retroactive" solution is very common in western international trade usage.[78] Furthermore, the problems related to the proof of the moment in which the loss or damages to the goods took place are avoided, if the risks are not divided during transport. Finally, in the contract of sales of *res in transit*, the seller usually provides the buyer with an insurance policy for the goods.[79]
b. If the circumstances so indicate, the risk passes to the buyer when the contract is concluded. Therefore, the buyer bears the risk only from the time when the contract is concluded if "the circumstances so indicate". But, what does this ambiguous expression mean? The use of this vague and indeterminate sentence[80] is always reprehensible, as it is certain to lead to legal uncertainty.[81] Nonetheless, the lack of an insurance policy against transportation risks may be deemed as one of such circumstances.
c. If at the time of the conclusion of the contract the seller knew, or could be expected to have known, that the goods had been lost or damaged and did not disclose this to the buyer, the loss or damage is at the risk of the seller. Through this final rule, an exception to Article 146.3 CESL is introduced: if the seller acts with bad faith, he is punished with the burden of bearing the risk. This usually happens when the seller concludes the contract of sale despite knowing, at that moment, that the goods had been lost or damaged, and he does not disclose this fact to the buyer. However, the seller does not bear all the risks, but only those risks that he knew or could have known.[82]

[77] "A line of sellers and buyers of a single cargo of oil, traded on a forward basis on the expectation of making a profit on a short-time price movements", Grewal, p. 94, footnote n. 13.

[78] However, this rule is the exception in art. 68 CISG. In this author's opinion, the CESL's solution is to be welcomed, because it is in line with current commercial practice. *Vid.,* Oliva Blázquez, p. 155 et seq.

[79] Enderlein and Maskow (1992, p. 270); Hoffmann (1986, p. 293); Schlechtriem (1986, p. 89, footnote n. 361).

[80] The new art. 143. 2 b of the EPLR of 26 February 2014 also uses a vague phrase: "Depending on the circumstances".

[81] *Vid.,* Faust (2012), "Das Kaufrecht in Vorschlag für ein Gemeinsames Europäische Kaufrecht", in Shulte-Nölke, *Der Entwurf für ein optionales europäisches Kaufrecht*, Sellier, p. 273

[82] Enderlein and Maskow (1992, p. 272); Neumayer and Ming (1993, p. 439); Roth (1979, p. 299).

10.4 Passing of Risk in Consumer Sales Contracts

The passing of risk in a B2C contract is regulated in art. 142 CESL. This article is mandatory in nature; which means that the parties may not, to the detriment of the consumer, exclude its application or derogate from or vary its effects (art. 142.5 CESL). Nevertheless, there is nothing to prevent the level of protection for the consumer being raised by agreement between the parties.[83]

The rules governing the passing of risk in this type of sales are not completely new. In fact, both the DCFR and the Directive 2011/83/EU foresee specific provisions concerning the passing of risk in consumer sales contracts, and the CESL is clearly influenced by them.

Although art. 142 contains different rules, the basic principle underlying the CESL is that the consumer does not bear the risk before the moment in which he actually takes over the goods. The aim of the rule, according to the literal wording of the Official Comments to art. IV.A.-5:103 DCRF, is to avoid burdening the consumer unduly with unforeseen risks, which he or she will neither be able to anticipate nor be likely to have taken out insurance against.[84] Therefore, the CESL ensures a high level of consumer protection (art. 1.3 CESL).

Therefore, the risk passes to the consumer at the time when the consumer, or a third party designated by him (other than the independent carrier), has acquired physical possession of the goods or, the tangible medium on which the digital content is supplied (art. 142.1 CESL). This rule is an exception to the general regulation set out in art. 144.1 CESL. Indeed, if the buyer, in a B2B contract, delays taking over the goods, the risk passes to him at the time when the goods should have been taken over. On the contrary, the consumer only bears the risk when he has acquired actual physical possession of the goods, unless his failure to take over the goods cannot be excused. Furthermore, the risk passes to the consumer when a third party, designated by him, acquires physical possession of the goods.[85]

In the case of contracts for the supply of digital content not supplied on a tangible medium, the risk passes at the time when the consumer, or a third party designated by the consumer for this purpose, has obtained control of the digital content (art. 142.2 CESL). This rule deals with cases in which the digital content has normally been downloaded from the Internet[86], and determines that the risk is borne by the consumer when he has obtained full control of the digital content. Since this rule applies to contracts for the supply of digital content, in the case of contracts

[83] Zoll and Watson (2012, p. 607).

[84] Von Bar & Clive, IV.A.-Art. 5:103 DCFR. Comment A.

[85] "Therefore, the risk does not pass to the consumer via a third party if such third party has been designated by the seller", Zoll and Watson (2012, p. 606).

[86] "For downloads, when he or his designate has obtained control of the digital content (Art 142(2) CESL)", Schuller and Zenefels (2013), Obligations of Sellers and Buyers, in G. Dannemann, S. Vogenauer, *The Common European Sales Law in Context. Interactions with English and German Law*, Oxford, Oxford University Press, p. 608.

in which only access to the digital content is provided "the risk never passes to the customer but remains with the supplier"[87].

Paragraph 3 of art. 142 CESL contains an exception applicable to the above rules[88]: if the consumer fails to perform the obligation to take over the goods or the digital content and the non-performance is not excused under art. 88 CESL, the risk passes at the time when the consumer, or the third party designated by the consumer, would have acquired the physical possession of the goods or obtained the control of the digital content if the obligation to take them over had been performed[89]. It is important to point out that the risk only passes to the consumer when the failure to perform his obligation is not excused. Thus, if the consumer's non-performance of the obligation to take over the goods (art. 123(1)(b) CESL) is excused, such as when it is due to an impediment beyond his control (art. 88.1 CESL), the seller will bear the risk. Nonetheless, this exception does not apply in distance or off-premises contracts[90].

Finally, paragraph 4 of art. 142 CESL supposes a rather unusual situation. Indeed, as a general rule, if the sales contract involves carriage of goods, the risk only passes when the goods are actually handed over to the consumer. As a consequence, if the goods have been lost or destroyed, the consumer does not have to pay for them.[91] However, where the consumer arranges the carriage of the goods or the digital content supplied on a tangible medium, the risk passes when the goods are handed over to the carrier, without prejudice to the rights of the consumer against the carrier (cf. art. 20 Directive 2011/83/EU).[92] Hence, in this case, the allocation of risk is linked to the handing over of the goods to the carrier, just as what happens in B2B contracts[93]. However, this rule will only be applied when the consumer arranges the carriage in a way not offered by the trader; otherwise, the risk does not pass to the buyer.

---

[87] Zoll and Watson (2012, p. 607).

[88] This exception is inspired by art. IV.A.-5:103(2) DCFR: "Paragraph (1) does not apply if the buyer has failed to perform the obligation to take over the goods and the non-performance is not excused under III.–3:104 (Excuse due to an impediment) in which case IV.A.–5:201 (Goods placed at buyer's disposal) applies".

[89] "The formula in Article 142(3) CESL is rather cumbersome", De Wit, p. 179.

[90] It must be borne in mind that this paragraph 3 of Article 142 has been deleted by virtue of the amendment 209 of the EPLR of 26 February 2014. Hence, the seller shall bear the risk even when the consumer fails to perform the obligation to take over the goods and the non-performance is not excused. Obviously, this amendment seeks to improve the protection of the consumer, and in addition is fully coherent with the wording of art. 20 Directive 2011/83/UE, that did not take into consideration this exception.

[91] "Such a result will provide an incentive for the seller to exercise the utmost care in arranging transportation and in choosing a carrier." Von Bar & Clive, IV.A.-Art. 5:103 DCFR. Comment C.

[92] Article 20 Directive 2011/83/UE states that the risk shall pass to the consumer upon delivery to the carrier if the carrier was commissioned by the consumer to carry the goods and that choice was not offered by the trader, without prejudice to the rights of the consumer against the carrier.

[93] It seems "a logical exception", De Wit, p. 180.

References

Adame Goddard, J. (1984), La regla periculum est emptoris aplicada a la compraventa internacional de mercaderías, *Anuario Jurídico* (México D.F.), pp. 227–249.

Alazemi, E. (2012). Passing of Risk in International Contracts of Sale of Goods; A Comparative Study Between the United Nations Convention on Contracts for Sale of Goods 1980 and the English Sale of Goods Act 1979, http://www.cisg.law.pace.edu/cisg/biblio/alazemi.html#chIII.

Alonso Pérez, M. (1972), *El riesgo en el contrato de compraventa*, Madrid, Montecorvo.

Angelici, C. (1979),*"Consegna" e "proprietà" nella vendita internazionale*, Milano, Giuffrè.

Angelici, C. (1981), La disciplina del passaggio dei rischi. In *La Vendita Internazionale. Convegno S. Margherita Lugure, 26- 28.8.80*, Milano, Giuffrè.

Audit, B. (1990), *La vente internationale de marchandises.* Convention des Nations-Unies du 11 avril 1980, Paris, L.G.D.J.

Bernstein, H. & Lookofsky, J. (1997), *Understanding the CISG in Europe. A Compact Guide to the 1980 United Nations Convention on Contracts for the International Sale of Goods*, The Hague/London/Boston, Kluwer Law International.

Burke, P.A. (1981), International Trade: Uniform Law of Sales, *Harvard International Law Journal*, p. 473 a 479.

Dannemann, G. (2012), Article 129. In Shulze, R., (ed.), *Common European Sales Law (CESL). Commentary*, Baden-Baden, C.H. Beck, Hart, Nomos, pp. 565–568.

De Vries, H. (1982), The Passing of Risk in International Sales under the Vienna Convention 1980 as compared with Traditional Trade Terms, *European Transport Law*, pp. 495–528.

De Wit, R. (2013), Duties of buyer and seller. Transfer of risk, in Claeys, I. Feltkamp, R., *The Draft Common European Sales Law: Towards and Alternative Sales Law? A Belgian Perspective,* Cambridge (UK), Intersentia, pp. 155 a 184.

Del Duca, L.F. & Del Duca, P. (1996). Practice under the Convention on International Sale of Goods (CISG): a primer for attorneys and international traders, (Part II), *Uniform Commercial Code Journal*, p. 99–167.

Enderlein, F & Maskow, D. (1992), *International Sales Law. United Nations Convention on Contracts for the International Sale of Goods -Convention on the Limitation Period in the International Sale of Goods. Commentary.* New York/London/Rome, 1992.

Erauw, J. (2005–2006), "The Risk of Loss and Passing It", *Journal of Law and Commerce*, 25, pp. 203–217.

Faust, F. (2012), "Das Kaufrecht in Vorschlag für ein Gemeinsames Europäische Kaufrecht", in Shulte-Nölke, *Der Entwurf für ein optionales europäisches Kaufrecht*, Sellier, pp. 251–258.

Feltham, J.D. (1981), The United Nations Convention on Contracts for the International Sale of Goods, *The Journal of Business Law,* pp. 346–361.

Fiorillo, L. & Bodin, A. (1992), A., International Sale of Goods. In Barbero, L., *International Trade Law Post-Graduate Course. Participant's Review. Turín, 3 April–26 June 1992.* Turin. University Institute of European Studies Turín, International Training Centre of the ILO-Turín, pp. 351–363.

Fouchard, P. (1990), *Rapport de synthèse*. In Derains, Y. & Ghestin, J., *La Convention de Vienne sur la Vente Internationale et les Incoterms. Actes du Colloque des 1er et 2 décembre 1989*, París, L.G.D.J., pp. 149–169.

Gabriel, H.D. (1994), *Practitioner's Guide to the Convention on Contracts for the International Sale of Goods (CISG) and the Uniform Commercial Code (UCC)*, New York/London/Rome, Oceana.

Grewal, S.S. (1991), Risk of Loss in Goods Sold During Transit: a comparative study of the U.N. Convention on Contracts for the International Sale of Goods, The U.C.C. and the British Sale of Goods Act, *Loyola of Los Angeles International and Comparative Law Journal*, pp. 92–119.

Hager, G. (2005), Art. 66. In Schlechtriem, P. & Schwenzer, I., *Commentary on the UN Convention on the International Sale of goods (CISG)*, 2ª ed, Oxford, Oxford University Press.

Hancock, W.A. (1986), *The Convention on Contracts for the International Sale of Goods compared with the Uniform Commercial Code.* In Hancock, W.A., *Guide to the International Sale of Goods Convention*, Chesterland, OH, Business Laws.
Heuzé, V. (1992), *La vente internationale de marchandises.* Droit uniforme, París, GLN JOLY Éditions.
Honnold, J. (1984a), The new Uniform Law for International Sale of Goods and the UCC: a comparison. In. Symposium on International Sale of Goods, *The International Lawyer*, pp. 21–28.
Honnold, J. (1984b), Risk of Loss. Chapter 8, in Galston, N. & Smit, H., *International Sales: The United Nations Convention on Contracts for the International Sale of Goods. Conference held by the Parker School of Foreign and Comparative Law, Columbia University, October 1983*, New York, Matthew Bender, pp. 8-–1—8-–15.
Honnold, J.O. (1991), *Uniform Law for International Sales under the 1980 United Nations Convention*, Deventer/Boston, Kluwer.
Ionasco, T. & Nestor, I. (1966), *Le risque de perte en transit: existe-t-il des différences quant aux effects de certaines clauses similaires concernant le risqué*, in Honnold, J., *Unification of the Law Governing International Sale of Goods, The Comparison and Possible Harmonization of National and Regional Unifications*, Paris, Librairie Dalloz, p. 151.
Kahn, P (1996), Vente Commerciale Internationale. In *Juris-Classeur de Droit International.* 9, Fascicule 565-A- –5, París. Éditions du Juris-Classeur, pp. 1–29.
Lilleholt, K. (2011), Passing of Risk and the Risk of Mystification: Some Drafting Issues, *European Review of Private Law*, 19, 6, pp. 921–929.
López y López, A. (1993), Artículo 1452. In *Comentario del Código Civil*, Tomo II, Madrid, Ministerio de Justicia, pp. 895–898.
Neumayer, C.H. & Ming, C. (1993), *Convention de Vienne sur les contrats de vente internationale de marchandises. Commentaire,* Lausanne, CEDIDAC.
Nicholas, B. (1962), *An Introduction to Roman Law, Oxford,* Clarendon Law Series.
Nicholas, B. (1989), The Vienna Convention on International Sales Law, *The Law Quarterly Review,* pp. 201–243.
Oliva Blázquez, F. (2000), *La transmisión del riesgo en la compraventa internacional de mercaderías*, Valencia, Tirant lo Blanch.
Rabel, E. (1938), A Draft of an International Law of Sales, *The University of Chicago Law Review*, 1938, pp. 543–565.
Rabel, E. (1958), *Das Recht des Warenkaufs*, Berlin, Tübigen.
Rosset, A. (1997), *Improving the Uniform Commercial Code*, Centro di studi e ricerche di diritto comparato e straniero, Saggi, Conferenze e Seminari, Roma.
Roth, P.M. (1979), The Passing of Risk, *The American Journal of Comparative Law*, pp. 291–310.
Schlechtriem, P. (1986), *Uniform Sales Law: The UN-Convention on Contracts for the International Sale of Goods,* Wien, Manz.
Schuller C., & Zenefels A. (2013), Obligations of Sellers and Buyers, In G. Dannemann, S. Vogenauer, *The Common European Sales Law in Context. Interactions with English and German Law,* Oxford, Oxford University Press, pp. 581–611.
Seymour, A. (2008), The Passing of Risk in Contracts for Sale in Roman Law and Australian Law: A Comparative Perspective, *Queensland Law Student Review*, Number 1, Volume 1, pp. 25–35.
Stocks, M. (1993), *Risk of loss under the Uniform Commercial Code and the United Nations Convention on Contracts for the International Sale of Goods: a comparative analysis and proposed revision of UCC Sections 2—509 and 2 510*, Northwestern University Law Review, pp. 1415–1457.
Thieffry, J. (1988), Sale of Goods between French and U.S. Merchants: Choice of Law considerations under the U.N. Convention on Contracts for the International Sale of Goods, *The International Lawyer*, p. 1017–1035.
Von Bar, C. & Clive, E. (2011), *Draft Common Frame of Reference, Full Edition*, Vol. 2. München, Sellier.
Von Hoffmann, B. (1986), Passing of Risk in International Sales of Goods, in Sarcevic, P. & Volken, P. *International Sale of Goods: Dubrovnik Lectures*, Oceana, pp. 265–303.

Wiese, V. (2012), Gefahrübergang nach Artt. 140 ff. GEKR, in Schmidt-Kessel, M. *Ein einheitliches europäisches Kaufrecht? Eine Analyse des Vorschlags der Kommission*, Munich, Sellier.
Zoll, F. & Watson, J. (2012), "Articles 141–146", in Shulze, R., (ed.), *Common European Sales Law (CESL). Commentary*, Baden-Baden, C.H. Beck, Hart, Nomos, pp. 602–615.

Chapter 11
Contract for the Supply of Digital Content

Javier Plaza Penadés

Abstract The main aspects of a contract for the supply of digital content are analysed in this chapter. This can be seen as the most novel part of the proposed Regulation of the European Union, and is certainly a very important part of the final content of the proposal. This type of contract is a logical consequence of the development of information technology and communication, and the evolution of an information society and knowledge economy.

Its inclusion as part of the European sales contract needed specific regulation with regard to certain aspects, and also required a degree of coordination with other areas of the Law, such as copyright, competition law, consumer law or ICTs Law.

The main aspects of these digital content contracts are here explained and discussed in a clear and systematic way.

Keywords Digital content · Copyright law · Consumer law · Services of information society and E-commerce law

11.1 Introduction

The development of E-commerce and the transfer of digital content for storage, processing or access, and repeated use, such as the download of music or movies, has been growing rapidly and holds a great potential for further growth, but is still surrounded by a considerable degree of legal diversity and uncertainty. The Common European Sales Law (CESL) should, therefore, cover the supply of digital content irrespective of whether or not that content is supplied on a tangible medium or supplied online.

In accordance with the increasing importance of the digital economy day by day, art. 1 CESL, on the objective and subject matter, includes and incorporates within the objective of this proposal for a Regulation on cross-border transactions

---

J. Plaza Penadés (✉)
University of Valencia, Valencia, Spain
e-mail: javier.plaza@uv.es

© Springer International Publishing Switzerland 2015
J. Plaza Penadés, L. M. Martínez Velencoso (eds.), *European Perspectives on the Common European Sales Law,* Studies in European Economic Law and Regulation 4,
DOI 10.1007/978-3-319-10497-3_11

"the supply of digital content and for related services where the parties to a contract agree to do so".

Moreover, art. 5, together with sales contracts of goods, provides that the Common European Sales Law may be used for "contracts for the supply of digital content", which "can be stored, processed or accessed, and re-used by the user", irrespective of whether the digital content is supplied in exchange for the payment of a price, and irrespective of whether a separate price was agreed for the related service, or also whether or not supplied on a tangible medium. In this sense, art. 5 emphasises the most remarkable aspect of this type of contract: that it "can be stored, processed or accessed, and re-used by the user".

On the other hand, digital content is often supplied not in exchange for a price but alongside separate paid goods or services, involving non-monetary consideration such as giving access to personal data, or being supplied free of charge in the context of a marketing strategy based on the expectation that the consumer will purchase additional or more sophisticated digital content products at a later stage. In view of this specific market structure and of the fact that defects in the digital content provided might harm the economic interests of consumers irrespective of the conditions under which it has been provided, the availability of the Common European Sales Law should not depend on whether a price is paid for the specific digital content in question.

With a view to maximising the added value of the Common European Sales Law, its material scope should also include certain services provided by the seller that are directly and closely related to specific goods or digital content supplied on the basis of the Common European Sales Law, and in practice often combined in the same, or a linked, contract at the same time, most notably repair, maintenance or installation of the goods or the digital content.

However, the Common European Sales Law should not cover any related contracts by which the buyer acquires goods or is supplied with a service, from a third party. This would not be appropriate because the third party is not part of the contracting parties' agreement to use the Regulation of the Common European Sales Law. A related contract with a third party should be governed by the respective national law, which is applicable according pursuant to Regulations (EC) No 593/2008 and (EC) No 864/2007 or any other relevant conflict of law rule.

The Common European Sales Law should identify well-balanced solutions, taking into account the legitimate interests of the parties, for designating and exercising the remedies available in the case of non-performance of the contract. In business-to-consumer (B2C) contracts the system of remedies should reflect the fact that the nonconformity of goods, digital content or services falls within the trader's sphere of responsibility.

Finally, it should be noted that, in order to enhance legal certainty by making the case law of the Court of Justice of the European Union and of national courts on the interpretation of the Common European Sales Law or any other provision of this Regulation accessible to the public, the Commission should create a database containing all relevant final judgments. With a view to making this task possible, and the Member States must ensure that these national judgments are quickly communicated to the Commission. This communication from each Member State to the Commission should be obligatory in order to develop an inventory of the relevant case law of the different States of the European Union and, therefore, it would be desirable, regardless of the language of each country, for the decisions and any appeals to be in English and in an open access database.

11.2 Concept of "Digital Content"

According to art. 2, which contains the definitions for the purposes of this Regulation, "'digital content' means data which are produced and supplied in digital form, whether or not according to the buyer's specifications, including video, audio, picture or written digital content, digital games, software and digital content which makes it possible to personalise existing hardware or software".

This definition determines the legal concept of "contracts for the supply of digital content" (art. 5), delimiting the specific objects of the provision for the supply or delivery of digital goods.

Article 2(j) also specifically excludes, as the possible objects of a contract for "the supply of digital content", the following goods and services: "financial services, including online banking services; legal or financial advice provided in electronic form; electronic healthcare services; electronic communications services and networks, and associated facilities and services; gambling; the creation of new digital content and the amendment of existing digital content by consumers or any other interaction with the creations of other users". The reason for the exclusion of these types of contracts is, in most cases, the existence of another specific European regulation.

On the other hand, a "related service" can be the object of a contract for the supply of digital content. A related service "means any service related to goods or digital content", such as installation, maintenance, repair or any other processing, provided by the seller of the goods or the supplier of the digital content under the sales contract, the contract for the supply of digital content or a separate related service contract which was concluded at the same time as the sales contract or the contract for the supply of digital content; it excludes: (i) transport services, (ii) training services, (iii) telecommunications support services; and (iv) financial services (art. 2(m)).

In electronic contracts for the supply of digital content the seller is also a 'service provider'; and, therefore, falls under the provisions of arts. 9–11 of Directive 2000/31/CE of the European Parliament and of the Council of 8 June 2000 on certain legal aspects of information society services, in particular electronic commerce, in the Internal Market ("Directive on electronic commerce").

In Case C128/11, 3 July 2012, the Judgment of the Court (Grand Chamber) of European Union, on legal protection of computer programs in proceedings between UsedSoft GmbH ('UsedSoft') and Oracle International Corp. ('Oracle') concerning the marketing by licensee of used licences for Oracle computer programs downloaded from the Internet, and the exhaustion of the distribution right on copyright by application of first sale doctrine, are analysed several questions on sale contracts for the supply of digital contents (on computer software).

The facts of this Case are that software owner develops and markets computer software. It is the proprietor of the exclusive user rights under copyright law in those programs. It is also the proprietor of the German and Community word marks the software owner, which are registered inter alia for computer software.

The right holder distributes the software at issue in the main proceedings, namely databank software, in 85 % of cases by downloading from the internet. The customer downloads a copy of the software directly to his computer from Software owner's website. The software is what is known as 'client-server-software'. The user right for such a program, which is granted by a licence agreement, includes the right to store a copy of the program permanently on a server and to allow a certain number of users to access it by downloading it to the main memory of their work-station computers. On the basis of a maintenance agreement, updated versions of the software ('updates') and programs for correcting faults ('patches') can be downloaded from software owner's website. At the customer's request, the programs are also supplied on CD ROM or DVD.

Software owner offers group licences for the software at issue in the main proceedings for a minimum of 25 users each. An undertaking requiring licences for 27 users thus has to acquire two licences.

Right holder's licence agreements for the software at issue in the main proceedings contain the following term, under the heading 'Grant of rights':

> With the payment for services you receive, exclusively for your internal business purposes, for an unlimited period a non-exclusive non-transferable user right free of charge for everything that software owner develops and makes available to you on the basis of this agreement.

The licensee markets used software licences, including user licences for the computer programs at issue in the main proceedings. For that purpose licensee acquires from customers of the software owner such user licences, or parts of them, where the original licences relate to a greater number of users than required by the first acquirer.

In October 2005 the licensee promoted a 'Special Offer' in which it offered for sale 'already used' licences for the software owner programs at issue in the main proceedings. In doing so it pointed out that the licences were all 'current' in the sense that the maintenance agreement concluded between the original licence holder and it was still in force, and that the lawfulness of the original sale was confirmed by a notarial certificate.

Customers of the licensee who are not yet in possession of the software in question download a copy of the program directly from right holder's website, after acquiring such a used licence. Customers who already have that software and then purchase further licences for additional users are induced by the licensee to copy the program to the workstations of those users.

On these facts, the Court clarifies that the wording of Directive 2009/24 does not make any reference to national laws as regards the meaning to be given to the term 'sale' in Article 4(2) of the directive. It follows that that term must be regarded, for the purposes of applying the directive, as designating an autonomous concept of European Union law, which must be interpreted in a uniform manner throughout the territory of the European Union. That conclusion is supported by the subject matter and purpose of Directive 2009/24. Recitals 4 and 5 in the preamble to that directive, which is based on Article 95 EC, to which Article 114 TFEU corresponds, state that its objective is to remove differences between the laws of the Member States which have adverse effects on the functioning of the internal market and concern computer programs. A uniform interpretation of the term 'sale' is necessary in order to avoid the protection offered to copyright holders by that directive varying according to the national law applicable.

According to a commonly accepted definition, a 'sale' is an agreement by which a person, in return for payment, transfers to another person his rights of ownership in an item of tangible or intangible property belonging to him. It follows that the commercial transaction-giving rise, in accordance with Article 4(2) of Directive 2009/24, to exhaustion of the right of distribution of a copy of a computer program must involve a transfer of the right of ownership in that copy.

The seller submits that it does not sell copies of its computer programs at issue in the main proceedings. It says that it makes available to its customers, free of charge, on its website a copy of the program concerned, and they can download that copy. The copy thus downloaded may not, however, be used by the customers unless they have concluded a user licence agreement with the software owner. Such a licence gives right holder's customers a non-exclusive and non-transferable user right for an unlimited period for that program. The software owner submits that neither the making available of a copy free of charge nor the conclusion of the user licence agreement involves a transfer of the right of ownership of that copy.

In this respect, it must be observed that the downloading of a copy of a computer program and the conclusion of a user licence agreement for that copy form an indivisible whole. Downloading a copy of a computer program is pointless if its possessor cannot use the copy. Those two operations must therefore be examined as a whole for the purposes of their legal classification (see, by analogy, Joined Cases C145/08 and C149/08 *Club Hotel Loutraki and Others* [2010] ECR I4165, paragraphs 48 and 49 and the case law cited).

As regards the question whether, in a situation such as that at issue in the main proceedings, the commercial transactions concerned involve a transfer of the right of ownership of the copy of the computer program, it must be stated that, according to the order for reference, a customer of software owner who downloads the copy of the program and concludes with that company a user licence agreement relating to that copy receives, in return for payment of a fee, a right to use that copy for an unlimited period. The making available by the software owner of a copy of its computer program and the conclusion of a user licence agreement for that copy are thus intended to make the copy usable by the customer, permanently, in return for payment of a fee designed to enable the copyright holder to obtain a remuneration corresponding to the economic value of the copy of the work of which it is the proprietor.

In those circumstances, the operations of sale examined as a whole, involve the transfer of the right of ownership of the copy of the computer program in question.

It makes no difference, in a situation such as that at issue in the main proceedings, whether the copy of the computer program was made available to the customer by the right holder concerned by means of a download from the right holder's website or by means of a material medium such as a CD-ROM or DVD. Even if, in the latter case too, the right holder formally separates the customer's right to use the copy of the program supplied from the operation of transferring the copy of the program to the customer on a material medium, the operation of downloading from that medium a copy of the computer program and that of concluding a licence agreement remain inseparable from the point of view of the acquirer, for the reasons set out before. Since an acquirer who downloads a copy of the program concerned by means of a material medium such as a CD-ROM or DVD and concludes a licence agreement for that copy receives the right to use the copy for an unlimited period in return for payment of a fee, it must be considered that those two operations likewise involve, in the case of the making available of a copy of the computer program concerned by means of a material medium such as a CD ROM or DVD, the transfer of the right of ownership of that copy.

Consequently, in a situation such as that at issue in the main proceedings, the transfer by the copyright holder to a customer of a copy of a computer program, accompanied by the conclusion between the same parties of a user licence agreement, constitutes a 'first sale … of a copy of a program' within the meaning of Article 4(2) of Directive 2009/24.

11.3 European Regulation on Digital Contents

The specific objects of contracts for digital contents, according to art. 2(j) of the proposal for a Regulation, are data that are produced and supplied in a digital format, such as online digital material support, and are regulated by different articles, which are basically those related to copyright, consumer protection and information society services. However, it can also include other topics, such as Competition Law or data protection. This is the reason why digital content must conform to the specific requirements of the different Regulations and Acts.

11.3.1 Copyright Law

One of the most important aspects of the contract for the supply of digital content is derived from the application of the rules on copyright and neighbour rights, and much of the content of the contracts may be protected by copyright and other related rights, such as literary, artistic or scientific digitised works, computer programs, databases, performance, artistic photographs and simple photographs, broadcasting, movies, etc.

Obviously, the object of this type of contract must respect the rules on copyright. However, the seller should know that the contract does not include the acquisition of any copyright on its digital content (*corpus mysticum*); and the buyer will only acquire the material property under the contract (*corpus mechanicum*).

On the other hand, the exhaustion of copyright occurs by the derivation of the "first sale doctrine", which has recently been reformulated by the Court of Justice of the European Union in *UsedSoft GmbH v Oracle Int. Corp.* (Case C-128/11 of 3 July 2012 regarding the ability to resell licenses for computer programs that have been lawfully acquired but have not been used by the purchaser of such licenses).

At least, the copyright law of the European Union has been harmonised by the various copyright Directives of the European Union, which the Member States are obliged to enact into their national laws, and by the judgments of the Court of Justice of the European Union, (that is, the European Court of Justice and the General Court). This has involved a high level of harmonisation in the different Member States in this field.

The first Directive was *Directive 92/100/EEC,* which has been repealed and replaced by *Directive 2006/115/EC*. The last, for the time being, is Directive 2012/28/EU of the European Parliament and of the Council of 25 October 2012 on certain permitted uses of orphan works; but there are others, such as Directive 2011/77/EU of the European Parliament and of the Council of 27 September 2011 amending Directive 2006/116/EC on the term of protection of copyright and certain related rights; or Directive 2011/29/EU.

The Directive on the legal protection of computer programs (91/250/EEC) was a real European "first" for copyright law, the first copyright measure to be adopted following the publication of the White Paper on completing the Single Market by 1992. The objective of the Directive was to harmonise Member States' legislation regarding the protection of computer programs in order to create a legal environment that would afford a degree of security against unauthorised reproduction of such computer programs.

The Database Directive (Directive 96/9/EC of the European Parliament and of the Council of 11 March 1996 on the legal protection of databases) created a *sui generis* protection for databases that do not meet the criterion of originality for copyright protection. It is specifically intended to protect "the investment of considerable human, technical and financial resources" in creating databases (para. 7 of the preamble), whereas the copyright laws of many Member States specifically exclude effort and labour from the criteria for copyright protection. To qualify, the database must show "qualitatively and/or quantitatively a substantial investment in either the obtaining, verification or presentation of the contents…". Their creators have the right "to prevent extraction and/or re-utilization of the whole or of a substantial part, evaluated qualitatively and/or quantitatively, of the contents of that database." (art. 7(1)). This is taken to include the repeated extraction of insubstantial parts of the contents if this conflicts with the normal exploitation of the database or unreasonably prejudices the legitimate interests of the creator of the database (art. 7(5)).

Finally, the objectives of Directive 2001/29/EC of the European Parliament and of the Council of 22 May 2001 on the harmonisation of certain aspects of copyright and related rights in the information society are to adapt legislation on copyright and related rights to reflect technological developments and to transpose into

Community law the main international obligations arising from the two treaties on copyright and related rights adopted within the framework of the World Intellectual Property Organisation (WIPO) in December 1996. It is an essential building block for the Information Society. The final text is a result of over three years of thorough discussion and an example of co-decision making where the European Parliament, the Council and the Commission have all had a decisive input.

11.3.2 Consumer Law

European consumer law is in exactly the same situation, since there is a high number of Directives that overlap the rights of European trading, and since there is a large number of Directives on the subject that establish a set of imperatives and inalienable rights for the consumer, and which are applicable to the contract for the supply of digital content[1].

---

[1] Council Directive 85/577/EEC of 20 December 1985 to protect the consumer in respect of contracts negotiated away from business premises (OJ L 372, 31.12.1985, p. 31); Council Directive 87/102/EEC of 22 December 1986 for the approximation of the laws, regulations and administrative provisions of the Member States concerning consumer credit (OJ L 42, 12.2.1987, p. 48); Council Directive 89/552/EEC of 3 October 1989 on the coordination of certain provisions laid down by law, regulation or administrative action in Member States concerning the pursuit of television broadcasting activities: Articles 10–21 (OJ L 298, 17.10.1989, p. 23); Council Directive 90/314/EEC of 13 June 1990 on package travel, package holidays and package tours (OJ L 158, 23.6.1990, p. 59); Council Directive 93/13/EEC of 5 April 1993 on unfair terms in consumer contracts (OJ L 95, 21.4.1993, p. 29); Directive 97/7/EC of the European Parliament and of the Council of 20 May 1997 on the protection of consumers in respect of distance contracts (OJ L 144, 4.6.1997, p. 19); Directive 1999/44/EC of the European Parliament and of the Council of 25 May 1999 on certain aspects of the sale of consumer goods and associated guarantees (OJ L 171, 7.7.1999, p. 12); Directive 2000/31/EC of the European Parliament and of the Council of 8 June 2000 on certain legal aspects on information society services, in particular electronic commerce, in the internal market (Directive on electronic commerce) (OJ L 178, 17.7.2000, p. 1); Directive 2001/83/EC of the European Parliament and of the Council of 6 November 2001 on the Community code relating to medicinal products for human use: Articles 86–100 (OJ L 311, 28.11.2001, p. 67); Directive 2002/65/EC of the European Parliament and of the Council of 23 September 2002 concerning the distance marketing of consumer financial services (OJ L 271, 9.10.2002, p. 16); Directive 2005/29/EC of the European Parliament and of the Council of 11 May 2005 concerning unfair business-to-consumer commercial practices in the internal market (OJ L 149, 11.6.2005, p. 22); Directive 2006/123/EC of the European Parliament and of the Council of 12 December 2006 on services in the internal market (OJ L 376, 27.12.2006, p. 36); Directive 2008/122/EC of the European Parliament and of the Council of 14 January 2009 on the protection of consumers in respect of certain aspects of timeshare, long-term holiday product, resale and exchange contracts (OJ L 33, 3.2.2009, p. 10); Directive 2008/48/EC of the European Parliament and of the Council of 23 April 2008 on credit agreements for consumers (OJ L 133, 22.5.2008, p. 66); Directive 2009/22/EC of the European Parliament and of the Council of 23 April 2009 on injunctions for the protection of consumers' interests (Codified version) (Text with EEA relevance). Finally, Directive on Consumer Rights (2011/83/EC) replaces, as of 13 June 2014, Directive 97/7/EC on the protection of consumers in respect of distance contracts and Directive 85/577/EEC protect consumer in respect of contracts negotiated away from business premises. Directive 1999/44/EC certain aspects

11.3.3 Services of Information Society and E-commerce Law

There is basic distinction between that which is related to "contracts concluded by electronic means" and to "contracts for the supply of digital content". Obviously, a contract for the supply of digital content can be concluded online by electronic means, but this is not necessarily so, because it is possible for it to be concluded offline, through digital or material support, such as a CD or DVD.

An electronic contract allows the contract itself to be perfected through other instruments or devices that allow access to various computer or electronic networks, expanding the horizon of e-commerce to the contracts perfected through the television screen (t-commerce) or mobile phone (m-commerce), or any other device that allows access to the telecommunications network, as is the case with the latest applications that are connected to the Internet of Things.

Therefore, in the Annex to the Regulation, in which the substantive content of the contract of sale is developed, there is a specific provision for an electronic contract whose application overlaps the contract of sale where this type of contract is concerned.

In this sense, art. 24 provides additional duties for distance contracts concluded by electronic means. In the first place, when "… a trader provides the means for concluding a contract and where those means are electronic and do not involve the exclusive exchange of electronic mail or other individual communication. The trader must make available to the other party appropriate, effective and accessible technical means for identifying and correcting input errors before the other party makes or accepts an offer" (art. 24(1) and (2)).

In addition, "The trader must provide information about the following matters before the other party makes or accepts an offer:

a. the technical steps to be taken in order to conclude the contract;
b. whether or not the trader will file a contract document and whether it will be accessible;
c. the technical means for identifying and correcting input errors before the other party makes or accepts an offer;
d. the languages offered for the conclusion of the contract; and
e. the contract terms. (art. 24(3))"

Actually, these information duties are identical to those that Directive 2000/31/EC of the European Parliament and of the Council of 8 June 2000 on certain legal aspects of information society services, in particular electronic commerce, in the Internal Market ("Directive on electronic commerce") requires for electronic contracts, with the only addition being the terms of contract, which is a legal duty that is already implicit in the mandatory provisions for consumer contracts. For this reason, art. 27, provides for the mandatory nature of these rules in that it establishes that "In relations between a trader and a consumer, the parties may not, to the

of the sale of consumer goods and associated guarantees as well as Directive 93/13/EEC unfair terms in consumer contracts remains in force.

detriment of the consumer, exclude the application of…" these duties and obligations. This has been stipulated in art. 27 because in relations between a trader and a consumer, the trader bears the burden of proof that it has provided the information required by the proposal of Regulation (art. 26).

However, what really is new in the case of distance contracts concluded by electronic means is that art. 25 provides additional requirements when the consumer is obligated to make a payment to the trader. In this case, "the trader must make the consumer aware in a clear and prominent manner, and immediately before the consumer places the order, of the information required…" concerning the main characteristics of the digital content or related services that are to be supplied, the total price of the digital content or related services inclusive of taxes, the arrangements for payment, the content, and the time when the supply of the digital content or performance of the related services will be effected, as well as the time by which the trader undertakes to supply the digital content or to perform the related services.

Also, "The trader must ensure that the consumer, when placing the order, explicitly acknowledges that the order implies an obligation to pay. Where placing an order entails activating a button or a similar function, the button or similar function must be labelled in an easily legible manner only with the words "order with obligation to pay" or similar unambiguous wording indicating that placing the order entails an obligation to make a payment to the trader. Where the trader has not complied with this paragraph, the consumer is not bound by the contract or order." (art. 25(2)). Additionally, "The trader must indicate clearly and legibly on its trading website at the latest at the beginning of the ordering process whether any delivery restrictions apply and what means of payment are accepted." (art. 25(3)).

As can be seen, the e-procurement model is based on a contract formed via a web page and directed towards a massive contract with a plurality of people (traders or consumers, in which case the duties have a mandatory or imperative nature).

Finally, there is a similar distinction between "electronic contract" and "informatics contract", which, while seemingly obvious, has occasionally led to some confusion.

An informatics contract is one that aims to provide computer programs and computer equipment (sale, leasing, renting computer equipment) or programs for software licensing, copyright transfer, escrow, and outsourcing of the computer; while "electronic contract" is one contract that is executed by electronic means.

Obviously any informatics contract, like other contracts (where also internet access or hosting is included), can be concluded online, through an electronic network.

11.4 Obligations and Remedies in Contract for the Supply of Digital Content

Part IV of CESL looks closely at the rules specific to sales contracts and contracts for the supply of digital content that contain the obligations of the seller and of the buyer. This part also contains rules on the remedies for non-performance of buyers and sellers; and, finally, sets out general provisions on the passing of risk.

For reasons of coordination, this Part analyses only the main aspects of the regulation of contracts for the supply of digital content: the obligations of sellers and buyers in contracts for the supply of digital content; because the remedies for the sellers and buyers, as well as the passing of risk and the change of circumstances are developed in others parts of this instrument.

In this area, the Regulation is less original, because it is limited to the typical duties of the seller and the buyer of the various States, which is already included in the Principles of European Law Sales (PELS).

11.4.1 Seller's Obligations in Contracts to Supply Digital Content

Chapter 11 contains the seller's obligations.

There are five basic or main obligations of the seller listed in art. 91:

Supply the digital content.

- Transfer the ownership of the goods, including the tangible medium on which the digital content is supplied.
- Ensure that the digital content are in conformity with the contract.
- Ensure that the buyer has the right to use the digital content in accordance with the contract.
- Deliver such documents relating to the digital content as may be required by the contract

This article develops the basic obligations of seller more than art. 1:2001 PELS, because it includes: the obligation of transferring the ownership of the digital contents, excluding, obviously, the copyright, which has its own system of transfer and which normally remains with his owner; and that the buyer is bound by the specifications of the licence of use.

With regard to the place of delivery, art. 93 of the annex to the Proposal of a Regulation lays down as a place of delivery the consumer's place of residence at the time of the conclusion of the contract, where the place of delivery cannot be otherwise determined in the case of a contract for the supply of digital content, which is a distance or off-premises contract, or in which the seller has undertaken to arrange for the carriage to the buyer. This solution offers a high degree of legal certainty, since it avoids the possibility of the place of delivery being where the servers are housed in the case of electronic contracts.

In any other case, the place of delivery where the contract of sale involves carriage of the goods by a carrier or series of carriers is the nearest collection point of the first carrier or where the contract does not involve carriage, the seller's place of business at the time of conclusion of the contract (art. 93(1)(b)).

If the seller has more than one place of business, the place of delivery is that which has the closest relationship to the obligation to deliver (art. 93(2)).

Article 94 of the annex concerns the method of delivery, distinguishing between three situations in which the seller fulfils the obligation to deliver:

(a) in the case of a consumer sales contract or a contract for the supply of digital content which is a distance or off-premises contract or in which the seller has undertaken to arrange carriage to the buyer, by transferring the physical possession or control of the goods or the digital content to the consumer;
(b) in other cases in which the contract involves carriage of the goods by a carrier, by handing over the goods to the first carrier for transmission to the buyer and by handing over to the buyer any document necessary to enable the buyer to take over the goods from the carrier holding the goods; or
(c) in cases that do not fall within points (a) or (b), by making the goods or the digital content, or where it is agreed that the seller need only delivery documents representing the goods, the documents, available to the buyer.

In relation to the time of delivery, art 95 provides that "(1) Where the time of delivery cannot be otherwise determined, the goods or the digital content must be delivered without undue delay after the conclusion of the contract.

(2) In contracts between a trader and a consumer, unless agreed otherwise by the parties, the trader must deliver the digital content not later than 30 days from the conclusion of the contract."

Therefore, the main obligations of the seller are fulfilled by complying with his obligations regarding the carriage of the goods.

As can be seen, this duty of the seller in a contract for the supply of digital content is a relative novelty, because it applies the basic duties of the seller in a sale of goods contract to this digital content type of contract. In this sense, these duties are an adaptation of the principles of the PELS (art. 2:001: Overview of obligation of the seller).

11.4.2 Buyer's Obligations in Contracts to Supply Digital Content

According to art. 123 of the proposal of a Regulation, the main obligations of the buyer are:

- to pay the price.
- to take delivery of the goods or the digital content.
- to take over documents representing or relating to the goods or documents relating to digital content as may be required by the contract.

But this duty of the buyer does not apply to contracts for the supply of digital content where the digital content is not supplied in exchange for the payment of a price.

This article lists three basic obligations of the buyer for this type of contract; and it is an adaptation of art. 3:001 PELS. However, these basic duties, which are a reflection of the seller's duties, are not mandatory; and for this reason the buyer, as well as the seller, may not always be subject to all the obligations set out in this article.

There is a very important degree of coincidence with the PELS in relation to the means, place and time of payment, but subject to certain necessary adaptations.

Article 124 sets out that:

(1) Payment shall be made by the means of payment indicated by the contract terms or, if there is no such indication, by any means used in the ordinary course of business at the place of payment taking into account the nature of the transaction.
(2) A seller who accepts a cheque or other order to pay or a promise to pay is presumed to do so only on condition that it will be honoured. The seller may enforce the original obligation to pay if the order or promise is not honoured.
(3) The buyer's original obligation is extinguished if the seller accepts a promise to pay from a third party with whom the seller has a pre-existing arrangement to accept the third party's promise as a means of payment.
(4) In a contract between a trader and a consumer, the consumer is not liable, in respect of the use of a given means of payment, for fees that exceed the cost borne by the trader for the use of such means.

With regard to the place of payment, art. 125 provides: "Where the place of payment cannot otherwise be determined it is the seller's place of business at the time of conclusion of the contract. If the seller has more than one place of business, the place of payment is the place of business of the seller which has the closest relationship to the obligation to pay."

Regarding the time of payment, art. 126 of the annex follows by determining that "Payment of the price is due at the moment of delivery. The seller may reject an offer to pay before payment is due if it has a legitimate interest in so doing."

One of the principal novelties regarding payment in this proposal of a Regulation is to allow payment by a third party, but the buyer who entrusts payment to another person remains responsible for that payment. (art. 127).

Moreover: "The seller cannot refuse payment by a third party if (a) the third party acts with the assent of the buyer; or (b) the third party has a legitimate interest in paying and the buyer has failed to pay or it is clear that the buyer will not pay at the time that payment is due." (art. 127(2)). In this case, the payment by a third party discharges the buyer from liability to the seller (art. 127(3)). Article 127.4 then continues to lay down that where the seller accepts payment by a third party without the buyer assent or without a legitimate interest in paying, he is discharged from this liability to the seller but the seller is liable to the buyer for any loss caused by that acceptance.

Another novelty in this proposal is the inclusion of rules on the imputation of payment, in accordance with art. 129 of the annex. In the first place, sub-art. 1 provides that the buyer may at the time of payment notify the seller of the obligation to which the payment is to be imputed where a buyer has to make several payments to the seller and the payment made does not suffice to cover all of them. Therefore, the principle of freedom of choice for the buyer applies.

If the buyer does not make this notification, the seller may impute the performance to one of the obligations, except if obligation is not yet due or is disputed. (art. 128(2) and (3)).

Finally, "In the absence of an effective imputation by buyer or seller, the payment is imputed to that obligation which satisfies one of the following criteria by this order:

a. the obligation which is due or is the first to fall due;
b. the obligation for which the seller has no or the least security;

c. the obligation which is the most burdensome for the buyer;
d. the obligation which arose first.

If none of those criteria applies, the payment is imputed proportionately to all the obligations." (art. 128(4)). Proportionality is, thus, the final and residual solution.

A different question arises on the imputation of payments when the buyer pays an insufficient amount to cover his obligation with regards to the principal, interests and expenses. In relation to any one of these obligations a payment by the buyer is to be imputed, first, to expenses, secondly, to interest, and thirdly, to principal, unless the seller makes a different imputation (art. 128(6)).

11.5 Obligation of Taking Delivery

Special attention must be paid to the issue of the obligation of taking delivery in relation with the lack of conformity in this type of contract on digital contents.

Article 129 provides that: "The buyer fulfils the obligation to take delivery by (a) doing all the acts which could be expected in order to enable the seller to perform the obligation to deliver; and (b) taking over the goods, or the documents representing the goods or digital content, as required by the contract".

As we have seen, the supply of digital content has to be done at the agreed time (*dies a quo*), but advance payment is possible, "If the seller delivers the goods or supplies the digital content before the time fixed, the buyer must take delivery unless the buyer has a legitimate interest in refusing to do so" (art. 130(1)), wherever the digital content is supplied in exchange for the payment of a price.

Furthermore, "If the seller delivers… a digital content less than that provided for in the contract the buyer must take delivery unless the buyer has a legitimate interest in refusing to do so" (art. 130(2)).

Equally, "If the seller delivers a quantity of goods or digital content greater than that provided for by the contract, the buyer may retain or refuse the excess quantity" (art. 130(3)); but "If the buyer retains the excess quantity it is treated as having been supplied under the contract and must be paid for at the contractual rate" (art. 130(4)). Also, in a consumer sales contract, this not apply "if the buyer reasonably believes that the seller has delivered the excess quantity intentionally and without error, knowing that it had not been ordered" (art. 130(5)).

11.6 Conformity of Digital Content

Finally, one of the most interesting parts of the Proposal of a Regulation is that relative to conformity of the digital content, which is regulated together with the conformity of goods.

Article 99 provides that, "In order to conform to the contract, the digital content must:

a. be of the quantity, quality and description required by the contract;
b. be contained or packaged in the manner required by the contract; and
c. be supplied along with any accessories, installation instructions or other instructions required by the contract."

Following on, art. 100 contains the criteria for conformity of the goods and digital content. So, the digital content must:

> (a) be fit for any particular purpose made known to the seller at the time of the conclusion of the contract, except where the circumstances show that the buyer did not rely, or that it was unreasonable for the buyer to rely, on the seller's skill and judgement;
> (b) be fit for the purposes for which goods or digital content of the same description would ordinarily be used;
> (c) possess the qualities of goods or digital content which the seller held out to the buyer as a sample or model;
> (d) be contained or packaged in the manner usual for such goods or, where there is no such manner, in a manner adequate to preserve and protect the goods;
> (e) be supplied along with such accessories, installation instructions or other instructions as the buyer may expect to receive;
> (f) possess the qualities and performance capabilities indicated in any pre-contractual statement which forms part of the contract terms by virtue of Article 69; and
> (g) possess such qualities and performance capabilities as the buyer may expect. When determining what the consumer may expect of the digital content regard is to be had to whether or not the digital content was supplied in exchange for the payment of a price.

Article 101 provides legal solutions in order to correct any errors in installation under a consumer sales contract, specifically providing that: "(1) Where goods or digital content supplied under a consumer sales contract are incorrectly installed, any lack of conformity resulting from the incorrect installation is regarded as lack of conformity of the goods or the digital content if: (a) the goods or the digital content were installed by the seller or under the seller's responsibility; or (b) the goods or the digital content were intended to be installed by the consumer and the incorrect installation was due to a shortcoming in the installation instructions. (2) The parties may not, to the detriment of the consumer, exclude the application of this Article or derogate from or vary its effects."

Another basic principle of a sales contract, and one which contains a duty of the seller, is contained in art. 102 of the annex, this being that the digital content "must be cleared of any right or not obviously unfounded claim of a third party."

With regard to rights or claims based on intellectual property (basically copyright), "the goods must be free from and the digital content must be cleared of any right or not obviously unfounded claim of a third party:

a. under the law of the state where the goods or digital content will be used according to the contract or, in the absence of such an agreement, under the law of the state of the buyer's place of business or in contracts between a trader and a consumer the consumer's place of residence indicated by the consumer at the time of the conclusion of the contract; and
b. which the seller knew of or could be expected to have known of at the time of the conclusion of the contract."

In these cases, the protection of copyright is based in principle of national treatment, that is, the author or owners of copyright have the same protection as nationals of that country.

Article 102 continues: "In contracts between businesses, paragraph 2 does not apply where the buyer knew or could be expected to have known of the rights or claims based on intellectual property at the time of the conclusion of the contract," (para. 3); and "In contracts between a trader and a consumer paragraph 2 does not apply where the consumer knew of the rights or claims based on intellectual property at the time of the conclusion of the contract" (para. 4).

However, "In contracts between a trader and a consumer, the parties may not, to the detriment of the consumer, exclude the application of this Article or derogate from or vary its effects" (para. 5).

According to art. 103: "Digital content is not considered as not conforming to the contract for the sole reason that updated digital content has become available after the conclusion of the contract."

Article 104 respects the buyer's knowledge of the lack of conformity in a contract between traders, and says that "In a contract between traders, the seller is not liable for any lack of conformity of the goods if, at the time of the conclusion of the contract, the buyer knew or could not have been unaware of the lack of conformity."

Article 105 determines the relevant time for establishing conformity:

1. The seller is liable for any lack of conformity which exists at the time when the risk passes to the buyer under Chapter 14.
2. In a consumer sales contract, any lack of conformity which becomes apparent within six months of the time when risk passes to the buyer is presumed to have existed at that time unless this is incompatible with the nature of the goods or digital content or with the nature of the lack of conformity.

...

4. Where the digital content must be subsequently updated by the trader, the trader must ensure that the digital content remains in conformity with the contract throughout the duration of the contract.
5. In a contract between a trader and a consumer, the parties may not, to the detriment of a consumer, exclude the application of this Article or derogate from or vary its effect.

On the other hand, and finally, art. 97 establishes the procedure for the delivery of digital contents avoiding the effects of breach of contract by a seller who is left in possession of the digital content because the buyer, when bound to do so, has failed to take delivery. Obviously the seller must take reasonable steps to protect and preserve them and avoid *mora creditoris*. "In this case, the seller is discharged from the obligation to deliver if the seller (a) deposits the digital content on reasonable terms with a third party to be held to the order of the buyer, and notifies the buyer of this; or (b) sells the goods or the digital content on reasonable terms after notice to the buyer, and pays the net proceeds to the buyer (art. 97(2)). Also "The seller is entitled to be reimbursed or to retain out of the proceeds of sale any costs reasonably incurred" (art. 97(3)).

11.7 Summary

After studying the main aspects of the contract for the supply of digital content in the CELS, a superficial reader might conclude that he knows the specifics rules contained therein, and the different solutions available; however, at the same time, he should be aware of one of the most important and novel parts of this Regulation, because it has made a very important attempt to adapt the solutions of sale of goods contracts to this type of contract. For this reason, the various rules regarding the contract for the supply of digital content are disseminated throughout the whole text, and jurists must look in each article to find the legal solutions applicable to these digital content contracts, which is a logical consequence of the development of information technology and communication, and the implementation of the knowledge economy.

One of the most important aspects of the contract for the supply of digital content is derived from the application of the rules on copyright and neighbour rights, and much of the contents of the contracts may be protected by copyright and related rights, such as literary, artistic or scientific digitised works, computer programs, databases, performance, artistic photographs and simple photographs, broadcasting, movies, etc. However, the seller should know that the contract does not include the acquisition of any copyright on its digital content (*corpus mysticum*); and the buyer will only acquire the material property under the contract (*corpus mechanicum*).

Certainly its inclusion as part of the European sales contract needed in some aspects of a specific regulation, and also requires some coordination with other parts of the Law, such as copyright, competition law, consumer law or ICTs Law.

Another basic distinction is the related to "contracts concluded by electronic means" and "contract for the supply of digital content". Obviously a contract for the supply of digital content could be concluded Online by electronic mean, but not necessarily, because it is possible to be conclude out line, in a digital or material support. Therefore, in the Annex to Regulation, in which the substantive content of the contract of sale Europe develops, we can find a specific regulation of electronic contract whose application overlaps the contract of sale where this kind of contract is given.

The truth is that the core of the regulation of this type of contract is in the rights and duties of the buyer and seller, because the contract supply of digital content is integrated into the regulation of sale of goods, with appropriate adaptations.

Finally, it should be noted also in order to enhance legal certainty by making the case law of the Court of Justice of the European Union and of national courts on the interpretation of the Common European Sales Law or any other provision of this Regulation accessible to the public the Commission should create a database comprising the final relevant decisions. With a view to making that task possible, and the Member States must ensure that such national judgments are quickly communicated to the Commission. I believe this step forced to develop inventory of case Law of the different States of European Unions, and therefore it would be desirable, regardless of the language of each country, the decisions and appeals were in English and in an open access database.

Biblography

Beale, Hugh (ed.) (2012) Chitty on Contracts, 31st ed., Sweet & Maxwell, London.
European Law Institute, Statement on the Proposal for a Regulation on a Common European Sales Law, COM (2011) 635 final, 2012, available at http://www.europeanlawinstitute.eu (last visited 3 December 2013).
Expert Group on European contract, A European contract law for consumers and businesses, 3 May 2011, (so-called Feasibility Study), available at http://ec.europa.eu/justice/contract/files/feasibility_study_final.pdf (last visited 3 December 2013).
Grigoleit C Hondius E (2011) Unexpected circumstances in European Contract Law, Cambridge University Press, New York.
Hegel, Georg Wilhelm Friedrich, Elements of the Philosophy of Right (translation S.W. Dyde, Batoche Books, Kitchener, Ontario , 2001).
Hondius, Huetger, Jeloschek, Sivesand and Wiewiorrowska (2008) Principles of European Law PELS, Study Group on a European Civil Code, Oxford University Press. UK
Jauernig, Othmar (ed.), (2011) Bürgerliches Gesetzbuch, 14th ed., CH Beck, Munich.
Keirse, Anne (2011) Why the Proposed Optional Common European Sales Law Has Not, But Should Have, Abandoned the Principle of All or Nothing: A Guide to How to Sanction the Duty to Mitigate the Loss, ERPL, p. 951 et seq.
Lando and Beale (2000) Principles of European Contract Law, Parts I and II, prepared by the Commission on European Contract Law, 2000.
Larenz K (1957) Geschäftsgrundlage und Vertragserfüllung: die Bedeutung "veränderter Umständen" inm Zivilrecht. C.H. Beck, München.
Momberg Uribe R (2011) Change of Circumstances in International Instruments of Contract Law. The Approach of The CISG, PICC, PECL and DCFR, 15(2) VJ, pp. 233 ff. http://www.cisg.law.pace.edu/cisg/biblio/uribe.pdf
Peer GM (2001) Die Rechtsfolgen von Störungen der Geschäftsgrundlage. Ein Vergleichzwischen § 313 Reg Eeines Schuldrechtsmodernisierungsgesetzes und demgeltendendeutschen und österreichischen Rechtsowiemodernen Regelwerken, in Helms T Neumann D Caspers G Sailer, R Schmidt-Kessel M (ed.), Jahrbuch Junger Zivilrechtwissenschaftler. Das neue Schuldrecht, Freiburg, pp. 61 et sEq.
Posner, Richard, Economic Analysis of Law, 7th ed., Aspen, Austin et al. 2007.
Remien, Oliver (2012) Schadensersatz und Zinsennach EU-Kaufrecht, in: Schmidt-Kessel, Martin (ed.), Eineinheitlicheseuropäisches Kaufrecht?, sellier, Munich, p. 503 *et seq*.Remien, Oliver, Herrler, Sebastian, and Limmer, Peter (eds.) (2012) Gemeinsameseuropäisches Kaufrechtfür die EU?, Beck, Munich, S. 331 *et seq*.
Schmidt-Kessel, Martin, (2012) Strukturfragen des Schadensersatzesim Draft Common Frame of Reference füre in Europäisches Privatrecht, in: Remien, Oliver (ed.), Schadensersatzimeuropäischen Privat- und Wirtschaftsrecht, Mohr Siebeck, Tübinge.
Schmidt-Kessel M (2013) Der Entwurffürein Gemeinsames Europäisches Kaufrecht Kommentar, Sellier, Munich.
Schulze, Reiner (ed.), (2013) Common European Sales Law, Hart, Nomos, Baden-Baden.
Schwenzer (ed.), Commentary on the UN Convention on the International Sale of Goods, 3rd ed., OUP, Oxford, 2010.
Shavell, Steven, Foundations of Economic Analysis of Law, Belknap Press of Harvard University, Cambridge, Massachusetts, 2004.
Treitel, Guenter H., Contracts in General, in: International Encyclopedia of Comparative Law, vol. 7 chapter 16, Mouton, The Hague and Mohr Siebeck, Tübingen, 1976.
Unberath, Hannes, Die Vertragsverletzung, Mohr Siebeck, Tübingen, 2007.
UNIDROIT, Principles of International Commercial Contracts, Official Commentary, Rome 2010.
Van Houtte H (1993) Changed Circumstances and Pacta Sunt Servanda, in: Gaillard E (ed), Transnational Rules in International Commercial Arbitration, ICC Publ. Nr. 480,4, Paris, pp. 105 et seq.
Vogenauer, Stefan, & Kleinheisterkamp, Jan (eds.), Commentary on the UNIDROIT Principles of International Commercial Contracts (PICC), 2009.

Chapter 12
Obligations and Remedies Under a Related Service Contract

M. José Reyes López

Abstract Following the model of Directive 2011/83/EU of the 25 October 2011 on consumer rights, the proposed CESL regulation is structured on the basis of sales and service contracts. With regard to service contracts, however, the CESL only regulates those service contracts whose existence is justified by their direct link to sales contracts.

The provisions of service contracts, that are regulated, are equivalent to the performance of the 'giving'. Therefore, the CESL refers in its formulation to the traditional distinction between obligation of means and the obligation of results, requiring in this case, the performance of a particular result, regardless of whether it is free of charge or onerous.

This treatment justifies that the breach of related services has to be redirected, in order to consider it as a lack of conformity in the contract of sale or supply of digital content.

However, the regulation of services provided by the DCFR is more extensive. This regulation, unlike that of the CESL, which is limited to the regulation of sales contracts, is contained in a generally applicable section of the instrument. This regulation is applicable to all services and, in particular, to the related services contracts, and is followed by the regulation of six types of contract: construction, processing, storage, design, information and advice, and treatment; which are omitted in the CESL.

Nor do the national laws of each Member State of the EU offer a regulation of related services contracts in particular. Therefore, the incorporation of Part V of the CESL should not, in principle, be considered as a potential source of conflict when there is an agreement between the parties, but a mechanism that will help to resolve situations that are difficult to fit into a concrete legal framework. However, it is important to highlight that, in the same way as it is intended to unify the rules of sale, it would be desirable to advance a model to establish at least a uniform regulation in the basic rules of the provision of services.

M. J. Reyes López (✉)
University of Valencia, Valencia, Spain
e-mail: maria.j.reyes@uv.es

© Springer International Publishing Switzerland 2015

J. Plaza Penadés, L. M. Martínez Velencoso (eds.), *European Perspectives on the Common European Sales Law,* Studies in European Economic Law and Regulation 4,
DOI 10.1007/978-3-319-10497-3_12

Keywords Related services contract · Right to withdraw · Obligations of the parties in the service contract · Remedies in the service contract · Duty to disclose information

12.1 The Nature of the Issue

12.1.1 Background and Explanation for the Regulation

The existence of a single market implies the existence of a set of rules to facilitate the exchange of goods and services within the EU, the fewer inequalities there are between the rules of the Member States the better the free circulation of goods will be.

Given the existence of the different content of the rules in the EU, as highlighted by the Communication of 2001, which identified the fragmented legal framework in the field of contract law together with the obstacles that this carries with it to cross-border trade. In July 2010, the Commission launched a public consultation with the Green Paper on policy options for progress towards a European contract law for consumers and businesses, setting out policy options in order to strengthen the growth of the internal market in the area of European contract law.

On the 8 June 2011, in response to the Green Paper, the European Parliament issued a Resolution expressing its strong support for the development of an instrument that would improve the establishment and functioning of the internal market, benefiting traders, consumers and judicial systems of the Member States.

To this end, the instrument chosen to develop this initiative is a Regulation on a Common European Sales Law (CESL).

The CESL focuses on the harmonisation of the contract laws of Member States, not by modifying the existing national contract laws in force, but creating within the legal systems of each Member State, a second regime of contract law for contracts that fall within its scope of application, which must be identical throughout the European Union and coexist with the rules of the national contract laws in force in each Member State, on a voluntary basis and upon the expressed agreement of the parties.

Among the innovations introduced by this proposal, it is worth noting the unification in the regulation of the model of sales contracts, the sale of digital content and the related services contract. As set out in its recital number 19, its aim is to maximise the added value of the common European sales law, which justifies the inclusion in its material scope of certain services provided by the seller that are directly and closely related to the specific goods or digital content supplied on the basis of the said rules. These are, in practice, often mixed in the same contract or in a related contract concluded at the same time, as happens in relation to repair services, maintenance or installation of the goods or the digital content, or temporary storage of digital content in the provider's cloud, whose execution is very close to the sale, as if it were another provision.

12.2 Related Services Contracts

12.2.1 Concept

The proposal for an optional instrument is structured on the basis of the sale-services dichotomy, so that the contracts to which it is applied can only be sales contracts or contracts related to specific services. It should also not be forgotten that this concept is closely linked with initial Part IV, which regulates the obligations and remedies of the parties to the sales contract.

The CESL does not contain any definition of the services contract; it only defines related services, redundantly, for example: placing, installation, maintenance, repair or other treatment provided by the seller of goods or provider of digital content. For this reason it is important to underline that the CESL does not affect all service contracts but only those very specific services that are linked to the sale of goods or digital content.

Specifically, art. 2(m) defines " related services" as "any service related to goods or digital content, such as storage or any other processing, including installation, maintenance, repair or any other processing, provided by the seller of the goods or the supplier of the digital content under the sales contract, the contract for the supply of digital content or a separate related service contract which was concluded at the same time of the contract for the supply of digital content".

Therefore, the definition given by the Proposal covers two cases.

The above article links, firstly, a service to a sale of goods or digital content that has been executed. Then, the article defines the related services as: any goods or digital content related services; such as: storage or any other processing, installation, maintenance, repair or any other treatment that has been provided by the seller of the goods or provider of digital content under the sales contract or under the digital content contract. However, the second meaning of related services has a different scope because it also includes related services contracts that are concluded separately and at the same time as the sales of goods contract or the supply of digital content contract or provided for, even if only as an option, in the sales contract or in the contract for the supply of digital content.

This systematic framework makes it clear that the treatment given to the related service has no autonomy, but it is subject to the main contract. For instance, the conclusion of the sales contract or the supply of digital content contract, being the first main contract, will initiate the second contract. The same interpretation is to be given to the third case because they are contracts that have been formed at the same time and with the aim of completing the main contract.

In addition, art. 5 sets out that the CESL may be used for: "c) related service contracts, irrespective of whether a separate price was agreed for the related service".

However, pursuant to art. 7, the CESL "may be used only if the seller of goods or the supplier of digital content is a trader. Where all the parties to a contract are traders, the Common European Sales Law may be used if at least one of those parties is a small or medium-sized enterprise ('SME')".

The following are excluded from this scheme:

a. transport services,
b. training services,
c. telecommunications support services, and
d. financial services.

That is to say, it excludes all those contracts that are not subject to the performance of an agreed sales contract. The intention of the Proposal for a Regulation is very clear: to establish exclusively a regulation on the sale of goods or digital content.

Moreover, the regulation of these services is not independent from the sales contract; and the regulation only includes those services related to a sales contract of personal property that has been concluded at the same time. Mixed contracts also opt for the application of the rules of the sale to apply to the services.

This regulation is not compiled in this way in any EU Member State—although, for example, there is extensive regulation of the service contract in the German BGB (sections 607–630 BGB), but it is redirected in his treatment to that provided thereby for the service contract or, where appropriate, in its treatment of work contracts.

12.2.1.1 Regulation in the DCFR

The regulation contained in the DCRF has a different purpose as it is applicable to all services, while the rules included in the CESL are only applicable to the related services included in it. In contrast to those mentiones in the DCFR, the CESL only includes the processing service, expressly excluding the others.

The DCFR contains a general category applicable to all the services, which highlights the common aspects of the performances to be carried out, and then a general category that regulates and has special implications in each field of business: construction, processing, storage, design, information and advice, and treatment.

The regulation of services in the DCFR is contained in Book IV that is entitled "Specific contracts and the rights and obligations arising from them"; and which, in art. IV.C.-1:101, includes the scope of the service contract as being "contracts under which one party, the service provider, undertakes to supply a service to the other party, the client". The CESL excludes, specific types of contractual services included in chapters 3–8 of Book IV, Part C DCFR, following the recommendation of the Green Paper on policy options for progress towards a European contract law for consumers and businesses, since this Paper stated that the regulation of sales contracts shall be included, but not services contracts. The purpose of the DCFR, unlike the CESL, is to regulate the activity undertaken by a multitude of economic agents, which undertake the tasks of: construction, maintenance and repair of goods, storage and safekeeping, design and project development, information and professional advice, and medical activity; but excludes a systematic regulation of the service contract citing the existence of sector-specific regulations and the heterogeneity of the issue. The DCFR only provides a collateral regulation of the related services to the sale of goods and digital content, some of which could be described as post-sales services, for which specific obligations and remedies of the parties are stated.

The DCFR also differs as to the scope of application of the service contract, defined as a contract under which one party undertakes to supply a service to the other party in exchange for remuneration. However the CESL expands this concept to the contracts in which the provider performs a service without the right to receive payment from the client.

12.2.2 The Parties

Pursuant to art. 2of the CESL, two parties are involved: the service provider and the costumer.

The "'service provider' means a seller of goods or supplier of digital content who undertakes to provide a customer a service related to those goods or that digital content;" and, the "'customer' means any person who purchases a related service".

The concept of customer does not clarify if this definition includes consumers and businesses or only consumers. It is not clear whether the contracts shall be concluded between a trader and a consumer or, on the contrary, the contract may be concluded between traders. In this event, we cannot assume that the customer may only be a consumer. This matter is completely clear in other types of contracts, such as the ones set out in art. 2(p), which defines the concept of distance contracts and off-premises contracts, stating expressly that these contracts must be entered into between a consumer and a trader.

Following the policy of different Community Directives, the reference to the term 'person' must be understood as referring exclusively to the natural person and not to legal persons, which would exclude a customer from being a business. In this regard, the DCFR defines 'consumer' as "any natural person who is acting any primarily for purposes which are not related to his or her trade, business or profession" (art. I.-1:106).

12.2.3 Application of Certain General Rules to Related Services

12.2.3.1 The Duty to Disclose Information About the Goods and Related Services

This obligation is contained in art. 23 of the CESL, located in section 2, which regulates the pre-contractual information to be provided by the trader who deals with another trader, stating that:

1. Before the conclusion of a contract for the sale of goods, supply of digital content or provision of related services by a trader to another trader, the supplier has a duty to disclose by any appropriate means to the other trader any information concerning the main characteristics of the goods, digital content or related

services to be supplied which the supplier has or can be expected to have and which it would be contrary to good faith and fair dealing not to disclose to the other party.

2. In determining whether paragraph 1 requires the supplier to disclose any information, regard is to be had to all circumstances, including:

   a. whether the supplier had a special expertise;
   b. the cost to the supplier of acquiring the relevant information;
   c. the ease with which the other trader could have acquired the information by other means;
   d. the nature of the information;
   e. the likely importance of the information to the other trader; and
   f. good commercial practice in the situation concerned.

In the DCFR, pre-contractual obligations of notice or information are regulated by establishing, in advance, before the conclusion of the contract; that the trader is bound by an obligation to warn the client (art. IV.C.-2:2102 DCRF).

12.2.3.2 Right to Withdraw

The right to withdraw will not apply to "a contract for the supply of goods or related services for which the price depends on fluctuations in the financial market which cannot be controlled by the trader and which may occur within the withdrawal period" (art. 40.2(c) CESL).

Neither will this right apply where "the consumer has specifically requested a visit from the trader for the purpose of carrying out urgent repairs or maintenance. Where on the occasion of such a visit the trader provides related services in addition to those specifically requested by the consumer or goods other than replacement parts necessarily used in performing the maintenance or in making the repairs, the right of withdrawal applies to those additional related services or goods" (art. 40.3(e)).

In the cases in which the right of withdrawal applies, the withdrawal period of 14 days shall run from the day of the conclusion of the contract (art. 42(e) CESL).

12.2.4 Obligations and Remedies of the Parties to a Related Service Contracts

12.2.4.1 Application of Certain General Rules on Sales Contracts

Part V of the CESL is structured in two parts. The first part refers to the rules set out in Chapter 9 (see below), whereas the remaining rules provide a regulation applicable only to the related services.

Of particular importance is art. 147.2, which sets out the incidental and dependent nature of the provisions concerning related services establishing that "where a sales contract or a contract for the supply of digital content is terminated, any related service contract is also terminated".

Thus, a new kind of provision is implemented, bound to the main contract, that has a rather different regulation to the service provisions included in the DFCR, and which includes the features discussed below.

12.2.4.2 Obligations of the Service Provider

The obligations of the service provider are specifically regulated in section 2 of Part V CESL. In particular, its art. 148 regulates the obligation to achieve result and the obligation of care and skill.

This regime puts an end to the discussions arising from the doctrine as to whether the provision of a service is an obligation to provide care and skill or to achieve results, because this article establishes conclusively that the provision of a service is an obligation to achieve results: those specifically agreed in the contract.

In this sense, it can be understood that the proposal of the CESL has followed the approach of the DCFR, which in its art. IV.C.-2:106 contains the obligation to achieve results, highlighting the close relationship that this legal regime has with the new construction of infringement, which it is in force in the European contractual laws.

In addition, the approach between the sales contract and the service contract is also included in para. 2 of art. IV.C.-2:106, which makes an express reference to the rules on conformity in the provision of services in the same way as provided for the sales contract. However, it is submitted that in considering these provisions, which denote installation, maintenance, repair, etc. as services, perhaps it would have been more successful if this had been included as one more provision, generally for contracts for the sale of goods or digital content, since it is important to specify in advance the result required so that any non-compliance would cause the lack of conformity of the related service contract. This also seems to be the approach of the CESL, since art. 147 makes reference to the application of certain rules that regulate the infringement of the sales contracts or a contract for the supply of digital content, contained in article 87, thereby expressly connecting the aims of the sales and the aims of the service contracts, *per* art. 147.2. Moreover, art. 147 highlights the reference to the rules concerning the infringement of the sale, which states that the breach of the obligation is based on the idea of the lack of conformity of the provision, because in the CESL, the contractual responsibility system is based on the objective concept of non-performance.

In the provisions governing these related services, non-performance includes any failure to perform an obligation that results from the contract. This concept includes faulty compliance or delay, and does not take into account the criteria of subjective imputation.

Therefore, art. 148.1 CESL includes, unless otherwise agreed, the obligation of the service provider to achieve a result, without subjectively valuing their conduct in order to determine whether there is compliance or not.

The distinction between 'obligations to achieve result' and 'obligations of care and skill' may make sense in the DCFR that regulated medical treatment contracts, but the CESL proposal includes a related services contract that is very close to the maintenance contract, in which fault does not merit special consideration.

The article sets out that "In the absence of any express or implied contractual obligation to achieve a specific result, the service provider must perform the related service with the care and skill which a reasonable service provider would exercise and in conformity with any statutory or other binding legal rules which are applicable to the related service". This means, in the absence of having to achieve a certain result, certain criteria are established to ensure that the obligation is performed with the care and skill that can reasonably be required from the service provider. In particular, regard is to be had, amongst other things, to:

a. the nature, the magnitude, the frequency and the foreseeability of the risks involved in the performance of the related service for the customer;
b. if damage has occurred, the costs of any precautions which would have prevented that damage or similar damage from occurring; and
c. the time available for the performance of the related service.

This obligation is also found in art. IV.C.-2:105 DCFR, in which the regulation of service contracts also includes an obligation of skill and care.

In addition, in the case of dealings between a trader and a consumer, the parties may not exclude the application of art. 148.2, and also may not introduce any exceptions or modify their effects to the detriment of the consumer. But, art. 148.4 provides that if, in a contract between a trader and a consumer, the related service includes installation of the goods, this should be done so that the installed goods conform to the contract, as required by art. 101. This obligation redirects the assessment of compliance or non-compliance of the contract, since this article states that the lack of conformity of the installation causes the lack of conformity of the goods if the incorrect installation is due to the seller or someone acting on the seller's behalf, or due to the instructions for the installation.

The implementation of these criteria does not introduce anything new in any way, and they are not exclusive to the service contract. These are general criteria for determining fault, which must also be considered as an expression of the duty of cooperation set out in art. 3 of Annex 1 CESL.

The following precepts list other obligations, related to payment, of the related service provider that cannot be considered typical or defining of the service contract, but are rules that govern any contract as manifestations of the principle of good faith, in addition to highlighting once again the non-principal character of the services in relation to the sale. In particular, art. 150 introduces a rule that is not exclusive of the service contract and would be more appropriate for a general theory of the obligation, as it establishes that the performance of the service by another person does not mean that the contracted provider is not responsible to the client.

Closely linked with the conformity of the contract and with the legal remedies for the breach, the obligation of the service provider is included to provide for "where a separate price is payable for the related service, and the price is not a lump sum agreed at the time of the conclusion of the contract, the service provider must provide the customer with an invoice which explains, in a clear and intelligible way, how the price was calculated" (art. 151).

Article 152 then proceeds to state:

> 1. The service provider must warn the customer and seek the consent of the customer to proceed if:
> (a) the cost of the related service would be greater than already indicated by the service provider to the customer; or
> (b) the related service would cost more than the value of the goods or the digital content after the related service has been provided, so far as this is known to the service provider.

Article 152(2) then provides that the service provider who does not obtain the consent of the customer after having provided the required information will not then be able to charge a higher price than that already agreed or neither he will be able to charge more for the related service than the value of the goods or digital content after the related service has been carried out.

This contractual obligation of the service provider to give such information is laid down as a duty in art. IV.C.-2:108 DCFR in para. (c). Where such information is required, however, the CESL imposes an obligation on the service provider to inform, but during the performance of the service, unlike art. IV.C.-2:102, which requires it to be given before the conclusion of the contract.

12.2.4.3 Customer Obligations

Articles 153 and 154 CESL list two obligations for the customer.

The first of these is that "The customer must pay any price that is payable for the related service in accordance with the contract". Then "This price is payable when the related service is completed and the object of the related service is made available to the customer" (art. 153).

The second obligation is to provide access in the cases "where it is necessary for the service provider to obtain an access to the customer's premises in order to perform the related service the customer must provide such access at reasonable hours" (art. 154).

The first rule coincides in part with the one in art. IV.C.-4:106 DCFR for processing contracts, although this rule has overlooked some aspects that could be generalised to all contracts.

On the other hand, art. 154 imposes an obligation, which is not specific to the service contract, but that represents a realisation of the duty to cooperate that is incumbent on any contractual party by virtue of art. 3 CESL.

In the DCFR the obligation to provide access is contained in art. IV.C.-4:102 para. (a), in the regulation of processing contracts and within a general obligation of the customer to cooperate, contained in art. IV.C.-2:103 DCFR, within the general part of the service contract regulation.

12.2.5 Remedies

When the existence of a breach is determined, in order to satisfy the interest of the injured party, Section IV of Part V CESL summarises the "remedies" available for both the customer and the service provider, in contrast to the provisions for sales contracts, which specifies these "remedies" in separated sections.

This section contains two provisions that are intended to regulate customer remedies and two subsequent provisions that establish the remedies of the service provider.

Despite the remedies being in different articles, as noted previously, art. 155 and 157 contain the same protection mechanisms for both parties. In addition, the remedies are set out according to whether the contract is established between traders or between a trader and a consumer.

The system of remedies in the DCFR, and its precedents, has its basis in the sales contract. In the case of services, the DCFR generically refers to Book III, and then apply them specifically to the service contract.

12.2.5.1 Customer Remedies

The customer will have at his disposal, subject to the adjustments made by art. 155, the same remedies as those provided to the purchaser in Chapter 11 CESL, which are:

a. To require specific performance

In the DCFR, the remedy of enforcement is contained in art. III.-3:302, where there has been a failure to effect delivery of the service, which is extended to any faulty performance.

Together with faulty performance, this may also cover the case of non-compliance by the customer of his cooperation duties (art. IV.C.-2:103 DCFR).

b. To withhold the customer's own performance

This can be found in art. IV.C.-3:107 DCFR. This precept determines that the moment of the creation of the obligation is the moment the thing is delivered; moreover, this is also the moment when the obligation to pay arises.

c. To terminate the contract

In the DCFR, termination of the contract is governed by art. IV.C.2:11 as far as the client is concerned, when the result laid down in the contract has not been achieved; whereas art. IV.C.2:111 regulates this generally.

In any case, by reference to the rules of Book III, it can be seen that termination has an *ex nunc* effect, and it does not affect any contractual rights acquired by any party prior to the termination of the contract.

The termination does not affect the obligations already executed but it releases the service provider from the obligation to continue performing his activity.

Where the customer is a consumer, he shall be entitled to terminate the contract for any lack of conformity in the provision of the related service, unless the lack of conformity is insignificant, in the same way as provided for in art. 3.6 of Directive 1999/44. Article IV.A.-4:201DCFR also excludes the possibility of termination in consumer sales when the lack of conformity is minor.

Unlike the CESL, the DCFR regulates various causes that can give rise to the termination of the contract.

The first of these is produced by a fundamental breach of the provision, which appears to be linked to the failure to achieve the result of the service (art. IV.C.2:106). In these situations, the remedy of termination is also provided when the client is sure that the result is not going to be produced, as well as for cases in which the infringement of a service specifically identified by the parties as an obligation to achieve skills and care.

Chapter 1, Book II and art. IV.C.-2:105 DCFR regulates situations relating to the rules governing the capacity of service providers at the time when prior information is given to the client; therefore, if the service provider has a special skill or training to undertake the performance of the service, then it is not true the client may be entitled to claim a fundamental breach of the contract and request the termination.

Secondly, termination by supervening circumstances is regulated in art. IV.C.-2:109, which provides the possibility that any party may make a unilateral modification to the contract in order to achieve the required results subject to the criterion of reasonableness, and taking into account any substantial change of circumstances.

d. To reduce the price

This remedy will take place in situations where a defective infringement is foreseen, unless it is an essential term of the contract.

e. To claim damages, under Chapter 16

This remedy is a way to punish any conduct that is contrary to the obligations of care and skill of the agent or the client.

This is also reflected in the general section of the DCFR, in article III.-3:701, as a resource that can be chosen together with the mechanisms already discussed above.

The DCFR includes this remedy in the service contract relating to the client's obligation of cooperation(art. IV.C.-2:103) and to the obligation of information, warning or advice by the service provider.

It should be highlighted in particular that art. IV.C.-2:102 regulates the right to claim compensation if the customer does not notice unusual events that may affect to the performance of the service. Article IV.C.-2:110 uses compensation to punish the customer who does not notify the lack of conformity to the provider in a timely fashion, and also if the customer chooses to withdraw from the contract without just cause (art. IV.C.-2:111).

With regard to the service provider, art. IV.C.-2:108 states that if the foreseen risk occurs but other interests of the client are also damaged, then the lack of warning entitles the right to claim for compensation.

Given the variety of cases that can be included in an obligation to 'do' something both the CESL (art. 106) and the DCRF ((art. III.-3:303 (2)(c))) regulate the possibility that in the case where the provisions of the contract are personal in nature, or when the customer does not want this provision to be performed by a provider who has breached the contract, the customer may request the compensation for damages.

A) The right to cure

Following the principle of good faith, the remedies available to the customer are subject to the right of the service provider to amend the terms of the contract, whether or not the customer is a consumer.

In particular:

> in a related service contract between traders, the customer may rely on a lack of conformity only if the customer gives notice to the service provider within a reasonable time specifying the nature of the lack of conformity. (art. 156.1)

Article 156.2 also provides that the service provider may not rely on any lack of conformity where it concerns facts, which the service provider knew or could be expected to have known, and which were not disclosed to the customer. Moreover, in the case of incorrect installation under a consumer sales contract as referred to in art. 101, the remedies available to the consumer are not subject to a service provider's right to amend.

B) Notification of lack of conformity

Applying the principle of good faith, art.156 of the Proposal sets out the obligation to notify the lack of conformity in related service contracts between traders.

However, the DCFR sets out in art. IV.C.-2:110 that the client must notify the service provider of the anticipated non-conformity before the breach occurs.

This notification is not required to be carried out with any formal requirement. The notification must specify the nature of the lack of conformity within a reasonable time: either from the time the related service is completed, or when the customer discovers or could be expected to discover the lack of conformity, whichever is later. This requirement is related to art. IV.C.-2:110 DCFR, which lays down the obligation of the client to notify of the anticipated non-conformity.

The service provider is not entitled to rely on the lack of notification set out in art. 156 if the lack of conformity is due to fraud; that is to say, "if the lack of conformity relates to facts of which the service provider knew or could be expected to have known and which the service provider did not disclose to the customer".

12.2.5.2 Remedies of the Service Provider

The remedies for the services provider are contained in two articles.

The first of them includes the situation of non-performance by the customer and the right of notification.

In the case of a non-performance by the customer, the service provider has recourse to the same remedies as are provided for the seller. Namely:

a. to require performance;
b. to withhold the service provider's own performance;
c. to terminate the contract; and
d. to claim interest on the price or damages, under Chapter 16 (art. 157.1).

The second article includes the right of the customer to decline the performance. In relations between a trader and a consumer, the application of this article cannot be excluded or be derogated from, and nor can its effects be varied to the detriment of the consumer (art. 158.3).

The termination of the contract may happen at any time, even before the service starts to be performed. Where notice is given by the customer to the service provider, the provider no longer has the right or obligation to provide the related service (art. 158.2(c)). However, the customer "remains liable to pay the price less the expenses that the service provider has saved or could be expected to have saved by not having to complete performance" (art. 158.2(b)). The aim of this regulation is to prevent unjust enrichment.

This Article distinguishes between two situations, whether or not there is any ground for unilateral termination under any provision. Thus, if there is not any ground for termination under any other provision, the customer remains liable to pay the price less expenses.

Finally, it is important to underline that, pursuant to art. 173.3 "where a related service contract is avoided or terminated by the customer after the related service has been performed or partly performed, the monetary value of what was received is the amount the customer saved by receiving the related service".

12.2.6 Regulation in Spanish Law

Both the regulation of the CESL and the regulation of the DCRF are different from that governing the service contract as regulated in the Spanish Civil Code. Any regulation concerning services contracts is very scarce and obsolete, and there is no specific regulation on related service contracts.

Unlike the CESL, the Civil Code regulates the performance of services exclusively relating to onerous contracts. Moreover, there is not a general section that covers a general category for all contractual services, nor a special part to regulate each type of service. The Civil Code only distinguishes between works contracts and services contracts, and distinguishing between obligations of conduct and result.

However, with regard to the obligations of the service provider, the Spanish consumer protection rules states in art. 116.2 Texto Refundido de la Ley General para la Defensa de los Consumidores y Usuarios y Otras Leyes Complementarias (TRLGDCU) that the "lack of conformity resulting from the incorrect installation of the goods will be equal to the non-conformity of the goods when the installation is included in the sales or supplying contract regulated in Article 115.1 and this has been performed by the seller or under his liability, or by the consumer where the incorrect installation is due to a shortcoming in the installation instructions". In this regard, this article is similar to the CESL in regulating this issue more by the rules of sales contracts than by the rules of the services contracts in particular.

In this sense, the duty of disclosure is set out generally in arts. 20 and 21 TRLGDCU, which are directly related to the notion of conformity of the product sold to the consumer, as well as art.60 and art. 148.2.

12.2.7 *Regulation in Italian Law*

The problems linked to the related services contract does not have a specific regulation in Italian law, neither in the Italian Civil Code nor in the rules related to sales contracts.

These services are governed by the general rules of the Civil Code relating to specific contracts, generally the performance of works contracts, for instance, maintenance etc., and, where appropriate, the special provisions applicable to each case that have been agreed. What it is created is a link between the main contract (the sales contract) and the secondary contract (the services contract).

The concept of "related service" is only mentioned in art. 69,(g) of the Codice dei Consumatori, where in respect of timeshare contracts, it sets out that "ancillary contracts" should be understood as a contract under which the consumer buys related services to a timeshare contract or to a contract of a product for long term holidays and provided by the operator or by a third party on the basis of an agreement between the third party and the operator.

Based on this connection, the consequences of a possible termination of the main contract are listed in art. 77 of the Codice dei Consumatori which states:

1. Where the consumer exercises the right to terminate the timeshare contract or of the contract of a product for long term holidays it will automatically involve, Without expenses to the consumer, the termination of all the exchange contracts related and any other ancillary contract.
2. Notwithstanding the provisions of Articles 125-ter and 125-quinquies of the Legislative Decree 1 September 1993 n.385, on credit contracts for consumers, if the price is fully or partly covered by credit granted to the consumer by the operator or by a third party based on an agreement between the third party and the trader, the credit contract will be terminated without any expenses to the consumer when the consumer exercises the right of rescission timeshare contract, the contract for products for long-term holidays, or the contract to resell or exchange.

The case law, based on the close connection between contracts and the unity of the interest has applied, in these circumstances, the general principle *simul stabunt, simul candent*. In this sense, the judgment of 22 March 2013, n. 7255, has stated that: "… if there is a functional link between several contracts, they remain thus subject to the discipline of the respective negotiating scheme, while their interdependence produces a unitary regulatory development concerning the permanence of the contractual relationship, for them "*simul stabunt, simul cadent*".

This principle seems to apply also to related services that, provided they are based on independent contracts, are closely linked to the main sales contract and dependent on it. Events that affect the validity or effectiveness of the main contract (invalidity, annulment, rescission, termination, withdrawal, etc.), also influence its effects on the ancillary contract concerning the provision of the related services.

12.2.8 Regulation in Dutch Law

The Dutch law does not include specific rules for the related services contracts.

Since 1992, the Dutch Civil Code has contained specific rules for the services contract ("overeenkomst van opdracht"), including the peculiarities of the agency contract ("lastgevingsovereenkomst"), the conciliation contract ("bemiddelingsovereenkomst"), the business agency contract ("agentuurovereenkomst") and the performance of medical services ("Geneeskundigebehandelingsovereenkomst"). Also, the travel contract ("reisovereenkomst") and the deposit contract ("bewaarnemingsovereenkomst") are governed by the Civil Code.

Apart from this, the services contract is included in several general rules. Thus, the contract of employment rules ("overeenkomst tot aanneming van werk" or " aanneming van werk") contain the traditional rules that, due to the lack of rules for other services, apply to many other services, such as auto repair, plumbing, etc. (LOOS).

12.2.9 Regulation in French Law

The regulation of services linked to sales contracts is not specifically regulated in the French legal system, neither in its Civil Code, nor in the Code de la Consummation. Therefore, its regulation depends on the previous operation of categorising the contract as a service (arts. 1779–1789 CC) or as a sale of goods (arts. 1582–1688 CC).

12.3 Conclusions

The regulation of the related services contracts included in the CESL is one of the most problematic aspects of this proposal.

The regulation of the related services contracts included in the CESL is a very partial regulation, which has been targeted to the maintenance services contracts and others linked to the sales contract.

The regulation of the regime follows the general aim of the DCRF in order to establish a single category for services contracts. Specifically, Book IV, entitled 'Specific contracts and the rights and obligations arising from them', in Part C, following the line taken in the Principles of European Contract Law (PECL), proposes rules for services contracts with a general part applicable to all services contracts and a special part with several chapters containing specific provisions for each kind of services.

Unlike the Directive 2011/83/EU on consumer rights and the DCFR, however, the new regulation explicitly introduces for the first time the regulation of cloud computing, due to the fact that this is one of the main problems related to contracts to provide digital content.

However, the rules of the CESL have not aimed at establishing general rules for the services contract. True to its name, the CESL has intended to establish general rules for sales contracts, and that is what the CESL has regulated, which justifies that, in this case, the related services are restricted to being considered as ancillary services of the main sales contract, without prejudice to the regulation of this regime in articles 149 and 152 CESL, different from that of the sales contract, that establish the obligation to prevent any damage to the customer and to warn him of the existence of unexpected or uneconomic costs.

Finally, it should be said that, in addition to the differences noted above regarding the European existing texts, in particular the DCRF and the Directive 2011/83/EU, the CESL leaves unresolved the problem of what would happen if the subordination to the CESL were agreed regarding the main sales contract but the service with the provider of the related service were not; this makes it necessary to continue applying the criteria laid down by the Regulation (EC) of June 2008 on the law applicable to contractual obligations (Rome I).

In the laws of the Member States of the EU there is no specific regulation on related services, so that the regulation offered in the CESL, far from offering problems for their implementation in each national law, will provide a more effective response to the problems that may arise from a breach of these services, avoiding having to determine whether these performances must fit within a specific type of services contract or as a mandatory performance in the sales contract, this should however not prevent the unmet obligations under the service contract from purporting to restitute the contract, but to terminate it, with the consequent non-application of the disagreement rules that follow from the Directive 99/44/CE on certain aspects of the sale of consumer goods and associated guarantees.

Bibliography

AAVV. Derecho contractual europeo: problemática, propuestas y perspectivas. (Esteve Bosch Capdevila, coord.), (2009).

AAVV. La revisión de las normas europeas y nacionales de protección de los consumidores: más allá de la Directiva sobre derechos de los consumidores y del Instrumento Opcional sobre un derecho europeo de la compraventa de octubre de 2011. (Sergio Cámara Lapuente, Esther Arroyo i Amayuelas, coords), (2012a).

AAVV. Derecho europeo de los contratos: libros II y IV del marco común de referencia. (Antoni Vaquer Aloy, Esteve Bosch Capdevila, María Paz Sánchez González, coords.), vol. 2, (2012b).
AAVV. Nuevas perspectivas del derecho contractual. (Esteve Bosch Capdevila, dir.), (2012c).
Antonopoulus, N., Gillan, L., Cloud computing. Principles, systems and applications, Springer, Berlin, (2010).
Barendrecht, M., et al., Principles of European Law Services Contracts, Munich, (2007).
Barrón Arniches, P. Cuestiones sobre el contrato de servicios diseñado en el Marco Común de Referencia. Indret, 3, (2008).
Barrón Arniches, P. El contrato de servicios en el Nuevo Derecho contractual europeo, Madrid, (2011).
Common market law review. Editorial comments. A Common European Sales Law (CESL) ahead?, vol 49, 4, 1267–1278, (2012).
Common market law review. Chicago conference, vol. 50, (2013).
Eidenmüller, H., Jansen, N., Kieninger, E.M., Warner, G., Zimmermann, R., "Der Vorschalg für eine Verordung über ein Gemeinsames Europäisches Kaufrecht", JZ 2012, 67–6, pp. 269–320.
Hesselink, "How to opt-into the Common European sales Law? Brief comments on the Commission's proposal for a Regulation". Centre for the Study of European Contract Law, WP Series 2011–15, pp. 1–12.
Lando O, Beale H., Principles of European Contract Law, Parts I and II. Kluver, The Hague, (2000).
Leine, J., "Finish report", Helberger, N., Guibault, L., Van der Sloot, B. Digital content services for consumers: comparative analysis of the applicable legal frameworks and suggestions for the contours of a model system of consumer protection in relation to digital content services. Report 1: country reports (http://www.ivir,nl/publications/helberger/Digital_content_services_for_consumers_1.pdf, pp. 6–39, (2011).
Loos, B.M., Analysis of the applicable legal frameworks and suggestions for the contours of a model system of consumer protection in relation to digital content contracts. http://www.ivir.nl/publications/helberger/digital_content_contracts_for_consumers.pdf, (2011).
Micklitz y Reich, The Commission Proposal for a "Regulation on a Common European Sales Law" (CESL)-Too broad or not broad enough?, EUI Working Paper LAW 2012/04, pp. 1–38. http://cadmus.eui.eu/bits-tream/handle/1814/20485/LAW_2012_04_Micklitz_Reich.pdf, (2012).
Pasa, B., Morra, L., et al., Translating the DCFR and Drafting the CESL. Sellier. Munich (2014).
Schmidt Kessel, M., "The application of the Consumers Right Directive to digital content". http://www.europarl.europa.eu/document/activities/cont/20110825att25288/20110825ATT25288EN.pdf, (2011).
Schulte-Nölke et al (eds), Der Entwuff ein optionales europäisches Kaufrecht: Schulte-Nölke, Hans/Zoll, Fryderyk/Jansen, Nils/Schulze, Reiner (eds), Der Entwuff ein optionales europäisches Kaufrecht, Sellier, Munich (2012).
Shulze (ed), Common Frame of Reference and Exinting EC Contract Law: Schulze, Reiner (ed), Common Frame of Reference and Exinting EC Contract Law, Sellier: Munich (2008).
Shulze (ed), Common European Sales Law (CESL), -Commentary- C.H. Beck.Hart.Nomos. Baden-Baden, (2012).
Tijon Tjin Tai, T.F. E., "Service contracts in the Dutch Civil Code". Zimmermann, R., Service Contracts, Mohr, Tübingen, pp. 167–180, (2010).
Von Bar, C., Clive, E., Draft Common Frame of Reference, v. 2, Sellier, Munich (2010).

Chapter 13
Damages and Interest

Matthias Lehmann

Abstract The right to rescind the contract and to withhold or reduce the price does not fully compensate the creditor for his loss in every case. Therefore, each system of contract law must provide for an additional level of remedy as a backup. In most cases, this additional level of remedies consists in claims for damages and interests. Damages are the general remedy available for all kinds of breaches of contract. If monetary obligations are not performed, interest may be added as an additional remedy that does not exclude the simultaneous awarding of damages.

Damages and interest is regulated in Chapter 16 of the CESL. One could consider Chapter 16 as a sort of distilled experience of national and international law. Nevertheless, this does not prevent its articles from occasionally deviating from them. This chapter will first focus on general aspects of Chapter 16 (II) and then turn to the provisions on damages (III) and interest (IV).

Keywords Damages · Strict liability · Fault-based liability · Principle of full compensation · Mandatory nature · Monetary damage · Tort law · Interest · Claim for interest · Period of interest · Interest rate

13.1 Introduction

13.1.1 Theoretical and Economic Background

It is hard, if not impossible, to enforce contractual obligations literally against an unwilling or incapable debtor. The right to rescind the contract and to withhold or reduce the price does not fully compensate the creditor for his loss in every case. Therefore, each system of contract law must provide for an additional level of remedy as a backup. In most cases, this additional level of remedies consists in claims for damages and interests. Damages are the general remedy available for all kinds of breaches of contract. If monetary obligations are not performed, interest may be

M. Lehmann (✉)
Martin-Luther University Halle-Wittenberg, Halle, Germany
e-mail: matthias.lehmann@jura.uni-halle.de

© Springer International Publishing Switzerland 2015

J. Plaza Penadés, L. M. Martínez Velencoso (eds.), *European Perspectives on the Common European Sales Law,* Studies in European Economic Law and Regulation 4,
DOI 10.1007/978-3-319-10497-3_13

added as an additional remedy that does not exclude the simultaneous awarding of damages.

There are deontological and teleological reasons for allowing these types of claims (Unberath 2007, pp. 285–310). Damages and interest serve the immediate goal of dispensing justice by making the creditor whole. In the words of Hegel, they re-establish the law's authority by "negating its negation" that has come about through the non-performance of the debtor's contractual obligations (Hegel 2001, § 82, No. 172). They thus compensate for the wrong that is caused by the non-performance of contractual obligations. In the Aristotelian system, they are part of the corrective justice that complements commutative and distributive justice (Aristotle 2013, No. 4).

Damages and interest are also required from an economical perspective (Baird 1994; Unberath 2007, pp. 310–321). If the debtor did not have to pay them, he may be incentivised to break the contract where it is convenient for him to do so. A rescission of the contract or the withholding or reduction of price may not adequately reflect the loss suffered by the creditor. The breach, therefore, is not an "efficient breach" in the sense that the creditor would be fully compensated and the debtor may still gain (cf. Posner 2007, p. 120). Rather, the breach only unilaterally improves the creditor's position.

From the vantage point of law and economics, it also becomes clear that damages and interest redistribute the risk of non-performance (Shavell 2004, p. 311; see also Posner 2007, p. 120). A contract is not always breached because one of the parties is at fault. It can also come about by random events that none of them has caused intentionally or negligently. One can think, for example, of a case in which contractual duties are not performed because of a breakdown of production in the seller's plant. In this case, the awarding of damages does not serve as an incentive mechanism, but rather as a mechanism to redistribute the risk of such a breakdown to the seller.

Against this theoretical and economic background that strongly favours damages and interest, it is hardly surprising that the CESL includes rules on these remedies. Indeed, any sales law would be incomplete if it did not contain provisions in this regard. The EU legislator, however, had to venture into territory that was relatively new to him. The Directive on Consumer Sales[1] skipped over the topic and left it to the Member States to provide for damages. It is true that the Late Payment Directive deals with the apportionment of interest, but only in the context of B2B contracts.[2] There is, thus, no pre-existing EU law on damages in general and on interest in B2C relationships.

13.1.2 Historical Antecedents in Uniform Law

Fortunately for the EU legislator, he could build upon many rules of uniform law that provide for damages and interest as remedies. Such rules have a long tradition. They exist both on the international and the European level.

[1] Directive 1999/44/EC of the European Parliament and of the Council of 25 May 1999 on certain aspects of the sale of consumer goods and associated guarantees, OJ L 171, 7.7.1999, p. 12.

[2] Directive 2011/7/EU of the European Parliament and of the Council of 16 February 2011 on combating late payment in commercial transactions, OJ L 48, 23.2.2011, p. 1.

The first among these rules was laid down in the Convention relating to a Uniform Law on the International Sale of Goods (ULIS) adopted as early as 1964. Articles 74, 82–83 ULIS deal with damages and interest. Upon these provisions, the Vienna Convention on the International Sale of Goods (CISG) of 1980 bases its damages and interest regime, which is contained in its arts. 45(1)(b), 61(1)(b), 74 and 78. It is remarkable that both the ULIS and the CISG rules are contained in conventions binding under Public International Law.

A new stage was achieved, in some sense, with the adoption of the Principles of European Contract Law (PECL), arts. 9:501–9:508. Although these provisions incorporate insights from the ULIS and the CISG, they also contain the first comprehensive and detailed uniform regime for damages and interest. The ensuing UNIDROIT Principles of International Commercial Contracts (UPICC), arts. 7.4.1–7.4.12, are not fundamentally different, though more explicit on some points. Both texts are not binding conventions, but rather are soft law projects. Nevertheless, they exert considerable influence on legal practice and on law reform projects in the Member States.

From the PECL runs a direct line to the Draft Common Frame of Reference (DCFR), which deals with damages and interest in its arts. III.-3:701 to III.-3:708. These provisions, in turn, have served as a model for Chapter 16 of the CESL. If the rules of the proposal were to be formally adopted, soft law would thus be turned into "hard" EU law. One must not forget, however, that the rules of the PECL, the UPICC, and the DCFR are themselves not without antecedents. They are the result of a careful analysis of the pre-existing conventional law, namely that of the CISG, and of in-depth comparative research into the national legal systems of different states.

It is thus accurate to consider Chapter 16 as a sort of distilled experience of national and international law. Its content is hardly new, but instead rests on solid foundations. Given the origins of the proposal, it is not surprising that the provisions on damages follow lines that are similar to national legal systems and international uniform texts. Nevertheless, this does not prevent them from occasionally deviating from them. This discussion will first focus on general aspects of Chapter 16 (II) and then turn to the provisions on damages (III) and interest (IV).

13.2 Chapter 16 CESL Within the Context of European National Legal Systems

13.2.1 Special Treatment of Damages and Interest

If one compares the CESL to national legal systems for possible doctrinal insights, the first thing that one remarks is that the former dedicates a separate chapter to the topic of damages and interest. This is, of course, inherited from international conventions (ULIS and CISG) that adopt the same approach. It stands, however, in marked contrast to the soft law texts (PECL, UPICC and DCFR) that all rank damages and interest as one of several remedies and do not treat them independently.

One may speculate as to why the drafters of the CESL decided to follow the conventions and to deviate from the more recent soft law. To a certain extent, this decision was already predetermined by the structure that the drafters had chosen. By following a division of the seller's obligations and remedies on the one hand and the buyer's obligations and remedies on the other, it was inevitable that the outline would be more similar to that of the conventions, and contrary to the soft law, CESL. Specifically, such a structure makes a separate chapter on damages and interest almost inevitable if one does not want to repeat the rules on them in the context of each party's remedies.

However, the drafters may also have had more in mind than to simply follow the tables of content of the international conventions. One of the shortcomings of the proposal for the CESL is that it is very specific to sales contracts when seen from the point of view of European private law, in general. In contrast to the soft law texts and national legal system such as the Common law or German law, the CESL does not contain general provisions of contract law. It is drafted in a very specific way tailored to sales and related service contracts. For instance, the CESL carefully avoids the terms "debtor" and "creditor". Instead, it uses the terms "seller", "buyer", "service provider", and "customer". Because of this specificity, it will be very hard to build new instruments upon it that may concern other types of contracts, for instance general service contracts, loan contracts or franchise contracts. Chapter 16 remedies this shortcoming to a certain extent since its content is not specific to sales contracts. Because of their general character, its rules can be easily incorporated by reference to other instruments. Together with other provisions, such as those in Chap. 4 on the conclusion of the contract or those in Chap. 6 on defects in consent, it may, thus, serve as a nucleus for a European private law, and also as a source for a Common Frame of Reference, as originally envisaged by the Commission.

It is of course merely speculative whether the drafters indeed aimed at creating some sort of general rules of European private law. Should this have been their goal, they could have achieved it much more easily and to a much higher degree by eliminating the distinctions between buyers, sellers, service providers and customers. This simple step would have allowed them to enact a truly "general part" of remedies, and to also avoid a lot of repetition. For this reason, the proposal of the ELI which adopts this alternative approach should be applauded (see ELI 2011, p. 105 et seq., Chapter 15). If one were to follow this proposal, there would no longer be any need to treat damages and interest separately. Their respective rules could be incorporated into the same chapter as those on other remedies, such as termination or price reduction.

13.2.2 Unitary Concept of Damages

The next point that is remarkable is that Chapter 16 contains a single set of rules for all types of non-performance. Its provisions cover all cases of total absence of performance, late performance, and defective performance. The CESL, thus, contains a unitary regime for all cases in which a claim for damages or interest may arise.

In this respect, it deviates e.g. from German law, which even after its modernisation in 2002 continues to distinguish between different types of damages (see § 280

German Civil Code—*BGB*). The unitary regime is much more in line with the Romanic approach. From French law stems the concept of *inexécution du contrat* (see art. 1147 French *Code Civil*), which covers different kinds of non-performance, even though different remedies are provided in cases of missing title (*garantie d'eviction*—art. 1690 *Code Civil*) or defective performance (*garantie des vices cachés*—art. 1645 *Code Civil*). In its purest form, the unitary regime can be found in the Common law, which knows only one comprehensive category for all kinds of "breach of contract" (Beale, in Beale 2013, p. 1758, No. 26-001).

From a view of legislative methods, the approach chosen by the drafters for the CESL deserves reward because it makes intricate distinctions unnecessary. For instance, in Germany, the delimitation between late or defective performance has occupied the literature and the courts for some time (see e.g. Stadler in Jauernig 2011, § 280 No. 4). The CESL effectively avoids these problems by accepting only one type of damage.

That does not mean that all distinctions are unnecessary because every type of damage claim would fall under the same provision. It will be shown that Chapter 16 does not cover all types of damages that may arise under the CESL (see infra III 1). It is, therefore, necessary to distinguish the cases covered by Chapter 16 from those that are regulated in other provisions. This distinction, however, does not pose a major problem. For instance, the type of damage dealt with in art. 55 CESL only arises in the particular situation where one party has relied on the validity of the contract when in fact the agreement was null and void. In other words, the provision deals with the reliance interest (cf. Treitel 1976, p. 28, No. 50). In contrast, Chapter 16 deals with damage that occurs because one party has not properly fulfilled its (valid) contractual obligations.

13.2.3 Strict Liability vs. Fault-based Liability

The damages and interest claims provided for under Chapter 16 arise as soon as a contractual obligation is not performed. The expert group and the European Commission, which have proposed the CESL, have thus opted for a system of strict liability. This system is based on the idea that the debtor owes the creditor a guarantee for performance of his duties and will, therefore, be liable each time that he does not perform, except if his non-performance is excused. In this, the CESL follows the model set by international conventions (see arts. 82 and 83 ULIS, arts. 74 CISG) and by soft law texts on uniform law (art. 9:501 PECL, art. 7.4.1. UPICC).

Many other national legal systems decide otherwise. They opt instead for a system where liability is based on fault. For instance, under Austrian and German law, the debtor does not have to pay damages for a breach of his contractual obligations if he is not responsible for the violation of his duties (§ 1295(1) Austrian Civil Code—*ABGB*; § 280(1) 2 *BGB*). French law, in principle, also follows the model of fault-based liability (see art. 1137 *Code Civil*), even though in the case of sales contracts this is largely superseded by important guarantees (see supra 2).

In order to see which system is more appropriate, it is necessary to consider a "hard case", i.e. one where the debtor is not at fault but where nevertheless there is no excusing supervening event. A case in point is a defective product delivered by a supplier of the seller where the seller had no possibility of recognising the defect before delivery to the buyer. In a fault-based system, the seller will not be liable for any loss that the buyer suffers because he has not acted intentionally or negligently. In a system of strict liability, by contrast, he will owe damages because the impediment was not "beyond his control" (see art. 79(2) CISG; the same applies under art. 7.1.7 UPICC, see Kleinheisterkamp, in Vogenauer and Kleinheisterkamp 2009, art. 7.1.7 No. 16 footnote 212). The same also seems to be true for art. 88(1) CESL (cf. Zoll, in Schulze 2013, Article 88 No. 9). From an economic perspective, this result is to be preferred because the problem arose in the sphere of the seller, and it was, thus, easier for him to avoid (cheapest cost avoider). In a way, the principle of strict liability forces him to choose his suppliers more carefully. The result reached can also be justified from a deontological perspective because reasonable parties would have provided that such an event must be attributed to the seller (Unberath 2007, p. 334).

The formulation of the excuse in the CESL also closely follows the models of uniform law. Indeed, art. 88 CESL, which speaks of an "impediment beyond the debtor's control", is copied almost word for word from the CISG (art. 79(1)). It can also be found in the PECL (art. 8:108(1)) and under the title "force majeure" in the UPICC (art. 7.1.7). One can, therefore, speak of an internationally excepted axiom that applies to strict liability. The only difference is that the excuse under the CESL also exempts the debtor from the creditor's claim for interest (on this, see infra IV 2).

In principle, the CESL drafters' preference for the strict liability model with the *force majeure* exception can be defended with good arguments. One must, however, be aware that the parties can deviate to a certain extent from Chapter 16.

13.2.4 Mandatory Nature

From the debtor's perspective, the liability under Chapter 16 will often be too burdensome. One only needs to think of a seller from a Member State whose law follows the fault-based principle. If he bases his contracts on the CESL, he will also be liable for the mistakes of his suppliers, whereas under the national regime, he is not. Against this background, it would be very difficult to convince a seller of the advantages of opting into the new European instrument.

This raises the immediate question as to whether, and to what extent, the benefits of the CESL can be combined with a limitation of liability in the case of non-performance. In this regard, a distinction between the rules on damages and on interest becomes visible. In principle, the parties can change the damages regime as they wish. The parties are free to discard strict liability under Chapter 16 and to agree on a fault-based system. Article 108 CESL, which excludes any derogation from remedies to the detriment of the consumer, only applies to Chapter 11 and not to Chapter 16 (this is ignored by Možina, in Schulze 2013, art. 159 No. 11). The parties cannot, however, agree to clauses that exclude the trader's liability for death or personal injury to a consumer by an act, an omission, or by someone acting on his behalf (art. 84(a) CESL). In this case, strict liability is the norm and cannot be derogated from. Moreover, it is impossible to exclude the liability of the trader for any loss or damage to the consumer caused deliberately or as a result of gross negligence (art. 84(b) CESL). This means that the parties cannot go beyond the fault-based system to immunise the seller from liability in cases where he acted with intent or with gross negligence. The fundamental core of the CESL is, thus, constituted by fault-based liability, which cannot be contracted around. These two limits are completed by a third limit restricting clauses that require the consumer who fails to perform an obligation to pay a disproportionally high amount by way of damages or a stipulated payment for non-performance (art. 85(e) CESL). One notes a certain degree of liberty in this provision, which is only restricted in order to favour the consumer.

In contrast to Chapter 16's rules on damages, the rules on interest are much more resistant to change. Article 167(5) CESL sets out that they cannot be deviated from to the detriment of the consumer. Moreover, according to art. 171 CESL, they are even completely mandatory in B2B contracts. These two provisions are in some sense misleading because the rules that are declared to be "mandatory" permit a certain degree of derogation, subject only to a fairness test (see art. 167(3) and art. 170 CESL). This means that not all changes are *per se* excluded. However, what is remarkable is that the rules on interest in B2B contracts contained in section 2 are mandatory to an even larger extent than the rules on interest in B2C contracts contained in section 3. The explanation for this ostensible paradox is the Late Payment Directive[3] because it only applies to commercial transactions. The goal of this Directive is to discourage late payments in commercial relationships and to remove all such incentives.[4] For this reason, it provides particularly harsh sanctions for any delay in the payment of the price for B2B contracts. Understandably, the drafters of the CESL did not want to apply the same drastic sanctions to debtors that double as consumers. They, therefore, permitted more lenient contractual rules for late payment by consumers. This different treatment for B2B and B2C contracts certainly reflects the current state of EU law (*acquis*). However, to see it face to face in one instrument shows the confusion that results if one infuses macroeconomic policies into private law. Whatever the policy behind it, it is hardly convincing from a perspective of private law justice to restrict freedom of contract in B2B relations more than in B2C relations.

[3] Directive 2011/7/EU of the European Parliament and of the Council of 16 February 2011 on combating late payment in commercial transactions, OJ L 48, 23.2.2011, p. 1, art. 1.

[4] See Preamble 16 Directive 2011/7/EU.

13.3 Damages

13.3.1 Scope of Section 1 of Chapter 16 CESL

The first section of Chapter 16 is entitled "damages". In spite of this designation, the provisions contained in it are tailored to a specific type of damage, i.e. the loss that arises from the non-performance of the contractual duties by the debtor. The extent of liability under the CESL, however, is broader. There are a number of instances in which a party is liable for loss other than the case of non-performance. For instance, under art. 55 CESL, the debtor must repair, after the avoidance of the contract, the loss that the creditor suffered because he relied on the validity of the contract. Further examples of liability that may arise are those for the violation of information duties (art. 29(1) CESL), the liability for diminished value of the good after withdrawal from the contract (art. 45(3) CESL), and the liability in case of a violation of the duty of good faith and fair dealing (art. 2(2) CESL).

The question as to how these other liabilities shall be dealt with is already subject to a dispute in the literature, even though the CESL has yet to enter into force. According to one opinion, these types of remedies should in principle be submitted to Chapter 16 (Remien 2012, p. 505). However, the provisions mentioned carefully avoid the term "damages" and instead speak of a liability for "loss", for "diminished value", and simply of "liability". Moreover, many of the provisions contained in Chapter 16 do not fit this type of liability; for instance, art. 165 or art. 166 CESL. It, therefore, seems more appropriate to say that Chapter 16 does not apply to these types of liabilities directly, but instead leaves open the possibility that some of its provisions can be applied by analogy (in this sense, see Pfeiffer, in Schulze 2013, art. 55 margin No. 4; see also Koch 2011, p. 231).

Section 1 of Chapter 16 misses out on some important points. For instance, it does not address the issue of liquidated damages clauses or other stipulated payments for non-performance. This has been regretted in the literature (Koch 2011, p. 237), and a proposal to fill the gap has been made by the European Law Institute (ELI 2011, p. 109, art. 150). Section 1 of Chapter 16 also does not contain any provision on the certainty of harm required to award damages, which can be found in other texts (see art. 7.4.3 UPICC). To leave this question exclusively subject to the rules of national procedure may prove to have been a mistake given the differences in Member State laws in this field. The chapter also does not answer the notoriously difficult question of in which currency damages must be paid (Koch 2011, p. 238; Remien 2012, p. 510). It is strongly to be hoped that these shortcomings will be resolved in the final version.

13.3.2 Notion of Damage

Damages are only owed for damage. Any discussion of the notion of "damages" must, therefore, begin with an analysis of the concept of "damage". A definition can be found in art. 2(g) CESL Regulation. Accordingly, damage means "a sum of money to which a person may be entitled as compensation for loss, injury or damage". The reference to the word "damage" for defining "damage" is obviously not helpful. The rule, thus, shifts the problem of interpretation towards understanding the terms "loss" and "injury". Moreover, since the CESL does not define "injury", the emphasis is on the meaning of "loss". According to art. 2(c) of the Regulation, "loss" is "economic loss and non-economic loss in the form of pain and suffering".

We hereby learn that damage may consist of economic loss. At the same time, damage may also be suffered by non-economic loss, such as pain and suffering. Such damage is, therefore, to be repaired under the CESL.

Crucially, however, art. 2(c) of the Regulation excludes "other forms of non-economic loss such as impairment of the quality of life" from the scope of the term "damage". What this means is subject to doubt. One can imagine that this term covers the loss felt by the inability to use one's body parts, which is known as "loss of amenity" in English law or as "danno biologico" in Italian law (Wendehorst, in Schulze 2013, art. 2 Regulation, margin No. 8). However, historically this kind of damage has a close connection to pain and suffering (see Koch 2011, p. 226, n. 8). One must also not forget that such damage is the direct consequence of an "injury" and could, thus, become the subject of compensation, independent of how the term "loss" is to be defined. It is, therefore, not unlikely that the drafters had a different meaning in mind for the term "other forms of non-economic loss such as impairment of the quality of life". It is possible that they meant damage that is less directly related to a personal injury or "pain and suffering". As examples, the literature cites the inconvenience generated by a defective camera that fails to take holiday photos, or by music not perfectly delivered digitally which spoils a party (Remien 2012, p. 507).

The CESL excluded this type of damage from the definition of loss. At first sight, this seems to be contrary to the case law of the ECJ. In the famous decision in *Simone Leitner*, the Court held that a traveller can ask for compensation for non-material damage arising from the loss of enjoyment of a holiday.[5] Following this ruling, the DCFR generally defines 'loss' as also encompassing non-economic loss in the form of impairment of the quality of life (art. III.-3:701(3) DCFR). The expert group adopted the same position (see their Feasibility Study, art. 2 No. 12).

The fact that the CESL is more restrictive in this regard is most likely due to political considerations. The drafters apparently thought it would make the instrument unattractive to sellers if it were to include damages for the impairment of quality of life. In this case, businesses would rather stick to their national laws, which generally do not provide compensation for this type of damage (Koch 2011, p. 227). However, there can also be a deeper justification for the exclusion of this type of non-economic damage. The *Simone Leitner* case concerned the interpretation of the Package Travel Directive.[6] By its very nature, this directive is focused

[5] See ECJ, decision of 12 March 2002, Case C-168/00, [2002] E.C.R. I-2631, at 20–24.

[6] Council Directive 90/314/EEC of 13 June 1990 on package travel, package holidays and package tours, OJ L 158, 23.6.1990, p. 59.

on compensating the consumer for the loss of enjoyment of her holiday. It, thereby, wants to re-establish the equivalence of the performances of both parties. Because the enjoyment is of particular importance to the consumer, reasonable parties would have inserted a damages clause covering this type of loss in their contract. This goal of the Directive has also influenced the ECJ's decision to award damages for this type of loss.[7] With sales contracts, it is different. When entering into the agreement, the parties do not have a particular enjoyment of the product in mind, but rather the property transfer. The way in which the buyer enjoys the goods is hardly foreseeable and is, in essence, his own personal matter. Often, it is much easier for him to take precautions against the loss than for the seller (see Posner 2007, p. 126). From the seller's perspective, the possible damage is very hard to predict and consequently almost impossible to insure. If he would have to make guarantees for this kind of damage, he would probably have to raise the price considerably. For these reasons, reasonable parties would rarely submit a damages claim for loss of enjoyment.

It, therefore, makes sense to exclude from the liability of the seller damages resulting from the loss of enjoyment of a product. The CESL only codifies what reasonable parties themselves would have agreed to. Any other position would also have led to considerable divergences from the laws of the Member States (Koch 2011, p. 227). True, the result is, at first sight, less favourable for consumers (see Remien 2012, p. 508). But in the long run, they may prefer cheaper prices than a guarantee from the seller, which may invite abuse by certain types of buyers for which all consumers will ultimately have to pay. The exclusion of damages for the loss of enjoyment of the product by the CESL is thus not wrong. Rather, the mistake was made by the drafters of the DCFR and the expert group, who generalised a particular ruling of the ECJ to apply to all sorts of contract. This example should serve as a warning against inferring too much from the ECJ case law, which mostly deals with specific texts of secondary law, for European private law in general.

13.3.3 Principle of Full Compensation

The CESL provisions on damages are built upon the principle of full compensation (*restitutio in integrum*). According to art. 159 CESL, every damage caused by the non-performance has to be repaired. This covers, in the first place, the expectation interest (Možina, in Schulze 2013, art. 160 margin No. 1; see also Treitel 1976, p. 27). Repairing this interest means that the creditor has to be put into the position he would have been in had the contract been duly performed, art. 160 CESL, first sentence.

The CESL makes it clear that the expectation interest comprises not only loss suffered (the so-called *damnum emergens*), but also the gain of which the creditor has been deprived (the so-called *lucrum cessans*), (see art. 160 CESL second sentence). An exception applies, however, with regard to sales contracts where

[7] See ECJ, decision of 12 March 2002, Case C-168/00, [2002] E.C.R. I-2631, margin no. 22.

(additional) digital content is delivered free of charge, such as software coming with a new computer. According to art. 107 CESL, in a case where the software is defective, the buyer can only demand damages for the loss or damage caused to his property, including hardware, software and data, but not for the gain of which he has been deprived. One can hardly criticise this exception; given that the buyer receives the software for free, he should not be able to recover a *lucrum cessans*. However, it is questionable whether it was really necessary to dedicate a separate provision to such a minor point, which could have been inferred from the fact that the software has not been "bought" in the proper sense of the word. If European private law is to focus on such details, it risks failing to address the bigger picture.

Some uniform texts explicitly provide compensation for the mere "loss of a chance" (see art. 7.1.3(2) UPICC). One may think, for instance, of the opportunity to submit a tender for the construction of an airport, which is missed because of the late delivery of a computer (cf. UNIDROIT 2010, Comment 2 to art. 7.4.3 UPICC). Under the CESL, the situation is more complicated. On the one hand, a similar provision on loss of a chance is missing. On the other hand, it does not matter whether the loss has already materialised. As art. 159(2) CESL clarifies that the loss for which damages are recoverable includes the future loss that the debtor could expect to occur. This standard must be applied to the loss of a chance as well (similarly Remien 2012, p. 512). The loss is, thus, only recoverable if there was a high probability that the chance materialise.

In addition to the disappointment to the creditor for not receiving the benefit of contractual performance, a breach of a contractual duty may also lead to the creditor's losses on other rights or goods, such as his life, health or property. This is called consequential damage (Treitel 1976, p. 30, No. 53; for different approaches see Herbots 2011, p. 936 *et seq.*). For instance, a defective electrical stove may start to burn and cause the destruction of the buyer's abode. There can be no doubt that such consequential loss has to be repaired under the CESL (Možina, in Schulze 2013, art. 160 margin No. 7).

It is generally assumed that the reliance interest may also be recouped with a damages claim (Možina, in Schulze 2013, art. 160 margin No. 1; for the CISG see Schwenzer 2010, in Schwenzer, art. 74 margin No. 3). The reliance interest covers expenditures made in reliance on the existence of the contract (Treitel 1976, p. 28). Compensation for these expenditures may be relevant if a party has terminated the contract for non-performance. While it is not doubtful that this kind of damage must be repaired, one cannot fail to notice that the wording of art. 160 CESL hardly provides an explicit ground for such a damages claim. If the creditor asks for reliance interest, he must be put into the situation that existed prior to entering the contract, and not as though the contract had been duly performed, as art. 160 CESL suggests. The correct basis for such damages, therefore, seems to be an analogy to art. 55 CESL.

The buyer also incurs loss if he terminates the contract for the seller's non-performance and buys the goods elsewhere. These so-called substitute transactions are dealt with in art. 164 CESL. It is not surprising that the extra costs to the buyer are to be compensated. This would, arguably, have followed already from the general principle of full compensation. The function of art. 164 CESL is, therefore, not to allow a damages claim, but to submit it to two restrictive conditions: the substitute transaction must have been made "within a reasonable time" and "in a reasonable manner". Obviously, the word "reasonable" is not a very precise standard. However, since the same criteria are used in the CISG (art. 75) and in the soft law (art. 9:506 PECL, art. 7.4.5 UPICC, art. III.-3.706 DCFR), one can fall back on previous decisions rendered by courts and arbitrators when interpreting this term.

The CESL also includes a provision on the calculation of damages if there is a current price for the performance (art. 165 CESL). This is in line with the model of uniform law, even though the latter is more detailed and sophisticated in this respect (see e.g. art. 76 CISG). The provision on the calculation of damages using a market price is, however, tailored to B2B contracts. It does not fit B2C contracts. If the trader is the terminating party, the provision allows him to effectively shift the risk of price movements to the consumer (see Remien 2012, p. 517; see also the example given by Posner 2007, p. 125). Article 165 CESL should, therefore, be restricted to B2C relations where the consumer has terminated the contract.

13.3.4 Limits

In spite of the principle of full compensation, not all losses incurred by the creditor are recoverable. The CESL restricts the debtor's liability for loss where the debtor either foresaw or could be expected to have foreseen the loss at the time when the contract was concluded (art. 161 CESL). The foreseeability criterion has a long tradition. Its origins go back to the ULIS (art. 82, second sentence); it can also be found in the CISG (art. 74, second sentence) and in the soft law (art. 9:503 PECL, art. 7.4.4 UPICC). The DCFR provides that "[t]he debtor in an obligation which arises from a contract or other juridical act is liable only for loss which the debtor foresaw or could reasonably be expected to have foreseen at the time when the obligation was incurred as a likely result of the non-performance, unless the non-performance was intentional, reckless or grossly negligent" (art. III.-3:703 DCFR). Although it follows the foreseeability criterion, the text of art. 161 CESL differs in certain respects from this model.

First, it limits the damages to foreseeable loss even where the non-performance was intentional, reckless or grossly negligent. In that sense, it is clearly more favourable to the seller. One reason for this could be to bring the CESL in line with the CISG (art. 74) and the UPICC (art. 7.4.4), which also do not provide for such an exception. Another possible explanation is the motive to not deter businesses from using the CESL. However, it is very hard to justify that a seller who intentionally or recklessly inflicts harm on a buyer will not be held responsible for all consequences of his actions, but rather only for those that he foresaw. Such a seller does not deserve the protection of the law. The drafters of the CESL here have gone too far in their ambition to make the instrument attractive by protecting the wrong kind of businesses.

Second, art. 161 CESL leaves out the words "reasonably" and "likely" that are used in the soft law. It has been speculated that these changes were motivated as well by a desire for a stricter limitation on the seller's liability (Možina, in Schulze 2013, art. 161 margin No. 6). Yet in reality, the omission of these words would rather lead to a strengthening of the seller's liability because he would now also have to compensate for a loss that he could "not reasonably" be expected to have foreseen, and which was an "unlikely" result of his non-performance. The illogical consequences show that such a literal reading of the provision is inappropriate. One should not make too much out of the omission of these two words (in this sense also Možina, in Schulze 2013, art. 161 margin No. 7). One must probably attribute it to the drafters' preference towards a more efficient and succinct style, which is unfortunately lacking in so many other parts of the CESL.

Article 162 CESL makes it clear that the debtor is not liable for loss suffered by the creditor to the extent that the latter has contributed to the non-performance and its effect. This limit of contributory negligence is also recognised in the conventional law (see art. 80 CISG) and in the soft law (art. 9:504 PECL, art. 7.4.7 UPICC, art. III.-3:704 DCFR). The same is true for the creditor's duty to reduce the loss as far as possible, which is enshrined in art. 163 CESL. It can be traced back to the duty to mitigate the loss in conventional law (see art. 77 CISG) and soft law (art. 9:505 PECL, art. 7.4.8 UPICC, art. III.-3:705 DCFR). However, it has been recently criticised for being at odds with many Member State laws, and, instead, a proportional approach has been called for (Keirse 2011, p. 970).

13.3.5 Monetary Damage

Article 2(g) of the proposed Regulation makes it clear that damages are to be understood as a sum of money. In this sense, the European law will be different from e.g. Austrian and German law, where a debtor owing damages must primarily restore the creditor back to the situation that he would have been in without the damaging event (the so-called Principle of restitution in kind or *Natural restitution*, see § 1323 *ABGB* and § 249 *BGB*). It is, however, true that these damages in kind will most often turn into a claim for monetary damages, for instance where the restoration is not possible or is not sufficient to compensate the creditor (see e.g. § 251 *BGB*).

13.3.6 Relation to Tort Law

One of the most interesting questions regarding the damages provisions in the CESL is their relation to causes of action that may arise under tort law. It is possible, for instance, that the delivery of a defective good causes damage to the life, health or the assets of the buyer. In this case, liability may arise in both contract and in tort. In this case, an alternative arises: either tort liability may be applied in addition to the

CESL provision on damages (in French called *cumul*), or the latter excludes liability under tort law (in French called *non-cumul*).

The problem thus raised is quite intricate. The CESL proposal specifically states that the question falls outside its scope (Recital 27, last sentence CESL). One must distinguish whether the concurrent non-contractual claim arises under autonomous national tort law or under tort law harmonised by the EU, in particular through the Product Liability Directive.

As for non-contractual claims under autonomous national tort law, given the reluctant stance of the CESL, one must necessarily conclude that it is the applicable national law that will decide on *cumul* and *non-cumul*. Under the influence of the principle of equivalence recognised in ECJ case law,[8] the national legislator must apply the same or similar rules as those that are used in this respect for domestic cases (see Schmidt-Kessel 2012, p. 340). This means, for instance, that the non-contractual claims will be excluded where French tort law applies, but may be pursued concurrently where German tort law applies. The applicable tort law must be determined according to art. 4(1) and (2) of the Rome II Regulation.

As for non-contractual claims arising under national tort law harmonised by the law, the clash in reality is between two European regimes, the CESL and the Products Liability Directive. The clash becomes relevant when a producer is directly selling its products to individual buyers. The question then becomes whether the standard of liability for damages is determined by the CESL or the Products Liability Directive. The ECJ has decided that the latter is completely harmonises the matters it regulates.[9] Now it is true that the CESL may also override those parts of other EU law that aim at full harmonisation (this point is underscored by Schmidt-Kessel 2012, p. 340). However, one must also take into account the specifics of the Product Liability Directive. As the ECJ has underlined, the goal of this directive is, inter alia, to ensure undistorted competition between traders and to avoid differences in levels of consumer protection.[10] It would run counter to these aims if a producer and a consumer could simply opt out of the product liability regime by agreeing on the CESL. By its very aim, the Product Liability Directive must prevail with regard to questions of liability for defective products that are addressed in it.

13.4 Interest

13.4.1 Structure and Scope of Sections 2 and 3

The outline of the provisions on interest lends itself to confusion. Section 2 is entitled "Interest on late payments: general problems". From this, one could get the

---

[8] See e.g. ECJ, Case C-118/08, [2010] E.C.R. p. I-635, Transportes Urbanos y Servicios Generales SAL, margin no. 33 et seq.

[9] See ECJ, Case C-52/00, [2002] E.C.R. p. I-3827, Commission v France, at 19.

[10] ECJ, Case C-52/00, [2002] E.C.R. p. I-3827, Commission v France, at 17.

impression that the section applies to all kinds of debtors. However, one provision contained in it, art. 167 CESL, is only concerned with consumer debts. The whole situation gets even more confusing by the fact that the CESL deals with "Late payment by traders" in a special section (section 3). It is not at all clear why these debts deserve a separate section, but not consumer debt. The ELI proposal is much more sensibly structured in this regard because it puts all provisions on interests in one Chapter (ELI 2011, p. 109, section 4).

The scope of section 3 is narrowly defined. According to the wording of its introductory provision (art. 168 CESL), it only covers cases in which the "payment of a price" has been delayed. For the late performance of all other monetary obligations, the general rule of art. 166 CESL applies. The practical consequence is that a trader who delays the payment of the price of a good has to pay a much higher interest rate than if he delays the payment for damages. In the literature, this has been criticised as being contradictory; and it was consequently suggested to interpret section 3 broadly so as to also cover late payment of damages and other claims (Možina, in Schulze 2013, art. 168 margin No. 16). However, the apparent contradiction directly reflects the restricted scope of the Late Payment Directive. This directive only applies to "payments made as a remuneration" for commercial transactions (art. 1(2) Directive 2011/7/EU). The special regime of the Directive only targets the delaying of these payments. If one is to look for a justification of this narrow scope, it is perhaps appropriate to say that other monetary claims, such as damages claims, comparatively lend themselves more to disputes rather than claims for the payment of a price because there is no pre-existing voluntary commitment to fulfil them. Thus, their late payment would not be sanctioned as harshly as that for a claim for remuneration. It is, however, not sure that this rationale really justifies the different treatment of the two types of claims because a claim for the payment of a price can be disputed as well, e.g. in the case of defects of the goods delivered or service rendered.

13.4.2 Conditions of a Claim for Interest

In accordance with the principle of strict liability generally applying under the CESL, interest is due whenever a monetary obligation is not duly performed. It does not matter whether the debtor acted intentionally, negligently or without fault.

However, interest is not due where non-performance is excused under art. 88 CESL. This exception is tucked away in the provisions of the CESL (see arts. 167(2), 168(2)). It deviates from the previous uniform laws. There, interests can be claimed even in a case of excused non-performance (see e.g. for the CISG Schwenzer, in Schwenzer 2010, art. 79 margin No. 56). Given that the interest claim is conceptually similar to a kind of lump sum damage, it seems more consistent to allow the money debtor to rely on *force majeure*, as it is foreseen by the CESL. However, the difference will seldom matter because with regard to monetary obligations, there are very few impediments beyond the debtor's control in the sense of art. 88 CESL. Examples in point are, for instance, the few instances where money cannot be paid because of exchange controls or the breakdown of a currency.

13.4.3 *Period of Interest*

As a general rule, art. 166(1) CESL provides that the creditor is entitled to interest from the time that payment is due. There are two exceptions to this rule: one in section 2 regarding consumer debts (art. 167), and one in the section 3 regarding claims against a trader for payment (art. 168). With regard to all other monetary obligations of a trader, the general rule in art. 166 CESL applies.

As far as consumer debt is concerned, the interest period only starts to run 30 days after the consumer has received a notice from the creditor (art. 167(2), first sentence CESL). This rule is different from many national regimes. For instance, under German law, the consumer owes interest from the very moment he receives a request for payment from the creditor or where the time of payment has been specified according to the calendar (§ 286(1), (2) No. 2 BGB); the 30 day-period only serves as a default rule and applies where such a request or specification is missing. The rule of art. 167(2) CESL is much more favourable to the consumer. It effectively means that he can withhold the price for 1 month without being obliged to pay any interest, except for those rare cases where he is able to send the notice before delivery (see art. 167(2), second sentence CESL). It is true that the money is due before the end of the one-month period, and that the creditor, therefore, could already bring a claim (Koch 2011, p. 240), but this option will remain largely theoretical because of the costs and hassle of litigation. The interest rule under the CESL is, thus, a heavy burden for businesses, and they must carefully weigh the implications when agreeing with their customers on the European instrument.

Regarding price obligations of traders, the interest period starts to run at the time of payment that is specified in the contract (art. 168(2), first sentence CESL). Failing such a provision in the agreement, the interest runs 30 days after the receipt of an invoice or equivalent request for payment (art. 168(2)(a) CESL), or 30 days after the receipt of the performance of the other party if the date provided for under (a) is earlier or uncertain (art. 168(2)(b) CESL). Apparently, this provision is intended to reproduce the Late Payment Directive (art. 3(3)(b) Directive 2011/7/EU). Nevertheless, it creates an ambiguity because it remains uncertain as to whether its reference to the "date provided for in (a)" refers to the time when the debtor receives the invoice (or equivalent request for payment) or to 30 days after that time. In the interest of clarity, it would be better to go back to the formula of the Directive, which simply states that the second 30 days-period always applies when the invoice is received earlier than the performance (see art. 3(3)(b)(iii) Directive 2011/7/EU).

13.4.4 *Interest Rate*

The rate of interest that the debtor has to pay is determined differently, depending on whether the creditor's habitual residence is in or outside the Eurozone. For creditors residing in a Eurozone country, the interest rate is calculated on the basis of the rate applied by the European Central Bank (ECB) in its last main refinancing operation before the first calendar day of the half-year in question, or, where a variable rate tender procedure has been used, the marginal interest rate that results from it (the so-called base lending rate, see arts. 166(2)(a), 168(5)(a) CESL). If the creditor resides in a Member State outside the Eurozone, then the provision points to the "equivalent rate set by the national central bank of that Member State" (arts. 166(2)(b), 168(5)(b) CESL). The interest rate so determined is generally raised by two percentage points (art. 166(2) CESL). In the case of late payment by a trader, however, the surplus added is eight percentage points (art. 168(5) CESL).

Surprisingly, the legislator does not make provision for any solution if the creditor happens to live outside the EU. This is lamentable because the instrument also applies to such contracts (see art. 4 CESL Regulation). Moreover, the reference to the base lending rate, which is well known from the Late Payment Directive (see art. 2(7) Directive 2011/7/EU), is very complex and can hardly be understood by the ordinary consumer to which the CESL is targeted (also critical in this regard: Koch 2011, p. 239). To see it here in action might raise the European legislator's awareness of how misplaced such a reference looks in a text on private law, although one may not base too many hopes that this would lead to a change in its position.

13.4.5 Further Claims

Interest is a kind of lump sum to compensate the creditor for damage he presumably suffers by late payment. Where he can prove that his actual loss was higher, the debtor must compensate him. This is clearly set out in the CESL (arts. 166(3), 168(3) CESL).

In addition to interest, art. 169 CESL also allows for recovery costs. This provision has been modelled on the Late Payment Directive (art. 6 Directive 2011/7/EU). It only applies to B2B contracts and only for obligations to pay a price. According to the provision, the creditor can ask for a minimum sum of 40 € each time that the debtor does not honour his payment obligations and is not excused under art. 88 CESL. A term providing for a lower amount is presumed to be unfair and is, therefore, always invalid, even if it has been negotiated between the two parties, (see art. 170(2) CESL). This strict standard goes beyond that of the Late Payment Directive (art. 7(3) Directive 2011/7/EU). One can hardly understand why such a restriction to freedom of contract is necessary (Možina, in Schulze 2013, art. 170 margin No. 12). Traders are professionals. If they waive the recovery costs, they should be presumed to have done it for a purpose. Certainly the claim for recovery costs is not so important as to justify an absolute mandatory nature.

13.5 Summary

"There is nothing new under the sun"—that is what a superficial reader might conclude after a perusal of the CESL's Chapter 16. Indeed, the provisions on damages and interest contain ingredients that are well known from uniform law texts—be they conventional or soft law. To this mixture, particles of different Directives have been added, especially the one on late payment.

To a certain extent, this approach has its advantages. First, the close tracking of uniform law means that there is a body of literature and case-law upon which the interpreter can draw when the meaning of certain provisions is unclear. Second, the copying of the Directives' rules means that the CESL will not fall behind the *acquis*, but at the same time also not gold plate its standards.

Yet there are also clear insufficiencies. The mix of uniform law with the more regulatory-type provisions of EU law results in a stylistic hodgepodge. While the provisions on damages are principle-based and extremely openly phrased, the rules on interest are, by contrast, sometimes detailed to an extreme degree. Moreover, these provisions do not always neatly fit together. Even if one does a copy-and-paste job, one needs to pay attention to the new context in which the rules are set. There is some indication that this has not always been carefully done.

The biggest deficiency that results from the mix of uniform with EU law is, however, the lack of intelligibility of the new text. In some instances it is too open, and in some instances it provides a rather confusing amount of detail. For instance, the parties will have problems in deducting what damages have to be paid for non-performance because of the relatively scarce and succinct rules on this subject. At the same time, they may have difficulties to know which interest is owed just because they are simply overwhelmed by the different clauses and exceptions on this topic.

It would have been sensible to strike a middle ground on both subjects, and provide easily readable and sufficiently informative rules on damages and interest. Certainly that would have also implied a change to the existing EU law, in particular the Late Payment Directive. Nonetheless, the planned enactment of directly applicable European rules on sales contracts—a *premiere* in legal history—could be a welcome occasion in which to rethink the style and content of the preceding legislation.

References

Aristotle (2013) Nichomachean Ethics book V (transl. W.D. Ross eBooks Adelaide).

Baird D G (1994). The Law and Economics of Contract Damages John M. Olin Law & Economics Working Paper 2d. series No. 30.

Beale H (ed) (2012) Chitty on Contracts 31st ed. Sweet & Maxwell London.

European Law Institute Statement on the Proposal for a Regulation on a Common European Sales Law COM (2011) 635 final 2012 available at http://www.europeanlawinstitute.eu (last visited 3 December 2013).

Expert Group on European contract A European contract law for consumers and businesses 3 May 2011 (so-called Feasibility Study) available at http://ec.europa.eu/justice/contract/files/feasibility_study_final.pdf (last visited 3 December 2013).

Hegel G W F (2001) Elements of the Philosophy of Right (translation S.W. Dyde Batoche Books Kitchener Ontario).

Herbots J (2011) Why Is It Ill-Advised to Translate Consequential Damage by *Dommage Indirect* ERPL p. 931 *et seq*.

Jauernig O (ed) (2011) Bürgerliches Gesetzbuch 14th ed. CH Beck Munich.

Keirse A (2011) Why the Proposed Optional Common European Sales Law Has Not But Should Have Abandoned the Principle of All or Nothing: A Guide to How to Sanction the Duty to Mitigate the Loss ERPL p. 951 *et sEq*.
Koch B A (2011) Schadensersatz und Rückabwicklung in: Wendehorst Christiane and Zöchling-Jud Brigitta (eds.) Am Vorabend eines Gemeinsamen Europäischen Kaufrechts Manz Vienna p. 225 *et seq*.
Magnus U (1987) Schaden und Ersatz Mohr Siebeck Tübingen.
Posner R (2007) Economic Analysis of Law 7th ed. Aspen Austin *et al.*
Remien O (2012) Schadensersatz und Zinsen nach EU-Kaufrecht in: Schmidt-Kessel Martin (ed) Ein einheitliches europäisches Kaufrecht? sellier Munich p. 503 *et seq*.
Remien O Herrler S and Limmer P eds (2012) Gemeinsames europäisches Kaufrecht für die EU? Beck Munich pp. 331 *et seq*.
Schmidt-Kessel M (2012) Strukturfragen des Schadensersatzes im Draft Common Frame of Reference für ein Europäisches Privatrecht in: Remien Oliver (ed) Schadensersatz im europäischen Privat- und Wirtschaftsrecht Mohr Siebeck Tübingen.
Schulze R (ed) (2013) Common European Sales Law Hart Nomos Baden-Baden.
Schwenzer (ed) (2010) Commentary on the UN Convention on the International Sale of Goods 3d. edition OUP Oxford.
Shavell S (2004) Foundations of Economic Analysis of Law Belknap Press of Harvard University Cambridge Massachusetts.
Treitel G H (1976) Contracts in General in: International Encyclopedia of Comparative Law vol. 7 chapter 16 Mouton The Hague and Mohr Siebeck Tübingen.
Unberath H (2007) Die Vertragsverletzung Mohr Siebeck Tübingen.
UNIDROIT Principles of International Commercial Contracts Official Commentary Rome 2010.
Vogenauer S & Kleinheisterkamp J eds (2009) Commentary on the UNIDROIT Principles of International Commercial Contracts (PICC).

Chapter 14
Restitution

Adela Serra Rodríguez

Abstract The restitution of benefits is one of the effects of avoidance or termination of the contract, along with the extinguishment of the obligation. The CESL contains, in Chapter 17, arts. 172–177, some rules on the scope and manner of exercising a restitution claim of whatever was supplied under a contract that has been subsequently avoided or terminated. The CESL regulates jointly restitution arising from avoidance and termination; an approach which is new compared to the different European legal systems, although these two remedies do not arise from an identical basis. The aim of this commentary is to analyse the most relevant aspects of this proposal, highlighting certain gaps in the text that could cause problems of interpretation and application.

Keywords Restitution · Avoidance · Termination · Natural fruits · Legal fruits · Full restoration · Unreturnable goods · Digital contents · Payment for use and interest · Compensation for expenditure

14.1 Restitution Effect of Avoidance and Termination

Where avoidance or termination of a contract has occurred, art. 172.1 CESL provides the typical effect of returning the benefits received by the parties under the contract.

Amendment 224 approved by the Legal Affairs Committee of the European Parliament (published at 24.9.13 A 170301/2013) proposed a modification of the title to art. 172, which also now includes restitution in the event of the contract being invalid or not binding for reasons other than avoidance (by mistake, fraud, threats or unfair exploitation) or termination, thereby expanding the initial scope of art. 172. Indeed, under the text of the amendment, art. CESL 172.1 expressly refers to restitution being the remedy for invalid or non-binding contracts—the justification for the amendment—in those cases where the seller has not complied

A. Serra Rodríguez (✉)
University of Valencia, Valencia, Spain
e-mail: adela.serra@uv.es

© Springer International Publishing Switzerland 2015
J. Plaza Penadés, L. M. Martínez Velencoso (eds.), *European Perspectives on the Common European Sales Law,* Studies in European Economic Law and Regulation 4,
DOI 10.1007/978-3-319-10497-3_14

with certain additional obligations, or where a specific requirement has not been fulfilled. Examples of this can be found: in art. 19(4), in respect of a signed offer or written consent sent by the consumer to a distance contract concluded by telephone; art. 25(2) concerning the obligation of the trader, in distance contracts concluded by electronic means, to use unambiguous words by which the consumer recognises that placing the order entails an obligation to pay; art. 71(2), relating to additional payments expressly allowed in consumer contracts, in particular where they have not been incorporated by the use of default options; art. 72(3), providing that a merger clause does not bind a consumer; art. 79(2), relating to unfair terms not being binding; art. 167(3), in respect of interest clauses set in breach of the provisions arts. 166 and 167.2; and, finally, art. 170(1) on unfair terms relating to the rate of interest payable for delay. In all these cases, the breach of the duties specifically imposed on the trader, or the presence of unfair terms, implies that the consumer may recover the amount paid under the contract or that part of contract that is not binding. European Parliament legislative resolution of 26 February 2014 on the proposal for a regulation of the European Parliament and of the Council on a Common European Sales Law [P7_TA-PROV (2014) 0159] has adopted its position at first reading taking over the report of the Committee on Legal Affairs. It is to be hope that the Council will eventually give a similarly positive reaction.

It is questionable whether restitution could also be applied to cases of invalidity for reasons other than the defects in consent caused by mistake, fraud, threats or unfair exploitation, such as invalidity based on illegality or immorality of the contract, or the incapacity of one of the parties, which are not covered by the CESL. The answer must be in the negative (Lehmann 2012, p. 682), which has been justified in relation to the PECL, given the diversity of assumptions and differences of treatment among the legal systems of Member States, and considering that invalidity for lack of ability is more a matter of the Law of Persons than of Contract (Lando and Beale 1995, p. 227; Morales Moreno 2003, p. 371).

Unlike some other European legislation and harmonising texts, CESL regulates restitution for the effects of both avoidance and termination of the contract together, which can sometimes cause a disturbing effect. The restitution, following termination for non-performance, is the result of considerations of fairness: if the defaulting party would not have to repay what they received, they would be unjustly enriched. At the same time, restitution is a natural consequence of the avoidance of the contract. An avoided contract should return the parties to their pre-contractual situation (status quo ante), either as if the contract had never been made or as a result of the retrospective effect of the avoided contract. Article 54.3 CESL, which includes the effects of avoidance, refers to the rules on restitution under Chapter 17 of the CESL; as does art. 8.3 CESL for the effects of termination of the contract with regard to the refund of the price and the return of the goods or digital content as well as its other effects.

Restitution of benefits is one of the consequences of avoidance, invalidity or termination of contracts in European legal systems, and there exists harmonisation texts in European contract law, although these contain differences in scope, conditions and the precise content of restitution. In many European legal systems (e.g. French[1], Italian[2] or Spanish[3]), when dealing with single performance contracts that have been executed by one or both of the parties, the termination and invalidity have retroactive effect, "*ex tunc*". This retroactive effect does not occur when either party has executed its performance, or where a contract for performance in successive parts or instalments is terminated or avoided after some parts of it have been performed [art. 172(3) CESL]. In these cases, the solution is that it may be terminated with regard to future obligations without affecting, in principle, what has already been completed by each party.[4]

On the other hand, the rule in English law is that termination of the contract has no retroactive effect, since this contemplates contracts in which neither party has performed, as well as contracts for successive performances. As discussed below, this is the same in the regulation of termination in the PECL where, in general, there is no retroactive effect. This can be distinguished from invalidity of the contract, where, as in English law, *restitutio in integrum* does exist (in the case of "*ab initio rescission*" by misrepresentation or mistake). From the perspective of English law, the non-performance of one party entitles the other to extinguish the relationship for the future only "*ex nunc*". However, when single performance contracts have been performed by one of the parties, termination is not only prospective in effect, but also "*ex tunc*", either through the exercise of a restitutory remedy,[5] or through compensation for damages accompanying the termination.

The starting point in the CESL is different. Restitution after termination or avoidance is the natural consequence when one or both parties have received a benefit from the other and is obliged to return what was received. Therefore, when only a part of a contract is avoided or terminated by one of the parties, each party is obliged to return what the recipient has received under the part affected by the avoidance or termination.

Restitution, as rule, does not depend on the reason for the avoidance or termination, no matter the parties have acted in good or bad faith; although the scope and precise content of the obligation to return may be affected by the occurrence of these circumstances.

---

[1] Articles 1117 and 1304–1314 CC for avoidance and invalidity; arts. 1183 and 1184 CC for termination. Picod, Y. (2013), *Encyclopédie Dalloz*, "Nullitè"; C. Chabas (2010), "Résolution", *Encyclopédie Dalloz*, Repertoire de droit civil.

[2] Articles 1422 and 2033 CC for avoidance of contract; art. 1458 CC for termination for breach of contract.

[3] Articles 1303 and 1308 CC; v. Clemente Meoro, p .495 et seq.

[4] Moreover, unlike avoidance, which is retroactive, the effect of termination is not absolute, since several effects of the contract remain. So, termination does not affect the application of clauses introduced precisely for that eventuality, such as exclusion or exemption clauses, or the arbitration clauses that were intended to apply despite any termination.

[5] McGregor, H., *Contract Code. Drawn up on behalf of the English Law Commission*, Milán, 1983, p. 83.

14.1.1 *Legal Antecedents*

14.1.1.1 The Regulation in the UN Convention on Contracts for the International Sale of Goods, in the UNIDROIT Principles and in PECL

Just as in art. 172(1) CESL, the Vienna Convention on the International Sale of Goods (CISG), in art. 81-2 first paragraph, provides, as a result of the termination, the right to claim the other party has supplied or paid under the contract. If both or either of the parties have carried out their performance, they may require restitution. Also, if both parties are bound to make restitution, this must be performed simultaneously (art. 81-2, second paragraph), and the buyer loses his right to terminate if, by his own actions, he cannot return the goods (cf. art. 82). However, the CISG does not deal with the invalidity of the sale by vitiated consent, nor its consequences.

The Principles of International Commercial Contracts UNIDROIT provides two restitution regimes dealing with the situation after a contract has been avoided (art. 3.2.15) or has been terminated (art. 7.3.5–7.3.7). The overall effect of the termination is in accordance with art. 7.3.5(1) in that the parties are relieved of the obligation to accept any future benefits (releasing effect).

In addition, under art. 7.3.6(1) "On the termination of a contract to be performed at one time either party may claim restitution of whatever it has supplied under the contract, provided that such party concurrently makes restitution of whatever it has received under the contract". It is established, therefore, that restitution can be claimed by either party, not only the aggrieved party, and reciprocity or interdependence between restitution obligations of each party are also available for contracts to be performed at one time.

However, unlike English law and the CISG, termination of contract is possible, even though restitution in kind is not possible. In fact, art. 7.3.6(2) provides: "If restitution in kind is not possible or appropriate, an allowance must be made in money whenever reasonable." It seems, therefore, that there will always be restitution, if not in kind, by paying money. Even when restitution in kind is possible, but is not appropriate, it can be possible to substitute the pay of money; so if the aggrieved party has received a benefit, he could choose to pay the monetary value in restitution.

This conclusion is apparently inconsistent with the provision of art. 7.3.6(1), which determines that the restitution claim means the return whatever was received. These two rules can be interpreted as meaning the impossibility of restitution in kind prevents the restitution claim only but does not prevent the termination of the contract. So, if a party who terminates and claims restitution can return in kind, but the other party cannot, he will have to repay the equivalent in money (Clemente Meoro 1998). As an exception, the party benefited by compliance is not required to compensate the other party in money if the impossibility of making restitution in kind is attributable to the other party (art. 7.3.6(3)).

In the case of contracts under which the characteristic performance is to be carried out over a period of time, the effect of restitution occurs only for the period after the termination, not for performances that have been carried out over a period of time before the contract is terminated (art. 7.3.7). In this way, successive goods delivered in instalments and payments made on a regular basis, do not affect the termination of the contract. Restitution will only operate with respect to that given and received after termination and will not have retrospective effect. Where restitution is appropriate, the provisions of art. 7.3.6. will apply.

With regard to avoidance, art. 3.2.15 UNIDROIT provides identical rules for the restitution of benefits delivered under the contract, or the part of contract that has been avoided; in accordance with paragraph (1) the restitutory claim means that party can return whatever he has received under the contract or the part of it that has been avoided. Article 3.2.15(2) contains the same rule as art. 7.3.6(2), that the impossibility of restitution in kind does not prevent avoidance, but if the party to whom restitution is claimed cannot do so, or it is not appropriate to do so, compensation in money has to be made "whenever reasonable". Finally, the recipient of a performance, which cannot be returned, does not have to make an allowance in money if the impossibility of restitution in kind is attributable to the other party.

As in the UNIDROIT Principles, the Principles of European Contract Law (PECL) 2002 regulate the effects of avoidance and termination in different locations.

With regard to the Termination of Contract (Section 3 Chapter 9 "Private remedies for non-performance"), art. 9:305(1) (ex art. 4.305) provides: "Termination of the contract releases both parties from their obligation to effect and receive future performance, but, subject to Articles 9:306–9:308 does not affect the rights and liabilities that have accrued up to the time of termination". Therefore, termination of the contract releases both parties from their duty of performance of the future obligations that have not yet expired, but does not, in principle, affect those that were, or should have been, fulfilled before the termination.

As a general rule, termination does not have a retroactive effect because it is not convenient to treat the contract as if it had not been concluded, since this conclusion might not let the aggrieved party claim damages; or might prevent the application of dispute resolution clauses and other clauses that should apply even if the contract were to be terminated (Lando and Beale 1995, p. 420); for example, the liquidated damages clause, and agreed, exclusion or exemption clauses, as referred to in art. 9.305(2) PECL: "Termination does not affect any provision of the contract for the settlement of disputes or any other provision which is to operate even after termination".

Articles 9.306–9.308 PECL provide, as an exception to the irretroactive effect of the termination, the right to recover performances that can be, or should be, returned. Article 9.306 deals with the aggrieved party who terminates the contract providing that he may reject property previously received from the other party (before termination) if its value has been substantially reduced as a result of the termination, as a result of the other party's non-performance. The buyer may receive a good that has depreciated substantially because, for example, as a result of a subsequent breach, the purpose for which it was purchased may no longer exist. So, where the contract is terminated, he could restore that benefit to the other party.

Since a party may terminate the contract if the other party's non-performance is fundamental, it would be inequitable not to allow a claim to recover whatever was paid or delivered to the other party if nothing has been received in return. Therefore, arts. 9:307–9:309 PECL deal with the restoration regime where this is possible. Firstly, art. 9:307 PECL provides: "On termination of the contract a party may recover money paid for a performance which he did not receive or which he properly rejected".

Secondly, on termination of the contract, where a party has delivered goods or supplied property that can be returned, this party has the right to recover this property if the other party (the recipient) who received it has not paid or made any other counter-performance (art. 9:308 PECL).

Finally, one must bear in mind that in some cases, after a contract has been terminated, one party carries out a performance that cannot be returned and for which it has not received payment or any other counter-performance. Applying art. 9:309, this party may recover a reasonable amount for the value of the performance to the other party (Vaquer 2003, p. 542).

To summarise, where benefits cannot be restored because, for example, it is a service or it has been sold to a third person, one party may require the other party to pay a reasonable amount for the value of the performance, even when the party that has received the benefit is the aggrieved party.

With regard to avoidance, art. 4:115 deals with the restitution effect, providing that either party may claim restitution of whatever it has given to the other based on the contract avoided or partially avoided, if it can return what he had received. If this cannot be returned for any reason, a reasonable sum would have to be paid for what was received. Avoidance means setting aside the contract or part thereof as it never existed. It is a natural consequence of this that the parties mutually return what they have received or its value if it cannot be returned.

This has to be interpreted as in accordance with arts. 7.3.6(1) and (2) and 3.2.15(1) and (2) UNIDROIT: the restitution claim depends on the party being able to repay in kind the equivalent to what he received. However, if the party against whom the restitution is claimed cannot return in kind, he must do so with its pecuniary value. It does not matter whether the impossibility to return in kind is attributable to the party who has to do the returning.

However, there is a difference in the regulation of the UNIDROIT Principles. According to art. 3.2.15(3), where he, who received the benefit of compliance, cannot return in kind, he does not have to pay any monetary sum if the impossibility is attributable to the other party (who is claiming the restitution). In contrast, in PECL, it is irrelevant whether the impossibility to make restitution in kind is attributable or not the other party. That party is still entitled to claim a reasonable sum in payment if the other party cannot return in kind.

14.1.1.2 The Regulation in the DCFR and in Acquis Principles

The principles of the existing EC Contract Law ("Acquis Principles" published in 2009) do not contain specific rules for the restitution of benefits arising from the avoidance of the contract; probably due to this issue not being addressed sufficiently in the European contractual acquis.

The Acquis Principles are limited to the releasing effect of the termination of the contract in art. 8:303(1), so that, from the moment that the termination is effective, both parties are released from the performance of their respective obligations. Moreover, art. 8:303(2) provides, within the effects of termination, that the obligation of each party is to effect restitution of whatever it has fulfilled under the contract. In case of partial termination, each party shall be obliged to return only that which each party received under the part of the contract affected by the termination.

The DCFR, in line with the PECL, and unlike the CESL, provides two regimes for the effects of avoidance and the effects of termination of the contract.

The effects of the termination of the contract for non-performance are governed by Book III, particularly in Chapter 3, Section 5, Sub-section 4: "Restitution". According to art. 3:510: "Restitution of benefits received by performance: (1) On termination under this Section a party (the recipient) who has any benefit received by the other's performance of Obligations under the terminated contractual relationship or terminated part of the contractual relationship is obliged to return it. Where both parties have obligations to return, the obligations are reciprocal".

This simultaneity or reciprocal restitution of benefits is expected when both parties have benefits restored; as provided by the Vienna Convention, although the CESL silent on this matter.

The DCFR also provides that the restitution must be made in kind, but if the benefit (not being money) cannot be transferred because it causes an unreasonable effort or expense, the recipient shall pay of a sum of money equivalent to its value (III.-3:510(3)). Here, the impossibility to return in kind does not preclude the restitution claim, unlike the PECL and the UNIDROIT Principles.

The restitution effect of termination does not require that, in the case of contracts for performance in separate parts or otherwise divisible, what was received by each party resulted from the due performance of a part for which counter-performance was duly made (III-.3:512 (I)). By way of exception, paragraph (I) shall not apply and, therefore, the party will be obliged to return (in kind or monetary equivalent) if what was rejected by the terminating party was rejected correctly, in accordance with III.-3:510, or if the value of the non-transferable allowance received by the terminating party had been eliminated or fundamentally reduced as a result of the failure of the other party. In this sense, the CESL simplifies this rule: on the termination of a contract for performance in instalments or parts the party is entitled to recover benefits when the nature of the contract is such that part performance holds no value for the party, who is not necessarily the aggrieved party.

DCFR, in II.-7:212(2), deals with the effects of avoidance, by referring to the rules on unjust enrichment, as to whether each party is entitled to recover whatever has been provided as a result of an avoided contract, or its pecuniary equivalent. According to paragraph 3, the restitution for the owner who correctly transferred the property under the void contract shall be governed by the rules for the transfer of property.

14.1.2 The Regulation in the CESL: Rules and Scope of Restitution

The Proposal for a Regulation on a Common European Sales Law in its Chapter 17 of Part VII regulates restitution; specifically, art. 172 provides: "Restitution on avoidance or termination

1. Where a contract is avoided or terminated by either party, each party is obliged to return what that party ('the recipient') has received from the other party.
2. The obligation to return what was received includes any natural and legal fruits derived from what was received.
3. On the termination of a contract for performance in instalments or parts, the return of what was received is not required in relation to any instalment or part where the obligations on both sides have been fully performed, or where the price of what has been done remains payable under Article 8(2), unless the nature of the contract is such that part performance is of no value to one of the parties".

Therefore, art. 172 CESL establishes several rules for restitution as a consequence of avoidance or termination of the contract: (1) restitution of benefits in kind, (2) restoration of these benefits to include all legal and natural fruits, and (3) restitution in contracts for performance in instalments or parts.

Amendments 225–228, introduced by the Legal Affairs Committee of the European Parliament, include a new art. 172.2a and a 172.2b, concerning the time and cost of restitution. Article 172.2c, as amended, allows a party to withhold the performance of an obligation to return if he has a legitimate interest in so doing; for instance, where this is necessary in order to ascertain the existence of a lack. Moreover, art. 172.2d, as amended, provides, in the case of non-performance of an obligation, for the return or payment under Chapter 17 by one party, and the right of the other party to claim damages under arts. 159–163. As we have seen the European Parliament has confirmed these amendments by the legislative resolution of 26 February 2014.

a. Restitution in kind ("*in natura*")

Restitution is the main effect of termination and avoidance of the contract. Each party, regardless of who has avoided or terminated the contract or who has caused the avoidance or termination, is required to return whatever he have received under the contract.

In the CESL, the rule is that benefits have to be returned in kind; that is, where avoidance or termination of the contract arises, the parties must have returned to them the same things that each received. This is in contrast to other legal systems, such as English law, where this is always an amount of money (money had and received).

Unlike art. 82-1 CISG, the impossibility of restitution in kind allows the party concerned to terminate the contract; neither is restitution conditional on what can be made in kind, as in the UNIDROIT Principles (art. 7.3.6). So, in the CESL, a party who cannot make restitution in kind is authorised to terminate or void the contract, and to claim restitution of the benefit supplied. Therefore, restitution arises whether or not the obligation of the parties consist in the transfer of any property or money; and the impossibility of returning the goods supplied does not preclude the right to termination or avoidance of the contract, nor the obligation of restitution, as in PECL (art. 9:309) and the DCFR (III.-3: 515 (3)).

Each party must return what that party ("the recipient") had received from the other in the same state as it was before the conclusion of the contract, because the goal of restitution is to return the parties to the *status quo ante*. However, it is possible that since the formation of the contract, the goods that have to be returned have been improved or have deteriorated for some reason.

Therefore, it should be questioned why the CESL has not specifically laid down the obligation to compensate any deterioration in the goods that have to be returned; since, in this way, one party will benefit from his own negligence, when, as shall be seen, he is allowed to claim compensation for any expenditure on goods or digital contents, even when that party knew, or could have been expected to know, the cause of the avoidance or termination (cf. art. 175). Moreover, as has been shown, this irresponsibility in cases of deteriorated goods contrasts with the rule based on withdrawal (art. 45), (Lehmann 2012).

Therefore, it should be asked, if the goods had deteriorated because of the actions of the recipient—whether this is the defaulting party or the aggrieved party—whether the "*accipiens*" should be obliged to compensate for that deterioration. Moreover, even in cases of accidental deterioration that occurred before the termination, the party who has to return the goods should be made to pay the difference between the value of the property before and after damage (deterioration).

The amended text, presented and approved by the Legal Affairs Committee of the European Union, and confirmed by European Parliament legislative Resolution of 26 February 2014, including, by Amendment 240, a new art. 174(3), addresses such considerations. So, this new article and subsequent parts (art. 174.3 b, c, d) regulates the responsibility of the recipient for the deterioration of goods, digital content or fruits that he obliged to return.

b. Non-reciprocal obligations of restitution

The language of the first paragraph of art. 172 CESL does not specify the reciprocal nature of the restitution when both parties have received benefits from the other as a result of a subsequently avoided or terminated contract. It is expressly stated, however, in the Vienna Convention (art. 81.2.II), the UNIDROIT Principles (art. 7.3.6(1)), DCFR (III-.3:511 (1)), and in some European systems, such as the Spanish.[6]

[6] Thus, art. 1303 CC, provides for restitution in respect of contractual invalidity, together with art. 1308 CC, which states: "While one of the contracting parties does not return that which he is obliged to return pursuant to the declaration of nullity, the other cannot be compelled to perform in his turn what is incumbent on him".

However, in the CESL the restitution obligation of each party is independent of the obligation of the other. The cause of one party's obligation to return, derived from the void or terminated contract, does not have its cause in the other's obligation to return, but rather in order to restore the status quo prior to the formation of the contract. When both parties have received benefits and if one of the parties does not return to the other whatever it had received, this would produce unjust enrichment; but that does not exactly mean that the restitution obligation is reciprocal, since the duty of each party to return is not the equivalent of the obligation of the other to return; it is seen simply as a means to restore the situation to how it was before the contract (López Beltrán de Heredia 2009).

No change has been proposed in the text following the Legal Affairs Committee report, and confirmed by European Parliament legislative resolution of 26 February 2014, so it remains the case that the restitution obligations of both parties are independent even if both of them are obliged to return.

c. Time and cost of the return

The original text of the proposal is silent as to the time when the restitution should be made and the cost of it.

In order to fill this gap, amendment 225 in the text of the Committee report introduces in the CESL a new art. 172.2.a, which provides that restitution shall be made without undue delay and in any event not later than 14 days, which corresponds to the provisions on the exercise of a right of withdrawal in the CESL (arts. 44(1) and 45(1)), and is in line with Directive 2011/83/EU of the European Parliament and of the Council of 25 October, on consumer rights (arts. 9 and 13). This period starts when the communication of avoidance or termination of the contract is received. Such a rule cannot be found in the DCFR or the UNIDROIT or the Vienna Convention Principles.

However, under this amendment, where the recipient who has to return is a consumer, this deadline shall be considered to have been met if the consumer takes all the necessary steps to do so before the expiry of 14 days. Although not stated, it appears that the burden of proof of having taken such steps lies with the consumer.

On the other hand, in the report, the approved amendments also introduce a new art. 172.c. This provides that the cost of the return will be borne by the recipient, a solution that is justified as being consistent with the rules on the exercise of a right of withdrawal (art. 44(2)) and the provisions of Directive 2001/83/UE. However, according to art. 14.1.II Directive 2001/83/UE, for contracts concluded away from business premises when the goods are delivered to the consumer's home, the trader must collect the goods at his own expense when, by their nature, they cannot be returned by mail. It appears that this rule does not apply to the obligation to return in cases of avoidance or termination of contract.

d. Right to withhold the performance of the obligation to return

Amendment 227, adopted by the Legal Affairs Committee and confirmed by European Parliament legislative resolution of 26 February 2014, introduces an art. 172.2c CESL in order to recognise that a party who is obliged to return, has the right to withhold this performance when he has a legitimate interest to do so; for example, where it is necessary to determine if there is a lack of conformity of the goods within the contract, which could justify the right to terminate the contract for non-conformity of either the goods or digital contents.

In CESL, the reciprocity of the return performance is excluded. Consequently, it is not possible to justify the withholding of the performance of the obligation to return based on the refusal to return of the other party. This would not be a legitimate interest. This party must instead claim compensation for damages incurred for non-performance of an obligation to return (compensating the positive interest of performance, as provided in art. 160 CESL).

e. Liability for breach of the obligation to repay

Lastly, but however not included in the text of the proposed CESL, in cases of the breach of the obligation to return, a party can claim damages, according to the rules of Chapter VII arts. 159–165, which also appears in III.-3:515 DCFR, for cases in which the benefit cannot be transferred when it should have been restored or it has lost value[7].

14.2 Restitution of Natural or Legal Fruits

Any restitution resulting from the avoidance or termination of the contract must be complete, i.e. made in full. Therefore, the parties should have returned all benefits in kind (as a general rule), along with any civil and natural fruits those benefits have produced. This is justified because it places the parties in the same position that they would have been in if the contract had not taken place, as if the object had remained in its original ownership and possession.

Article 172.2 CESL clarifies that the obligation to return includes any natural or legal fruits derived from what was received and is under an obligation to be returned; but it does not define in what way these can be made. However, certain European legal systems (French, Italian, Spanish and German) do clarify this.

From these systems, we can conclude that natural fruits are those spontaneously and naturally produced by animals and the soil, as well as those produced by cultivation. Civil fruits are the benefits obtained as a result of running a business, or a legal operation (such as leasing). Unlike other European legal systems, the obligation to return civil fruits does not necessarily or automatically include the interest on the money received, whose return is specifically governed by the rule in art. 174.

The recipient must return the natural and civil fruits derived from what was received by reason of the contract, regardless of good or bad faith.

Under Spanish law there are certain controversial provisions that are applicable to the restitution of fruits and interest in the case of termination for breach. It is the generally accepted opinion that art. 1123 CC, which states that the parties "must

[7] This is provided for by a new art. 172(2)d introduced by Amendment 228.

return to each other what they have received", is applicable here; and this includes even what could have been received (cf. art. 455 and 1896.1 CC), since the "*solvens*" should not bear the cost of any inactivity on the part of the "*accipiens*" (Clemente). The same solution is asserted in the French and German legal systems. However, based on art. CC 1307, in the case of invalidity, it is concluded that the parties must restore the fruits actually received from the time the goods were delivered, but not those that could have been received if they had acted diligently.

According to the Vienna Convention on the International Sale of Goods, the refund of the price by the seller includes the payment of interest thereon from the date that the payment was made (art. 84-1). However, art 84.2 states that "The buyer must account to the seller for all benefits which he has derived from the goods or part of them: (a) if he must make restitution of the goods or part of them; or (b) if it is impossible for him to make restitution of all or part of the goods or to make restitution of all or part of the goods substantially in the condition in which he received them, but he has nevertheless declared the contract avoided or required the seller to deliver substitute goods." That is, just as the seller has to pay interest on the price to be returned, the buyer has to pay the benefits derived from the goods, whether he has to return them or whether this is not possible although he has terminated or avoided the contract because he was not responsible for the impossibility of restitution (cf. art. 82-2).

The UNIDROIT Principles do not expressly provide that the obligation of restitution of the performances under the contract avoided or terminated includes fruits and interests. However, regarding compensation for damages, article 7.4.9 reaffirms the rule according to which the harm resulting from delay in the payment of a sum of money is subject to a special regime and is calculated by a lump sum corresponding to the interest accruing between the time when the payment of the money was due and the time of actual payment; and if the obligation is not monetary, interest on damages for non-performance will accrue from the time of non-performance, unless otherwise agreed (art. 7.4.10). It should also be noted that in the case of an indemnity rule, the fruits and interest accrues from the time of non-performance of the obligation, not from the time that the benefits were received.

There is no clause in the PECL regarding the benefits and interests owing on a return in the event of invalidity or termination; but the DCFR (III-.3:511 (5)) contains identical provisions to art 172.3 CESL.

Restitution includes only fruits derived from what was achieved and not what might have been achieved.

14.3 Exception to the Principle of Full Restoration in Case of Termination of a Contract to be Performed in Instalments or Parts

Following the general rule laid down in art. 172.1 CESL (full restitution of benefits), art. 172.3 CESL provides that in the case of contracts for performance in parts or instalments, in which there are successive deliveries of goods or payments, no refund will occur with respect "to any instalment or part where the obligations on both sides have been fully performed, or where the price for what has been done remains payable under Article 8(2), unless the nature of the contract is such that part performance does not have any value to one of the parties".

Restitution of benefits, as an effect of the termination of the contract, has a special rule for contracts to be performed in parts or over periods of time where the performances have been fully carried out by both parties. In these cases, the retroactive effect of termination is not applicable because it would make no economic sense or may lead to unfair results. Termination only has a prospective effect or consequences for the future, to the extent that in these contracts performed in parts or by instalments, each performance has economic and legal autonomy, so that they can be separated out from what constitutes the part of the contract in dispute.

Non-performance by a party of a part or instalment of the contract does not affect the creditor's interest in the part that has already been fully performed and, consequently, termination and restitution do not affect those parts already executed. This is also recognised by various European systems (French, Belgian, Luxembourgish, Italian and Common Law).

This means then, that the periodical or partial obligations that have been performed on a regular basis by both parties will not be subject to restitution because the parties would have no interest in so doing.

Moreover, there will be no refund if the price for what has been done remains payable under art. 8(2), which provides that payments due before the time of termination remain payable. Therefore, if goods or digital content have not been paid before the termination, once the contract is terminated those goods do not have to be returned by the party that received them, then the payment due remains binding on the part who is obliged to comply. Otherwise, the party who has fulfilled that part of the contract (providing goods or digital content) may terminate the contract with respect to that part.

In the case of sales contracts with successive deliveries and payments, art. 73 of the Vienna Convention provides in several rules.

a. "In the case of a contract for delivery of goods by instalments, if the failure of one party to perform any of his obligations in respect of any instalment constitutes a fundamental breach of contract with respect to that instalment, the other party may declare the contract avoided with respect to that instalment". In such a case the whole contract is not terminated, but only part of it, so restitution will only affect the particular delivery, or deliveries, and not those already made, for which the contract continues to have effect (cf. art. 81.2).
b. "If one party's failure to perform any of its obligations in respect of any instalment gives the other party good grounds to conclude that a fundamental breach of contract will occur with respect to future instalments, he may declare the contract avoided for the future, provided that he does so within a reasonable time" (art. 73.2). Termination or avoidance not only affects the defaulted delivery, but also any future deliveries, provided there are reasonable grounds to conclude that a fundamental breach will occur with respect to them.
c. If an unfulfilled delivery is interdependent with other deliveries, so that without the one the other deliveries cannot be used for the purpose contemplated by the

parties at the time of the conclusion of the contract, the buyer (not the seller) can declare the contract avoided, not only with regard to the unfulfilled delivery, but also with regard to "deliveries already made or of future deliveries" (art. 73.3). Then buyer can avoid or terminate the entire contract, because it can be considered that the breach is fundamental; so the restitution effect also extends to what the parties have received under the contract (art. 81.2).

As a rule, termination of a contract in art. 9:305 PECL does not have retroactive effect; but sometimes it is convenient for a contract that has been terminated to be cancelled retrospectively. On the other hand, where the contract was to be performed over a period of time, it is appropriate that termination only affects the future without undoing what has already been achieved, except as provided in arts. 9:306–9:308.

However, there is a possibility that the aggrieved party, who has right to terminate the contract, can reject any property previously received from the other party if its value to the first party has been fundamentally reduced as a result of the other party's non-performance. Article 9:306 regulates this right to reject the useless property. For example, where a computer system requires a specific type of computer and the seller delivers the computer but fails to provide the necessary programs to make the equipment work. In this case the buyer must return the received goods, the unwanted property. This could be more convenient for the aggrieved party than claiming damages under art. 9:502 or reducing the price under art. 9:401 (Lando and Beale 1995, p. 421).

The result provided in art. 9:306 PECL would also be applicable to contracts that are severable, in which restitution of the previous instalments, already received, would be possible if those are rendered useless by the later breach (Lando and Beale 1995, p. 427).

In this sense, the DCFR provides for contracts in which the performance is due in separate parts or is otherwise divisible, so that restitution is not required when what was received by each party resulted from due performance of a part of the contract for which counter-performance was duly made (III-. 3:51)2. However, this does not apply when its receipt by the terminating party was properly rejected, for being fundamentally devalued as a result of the other party's non-performance. In such a case, the terminating party may claim restitution of the parts duly carried out.

This last rule is the one that is reflected in art. 172.3 CESL, which contains an exception to the provision of art. 172.3: that is, if a partial performance of the contract has no value to a party—which can be either the defaulting or the terminating party—then, the party who does not satisfy the partial performance (because the value of the partial benefit has been eliminated or fundamentally reduced) is entitled to claim full restitution.

This rule, however, does not appear in art. 7.3.7 UNIDROIT Principles, in the case of contracts to be performed over a period of time, and when goods have to be delivered in instalments. Article 7.3.7 UNIDROIT sets out that restitution can only be claimed in respect of the period after termination, not in respect of what was given and received before. So if the contract contained successive performances, consisting of successive deliveries and payments, termination of the contract does not affect the deliveries or payments already made. To sum up, if the contract is divisible (in parts or instalments) termination is partial; the contract is terminated only for the future, and cannot be claimed for past performance. As far as what restitution has to be made, the provisions of art. 7.3.6 apply.

14.4 Payment of Monetary Value in the Case of Unreturnable Goods or Digital Contents

Article 173 CESL sets out several rules for restitution under the title "Payment of monetary value".

Article 173(1) lays down the principal rule: "Where what was received, including fruits where relevant, cannot be returned, or, in a case of digital content whether or not it was supplied on a tangible medium, the recipient must pay its monetary value." Here, the impossibility of restore the property does not preclude the right to terminate the contract or to claim restitution of what was provided; which is in contrast to English law, and the Vienna Convention (art. 82-1), as has been seen.

The report approved by the Legal Affairs Committee of the European Parliament, contains the amendments 233–236 that affect this provision, which must be read as being incorporated into these rules. The goal of the amendment 233 to art. 173(1) is to simplify this provision by deleting the reference to digital content, because the report proposes the introduction of a new art. 172a relating to digital content which can be considered as returnable. European Parliament has ratified once again these proposals by legislative resolution of 26 February 2014.

PECL also provides the rule that the impossibility of restitution for a certain performance does not preclude the entitlement to recover a "reasonable sum" for what should have been received. In cases of avoidance (art. 4:115) and termination (art. 9:309 PECL), where the benefits cannot be returned to the party which has rendered a performance, this party may demand a reasonable amount for the value of the performance to the other party.

The DCFR rules on restitution distinguish between transferable and non-transferable benefit. In the latter case, its value should be returned, according to III.-3:513 (Payment of value of benefit).

In the CESL, as in the PECL, as well as Spanish law, restitution must be made, primarily, in kind, so that the same goods or digital contents that were received have to be restored. If that is not possible, their monetary value will be payable, calculated in accordance with paragraphs 2–4 of art. 173.

There are other issues to be considered under Article 173:

a. Firstly, the impossibility of return can be based on the destruction or disappearance of the property and on the fact that it no longer belongs to that party, having been sold to a third party in good faith.

Furthermore, art. 173(1) provides the same outcome for cases where the goods could be returned, but it would cause unreasonable effort or expense to the recipient to do so. Here, the recipient may choose to pay the monetary value, "provided that this would not harm the other party's proprietary interest". It seems that if the ownership of the goods has been transferred to the recipient and he in turn has not transferred them to a third person, so that the property remains with the recipient, he cannot choose the alternative of paying its monetary value even though such restitution causes him unreasonable effort or expenses. The recipient is obliged to return the goods, and the other party is entitled to recover the property.

However, Lehmann (2012, p. 697) proposes a different interpretation of this clause. The legitimate interest of the other party to recover the goods delivered would lie in their being non-fungible, unique in nature, difficult to find in the market, or if there was a good chance to sell them on favourable terms.

Also, III-.3:511(3) DCFR, PECL (art. 9:309; Lando and Beale, 1995), and the UNIDROIT Principles (Art. 7.3.6(2)), provide for the case in which the return is possible but it is too expensive or would cause unreasonable effort. The unreasonableness of the costs of returning has to be assessed by economic criteria, taking into account the interests of both parties (Lehmann).

In addition, the monetary value rule also applies to the fruits due according to art. 172 (2), regardless of whether the recipient can return what, in the main, was received.

b. Secondly, the consequence for a case of impossibility to return what was received does not depend on the party to whom such impossibility is attributable. In effect, art. 173(1) CESL does not distinguish between avoided or terminated contracts; both parties must have their benefits returned, so that if one of them cannot do this—even if he is the defaulting party—because the good has perished (accidentally, intentionally or negligently), the risk is not suffered by the other party; the party who cannot restore whatever was received must return its monetary value. This is regardless of whether the inability to repay is, or is not, attributable to the party who is obligated.

Then, if the goods cannot be returned because the recipient was negligent, his obligation to return in kind becomes his obligation to pay their monetary value. Also, if the goods are lost accidentally, the *accipiens* bears the risk of this accidental loss and must pay its monetary value. In this case, the recipient may then demand restitution of the obligation that he carried out under the contract.

c. Thirdly, under the text proposed by the Commision to Parliament and Council it is always impossible to return digital content, in contrast with amendments 229–232, approved by Legal Affairs Committee of the European Parliament, and confirmed by legislative resolution of 26 February 2014, which introduced a new art. 172a concerning restitution in the case of the supply of digital content, clarifying many issues that might arise from the rules contained in the CESL Proposal.

According to art. 173(1) CESL, where the object of the contract is digital content, it is considered that its return is impossible.

However, in the amended text from the Legal Affairs Committee, ratified by legislative resolution of 26 February 2014, digital content is considered returnable: "(a) where the digital content was supplied on a tangible medium and the medium is still sealed or the seller did not seal it before delivery; or (b) it is otherwise clear that the recipient who sends back a tangible medium cannot have retained a usable copy of the digital content", (for example, because it is technologically protected to prevent copying); or "(c) where the seller can, without significant effort or expense, prevent any further use of the digital content on the part of the recipient, for instance by deleting the recipient's user account. In all these cases, the buyer would not have to pay any monetary value, provided that, in the case of (a) and (b), they had sent back the tangible medium that contains the digital content, e. g. sent back the CD" (Art. 172 a(2)).

Finally, it should be noted that the new paragraph 3 of art. 172 a CESL, derived from Amendment 232, deals with the situation in which digital content is exchanged for a counter-performance that cannot be returned: "Where digital content is supplied in exchange for a counter-performance other than the payment of a price, such as the provision of personal data, and that counter-performance cannot be returned, the recipient of the counter-performance shall refrain from further use of what was received, for instance by deleting received personal data". This amendment then adds an important qualification to this rule: that the consumer must be informed of this deletion.

Of course, it is always possible to return the money; this repayment rule for the monetary value is provided, in the CESL, for the buyer of specific goods or the receiver of digital content.

It has been questioned whether this rule would apply "*genus numquam perit*" for general obligations, as contained in some legal systems such as the French (cf. arts. 1129, 1245 and 1246 Civil Code) or Spanish (arts. 1182 and 1105 CC), so that the debtor cannot opt for the payment of monetary value in the case of loss or inability to restore certain goods that are generic in nature, since there will always be goods available of the same genus. Lehmann (2012, p. 696) concludes that this exception is not included in the CESL; so generic goods would have to be treated like any other goods.

d. Fourthly, art. 173 regulates various criteria in order to quantify the monetary value of what was received and is impossible to return.
1. Goods that are impossible to return or would cause unreasonable effort or expense to do so: the monetary value of goods is "the value that they would have had at the date that payment of the monetary value is to be made if they had been kept by the recipient without destruction or damage until that date" (Art. 173(2)).

Therefore, the goods are valued at the date of their liquidation, which is the date of the avoidance or termination of the contract, and dependent on the state they were in when they were delivered. If, as a result of the expenses or improvements made to the goods after they were delivered until such time that must be paid for, their value had increased, such an increase will not be taken into account for the payment of the monetary value of the goods (whose return would cause unreasonable effort), since they are valued taking into account the state they were in when one party delivered them to the other party. Moreover, the recipient cannot be compensated for his expenditure if they did not benefit the other party, or if the expenditure was made by the recipient when he knew, or could have been expected to know, that there were grounds for the avoidance or termination of the contract (Article 175(1)).

The risk of loss to the goods, even if incidental, falls to he who is required to make the return (the buyer), who will have to pay its value at the date of the avoidance regardless of whether or not he could have avoided or foreseen their destruction.

The solution to the allocation of the risk of deterioration or loss between parties would have to be the same both where it is possible to return what was received (restitution in kind) and where its return is impossible. In any case, the CESL may be modified by introducing a rule that explicitly provides that the risk of deterioration of the goods before the avoidance or termination is borne by the recipient.

The PECL provides, where there is a performance that cannot be returned to one of the parties, he would have the right to receive a "reasonable amount for the value of the performance to the other party" (Art. 9:309). Thus, it may be that the net benefit or gain to the receiving party does not cover the cost of the other party of having provided it. In this case, the receiving party should not be required to pay the other's costs (Lando and Beale 1995, p. 425). This rule is understandable because it is not limited to sales agreements, but also includes service contracts.

The DCFR provides that the recipient shall pay the value (at the time of performance) of a benefit that is not transferable, or that ceased to be transferable, before the time when it was to be returned. In addition, he must pay compensation for any reduction in the value of a returnable benefit as a result of a change in the condition of the benefit between the time of receipt and the time when it was to be returned (III.-3:513). The risk of deterioration of the benefits before the termination or avoidance is borne by the recipient, who is obliged to effect the return. In order to calculate the monetary value of this, it must be into account what was the price agreed between the parties and, where no price was agreed, the value of the benefit is the sum of money that a willing and capable provider and a willing and capable recipient would lawfully have agreed.

2. Related service contracts: When the seller provides services that are directly and closely related to the goods or digital content supplied through a related services contract (repair, installation or maintenance) and it is avoided or terminated by the customer after the related service has been performed or partly performed "the monetary value of what was received is the amount the costumer saved by receiving the related service" (art. 173(3)).

Here, the monetary value payable is linked to the savings that the consumer has had for total or partial performance of the related services, which is not necessarily the same as the cost of the service at the time of delivery; (cf. art. 9: 309 PECL).

Also, it should be noted that the rule regarding the calculation of the monetary value of the payment for the related service performed, or party performed, is applicable only when it is the customer who has avoided or terminated the contract, not the provider.

3. Digital content: the monetary value of what was received will be the "amount the consumer saved by making use of the digital content" (art. 173(4)). So, the sum of money the costumer has to pay is the amount of the benefit or utility obtained by the use of the digital content, which may, or may not be, the cost of the digital content when it was provided, or when payment was to be made.

However, when the net benefit to the consumer of the use of non-returnable digital content is greater than the cost of providing that digital content, it seems reasonable that this sets the limit of the monetary value of the digital content that should be paid. This can be concluded from art. 176, which allows for an equitable modification of the obligation to pay or return as a result of the application of Chapter VII.

If digital content is not provided in exchange for a price, but in exchange for a different counter-performance—as with the provision of personal data—or without counter-performance, and that counter-performance cannot be returned under art. 172(1), the recipient will not have to pay its monetary value (art. 173(6)). It has been said that it is difficult to justify that this rule does not extend to cases where goods or services have been provided free of charge (Lehmann 2012, p. 703).

Amendment 236 introduced into the original text by the Legal Affairs Committee, confirmed by legislative resolution of 26 February 2014, includes in art. 173, a new paragraph 6a: "Without prejudice to Article 172 a(3), where the digital content is supplied in exchange for a counter-performance other than payment of a price and that counter-performance cannot be returned, the recipient of the counter-performance does not have to pay its monetary value". As justification, it is stated that very often it is not possible to return what was received in exchange for digital content and, in addition, it is impossible or very difficult to establish the monetary value of the counter-performance. In this case, the best solution is to balance the interests of the parties so that neither party has to pay the monetary value of what it has received, without prejudice to the obligation of the recipient of the counter-performance to refrain from further using what he has obtained.

d. Finally, by applying art. 176, the consequences of the application of art. 173, as it affects the obligations of return or payment, may be modified when it produces unfair results, particularly if one considers that the party did not cause the ground for the avoidance or termination, or did not have any knowledge of it.

14.5 Payment for Use and Interest on Money Received

Article 174(1) and (2) regulates the payment by the recipient for using the goods received and the payment of interest on the money received, subject to certain conditions.

Article 174 CESL provides: (1) "A recipient who has made use of goods must pay the other party the monetary value of that use for any period where:

a. the recipient caused the ground for avoidance or termination;

b. the recipient, prior to the start of the period, was aware of the ground for avoidance or termination; or
c. having regard to the nature of the goods, the nature and amount of the use and the availability of remedies other than termination, it would be inequitable to allow the recipient the free use of the good for that period".

Amendment 238 introduced into the original art. 174 CESL by the Legal Affairs Committee, and adopted by Parliament on 26 February 2014, has added the express reference to a recipient who has made use of "digital content", applying the same rule.

Art. 174(2) provides: "A recipient who is obliged to return money must pay interest, at the rate stipulated in Article 166, where:

a. the other party is obliged to pay for use; or
b. the recipient gave cause for the contract to be avoided because of fraud, threats and unfair exploitation".

Finally, art. 174(3) states: "For the purposes of this Chapter, a recipient is not obliged to pay for use of goods received or interest on money received in any circumstances other than those set out in paragraphs 1 and 2". The amended text includes reference to digital content.

1. Payment for use of goods received: the buyer has to pay for use of goods, but only if the recipient was liable for the avoidance or termination of the contract or may be considered to have acted in bad faith (because he knew of the ground for the invalidity or termination of the contract), or, in the circumstances, it would be inequitable to allow its free use during that period. Among the circumstances to be taken into account in order to conclude that free use would be inequitable are: "the nature of the goods", "the nature and the amount of the use" and the "availability of remedies other than termination" (e.g. compensation). These criteria involve introducing some arbitrariness in determining whether or not the use of goods should be paid for. To the extent that the recipient is required to pay for such use, the amount to be paid shall be taken into account in determining the damage suffered by the party who has terminated or avoided the contract.

Amendment 241, approved by the Legal Affairs Committee, introduced an art. 174(3)b, whereby the payment for the use of goods may not exceed the agreed price for the goods. It adds a new art. 174(3)c, which provides that where digital content is delivered in exchange for counter-performance other than money or without any counter-performance, the recipient will not have to pay for the use. This is so even if he did not have to return digital content, considering the amended art. 173(6). These amendments have been confirmed by European Parliament legislative resolution of 26 February 2014.

This rule regarding payment for the use of goods is not present in the PECL. The DCFR, (III.-3:514(1)), merely provides that the recipient is required to pay a reasonable amount for any use that the recipient makes of the benefit, except in so far as the recipient is liable under III.-3: 513 (i.e. he is obliged to pay the value of a benefit which is not transferable), and does not limit this obligation to where the circumstances exist that are provided for in art. 174(1) CESL.

2. Payment of interest on money received: the recipient is obliged to pay interest calculated according to art. 166, only if the other party is obliged to pay for the use of goods or the recipient caused the contract to be avoided because of fraud, threats or unfair exploitation.

This means it is possible that a non-defaulting party acting in good faith is obliged to pay interest on the money received, regardless of the use or purpose to which this money has been put, if the buyer has had to pay compensation for the use of the goods received. The deal between buyer and seller certainly does not seem symmetrical.

The second situation in which the seller may be obliged to pay interest on money received is where he has been responsible for the avoidance of the contract through fraud, threats or unfair exploitation. However, the seller will not be obligated to pay interest on the money if the contract was avoided by a mistake caused by him, or simply because the contract was terminated for non-performance, which is hardly justifiable taking account the position of the buyer.

Some European legal systems provide for the obligation to repay money together with legal interest regardless of good or bad faith (art. 1303 Spanish CC; art 2033 Italian CC), or only in the case of bad faith (art. 1345 French CC). However, as has been seen, the obligation to return the legal fruits received *per* art. 172(2) does not include interest on money received, which is governed by art. 174(2).

Interest payable is calculated at the rate fixed by art. 166 for interest on late payments, which is applied to the defaulting professional debtor; and, here, the rate is quite high. This is a comparatively strict regime because the recipient of goods only has to pay for the use he has actually made of them (Lehmann 2012, p. 709).

3. Payment for the deterioration of the goods, digital content and fruits: Amendments 240–243, approved by the Legal Affairs Committee and confirmed by European Parliament legislative resolution of 26 February 2014, introduced the new paragraphs 3a, 3b, 3c and 3d, concerning the obligation to compensate for deterioration. This omission in the original text has been criticised (Lehmann 2012, p. 690). In the CESL, a buyer will be able to receive back his payments regardless of whether or not it is his fault that the goods have deteriorated. This conclusion is not fair, especially considering that a recipient that has improved the goods may claim compensation for expenditure under art. 175.

Article 174(3)a, introduced by amendment 240, establishes the liability of the recipient for the deterioration of the goods, digital content or fruits, to the extent that it exceeds depreciation for normal use. As has been seen, there is no a specific rule in the CESL concerning the risk of deterioration or damage to goods, which in any case is born by the seller.

Further, under art. 174(3)a, the buyer that returns severely damaged goods or goods that have significantly diminished in value, and exceeded depreciation through normal use, must pay the difference in the value of the goods before and after the damage; but with a limit: the payment shall not exceed the agreed price for the goods or digital content, with this preventing any enrichment to the assets of the seller.

Under art. 174(3)c, from amendment 242, where digital content is supplied in exchange for counter-performance other than the payment of a price, or without counter-performance, the recipient of the digital content will not have to pay for its diminished value, as seems to be applicable where the digital content is returnable by virtue of art. 172; but this is also the situation when there is no monetary value to pay for not being able to returnable the digital content (art. 173(6)). Similarly, where digital content is supplied in exchange for counter-performance other than the payment of a price, the recipient of the counter-performance (the seller) does not have to pay for the diminished valued of what was received, according to art. 174(3) d; but he must refrain from any further use of what was received.

14.6 Compensation for Expenditure

Article 175 CESL, entitled "Compensation for expenditure", includes two different rules.

Firstly, the recipient that has incurred expenditure on the goods or digital content is entitled to compensation if two conditions are met: "the expenditure benefited the other party" and "the expenditure was made when the recipient did not know and could not be expected to know the ground for avoidance or termination". Amendment 244, introduced by the Legal Affairs Committee and confirmed by European Parliament legislative resolution of 26 February 2014, modifies art. 175 (1), to also include expenditure on the fruits of the goods.

Therefore, if the recipient can establish that the expenditure is a benefit to the other contractual party, either because it is necessary for the conservation of the goods (to prevent loss or diminution in value) and for the production of fruits, or because it is a useful expense for an improvement in the item (providing increase in value), he shall be entitled to payment thereof, as long as he acted in good faith, that is, that he did not know the ground for the avoidance or termination when undertaking out this expenditure.

The CESL does not provide any limitation to the right to compensation for expenditure or improvements made on goods where the recipient has acted in good faith. If this compensation would cause a limitation on the ability of the aggrieved party to be able to terminate the contract, because, for example, he lacks the liquidity needed to meet its payment, he may choose to pay the market value of the goods in their original state by way of compensation (Clemente Meoro 1998, p. 534; Belfiore 1988, p. 399).

Under III.-3:513(2) DCFR, the recipient, who is obliged to return, is entitled "to payment of the value of the improvements made in the goods if the other party can readily obtain that value by dealing with the benefit unless: a) the improvement was a non-performance of a obligation owed by the recipient to the other party; or b) the recipient made improvement when the recipient knew or could reasonably be expected to know that the benefit would have to be returned".

The second rule of art. 175 provides that the recipient is entitled to compensation of expenditure that was necessary for the preservation of the goods or digital content, or the fruits, even if he knew or could be expected to know of the ground for avoidance or termination, but on the condition that the recipient had not had the opportunity to ask the other party for advice.

Indeed, in the case of a recipient acting in bad faith, when he knew or should have known the ground for the avoidance or termination of the contract (for example, because he is the defaulting party), even though he has incurred expenditure on the goods, he is only entitled to be compensated for necessary expenses to "protect the goods or the digital content from being lost or diminished in value"—not expenditure necessary for the production of fruits—and, provided he had the opportunity to do so, he asked the other party for advice. With regard to expenses necessary for the preservation of the goods received, these may be paid to any party, including the defaulting party.

Similarly, art. 86 Vienna Convention provides that: "If the buyer has received the goods and intends to exercise any right under the contract or this Convention to reject them, he must take such steps to preserve them as are reasonable in the circumstances". Furthermore, it recognises the buyer's right to retain them "until he has been reimbursed his reasonable expenses by the seller". Article 7.3.6(4) UNIDROIT Principles states that "Compensation may be claimed for expenses reasonably required to preserve or maintain the performance received", but does not distinguish between a recipient acting in good faith or one acting in bad faith. There is no provision in the text with regard to beneficial expenditure or improvements to the goods that have to be returned.

Also, the recipient will be entitled to reimbursement of expenses if he requested the other party's advice and where this party asked him to incur the necessary maintenance expenses. The burden of proof that the recipient requested advice from the other party, or had no opportunity to do so, is on that recipient.

14.7 Mandatory Nature

Article 177 sets out that: "In relations between a trader and a consumer the parties may not, to the detriment of the consumer, exclude the application of this Chapter or derogate from or vary its effect". In short, freedom of contract is limited in contracts between consumers and traders.

Amendment 246, adopted by the Legal Affairs Committee, introduces some final words to this provision: "before notice of avoidance or termination is given", in order to provide that after this notice is given, parties should be allowed to derogate from its restitution rules and be able to reach an amicable settlement. This amendment has been confirmed by European Parliament legislative resolution of 26 February 2014.

References

Belfiore, A. (1988), "Risoluzione per inadempimento e obbligazioni restitutorie", *Scritti in onore di Giuseppe Auletta*, vol. II, Milán, pp. 243 et seq.

Clemente Meoro, M. E. (1998) *La facultad de resolver los contratos por incumplimiento,* Tirant Lo Blanch, Valencia.

Chabas, C. (2010), "Résolution-résiliation", *Encyclopédie Dalloz*, Repertoire de droit civil.

Lando, O. and Beale, H. (1995), *The Principles of European Contract Law, Part I: Performance, Non-Performance and Remedies*, Dordrecht-Boston-London.

Lando, O. and Beale, H. (2003), *Principios de Derecho contractual europeo*, Partes I y II, ed. española a cargo de P. Barres, J. M. Embid, F. Martínez, Madrid.

López Beltrán de Heredia, C. (2009), *La nulidad de los contratos*, Tirant Lo Blanch, Valencia.

Lehmann (2012), "Part VII. Restitution", *Common European Sales Law (CESL)—Commentary—*, (ed.) R. Schulze, Baden-Baden-München-Oxford, pp. 679–721.

Morales Moreno, A. M. (2003), "Validez del contrato", *Derecho privado europeo*, (coord.) S. Cámara Lapuente, Madrid, pp. 371–397.

McGregor, H. (1993), *Contract Code. Drawn up on behalf of the English Law Commission*, Milan.

Picod, Y. (2013), "Nullité", *Encyclopédie Dalloz*, Repertoire de droit civil.

Vaquer Aloy, A. (2003), "Incumplimiento del contrato y remedios", *Derecho privado europeo*, (coord.) S. Cámara Lapuente, Madrid, pp. 525–554.

Chapter 15
The Rules on Prescription

Luz M. Martínez Velencoso and Andrew O'Flynn

Abstract The Common European Sales Law, although limited in its application to the sale of goods, contains a systematic and almost complete regulation of the prescription of actions that takes into account several new tendencies that have emerged from a number of national legal systems. Broadly speaking, it contains two expiry periods that vary depending on the way in which the *dies a quo* are fixed. The shorter of the two expiry periods employs a subjective criterion, while the longer period makes use of an objective criterion, although this period is not a preclusion period. The law allows the parties concerned a great deal of autonomy in determining the length of these periods. It further distinguishes between the interruption and the suspension of the prescription period. In terms of the effects of the limitation period, the legislator has opted for the weak effect: that is, while it paralyses the action of the claimant, it does not extinguish the claimant's right.

Prescription is undoubtedly a necessary doctrine; not only for obligations derived from contracts but for all types of obligations, and so its regulation in the Common European Sales Law could go on to form the basis of its regulation in a future European Civil Code.

Keywords Preclusion period · Acquisitive prescription · Extinctive prescription · Rights susceptible to prescription · Periods of prescription · Dies a quo · Interruption of prescription · Postponement of expiry · Renewal of the prescription period · Effects of prescription · Agreements concerning prescription

---

L. M. Martínez Velencoso (✉)
LL.M. Humboldt Universität Berlin, University of Valencia, Valencia, Spain
e-mail: luz.martinez@uv.es

A. O'Flynn
LL.M. Cambridge University, Valencia, Spain
e-mail: ajo34@cam.ac.uk

© Springer International Publishing Switzerland 2015
J. Plaza Penadés, L. M. Martínez Velencoso (eds.), *European Perspectives on the Common European Sales Law,* Studies in European Economic Law and Regulation 4,
DOI 10.1007/978-3-319-10497-3_15

15.1 Introduction

The Common European Sales Law (from here on the CESL), although limited in its scope of application to the sale of goods, regulates the prescription of actions in a way that is systematic and almost complete, and which furthermore takes into account the new regulatory tendencies apparent in various national legal systems (for example the reform of the German Civil Code with respect to the regulation of the limitation of actions, as well as the recent reforms of the PECL and the DCRF). These tendencies can be summarised as presenting five main strands Zimmermann 2002:

1. The shortening of the expiry period. The expiry periods should not be excessively long (nor too short) as is the case under the national law of some countries in which certain actions have an expiry period of 30 years.
2. In order to determine the K for the calculation of the expiry date, the legislator makes use of a subjective criterion; that is, the period commences when the subject who wishes to bring a legal action knows, or is in a reasonable position to find out, the circumstances that provide the foundation of the claim and the person against whom the claim may be directed.
3. The legislator allows the subjects a great deal of autonomy in deciding upon the lengthening or shortening of the expiry period.
4. A distinction is made between the interruption and the suspension of the limitation period. In the case of the interruption of the period, when the conditions given in the law are met, the expiry period begins again from zero; whereas in the case of the suspension of the expiry period, the clock is stopped temporarily and then begins to run again from the point it had reached previously.
5. The weak effect of the limitation period is preferred to extinction; the effect of the limitation period is to paralyse the action of the claimant but does not result in the extinction of the claimant's right or action.

The doctrine of prescription is necessary, not only for obligations derived from contracts, but for all types of obligations; and so the regulation of this doctrine in the CESL could serve as the template for its regulation in a future European Civil Code.

There has been some discussion among legal experts concerning the basis on which prescription has been established. One of the principle justifications put forward in the literature is that it favours legal certainty by removing any doubts about the temporal validity of rights, and this configures its role as an instrument of public order, which in turn explains the imperative nature of the rules that comprise it. The limitation period is not subject to the autonomy of the parties, even though the rights it affects normally are (García Goyena 1852).

Another argument put forward in favour of this doctrine is that it serves to protect the security of commercial traffic because it saves debtors the costs entailed by the conservation of proof of payment of their debts. This reasoning is of special relevance to short limitation periods.

Finally, it is frequently affirmed that the limitation period determines the cases in which it is objectively inadmissible for claimants to exercise their rights tardily; typifying this behaviour as unfair conduct that is contrary to the rules of good faith and obliging claimants to exercise their rights within the appropriate time-frame.

These last two reasons are equally directed towards the protection of the passive subject of a right or power, as the passing of time will deprive this subject of the means of proving his case, and because the subject needs to be protected from the prospect that the prolonged silence of the right holder may suddenly be broken with legal action (Díez-Picazo y Ponce de León 1964).

Apart from prescription, other types of time period may be used to limit the exercise of the rights of the buyer; as, for example, in the *United Nations Convention on Contracts for the International Sale of Goods* (CISG) and the *Directive on Certain aspects of the Sale of Consumer goods and Associated Guarantees*. Article 39.2 of the CISG determines that: "*the buyer loses the right to rely on a lack of conformity of the goods if he does not give the seller notice thereof at the latest within a period of two years from the date on which the goods were actually handed over to the buyer...*". While article 5.1 of the Directive stipulates that: "*The seller shall be held liable under Article 3 where the lack of conformity becomes apparent within two years as from delivery of the goods. If, under national legislation, the rights laid down in Article 3(2) are subject to a limitation period, that period shall not expire within a period of two years from the time of delivery.*"

The system employed in the CISG by which a claim based on lack of conformity is limited temporally is a method by which such claims may be regulated without the need to make use of the doctrine of prescription.

The limitation period begins to count from the moment in which the object purchased has been placed effectively in the possession of the buyer. This is an objective method of calculation that offers security to the seller but is to the detriment of the buyer whose interests would be better protected if the period began at the moment in which he became aware of the lack of conformity of the goods (Morales Moreno 2003).

A similar system is employed by *Directive 1999/44/EC of the European Parliament and of the Council of the 25th of May 1999 on certain aspects of the sale of consumer goods and associated guarantees*, in which the time limits for the provision of guarantees by the seller are not formulated as a period of prescription but rather as the set period within which the conditions for liability must be met (Cañizares Laso 2003). A different issue is the prescription period indicated for a claim that arises as a consequence of a lack of conformity. According to art. 3 of the Directive if, under national legislation, the rights laid down in Article 3(2) (which relate to rescission of the contract and a reduction in price of the goods) are subject to a limitation period, that period shall not expire within a period of 2 years from the time of delivery.

In German Law the question of the limitation of claims for defects in goods is regulated in Section 438 of the German Civil Code (§ 438 BGB). According to this Section: "*(1) The claims cited in section 437 nos. 1 and 3 become statute-barred*

1. *in thirty years, if the defect consists of*

   a. *a real right of a third party on the basis of which return of the purchased thing may be demanded, or*
   b. *some other right registered in the Land Register,*

2. *in five years:*

   a. *n relation to a building, and*
   b. *in relation to a thing that has been used for a building in accordance with the normal way it is used and* that has resulted in the defectiveness of the building.

3. *Otherwise in two years*".

The German legislator has opted for a set of special rules, different from the general rules regarding prescription, to govern defects in things. This is due to the fact that usually most actions are governed by a 3 year prescription period, covering both contractual and extra-contractual claims, which relies on a subjective criterion to determine the "*dies a quo*". This subjective criterion was considered prejudicial for the provision of guarantees against hidden defects and contrary to legal security, and an objective criterion was thought to be more appropriate.

The proposal for a Common European Sales Law does not follow this dual system of regulation. The lack of conformity must be present in the moment in which the risks are transmitted to the buyer, as stated in article 105 of the CESL:

"*1. The seller is liable for any lack of conformity which exists at the time when the risk passes to the buyer under Chapter 14.*

2. *In a consumer sales contract, any lack of conformity which becomes apparent within six months of the time when risk passes to the buyer is presumed to have existed at that time unless this is incompatible with the nature of the goods or digital content or with the nature of the lack of conformity*".

If, however, the contract is between traders, then article 121 stipulates that:

"*1. In a contract between traders the buyer is expected to examine the goods, or cause them to be examined, within as short a period as is reasonable not exceeding 14 days from the date of delivery of the goods, supply of digital content or provision of related services*". In order to determine the period within which a claim based on a lack of conformity may be made we must apply the general rules contained in Chapter 18 CESL.

15.2 The Relation Between Extinctive and Acquisitive Prescription (Usucaption) in European Law

As a consequence of certain technical aspects of Roman Procedural Law and the historical evolution of prescription in Roman Law, Roman jurists considered extinctive prescription to be a special form of acquisitive prescription (De Pablo Contreras 1992). This confusion is still present in European Private Law, particularly in German Law. In German Law the action for the recovery of ownership expires after 30 years, in accordance with § 197 BGB (this point was not affected by the latest reform of the law of obligations). When the action for the recovery of ownership has expired after the 30 year period, the possessor in bad faith acquires an exception that has the status of a right ("Einrede"), and which is transmitted to his heirs but not to a third party, for example someone who has robbed him of the object. German legal experts have treated this *dominium sine re* as a "*curiosity*", "*an amicable deviation from the system*" or "*an untenable situation*" (Peters and Zimmermann 1981).

The Italian Civil Code of 1942 declares in art. 948.3 that the action to reclaim ownership does not expire, except in the case in which another has acquired ownership through usucapion.

This point of law was reformed in the Dutch legal system by the promulgation of a new Civil Code in 1994. The previous Code, dating from 1839, had limited the acquisition of property by prescription to those that had possessed the property in good faith, while those who had possessed it in bad faith benefitted from extinctive prescription, which occurred after a period of 30 years. The owner lost the right to reclaim the goods when one or various persons had possessed those goods for a period of at least 30 years. Cases in which the ownership and the possession of goods could end up in different hands were more common in old Dutch Law than in German or Roman law, as the action to reclaim ownership could not be revived when the possessor in bad faith had involuntarily lost possession of the goods after the 30 year period had passed.

This system was thought of as an anomaly, as the possessor in bad faith could benefit from extinctive prescription but not acquisitive prescription. The position commonly held in legal doctrine was that both types of prescription should have the same effect, as connecting extinctive prescription to acquisitive prescription maximises legal security. The new art. 3:105 of the Dutch Civil Code establishes that the person who is in possession of the property in the moment that the action prescribes, due to the expiration of the legal time period, acquires the property even when he is a possessor in bad faith. Article 3:306 fixes this period at 20 years. When the owner has not had possession of the property for 20 years and a third party has possessed the property for the same period, the owner loses the action to reclaim ownership and the possessor acquires ownership of the property through acquisitive prescription. Some legal scholars believe that this amendment, which frees the legal system from the possibility of "*dominium sin re*" in order to guarantee legal certainty, pays too high a price to achieve its aim (Jansen 2012).

In French law the action to reclaim ownership does not prescribe as long as the property has not been acquired by a third party through acquisitive prescription; this is because the right of ownership is considered to be a perpetual right, and the right to property cannot exist without the corresponding right to reclaim ownership. The prescriptive acquisition of immovable objects is possible, but it requires public and pacific possession of the property. Article 277 of the French Civil Code (which was modified in 2008) states that the right to property is not subject to a statute of limitations. However, rights *in rem* for immovable objects expire 30 years from the date in which the right holder knew or should have known of the circumstances that permit the use of the action in question.

English Law does not allow for acquisitive prescription for either movable or immovable goods. This is because it does not protect absolute property rights but rather the best right to possession. By virtue of this, when an owner loses his right to make a claim through extinctive prescription (after a period of 12 years in the case of immovable objects in accordance with the Land Registration Act 2002), the possessor (the adverse possessor) has a better right (the adverse possessor is, therefore, comparable to the owner that possesses the object).

While this is not acquisitive prescription its affect is very similar. The adverse possessor can inscribe his better claim in the Land Registry (as stated in the Land Registration Act 2002). The person registered as the owner of the property is informed of this claim and is granted a period of time in which to react (Jourdan 2002).

In Spanish legal doctrine the question of whether the action to reclaim ownership is autonomous and unaffected by any statutory limitation has been a source of controversy. Some legal scholars (Albaladejo 1990, Yzquierdo Tolsada 1998) have maintained that the action to reclaim ownership can be extinguished without the necessity of any opposing claim to the property based on usucaption. Other scholars have argued for the simultaneous correlation between usucaption and the extinctive prescription of the action (Díez-Picazo 1989, Montés Penadés 1990, De Pablo Contreras 1992).

This debate was finally resolved in the judgment of the Spanish Supreme Court of the 11th of July 2012 (ROJ 6698/2012), in which the Court provided a conceptual and methodological interpretation of the rules of prescription governing actions *in rem* and the acquisition of rights *in rem* by usucaption. The judgment states that: "*it is worthwhile noting the primacy or preferential nature of the effects of acquisition of ownership with respect to extinctive prescription, to the extent that the first are a necessary precondition of the second achieving its full effects. The loss of the right of ownership due to the mere passing of time, implicit in the extinctive prescription of the action to reclaim ownership (as stipulated in article 348 of the Civil Code) and configured as a cornerstone of our system of property law, would be meaningless if it were not preceded by a loss of possession of the property that threatened the right of ownership of the titleholder of this action, that is, that represented a possession adequate to produce usucaption (articles 447 and 1941 of the Spanish Civil Code).*"

The Draft Common Frame of Reference avoids the term acquisitive prescription and replaces it with the expression acquisition of ownership by continuous possession. Ownership is only extinguished with the passing of time when a third party acquires the property by acquisitive prescription (Salomons 2011).

4:101: Basic rule

1. An owner-possessor acquires ownership by continuous possession of goods:
   a. for a period of ten years, provided that the possessor, throughout the whole period, possesses in good faith; or
   b. for a period of thirty years.
2. For the purposes of paragraph (1)(a):
   a. a person possesses in good faith if, and only if, the person possesses in the belief of being the owner and is reasonably justified in that belief; and
   b. good faith of the possessor is presumed.

3. Acquisition of ownership by continuous possession is excluded for a person who obtained possession by stealing the goods.

4:301: Acquisition of ownership

1. Upon expiry of the period required for the acquisition of ownership by continuous possession the original owner loses and the owner-possessor acquires ownership.
2. When the owner-possessor knows or can reasonably be expected to know that the goods are encumbered with a limited proprietary right of a third person, this right continues to exist as long as this right is not itself extinguished by expiry of the respective period, or a period of 30 years (VIII.-4:101 (Basic rule) paragraph (1)(b)) or 50 years (VIII.-4:102 (Cultural objects) paragraph (1)(b)) has passed.

15.3 A Comparative Analysis of the Regulation of Prescription in the CESL

Extinctive prescription refers to the effect of the passage of time on legal actions and rights due to the inactivity of their titleholders.

In principle it is not necessary that these rights are contractual in origin. This is evident in the Principles of European Contract Law (PECL) whose Chapter 14 (on prescription) is placed within the section of the text dedicated to the general part of obligations. The same may be said of the Draft Common Frame of Reference (DCFR) in which prescription is regulated in Chapter VII of Book III.

Doubts have arisen over whether the rules governing prescription in the CESL should be applied only to those rights and actions that originate from a sales contract, or, given that the text uses neutral terms such as debtor and creditor (rather than buyer and seller), if these rules might be applied to the prescription of actions that derive from related services; although again, it is not clear if these services could be the object of an autonomous contract.

The CESL regulates the prescription of the right to receive damages for personal injuries, and makes it clear that these damages need not necessarily derive from a contract. The rules concerning prescription in the CESL generally follow the provisions laid down in the PECL and the DCFR, although many of their rules have been omitted because they fall outside the scope of the CESL.

15.3.1 Rights Susceptible to Prescription

Article 178 CESL establishes that the object of prescription is the right to "*enforce performance of an obligation, and any right ancillary to such a right*". Legal experts have debated how the notion of ancillary rights should be interpreted here (Arroyo 2013). In order to clarify this point the European Parliament's Legal Affairs

Committee introduced an amendment to art. 178 CESL in order to include within the object of prescription "*the right to any remedy for non-performance except withholding performance*". This change was in line with art. 185.1 CESL, according to which, after expiry of the relevant period of prescription the debtor is entitled to refuse performance of the obligation in question and the creditor loses all remedies for non-performance except that of withholding performance. Furthermore, the justification for this amendment made it clear that "*the rules on prescription do not concern commercial guarantees as defined in Art. 2(s)*".

Determining the object of extinctive prescription in the harmonising texts has not proved to be an easy task. Article 14:101 PECL employs the term "claim" to refer to it, while art. III-7:101 of the DCFR speaks of the "*rights subject to prescription*".

Article 1930 of the Spanish Civil Code states that ownership and other rights *in rem* are acquired pursuant to prescription, and it adds that rights and actions of any kind are extinguished by the running of their statute of limitations. It would seem clear that in both arts. 14:101 PECL and III-7:101 DCFR the object of prescription is the "*right to enforce performance of an obligation*"; that is to say it is the "*claims*" that prescribe, a line that is also taken in § 194 I of the BGB (*Ansprüche*). In consequence, the effect of art. 14:501 PECL and art. III-7:505 DCFR is that once the given time limit has expired the debtor may refuse to make payment, but if he has already paid, he will no longer be able to reclaim his money. In conclusion it can be affirmed that prescription does not extinguish the obligation nor does it extinguish the action of the creditor to reclaim his property, but it simply provides the debtor with a special means of defence (Díez-Picazo 1964).

The situation is different in English Law. The equivalent to prescription in English law would be the "limitation of actions" (regulated in the Limitation Act 1980). The effect of this rule is that the right will not be affected but only the possibility of exercising that right in court. This approach is alien to the civilian tradition (Zimmermann 2010). The limitation of actions is inserted into a procedural frame of reference.

15.3.2 Periods of Prescription and Dies a Quo

Article 179 CESL establishes two generic periods of prescription and one specific period in the case of the right to damages for personal injuries. The short period of prescription is 2 years and the long period was originally 10 years but was later amended by the Parliament to 6 years. In the case of the right to damages the period of prescription is 30 years. The commencement of the period of prescription is subjective in the case of the short period and begins to run "*from the time when the creditor has become, or could be expected to have become, aware of the facts as a result of which the right can be exercised.*" In contrast the long period of prescription commences "*from the time when the debtor has to perform or, in the case of a right to damages, from the time of the act which gives rise to the right.*"

There has been some discussion over whether the period of 10 years should be considered a period of prescription or a period of preclusion ("long stop" period). If this were a period of preclusion, it would mean that beyond the temporal limit it would be impossible for prescription to produce its effects (as is the case with art. 14:307 PECL and art. III.-7:307 DCFR). However, it would seem that this is not the case as both periods may be suspended according to art. 181 CESL (see also, arts. 182, 183, 185(1), and 186 CESL).

The European Parliament introduced an amendment to art. 179 CESL in relation to this issue by which they inserted para. 2a, which states that: "*prescription takes effect when either of the two periods has expired, whichever is the earlier*".

The explanation for this is contained in the Draft Report to the European Parliament's Legal Affairs Committee, by Mr Lehne and Mr Berlinguer: "*Your rapporteurs are aware that the 10-year prescription period has triggered critical reactions, whereas others, including the Commission, explain that its practical relevance is limited. In order to mitigate concerns, and whilst agreeing that the practical effects for the long period are limited, your rapporteurs propose a six-year period, which they believe to be an adequate solution in the light of the existing long prescription periods in the Member States*".

The subjective system for the calculation of time periods can cause problems in cases in which claims are made for the lack of conformity of goods. In these cases the buyer can take legal action against the seller many years after the contract was agreed upon, and it has often been argued that in such cases it is more useful to fix a period that begins to run from the moment the goods were put in the possession of the buyer (as is the case in the CISG or the Directive 99/44).

The prescription periods in European legal systems, many of them inspired by the French Civil Code (as is the case with the Spanish Civil Code), employ a variety of different time limitations, yet normally fix a general prescription period that is excessively long, varying from 15 to 20 years, and then a number of shorter periods for specific cases. However in other legal systems, in which the doctrine of prescription has been reformed and systemised, there has been a tendency to reduce these periods. One such case is the BGB (§§ 195, 196, 197 BGB) in which the standard period of prescription is 3 years, with a 10 year period for rights *in rem* and a 30 year period for other particular rights.

The reform of the French Civil Code in 2008 simplified the regulation of prescription periods. Personal actions are given a generic period of prescription of 5 years (art. 2224) and a 10 year period for civil non-contractual liability that is extended to 20 years for more serious cases (art. 2226).

A 5 year prescription period for personal actions is also to be found in art. 3:307 of the Dutch Civil Code.

Article 2262 bis of the Belgian Civil Code (modified by a law that came into force on 10 of June 1998) establishes a general period for personal obligations of 10 years that is lowered to 5 years in cases of non-contractual responsibility.

The common law approach is also along the same lines, as there is one limitation period for all contractual claims that begins with the accrual of the action. In England this limitation period is 6 years (according to s. 5 of the Limitation Act 1980).

Articles 14:201 PECL and III-7:201 DCFR fix a general period of prescription of 3 years, and both texts also determine a special period of 10 years applicable to actions declared by judicial judgments, arbitration awards or other similar titles when they may be executed in the same way as a judgment.

In this case the longer of the two periods is not viewed as a cause of legal insecurity as the action has been declared by a judicial judgment and there is, therefore, no doubt concerning the application of the time period. This possibility is not contemplated in the CESL.

The PECL and DCFR follow a subjective system to determine the time from which the period of prescription begins to run. The general period of prescription begins from the moment when the performance of the debtor can be enforced and, in the case of a right to damages, from the moment of the acts which give rise to the right to make a claim.

According to art. 14:307 PECL and art. III-7:307 DCF, the period of prescription cannot be extended, by the suspension of its running or postponement of its expiry, to more than 10 years or, in the case of claims for personal injuries, to more than 30 years. In order to establish this rule the texts both take as their point of departure the rules governing the general period of 3 years (arts. 14:201 PECL y III-7:201 DCFR) and take into account the fact that this period may be suspended when the creditor does not know or cannot reasonably be expected to know the identity of the debtor or the facts giving rise to the claim (arts. 14:301 PECL y III-7:301 DCFR). These causes of suspension do not appear in the CESL.

As the possibility of suspending the period of prescription could result in its indefinite extension, the texts fix a given moment after which no legal claim can be made. After the maximum period (of either 10 or 15 years) the claim of the creditor can no longer be pursued regardless of any subjective considerations relating to his knowledge of the actions that gave rise to the claim. However, this rule does not apply in the cases where it is possible to suspend prescription, contemplated in arts. 14:302 and III-7:302 DCFR as being when the creditor initiates judicial or extra-judicial proceedings to assert his right. The creditor cannot influence the duration of these proceedings, so it would be unfair to limit them to a maximum period.

15.3.3 The Extension of the Prescription Period: Interruption and Postponement of Expiry

The extension of the prescription period is regulated in arts. 181 ff. CESL. The extension means that the time during which the prescription is suspended due to certain circumstances is not taken into account when calculating the legally established period.

The CESL follows the PECL and the DCFR in distinguishing between interruption and postponement of the period but it provides for fewer circumstances in which they may be employed.

Article 181.1 CESL states that:

"1. *The running of both periods of prescription is suspended from the time when judicial proceedings to assert the right are begun*".

While the BGB (§ 204 BGB) establishes clearly what it understands by the initiation of judicial proceedings, the text of the proposed Common European Sales Law does not provide any such clarification, and so in case of doubt one must refer to national legislation. Article 181 (3) CESL states that the same rules apply: "*to arbitration proceedings, to mediation proceedings, to proceedings whereby an issue between two parties is referred to a third party for a binding decision and to all other proceedings initiated with the aim of obtaining a decision relating to the right or to avoid insolvency*".

This question was not dealt with by the PECL or the DCFR but it was treated in art. 10.5(1) (b) PICC (Principles of International Commercial Contracts).

The original version of the CESL did not regulate one of the causes of interruption of prescription that appears in both the PECL and the DCFR. This is the existence of an impediment that is outside the control of the creditor that appears in art. 14:303 PECL and art. III-7:303 DCFR. It is also contained in § 206 BGB.

For this motive the Parliament proposed the introduction of art. 183 CESL that determines that:

"*1. The running of the short period of prescription shall be suspended for the period during which the creditor is prevented from pursuing proceedings to assert the right by an impediment which is beyond the creditor's control and which the creditor could not reasonably have been expected to avoid or overcome.*

2. Paragraph 1 shall apply only if the impediment arises, or subsists, within the last six months of the prescription period.

3. Where the duration or nature of the impediment is such that it would be unreasonable to expect the creditor to take proceedings to assert the right within the part of the period of prescription which has still to run after the suspension comes to an end, the period of prescription shall not expire before six months have passed after the impediment was removed".

The justification for this was the following: "*Art. 183 (Creditor's incapacity) and the general principle of good faith and fair dealing do not appear sufficient to avoid unreasonably harsh results of impediments preventing the timely initiation of proceedings under article 181. As the provision is only applicable to the short period of prescription, the effect on legal certainty is limited*".

The text also introduces a new cause of suspension in art. 181 to cover the case of repair or replacement. The article declares that:

"*1. Where a lack of conformity is remedied by repair or replacement, the running of the short period of prescription is suspended from the time when the creditor has informed the debtor of the lack of conformity.*

2. Suspension lasts until the time when the non-conforming performance has been remedied".

The CESL also regulates postponement of expiry. Postponement means that although the period of prescription continues to run its course it only comes to an end after the completion of an additional period. There are two circumstances in which this is possible: in the case of negotiations between the parties, and in the case of the incapacity of one of the parties.

In the case of negotiations, the regulation in the CESL is similar to that of the PECL and the DCFR. Article 182 states that: "*If the parties negotiate about the right, or about circumstances from which a claim relating to the right might arise, neither period of prescription expires before one year has passed since the last communication made in the negotiations or since one of the parties communicated to the other that it does not wish to pursue the negotiations.*"

The CESL does not define what it considers to be a negotiation nor does it specify any special formalities for the communications between the parties. Given this lack of precision it will be for the national courts to provide guidance on these matters. In other jurisdictions, such as Germany, the time limit is shorter (the "claim is statute-barred at the earliest three months after the end of the suspension" according to § 203 BGB).

Article 183 CESL regulates postponement of expiry in the case of incapacity and stipulates that: "*If a person subject to incapacity is without a representative, neither period of prescription of a right held by that person expires before one year has passed since either the incapacity has ended or a representative has been appointed.*" It seems incongruous that the CESL does not make any general provisions concerning capacity but includes incapacity as one of the causes of postponement of expiry.

Both the PECL and the DCFR (arts. 14:305 PECL y III-7:205 DCFR), in contrast to the CESL, regulate another form of postponement of expiry in the case of legal claims that arise between a person subject to a legal incapacity and his or her representative. The period of prescription of these claims does not expire before 1 year has passed after either the incapacity has ended or a new representative has been appointed. It is strange that this possibility is not contemplated in the CESL.

The CESL also fails to make any exceptions allowing for the postponement of the expiry of the period of prescription on claims against the deceased's estate following the death of the creditor or debtor. Such an exception is contained in both the PECL and the BGB. In the PECL, where the creditor or debtor has died, the period of prescription of a claim held by or against the deceased's estate does not expire before 1 year has passed after the claim can be enforced by or against an heir, or by or against a representative of the estate. In § 211 BGB this period is 6 months.

15.3.4 The Renewal of the Prescription Period

Article 184 CESL declares that: "*If the debtor acknowledges the right vis-à-vis the creditor, by part payment, payment of interest, giving of security, set-off or in any other manner, a new short period of prescription begins to run.*"

This article is in accordance with arts. 14:101 PECL and III.-7:401 (1) DCFR.

The text does not provide any definition of acknowledgement, but lists situations that have traditionally been considered as acts of acknowledgement. As a consequence of this, it will be for national tribunals to determine if new types of acts by the debtor constitute acknowledgement of the debt.

In all cases the debt must be acknowledged directly by the debtor and not by a third party.

This short period of prescription is generally 3 years, independently of whether the initial claim was subject to the general period or the 10 year period of prescription for claims declared by a court judgment.

Another cause of renewal that is present in the PECL and the DCFR but not in the CESL is the renewal by attempted execution (arts. 14:401 and 14:402 PECL, and III-7:401 and III-7:402 DCFR). This cause is also contained in § 212 (1) BGB and art. 2244 of the French Civil Code.

15.3.5 The Effects of Prescription

In their regulation of the doctrine of prescription, legal systems normally grant it two different effects. One of these effects is that the passing of time automatically extinguishes rights and legal actions. The other is that the expiry of the given period can be used as a legal defence by the debtor when faced with a claim or legal action by the creditor.

In the first case, if the debtor voluntarily pays the creditor after the legal obligation to pay has been automatically extinguished, then the payment will be legally considered as a donation. If the payment was not made voluntarily, then the debtor would have the right to reclaim the money handed over, as it would be regarded legally as a case of wrongful receipt of payment. Prescription in these cases is applied automatically by the courts.

In the second case, if the debtor renounces the benefit of prescription and voluntarily pays the amount, then the act of payment constitutes the satisfaction of an existing obligation and is not seen as the wrongful receipt of payment. This second system is that followed by the Spanish Civil Code and by both the PECL and the DCFR (arts. 14:501 PECL and III-7:101 DCFR). The UNIDROIT Principles of International Commercial Contracts states in art. 10.9 that the expiration of the limitation period does not extinguish the right and that for the expiration of the limitation period to have effect the debtor must assert it as a defence. Article 10.11 goes on to declare that where there has been performance in order to discharge an obligation, there is no right of restitution merely because the limitation period has expired.

The United Nations Convention on the Limitation Period in the International Sale of Goods of 1974 stipulates that "*expiration of the limitation period shall be taken into consideration in any legal proceedings only if invoked by a party to such proceedings*". While art. 26 of the same text declares that: "*Where the debtor performs his obligation after the expiration of the limitation period, he shall not on that ground be entitled in any way to claim restitution even if he did not know at the time when he performed his obligation that the limitation period had expired*".

This same effect is contained in art. 185 CESL, which says that:

1. After expiry of the relevant period of prescription the debtor is entitled to refuse performance of the obligation in question and the creditor loses all remedies for nonperformance except withholding performance.
2. Whatever has been paid or transferred by the debtor in performance of the obligation in question may not be reclaimed merely because the period of prescription had expired at the moment that the performance was carried out.

Consequently, the remedies available against non-performance are extinguished upon the expiration of the corresponding period of prescription (whether that is the short or the long period). This is coherent given the fact that the prescribed obligation can no longer be required and, therefore, cannot be said to be unfulfilled. The exception to this is when the creditor is able to exercise the *exceptio non adimpleti contractus* (arts. 106(1)(b), 113, 131(1)(b), 133 CESL), even though his right to require performance of the obligation has expired. This exception is designed to maintain the synallagmatic nature of the contract.

Another consequence derived from this effect of prescription is that the debtor may set off the obligation that has expired against a claim asserted by the other party (arts. 14:503 PECL, III-7:503 and 25(2)(b) of the United Nations Convention on the Limitation Period in the International Sale of Goods 1974). This possibility was written out of the final version of the CESL for two reasons: firstly because the text does not regulate the compensation between claims, and secondly because this effect is not normally admitted in national legal systems.

In art. 1290 of the French Civil Code, compensation operates automatically and *ipso iure*. However, in art. 1242 of the Italian Civil Code, prescription does not exclude the possibility of compensation, unless the time period had already expired at the moment in which the coexistence of both debts was verified. Similar regulations appear in art. 120 of the Swiss Civil Code, art. 6:131 of the Dutch Civil Code and § 215 of the BGB.

Article 185.3 of the CESL establishes that: "*The period of prescription for a right to payment of interest, and other rights of an ancillary nature, expires not later than the period for the principal right.*" This point is given the same treatment in arts. 14:502 PECL and III-7:502 DCFR. In these cases the ancillary nature of the right to claim interest is strictly enforced, and this prevents the claimant from demanding interest when the principal right has expired.

15.3.6 Agreements Concerning Prescription

Article 186 of the CESL regulates agreements concerning prescription. The article determines that:

1. The rules of this Chapter may be modified by agreement between the parties, in particular by either shortening or lengthening the periods of prescription.

2. The short period of prescription may not be reduced to less than one year or extended to more than ten years.
3. The long period of prescription may not be reduced to less than one year or extended to more than thirty years.
4. The parties may not exclude the application of this Article or derogate from or vary its effects.
5. In a contract between a trader and a consumer this Article may not be applied to the detriment of the consumer.

The first paragraph of art. 186 presents some interpretative problems as the meaning of the words "*in particular*" is not clear. It could be taken to mean that agreements between the parties might affect other aspects of prescription; such as for example, the possibility of introducing motives for postponement distinct from those contained in arts. 181 and 182 CESL.

What is clear is that if an agreement is reached it cannot worsen the situation of the consumer in relation to the legal application of prescription.

Different legal systems have provided varying solutions to the problems posed by permitting agreements in relation to prescription. Sometimes, even though modification of the rules relating to prescription is prohibited, the party is permitted to renounce their claim to employ the expired time limitation as a defence. This possibility is present in the Portuguese Civil Code (arts. 300 and 302), the Italian Civil Code (arts. 2936 and 2937.2) and the Dutch Civil Code (art. 3.322).

In other cases, the parties may agree to modify the time periods (or the possibility of postponing prescription) within certain limits. BGB § 202 establishes a maximum extension period of 30 years but excludes any agreements that seek to alter the rules regarding prescription for liability for malice.

The 2008 revision of art. 2254 of the French Civil Code expressly permitted agreements that shortened or lengthened the limitation period, but forbade periods of less than a year or in excess of 10 years.

In English Law, it is permitted that parties may agree to reduce the limitation periods for breach of contract and negligence claims from those stipulated in the Limitation Act. Nevertheless, any agreement to reduce the limitation period is subject to the test of reasonableness under s. 11 Unfair Contract Terms Act 1977. In considering whether or not the shorter limitation period is unreasonable, the courts will have regard to the relative bargaining power of the parties.

Article 1935 of the Spanish Civil Code prohibits the parties from renouncing the benefits of prescription in advance (1935(I) *in fine*), and legal experts have argued over whether agreements concerning prescription are permissible. However there is a general consensus that agreements that lengthen the limitation period excessively are equivalent to those that renounce the benefits of prescription in advance.

Those who are in favour of allowing limited modifying agreements have argued that the general rule in Civil Law is to respect the will of the parties concerned. It is also the case that the very nature of prescription means that its benefits may be renounced by the party who is favoured by them, given that the expiry of the time limit can only be used as a form of defence by one party, made in the event of a claim against him by another.

According to Díez-Picazo, it would be coherent to allow for alterations in the time limits that varied between legally established maximums and minimums (for example, between the period of 1 year stated in art. 1968 of the Spanish Civil Code and the 15 year period of art. 1964).

Articles 14:601 PECL and III.-7:601 DCFR allow for the modification of the regulations regarding prescription by agreement between the parties, in particular for the shortening or the lengthening of the time limits. These agreements are subject to certain limitations:

a. the period of prescription cannot be reduced to less than a year;
b. nor can it be increased to more than 30 years, calculated from the moment specified in art. 14:203 PECL (art. III.-7:203 DCFR).

Permitted agreements on prescription may affect different aspects of the doctrine such as the moment from which the time limit begins to run, or the causes of postponement.

Finally, the international texts in force do not provide a homogenous solution to the questions posed by permitting agreements on prescription. Article 22 of the United Nations Convention on the Limitation Period in the International Sale of Goods (1974) establishes, as a general rule, that the limitation period cannot be modified or affected by any declaration or agreement between the parties. However the same article provides for two exceptions:

a. The debtor may at any time during the running of the limitation period extend the period by a declaration in writing to the creditor. This declaration may be renewed.
b. A clause in a contract of sale may stipulate a shorter period for the commencement of arbitration proceedings than that prescribed by the Convention, provided that the clause is valid under the law applicable to the contract of sale.

However, art. 10.3 of the UNIDROIT principles establishes a general rule which states the opposite. The parties may modify the limitation periods, but with certain limitations. It is prohibited to: "(a) shorten the general limitation period to less than one year (b) shorten the maximum limitation period to less than four years (c) extend the maximum limitation period to more than fifteen years."

References

Albaladejo García M (1990) La prescripción de la acción reivindicatoria, Anuario de Derecho Civil, vol. 43, núm. 1, pp. 25 *et seq.*
Arroyo i Amayuelas E Vaquer A (2013) Prescription in the Proposal for a Common European Sales Law, European Review of Contract Law, Volume 9, Issue 1, pp. 38 *et seq.*
Cañizares Laso A (2003) "La prescripción en el BGB después de la reforma del derecho de obligaciones", in Estudios Jurídicos en Homenaje al Prof. Díez-Picazo, Madrid.
De Pablo Contreras PV (1992), Prescripción de la acción reivindicatoria, Tecnos, Madrid.
Díez-Picazo y Ponce De León L (1964) La prescripción en el Código civil, Bosch, Barcelona.

Díez-Picazo y Ponce De León L (1989) Las relaciones entre usucapión y prescripción extintiva de la acción reivindicatoria, in Homenaje al profesor Juan Roca Juan, Editum. Ediciones de la Universidad de Murcia, Murcia, pp. 221 *et seq.*

García Goyena F (1852) Concordancias, motivos y comentarios del Código civil español, IV, Imprenta de la Sociedad Tipográfico-Editorial, Madrid.

Jansen JE (2012) Thieves and Squatters: Acquisitive and Extinctive Prescription in European Property Law, *EPLJ*, pp. 153 *et seq.*

Jourdan S (2002) Adverse Possession, Bloomsbury Publishing Plc, 2002.

Montés Penadés V (1990) Comentario al art. 348 CC, in Comentarios al Código Civil y compilaciones forales, tomo V, vol. 1, Edersa, Madrid, pp. 205 *et seq.*

Morales Moreno AM (2003) Adaptación del Código Civil al Derecho Europeo: la compraventa, in El Dret Civil Català en el context europeu, Girona, pp. 142 *et seq.*

Peters F Zimmermann R (1981) Verjährungsfristen: Der Einfluss von Fristen auf Schuldverhältnisse; Möglichkeiten der Vereinfachung von Verjährungsfristen, in Gutachten und Vorschläge zur Überarbeitung des Schuldrechts, vol. I, Verlag Bundesanzeiger, Köln.

Salomons A (2011) The Purpose and Coherence of the rules on Good Faith Acquisition and Acquisitive Prescription in the European Draft Common Frame of Reference. A tale of two gatekeepers, Centre for the Study of European Contract Law. Working Paper Series, vol. 11, Available online papers.ssrn.com.

Yzquierdo Tolsada M (1998) Las tensiones entre usucapión y prescripción extintiva, Dykinson, Madrid.

Zimmermann R (2002), "Das neue deutsche Verjährungsrecht—ein Vorbild für Europa?", in Huber P, Faust F (eds), Schuldrechtsmodernisierung: Einführung in das neue Recht, C. H. Beck 2002, pp. 15 *et seq.*

Zimmermann R (2010) Comparative foundations of a European Law of Set-off and Prescription, Cambridge University Press.

[illegible] (2011) [illegible] Comentario [illegible]
[illegible]
[illegible] (2006) [illegible]

Bibliography

General

Basedow J. Hopt K Zimmermann R (ed.) (2012) Max Planck Encyclopaedia of European Private Law Oxford OUP.

Beale H Tallon D Vogenauer S Rutgers J W Fauvarque-Cosson B (2010) Contract Law (Ius Commune Casebooks for the Common Law of Europe vol. 5) 2nd rev. ed. Oxford Hart.

Brownsword R Micklitz H Niglia L Weatherill S (2011) The Foundations of European Private Law Oxford-Oregon Hart.

Graziano T K (2009) Comparative Contract Law Cases Materials and Exercises (translations by Eleanor Grant) Basingstoke Hampshire Palgrave Macmillan.

Hartkamp A S et al (eds.) (2011) *Towards a European civil code* 4th rev. and expand. ed. Nijmegen Ars Aequi Libri The Hague Kluwer Law International [available in dropbox].

Reimann M Zimmermann R (2008) *The Oxford Handbook of Comparative Law* Oxford OUP 2008 [available in dropbox]

Whincup M (2006) Contract Law and Practice the English System with Scottish Commonwealth and Continental Comparisons 5th rev. ed. The Hague Kluwer Law International.

CISG

Díez-Picazo y Ponce de León L (ed.) (1998) Compraventa internacional de mercaderías comentario de la convención de Viena Madrid Civitas, Madrid.

Honnold J O (2009) Uniform Law for International Sales under the 1980 United Nations Convention 4th. ed. edited and updated by Harry M. Fletchner Austin Boston Chicago New York Wolters Kluwer.

Honsell H (ed.) (2010) Kommentar zum UN-Kaufrecht Übereinkommen der Vereinten Nationen über Verträge über den Internationalen Warenkauf (CISG) Heidelberg Dordrecht London New York Springer.

Kröll S Mistelis L A Perales Viscasillas MP (ed.) (2011) UN Convention on Contracts for the International Sale of Goods (CISG) München Oxford Portland Beck Hart Nomos.

Schwenzer I Muñoz E (ed.) (2011) Schlechtriem & Schwenzer Comentario sobre la Convención de las Naciones Unidas sobre los contratos de compraventa internacional de mercaderías 2 vols. Cizur Menor Aranzadi Thomson Reuters.

© Springer International Publishing Switzerland 2015

J. Plaza Penadés, L. M. Martínez Velencoso (eds.), *European Perspectives on the Common European Sales Law,* Studies in European Economic Law and Regulation 4,
DOI 10.1007/978-3-319-10497-3

PICC

Instituto Internacional para la Unificación del Derecho Privado *Unidroit Principles of international Commercial Contracts* Rome Unidroit 2004.

Bonell M J (2005) An International Restatement of Contract Law The UNIDROIT Principles of International Commercial Contracts 3rd ed. Irvington-on-Hudson N.Y. Transnational Publishers.

Vogenauer S Kleinheisterkamp J (eds.) (2009) Commentary on the Unidroit Principles of International Commercial Contracts (PICC) Oxford Oxford University Press.

PECL

Busch D et al (2002) The principles of European contract law and Dutch law Kluwer.

Cristofaro G (ed.) (2009) Principi del Diritto comunitario dei contratti Torino.

Díez-Picazo y Ponce de León L Roca Trias E Morales Moreno AM (2002) *Los Principios del derecho europeo de contratos* Madrid Civitas.

Lando O Beale H (eds.) (2000) Principles of European Contract Law. Parts I and II combined and revised The Hague [etc.] Kluwer Law International.

Lando O Beale H (eds.) (2003) Principles of European Contract Law. Part III The Hague [etc.] Kluwer Law International.

Veneziano A L (2005) The principles of European contract law and Italian law Kluwer.

DCFR

Alpa G Perfetti U Zatti P Iudica G (2009) Il Draft Common Frame of Reference del diritto privato europeo Padova CEDAM.

Terryn E Sagaert V Storme M (2011) Draft common frame of reference a national and comparative perspective Antwerp Intersentia

Von Bar C Clive E (eds.) (2009) *Principles Definitions and Model Rules of European Private Law Draft Common Frame of Reference (DCFR)* 6 vols. Munich Sellier [available dropbox]

CESL

Balthasar S (2013) The draft common European sales law—overview and analysis/International *Company and Commercial Law Review* 24(2) pp. 43–49.

Feltkamp R Claeys I (2013) A European Sales Law, Intersentia.

Dannemann G Vogenauer S (ed.) (2013) *The Common European Sales Law in Context* Oxford OUP.

Ganuza J J Gomez F (2013) Optional law for firms and consumers An economic analysis of opting into the Common European Sales Common market law review v. 50 n. 1 pp. 29–50.

Jansen N (2012) Revision of the Consumer-Acquis? Twelve Propositions on the European Commission's Proposal for a Common European Sales Law and the Future of European Contract Law *Schriftenreihe des Zentrums für Europäisches Wirtschaftsrecht der Universität Bonn* 2012 33 p.

Posner E A (2012) The questionable basis of the Common European Sales Law The role of an optional instrument in jurisdictional competition Common market law review v. 50 n. 1 pp. 261–275

Schmidt-Kessel M (ed.) (2012) Ein einheitliches europäisches Kaufrecht? Eine Analyse des Vorschlags der Kommission Sellier München.

Schulze R Stuyck J (2011) Towards a European Contract Law Munich Sellier.

Schulze R (ed.) (2012) *Common European Sales Law* C.H. Beck. Hart. Nomos München.

Smits J M (2013) Party choice and the Common European Sales Law or How to prevent the CESL from becoming a lemon on the law market Common market law review v. 50 n. 1 pp. 51–68

Whittaker S (2012) The Proposed Common European Sales Law. Legal Framework and the Agreement of the Parties *Oxford Legal Studies Research Paper* No. 10 51 p.

Index

© Springer International Publishing Switzerland 2015

J. Plaza Penadés, L. M. Martínez Velencoso (eds.), *European Perspectives on the Common European Sales Law*, Studies in European Economic Law and Regulation 4,
DOI 10.1007/978-3-319-10497-3